A BIOGRAPHY OF THE TRIPIṬAKA MASTER OF THE GREAT CI'EN MONASTERY OF THE GREAT TANG DYNASTY

BDK English Tripiṭaka 77

A BIOGRAPHY OF THE TRIPIṬAKA MASTER OF THE GREAT CI'EN MONASTERY OF THE GREAT TANG DYNASTY

Translated from the Chinese
of Śramaṇa Huili and Shi Yancong

(Taishō, Volume 50, Number 2053)

by

Li Rongxi

Numata Center
for Buddhist Translation and Research
1995

First Printing, 1995
ISBN: 1-886439-00-1
Library of Congress Catalog Card Number: 94-073928

Published by
Numata Center for Buddhist Translation and Research
2620 Warring Street
Berkeley, California 94704

Printed in the United States of America

A Message on the Publication of the English Tripiṭaka

The Buddhist canon is said to contain eighty-four thousand different teachings. I believe that this is because the Buddha's basic approach was to prescribe a different treatment for every spiritual ailment, much as a doctor prescribes a different medicine for every medical ailment. Thus his teachings were always appropriate for the particular suffering individual and for the time at which the teaching was given, and over the ages not one of his prescriptions has failed to relieve the suffering to which it was addressed.

Ever since the Buddha's Great Demise over twenty-five hundred years ago, his message of wisdom and compassion has spread throughout the world. Yet no one has ever attempted to translate the entire Buddhist canon into English throughout the history of Japan. It is my greatest wish to see this done and to make the translations available to the many English-speaking people who have never had the opportunity to learn about the Buddha's teachings.

Of course, it would be impossible to translate all of the Buddha's eighty-four thousand teachings in a few years. I have, therefore, had one hundred thirty-nine of the scriptural texts in the prodigious Taishō edition of the Chinese Buddhist canon selected for inclusion in the First Series of this translation project.

It is in the nature of this undertaking that the results are bound to be criticized. Nonetheless, I am convinced that unless someone takes it upon himself or herself to initiate this project, it will never be done. At the same time, I hope that an improved, revised edition will appear in the future.

It is most gratifying that, thanks to the efforts of more than a hundred Buddhist scholars from the East and the West, this monumental project has finally gotten off the ground. May the rays of the Wisdom of the Compassionate One reach each and every person in the world.

NUMATA Yehan
Founder of the English
Tripiṭaka Project

August 7, 1991

Editorial Foreword

In January, 1982, Mr. NUMATA Yehan, the founder of the Bukkyō Dendō Kyōkai (Society for the Promotion of Buddhism), decided to begin the monumental task of the complete translation of the Taishō edition of the Chinese Buddhist canon into the English language. Under his leadership, a special preparatory committee was organized in April, 1982, and by July of the same year the Translation Committee of the English Tripiṭaka (Scriptures) was officially convened.

The initial Committee consisted of the following thirteen members: HANAYAMA Shōyū (Chairman); BANDŌ Shōjun; ISHIGAMI Zennō; KAMATA Shigeo; KANAOKA Shūyū; MAYEDA Sengaku; NARA Yasuaki; SAYEKI Shinkō; (late) SHIOIRI Ryōtatsu; TAMARU Noriyoshi; (late) TAMURA Kwansei; URYŪZU Ryūshin; and YUYAMA Akira. Assistant members of the Committee were as follows: KANAZAWA Atsushi; WATANABE Shōgo; Rolf Giebel of New Zealand; and Rudy Smet of Belgium.

Holding planning meetings on a monthly basis, the Committee has selected one hundred thirty-nine scriptures and texts for the First Series of translations, an estimated one hundred printed volumes in all. Scriptures and texts selected are not necessarily limited to those originally written in India but also include works written or composed in China or Japan. All the volumes in the First Series are scheduled for publication within the twentieth century. While the publication of the First Series proceeds, the scriptures and texts for the Second Series, which is expected to be published in the following ten- or twenty-year period, will be selected from among the remaining works; this process will continue until all the scriptures and texts, in Japanese as well as in Chinese, have been published.

Frankly speaking, it will take perhaps one hundred years or more to accomplish the English translation of the complete

Chinese and Japanese scriptures and texts, which consist of thousands of works. Nevertheless, as Mr. NUMATA wished, it is the sincere hope of the Committee that this project will continue unto completion, even after all its present members have passed away.

It must be mentioned here that the final object of this project is not academic fulfillment but the transmission of the teaching of the Buddha to the whole world in order to create harmony and peace among mankind.

More than eighty Buddhist scholars in the West and in the East, all well qualified to be translators of the Chinese and Japanese scriptures and texts, have agreed to translate certain selected works. It is really a great pleasure for the Committee to announce that more than forty-five translations have already been received as of the end of September, 1992.

The present members of the Translation Committee of the BDK English Tripiṭaka are HANAYAMA Shōyū (Chairman); BANDŌ Shōjun; ISHIGAMI Zennō; ICHISHIMA Shōshin; KAMATA Shigeo; KANAOKA Shūyū; MAYEDA Sengaku; NARA Yasuaki; SAYEKI Shinkō; TAMARU Noriyoshi; URYŪZU Ryūshin; and YUYAMA Akira. Assistant members are WATANABE Shōgo and SUZUKI Kōshin.

Commemorating the ninety-fourth birthday of Mr. NUMATA Yehan, the Committee published the following three texts in a limited edition in April, 1991:

(1) *The Lotus Sutra* (Taishō No. 262)
(2) *The Sutra on Upāsaka Precepts* (Taishō No. 1488)
(3) *The Summary of the Great Vehicle* (Taishō No. 1593)

In December, 1991, the Publication Committee headed by Prof. Philip Yampolsky was organized. New editions of the above volumes and the remaining texts will be published under the supervision of this Committee.

HANAYAMA Shōyū
Chairman
Translation Committee of
the BDK English Tripiṭaka

September 10, 1992

Publisher's Foreword

It was in December, 1991, at the Numata Center for Buddhist Translation and Research in Berkeley, California, that a publication committee was established for the purpose of seeing into print the translations of the Chinese and Japanese Buddhist works in the BDK English Tripiṭaka Series. This committee will perform the duties of copyediting, formatting, proofreading, indexing, consulting with the translators on questionable passages, and so on—the routine duties of any publishing house. Represented on the committee are specialists in Sanskrit, Chinese, and Japanese, who will attempt to ensure that fidelity to the texts is maintained.

This Publication Committee is dedicated to the production of lucid and readable works that will do justice to the vision of Mr. NUMATA Yehan in his desire to make available to Western readers the major works of the Chinese and Japanese Buddhist canon.

"Taishō" refers to the *Taishō Shinshū Daizōkyō* (Newly Revised Tripiṭaka Inaugurated in the Taishō Era), which was published during the period from 1924 to 1934. This consists of one hundred volumes, in which as many as 3,360 scriptures in both Chinese and Japanese are included. This edition is acknowledged to be the most complete Tripiṭaka of the Northern tradition of Buddhism ever published in the Chinese and Japanese languages.

The series number on the spine and title page of each volume will correspond to the number assigned to the work by the Translation Committee of the BDK English Tripiṭaka in Tokyo. A list of the volume numbers is appended at the end of the text. For the convenience of scholars who may wish to turn to the original texts, Taishō page and column numbers are provided in the left-hand margins of each volume. No attempt will be made to standardize the English translations of Buddhist technical terms; these are left to the discretion of the individual translators.

Those participating in the work of this committee are Diane Ames, William Ames, Brian Galloway, David Hall, Nobuo Haneda, and Rev. Kiyoshi S. Yamashita.

Philip Yampolsky
Chairman
Publication Committee

September 10, 1992

Contents

A Message on the Publication of the English Tripiṭaka		*NUMATA Yehan*	v
Editorial Foreword		*HANAYAMA Shōyū*	vii
Publisher's Foreword		*Philip Yampolsky*	ix
Translator's Introduction		*Li Rongxi*	1
Preface		*Shi Yancong*	5
Fascicle I	Beginning from His Birth at Goushi and Ending with His Arrival at Gaochang in the West		11
Fascicle II	Beginning with the Country of Agni and Ending with the Country of Kanyākubja		37
Fascicle III	Beginning with the Country of Ayodhyā and Ending with the Country of Īraṇaparvata		75
Fascicle IV	Beginning with the Country of Campā and Ending with the Invitation of the King of Kāmarūpa		107
Fascicle V	Beginning with the Prediction of a Nirgrantha about His Homeward Journey and Ending with His Arrival at the Western Canal in the Imperial Capital		137
Fascicle VI	Beginning with His Arrival at the Western Capital in the First Month of the Spring in the Nineteenth Year and Ending with His Thanks for the Preface Written by the Emperor to the Scriptures and the Emperor's Reply in the Sixth Month of the Summer in the Twenty-Second Year		173

Fascicle VII Beginning with the Composition of the "Statement of the Sacred Preface" by the Crown Prince in the Sixth Month of the Summer in the Twenty-Second Year and Ending with a Reply by the Master in the Second Month of the Spring in the Fifth Year of Yonghui 203

Fascicle VIII Beginning with the Translation of the *Nyāyamukha Śāstra* in the Fifth Month of the Summer in the Sixth Year of Yonghui and Ending with the Expression of Thanks by Court Officials for the Inscription Composed by the Emperor for the Monastery in the Third Month of the Spring in the First Year of Xianqing 237

Fascicle IX Beginning with a Letter of Thanks for the Completion of the Inscription of the Ci'en Monastery in the Third Month of the First Year of Xianqing and Ending with His Return to the Western Capital with the Emperor in the First Month of the Third Year 275

Fascicle X Beginning with His Return to the Western Capital with the Emperor from Luoyang in the First Month of the Third Year of Xianqing and Ending with His Demise at Yuhua Palace in the Second Month of the First Year of Linde 325

Glossary 351

Selected Bibliography 359

Index 361

A List of the Volumes of the BDK English Tripiṭaka (First Series) 377

Translator's Introduction

The Tripiṭaka Master Xuanzang (A.D. 600–64), whose deeds and career as a Buddhist monk are described in this biography, was a prominent figure not only in the history of Buddhist learning but also in other fields of culture. He played a role in the establishment of friendly contacts between China and the countries through which he travelled in search of more knowledge of Buddhism and incidentally but not insignificantly provided posterity with data of historical value in his detailed records about regions in Central Asia and particularly in ancient India. He is thus respected not only by the Buddhists and people of China but also by the peoples of other Eastern Asian countries who have benefitted from the Buddhist lore that he acquired through many hardships and perils during his seventeen-year journey, from 629 to 645, in foreign lands.

His position is important in the Buddhist world because he brought back to China as many as 657 Sanskrit texts, far surpassing the number of books brought back home by any one of his predecessors who travelled to India for the purpose of obtaining Sanskrit Buddhist works. Out of these 657 texts that he had brought back from India, he translated, with the assistance of both monastic and lay scholars, 74 books in 1,335 fascicles altogether. Some of them are quite voluminous works, such as the *Mahāprajñāpāramitā Sūtra* in 600 fascicles and the *Abhidharmamahāvibhāṣā Śāstra* in 200 fascicles. If he had not been an assiduous translator, wholeheartedly devoted to the dissemination of the Dharma through translating Buddhist texts into Chinese, he could not have translated such an enormous number of books in the nineteen years from 645 when he returned from India up to his death in 664. In his last years, when he was getting old and feeble, he worked particularly hard, because he was worried that, human life being limited, he might not be able to translate as many texts as he desired for his fellow monks and countrymen to read. His activities as a novice, his journey to India, and then his engaging himself in translation after returning home show that he was an enthusiastic Buddhist monk and scholar with a great devotion to his religion and a strong will to overcome all difficulties to achieve his goal until he paid for it with his life.

Because of his translation of Buddhist texts into Chinese, Xuanzang was an epoch-making figure in the history of Buddhism in China. After his translations came out, they were known as the New Translations, in contrast to the Chinese versions of Buddhist texts rendered by previous monks and lay devotees, whose works were then labelled Old Translations. This was because Xuanzang was working at a time when, through the efforts of the pioneer translators, a more mature literary form, one more acceptable to Chinese readers, had been developed for the translation of Buddhist literature, enabling Xuanzang to do his works in a more refined way. His personal literary accomplishments and good scholarship, however, also accounted for his outstanding achievements.

It was Xuanzang who initiated the Faxiang (Dharmalakṣaṇa) school, also known in China as the Weishi school (Vijñānavāda) of Buddhism, mainly through his translations of the *Saṃdhinirmocana Sūtra* (5 fascicles), Asaṅga's *Yogācārabhūmi Śāstra* (100 fascicles), and the *Vijñaptimātratāsiddhi Śāstra* (10 fascicles). This last is a work comprising Vasubandhu's *Triṃśikā* and excerpts from the commentaries of ten Indian exponents, headed by Dharmapāla, which was translated into Chinese at the suggestion of Kuiji, one of Xuanzang's chief disciples. Kuiji had written no less than a hundred treatises in exposition of the idealistic theory of Weishi (Mind Only) that holds that all external phenomena are nothing but manifestations of the mind; and his elucidation of the viewpoint of this sect was so complete and convincing that he was regarded as the actual founder of the school, although its basic texts were provided by his teacher.

Huili, the author of this biography who was born in 614, was a man of talent and intelligence. He became a monk in the third year of Zhenguan (629), when he was a youth of fifteen. He was so well known for his learning in Buddhism that he was appointed by the Emperor to take part in the tasks of the Scripture Translation Court, which was set up at the Great Ci'en Monastery. Out of his admiration for and veneration of the Venerable Xuanzang, he wrote this biography about how the Master went to India to seek Buddhist texts and translate them into Chinese, so that future generations might know about his noble deeds. When he had finished his writing in five fascicles, relating events up to the Master's arrival in the capital at the conclusion of his return journey from India, he did not publish it but hid it in a cave, fearing that the contents of his writing might be incomplete and inadequate for the public. Later, when he fell seriously ill, he asked his disciples to dig out the manuscript before he passed away. Several years afterward, as the manuscript had become scattered and partially lost, his disciples collected and purchased back the lost sheets and restored the work to its complete form.

Then they asked the monk Yancong, who, though not as erudite in Buddhist learning as his schoolmates under the tutorship of Xuanzang, was good at literary writing, to compile and edit the recovered manuscript into book form. He accepted the commitment and also added five more fascicles to Huili's original five fascicles to relate the Master's activities after his return to China up to his death at midnight on the fifth day of the second month in the first year of Linde (664). He thus produced a more complete biography of the Venerable Tripiṭaka Master Xuanzang, which is presented here in an English version.

Li Rongxi

December 20, 1990

Preface

by the Respectful Śramaṇa Shi Yancong

220c It is considered with deference that when Lord Śākyamuni came to this Land of Endurance, the Eightfold Noble Path was first propagated and the Triple Gem was revealed to refute the books of all heretical schools; hence the prevalence of the Buddha's teachings. The Vaipulya doctrine of the Ekayāna and the Ten Stages of the Perfect Sect are known as the Great Dharma for the exposition of the ultimate truth. The parables of the magic city and the wearing of defiled clothes, as well as the utilization of the cart drawn by a goat or the cart pulled by a deer, are known as lesser learning, as they are explanations of expedient gists. As regards the practice of meditation, the observance of the disciplinary rules, and the employment of the art of incantation, they are but myriad ways leading to the one goal of dispelling illusion and benefitting living beings. Therefore the wise and holy ones of the successive dynasties admired and treasured them. The [*Avataṃsaka*] *Sūtra* spoken at eight assemblies is the fundamental text, as it is the root of the teachings, while the Law that was taught in the three rotations of the Wheel of the Dharma is the branch, as it signifies the offshoot. As regards the rain of four kinds of divine flowers, the earth quaking in six ways, and the king untying the jewel from his topknot and exposing the hidden pearl in his garment, they are metaphors for the refutation of the hypothesis of Three Vehicles (*yānas*) by the One Buddha Vehicle and the absorption of the branches and offshoots into the root.

It is mentioned in the *Fu-fa-zang-[yin-yuan]-zhuan* (Record of the causes of transmitting the Dharma *Piṭaka*) that the holy Ānanda could memorize and recite all the Dharma *Piṭaka* of the Tathāgata as fluently as water pouring out from one vessel into another. This was the teaching taught by Śākyamuni, the Honored One, to different audiences in accordance with circumstances on opportune occasions in the course of forty-nine years of his preaching activities. But when the Ajitavatī River dried up and the scene of the grove of śāla trees became gloomy, the profound gist and abstruse theory almost came to extinction. At the time when the five-layer coffin [containing the remains of the Buddha] was closed and wrapped in a thousand pieces of cotton cloth, ready for cremation, our late Senior Brother Kāśyapa, lamenting over the loss of the Eye of Men and Celestials, which left nobody behind to save living beings, summoned the saintly monks to collect the subtle sayings [of the Buddha]. They studied the regulations to fix the methods of meditation and compiled the disciplinary rules to found the Vinaya school. With the discourses of the *upadeśa* as a basis, they analyzed the theories of emptiness and substantiality. They distinguished the views of annihilation and permanence to show the causes of cultivation and to elucidate the fruits of realization, so as to provide an example for the people of the time and to serve as standard instruction for the future, so that those who turned to them for advice might adhere to their teaching.

When Wang Zun and Qin Jing were sent as envoys tracing the light of the sun to seek the teachings of the Buddha, Kāśyapa-Mātaṅga and Dharmāraṇya came at their invitation to translate the scriptures and worked even in the moonlight. Thereafter,
221a the guests who had shaved their heads and had sincere hearts spread their good reputation abroad, and texts in the foreign tendril-like script engraved on palm leaves were elaborately translated in the Middle Land. But thinkers might mistake the nature and aspects of the most abstruse and most spiritual theories, and debaters might confuse the right and wrong of the subtle mysteries. Moreover, as we were further and further away from the Holy Buddha, and as those of his teachings that were brought in were mostly incomplete, different carriages proceeded in competition on different ways, and each went separately on its own path.

When the Master was born, a bow was hung to signify the birth of a son, and the chamber was regarded as a symbol of response to the emptiness of life. When he had grown up in the years of bumper harvests, his heart corresponded with the sincerity of wonderful virtue. He found that there was no ferry to go out of the sea of desire, but that a house was in the land of enlightenment for the spirit to dwell in. Thus he cut off his hair, changed his dress, and fixed his faith upon the theory of the twofold voidness. He travelled to other districts and mountains by boat and horse, going a thousand *li*. He often regretted that the books obtained and used by ancient sages contained miswritten words that led to erroneous interpretations, and that previous scholars heard and taught dubious points that gave rise to confusion in understanding. "I venture to say that under a tree where music has been performed, there must be echoes of the bell and chime stone, and in the five regions of India, the meanings of the ancient texts must be preserved." So the Master made such a firm resolve that he forgot his meals and crossed dangerous regions as fearlessly as if he were walking on level ground. He defied a myriad of deaths to cross the Pamirs and the Ganges, and for the sake of one word he travelled to the Āmravana Garden. At the Monkey Pond on Gṛdhrakūṭa Mountain, he visited the holy sites and saw the wonderful views. At the Deer Park of the Hermits he sought for remnant texts among moth-eaten books. Living through spring and autumn seasons of cold and hot weather, he spent seventeen years in travelling through or hearing about one hundred thirty countries. There he publicized the great exploits of our Emperor, which shocked the powerful and influential persons of those countries. He lowered the high carriages of the heretics and pulled down the big banners of those who studied with him under the same teacher. Famous kings bowed their heads to him and superior friends associated with him. He was the only person whose edification and morality will last through the ages.

The texts of both Mahayana and Hinayana schools of the Tripiṭaka in Sanskrit obtained by the Master in India amounted to a total number of 657 books. These were carried back through frost and snow by big elephants as well as postal steeds to bring the journey to perfect completion under the protection of Heaven. Braving the hardships of day and rainy weather at night, he journeyed smoothly under the favor of imperial prestige.

In the nineteenth year of Zhenguan (645) he returned to the capital. There he was welcomed by monks and laymen, who swarmed to the city in great numbers. Even the outer city was overcrowded and in a great bustle, with tinklings of jade ornaments. It was indeed a grand occasion. When he had an interview with the Son of Heaven, the latter inquired with solicitude about his journey and ordered by decree that the department concerned have the texts translated into Chinese. Everybody showed respect and homage to him, and it is hard to describe the events in detail. As for the nobility of his lineal ascendants and clansmen, his renunciation of his kinsmen to enter the religious life, his travels far and near, which were praised by the people in China and abroad, his manifestation of repose to return to eternity, and the extinction of the funeral flames with the exhaustion of the pyre, things of this kind are to be found in this biography.

This biography, originally in five fascicles, was composed by Huili, a monk formerly residing at Guoxi Monastery in the region of Wei. With the secular surname of Zhao, Huili was a descendant of Gongliu of the region of Bing, and the son of [Zhao] Yi, Personal Chronicler to the Emperor and Assistant Judicial Inspector of the Sui dynasty. He was learned in Confucian and Buddhist lore and was good at writing compositions. In debating his eloquence was
221b as fluent as a piece of floating cloud, and his thoughts overflowed like the gushing of a spring. He was, moreover, frank in words and solemn in appearance, never dreading any pressure or force. He would go through fire and water dauntlessly [to achieve his objects]. He saw the learning and practice of the Tripiṭaka Master and looked at his appearance and manners. The more he tried to penetrate them, the more unexpectedly firm they seemed to be; and the more he looked up to them, the higher above him they seemed to be. Thus the events in the Master's life were written down to be bequeathed to posterity for a long time to come. But when the manuscript was completed, the author feared that some of the virtuous points might have been overlooked, and so he had it stored in an underground chamber. It was then heard of no more. Later, when he was seriously ill and his breath hung around the

last moment counted by the bell and clepsydra, he ordered his disciples to dig it up from the chamber; but he died when the manuscript was about to be taken out. His disciples and others were so deeply grieved that they could not refrain from wailing and sobbing piteously. This biography was then scattered in segments to various places. Sometime later, after several years of searching and purchasing, it was recently brought together again in its complete form.

I was then asked to compose a preface to it and was encouraged to put it in proper order. Realizing how incompetent I am, I declined the request. Then I was told that the business of the Buddha Dharma should not be left to be done by a layman, and that I should not insistently refuse to perform what was a task of virtue. I yielded with a sense of shame, and after considering the matter for a long time I spread out paper and took up my writing brush, while shedding tears of worry and uneasiness. Then I mixed the original text with supplementary annotations, extending it into a work of ten fascicles, as if I were putting dogs and goats among tigers and leopards and mingling shards and pebbles with jade and jasper. I hope readers of posterity will not sneer at me.

The fifteenth day of the third month
in the fourth year of Chuigong (688)

Fascicle I

Beginning from His Birth at Goushi and Ending with His Arrival at Gaochang in the West

The Master, a native of Chenliu, was named Xuanzang with the family name of Chen. He was a descendant of [Chen] Zhonggong, who served as a magistrate of Taiqui Prefecture during the Han dynasty. His great grandfather [Chen] Qin was the Governor of Shangdang during the Later Wei dynasty. His grandfather [Chen] Kang, a man of distinguished learning, served in the court of Qi as a Professor of the National Academy, living upon the revenue of Zhounan. Thus his descendants made their home there and were also regarded as natives of Goushi. His father, [Chen] Hui, brilliant and spotless by nature with an elegant character, mastered the classics at an early age. With a tall figure—eight feet—he had handsome features, perfect eyebrows, and bright eyes. He used to dress himself in a loose garment with a broad belt in the manner of a Confucian scholar. Being compared by the people of his time to Guo Youdao, he was of a calm and simple nature and took no interest in official promotion. Moreover, as the political situation of the Sui dynasty was on the decline, he devoted himself to the study of the ancient classics. He was repeatedly offered the honorary post of *xiao-lian* (Distinguished Person of Filial Piety and Honesty) by the regional and prefectural authorities and was also summoned by the Emperor to take up the position of judicial inspector, but he declined to accept either appointment on the excuse of ill health. For this he won the praise of the learned men of the day. He had four sons of whom the Master was the youngest.

From his childhood the Master showed magnanimity of nature
221c and outstanding brilliance. Once when he was a child of eight, his

father, who was sitting at a small table, was teaching him orally from the *Book of Filial Piety.* When he came to the passage relating how Zengzi stood up respectfully from the mat on which he was sitting, the Master got up and straightened his dress. Being asked why, he replied, "Since Zengzi stood to listen to the lectures of his teacher, why should I sit comfortably while receiving instructions from my father?" His father was greatly pleased with the reply and had no doubt that his son would make great achievements in his life. When he invited his clansmen and told them about this incident, they complimented him, saying, "He is a filial son indeed!" This was an instance of the Master's precocity.

Afterward the Master was well versed in the classics, loved ancient things, and honored the sages. He never read any book that was vulgar or improper, and he never followed customs not practised by the saints and wise men. He kept apart from other children and never set foot at the gate of the market place. Even should there be a din of bells and drums in the street, or a performance of singing and dancing watched by a crowd of men and women in the lane, he would not go out to behold it. Since his youth, he knew how to serve his parents with a cheerful countenance, in a mild and pure as well as honest and scrupulous manner.

His second elder brother, Changjie, a monk who lived in the Pure Land Monastery in the Eastern Capital, observed that the Master was competent to receive instruction in the Dharma and brought him to his monastery to learn the scriptures. Shortly afterward an imperial decree announced that fourteen persons would be allowed to enter monastic life at Luoyang. There were then several hundred men who had studied well, but the Master, being too young, was not allowed to join the limited number of candidates. He stood beside the gate of the government house, when the envoy Zheng Shanguo, who was the Lord of Justice, a man able to discern other people's talents, saw him and found in him an unusual person. He asked the lad, "To whose family do you belong?" The Master told him of his family. The imperial envoy then asked, "Do you intend to enter monastic life?"

"Yes," replied the Master. "But as my learning is shallow and my merit small, I was not allowed to take part in the competitive examination."

The envoy asked again, "What is your purpose in becoming a monk?"

To this the Master replied, "I wish to carry on the Tathāgata's teachings far into the future and glorify his bequeathed Dharma in the present." Shanguo highly praised his ambition, and as he was pleased with his intelligence and manners, he granted him special permission to go in. He said to his official colleagues, "It is easy for one to complete one's studies in the scriptures, but it is difficult for us to find a person of noble quality. If we allow this lad to enter monastic life, he will surely become a great man in the religion of Buddhism, even though you and I, gentlemen, may not witness him soaring high in the clouds and sprinkling down Sweet Dew (*amṛta*). Besides, we must not neglect this scion of a distinguished family." Considering what happened, the words of Lord Zheng proved true.

Having become a monk, the Master stayed with his elder brother. At the time a reverend teacher, Sengjing, was preaching the *Mahāparinirvāṇa Sūtra* in the monastery. The Master, holding the scripture in his hands, memorized what he had heard in the lectures so absorbedly that he even forgot to eat and sleep. He also studied the *Mahāyānasaṃparigraha Śāstra* under the instruction of the reverend teacher Yan with even greater interest. He could remember almost the whole text at the first reading, and after the second reading he memorized the work without missing anything. Astonished by his extraordinary talent, the people invited him to mount the pulpit to repeat what the teacher had preached. He gave a detailed exposition with full analysis in complete concordance with the gist of the teacher's sermon. Thence his good name and fame became widely known. He was then aged thirteen.

Afterward, the House of Sui lost power, and the country fell into a state of great turmoil. The imperial capital became a nest of despots like Jie the Tyrant and brigands like Zhe the Bandit, and the region between the Yellow River and the Luo River turned into

222a a cavern for evil men as brutal as jackals and wolves. Civilization collapsed, and the Buddhist community dispersed. White skeletons were scattered at crossroads, and the region was depopulated; no smoke came out of cooking stoves. Even the tumult caused by the rebellions of Wang Mang and Dong Zhuo, and the catastrophic invasions of Liu Yuan and She Le, did not surpass this in slaughter and devastation.

Although he was still a youth, the Master realized the desirability of adapting oneself to circumstances, and he said to his elder brother, "Although this is the district of our parents, there is no reason, since it is in such a tumultuous condition, why we should stay here and wait for death. I have heard that the Emperor of Tang, with the multitude of Jinyang under his command, has occupied Chang'an, and all the people of the country are flocking to him as if they were going to their parents. I wish to go there with you to seek shelter." His elder brother consented, and they went to Chang'an in the first year of Wude (618).

At that time, as the foundation of the dynasty had just been laid and the war was still going on, the urgent matter of the moment was the military art of the strategists Sun Wu and Wu Qi. It was no time for carrying on either Confucian or Buddhist activities. Therefore to the Master's deep regret no preaching meeting was held in the capital.

Formerly, Emperor Yang of the Sui dynasty had constructed four monasteries in the Eastern Capital and invited well-known monks of the country to live in them. All those who were called in were men specializing in one or another particular subject of learning. Therefore there had been an army of learned Buddhist scholars, of whom Sengjing, Zhituo, Daoji, and Baoxian were at the head. During the last years of the Sui dynasty, when the country was in chaos, their support was cut off. Most of them moved to the regions of Mian and Shu, where a large number of Buddhist scholars assembled. So the Master said to his elder brother, "As there is no more Dharma activity here, we should not waste our time. We should go to the region of Shu to pursue our studies." His elder brother consented, and they again travelled through the

Ziwu Valley and arrived at Hanchuan, where they met with the two reverend teachers Kong and Jing, both of whom were men of great virtue among the Buddhists. They were delighted and excited at the unexpected encounter. Staying there for over a month, they studied under the two teachers every day and then proceeded together to Chengdu.

As many scholars assembled, they held meetings to propagate the Dharma extensively. Thus the Master attended the lectures given by Daoji and Baoxian on the *Mahāyānasaṃparigraha Śāstra* and the *Abhidharmasamuccaya Śāstra,* and he also studied the *Abhidharmajñānaprasthāna Śāstra* of Kātyāyana under the instruction of the reverend teacher Daozhen. Not wasting a moment of time, he studied with full effort tirelessly; and within two or three years he thoroughly mastered the Buddhist texts of different schools. At that time the whole empire was suffering from starvation and disorder except the region of Shu, where the people lived in peaceful abundance. Therefore large numbers of monks came from all quarters of the empire to live there. There were often several hundred people attending the preaching meetings. The Master's intelligence and talent surpassed them all, and his name became known in the regions of Wu, Shu, Jing, and Chu. The people respected and admired him for his learning and personality just in the same way as the ancient people had esteemed Li Ying and Guo Tai.

Consequently, the Master's elder brother lived in the Konghui Monastery at Chengdu. He was also a man of sturdy build, with refined manners similar to those of his father. He was fond of both Buddhist and worldly lore and had lectured on the *Mahāparinirvāṇa Sūtra,* the *Mahāyānasaṃparigraha Śāstra,* and the *Abhidharmasamuccaya Śāstra.* He was learned in the *Shang-shu* and its *Expositions* and was especially erudite in the works of Laozi and Zhuangzi, winning the estimation of the people of Shu. The governor, Zhan, especially respected him. His ability in writing, his eloquence in discussion, his magnanimity in manners, and his capacity to edify people were not inferior to those of his younger brother. But in loftiness of mind, without defilement by impurities;

in researches into the metaphysical aspects of the cosmos; in
222b ambition to clarify the universe, with a mind to continue the tasks of the saints, to rectify collapsed principles and suppress evil customs; in dauntless spirit in adverse circumstances; and in sense of self-respect even in the presence of the Emperor—in all these matters the elder brother did not show superiority over the younger one. But both brothers led lives of purity in accordance with the monastic rules and had such good reputations that even the two brothers of Lushan did not surpass them.

When the Master reached the age of twenty in the fifth year of Wude (622), he received full ordination at Chengdu, where he spent the summer retreat and studied the Vinaya rules. He learned the rules laid down in the five classifications and seven groups of the Vinaya by studying them only once. Having completed his studies of all the scriptures and commentaries that could be found in the region of Yi, he desired to go to the capital to make further studies of specialized subjects and to clear up the doubts that had embarrassed his mind. But as this was prohibited by regulations, his elder brother detained him and he could not fulfill his wishes. Later, he secretly sailed down the Three Gorges in company with some merchants and ran away along the Yanzi River until he reached Tianhuang Monastery at Jingzhou. There the monks and laity, having heard of his fame long ago, asked him to preach sermons for them, since he had favored them with his presence. From summer to winter, the Master lectured on the *Mahāyānasaṃparigraha Śāstra* and the *Abhidharmasamuccaya Śāstra,* each three times. At that time, the Prince of Hanyang, a man of great virtue, closely related to the imperial family, was governor of that region. He was very pleased to hear that the Master had arrived and paid homage to him in person. On the first day of the preaching meeting, when the title of the text was expounded, the Prince went at the head of his group of officials, learned monks, and laymen to the assembly to observe the function. In the congregation many people put questions and made inquiries for a better understanding of the preaching. In answering them the Master gave full explanations to the satisfaction of all. Those who acquired a deeper understanding were moved to tears, and the Prince also eulogized him in the highest terms. Donations and gifts were heaped on him, but he took none of them.

After the conclusion of his preaching activities, he travelled northward in search of erudite scholars of virtue. On his way he reached Xiangzhou, where he visited the reverend teacher Huixiu and inquired of him about the dubious points he had found in the texts. Then he went to Zhaozhou and visited the reverend teacher Daoshen, from whom he learned about the *Satyasiddhi Śāstra*. Then he entered Chang'an and stayed at the Great Enlightenment Monastery, where he learned about the *Abhidharmakośa Śāstra* from the reverend teacher Daoyue. He grasped the essential meanings of all these texts by studying them only once, and could memorize whatever had passed his eyes, an ability unsurpassed even by senior scholars of deep learning. He studied with such profundity that he could comprehend subtle meanings and reveal what was hidden in the texts when others failed to reach it. On more than one abstruse point he had his own particular views.

At that time, there were at Chang'an two teachers of great virtue, Fachang and Sengbian, who were learned in both Mahayana and Hinayana teachings and whose conduct was in full concordance with the Three Studies of discipline, meditation, and wisdom. As they were great teachers of the Dharma in the capital, both monks and laymen flocked to them to be their disciples. Their morality was known throughout the country and their fame spread beyond the seas, with students following them like clouds grouping in the sky. They were comprehensively versed in all scriptures. They had, however, a special liking for expounding the *Mahāyānasaṃparigraha Śāstra*. Although the Master had gained achievements in the regions of Wu and Shu, he continued after his arrival at Chang'an to pursue learning under their instruction; but very soon he exhausted their store of knowledge. Both the two teachers highly praised the Master and said to him, "You are indeed an outstanding person in the religion of Buddhism. The re-illumination
222c of the Sun of Wisdom will have to depend upon you. We regret to say that we are getting old and may not be able to witness your

success." After that his fellow students had a different opinion of him, and his fame spread throughout the capital.

Having visited various teachers and learned their theories, the Master scrutinized their teachings and found that each of them specialized in some particular sect. When compared with the holy scriptures, they showed differences either vaguely or manifestly, so that he was at a loss to decide which of the theories he should follow. Thus he resolved to travel to the West to clear his doubts and to bring back the *Saptadaśabhūmi Śāstra,* which is now known as the *Yogācārabhūmi Śāstra,* to resolve the doubts of all. He also said, "Since Faxian and Zhiyan, prominent figures of former times, could travel to seek the Dharma for the benefit of all living beings, why should there be nobody to follow in their footsteps, so that the line of noble tasks should be discontinued? A real man should have the ambition to carry forward their tradition." Thus he associated with some companions and submitted a petition to the court, but a decree was issued forbidding them to travel abroad. The others withdrew from the attempt; the Master alone did not give up his aspiration.

In preparation for the journey to be undertaken by himself alone, and in view of the dangers on the road to the West, he tested his resolution by inflicting upon himself various pains known in the world to temper his willpower. He endured them all without flinching. Then he entered a pagoda to say prayers and to make up his mind, invoking all the saints to protect him with their divine influence so that he might go and return without encountering any obstacle. When the Master was born, his mother had had a dream in which she saw him dressed in white going toward the West. She said, "You are my son. Where do you wish to go?" The Master replied, "I am going to seek the Dharma." This was indeed a presage of his journey to the West.

In the eighth month in the autumn of the third year of Zhenguan (629), when the Master was about to start on his journey, he prayed again for a good omen. In the night he dreamed that he saw Mount Sumeru most beautifully made of the four precious substances, standing in the middle of the great sea. He desired to climb up the mountain, but the billows were turbulent and there was neither boat nor raft in sight. He was not daunted at all but decided to go into the sea. Suddenly he saw stone lotus flowers emerging out of the waves below his feet. When he turned back to look at the flowers, they disappeared as soon as he lifted his feet. In a moment he reached the foot of the mountain, which was so precipitous that it was impossible for him to climb up. While he was trying to ascend the mountain by leaping, a strong whirlwind came and carried him up to the top of the mountain. He looked around and saw that everything was clear in sight without any hindrance. Then he awoke from the dream elated with joy. After that he started on his journey, when he was twenty-six years of age.

There was then a monk named Xiaoda from Qinzhou, who had been studying the *Mahāparinirvāṇa Sūtra* in the capital and was about to return home after the completion of his learning. So the Master travelled with him to Qinzhou, where he stayed for one night and met a fellow traveller from Lanzhou, with whom he journeyed to Lanzhou. After spending one night there he met a man from Liangzhou, who was sending back horses for official use, and so he went there with that man. He stayed there for more than one month, and at the request of the local monks and laymen he expounded the *Mahāparinirvāṇa Sūtra,* the *Mahāyānasaṃparigraha Śāstra,* and the *Mahāprajñāpāramitā Sūtra.*

Liangzhou, the capital city of the Hexi region, was a linking place with the western tribes and the various countries located to the east of the Pamirs. Merchants came and went from there without intermission. On the days when the Master was preach-
223a ing, many of them came to offer him gems and jewels with worship and praise. After returning to their own countries, they extolled the virtues of the Master in the presence of their rulers, saying that he was coming to the West with the intention of seeking the Dharma in the Brahmanic countries. So it was that the people of various cities in the Western Region made preparations in happy anticipation of his arrival.

On the day when the preaching meeting was concluded, abundant precious alms of gold and silver coins and a large number of horses of good breed were offered to the Master, but he accepted only half of the gifts for his own religious purpose and shared the rest with various monasteries.

At that time, as the regime was newly established and the boundaries of the country were limited, common people were prohibited from going to the regions of the western tribes. Li Daliang, the governor of Liangzhou, enforced the prohibition very rigorously under strict imperial decree. It was reported to him that a certain monk from Chang'an intended to go to the countries in the West for an unknown purpose. Out of fear, the governor questioned the Master about his intentions. The Master told him that he intended to travel westward to search for the Dharma. On hearing this, the governor ordered him to return to the capital.

There was then a reverend teacher Huiwei, a leader of the Buddhists in the region of Hexi, who was a man of brilliant intelligence and great wisdom. He respected the Master for his eloquence in preaching and deeply sympathized with him when he heard about his ambition of going to seek the Dharma. He secretly sent two of his disciples, Huilin and Daozheng, to escort the Master furtively to the West. Thus he dared not go out openly but hid himself in the daytime and travelled by night, until he reached Guazhou, where the prefectural governor Dugu Da was very pleased to hear the news of his arrival and treated him with good hospitality. The Master inquired about the westbound route and was told that over fifty *li* to the north was the Hulu River, which was broad at the lower reaches and narrow at its upper part. As the current was rapid and the water deep, it was impossible to ferry across. Situated at its upper part was the Yumen Pass, which was the only way for travellers to follow as it was the key to the West region. Beyond the pass in the northwest were five watchtowers, set apart at a distance of one hundred *li* from each other with garrisons stationed in them, and there was neither water nor grass in between. Beyond the five watchtowers was the Mohoyan Desert in the territory of the country of Yiwu. On hearing this, the Master was worried and disturbed, and the horse he rode died at this juncture. Not knowing what to do, he brooded over the situation in silence for more than a month.

Before he could continue his journey, a warrant of arrest arrived from Liangzhou, stating that a monk by the name of Xuanzang was trying to enter the regions of the western tribes and that all prefects and magistrates through whose domain he might pass should take every precaution for his arrest. Li Chang, the prefect, who was a pious Buddhist, suspected that the Master was the wanted man. He secretly showed him the warrant and asked him, "Is the reverend teacher not the man mentioned in it?"

The Master hesitated and did not reply.

Li Chang said, "You must tell me the truth. If you are, I'll try to help you."

Then the Master told him the truth. On hearing it, Li Chang highly praised him as a man trying to achieve an unusual thing and said, "If you are truly trying to do what you have said, I shall destroy this document." So saying, he tore the warrant to pieces in the presence of the Master, but still he advised him, "You should leave here as soon as possible."

Now the Master worried all the more. Of the two junior monks,
223b Daozheng had already gone to Dunhuang, and only Huilin remained with him. Knowing that he could not stand the hardships of the long journey ahead, the Master dismissed him and let him go home. He bought a horse, but the trouble was that he had nobody to be his guide. Before the image of Maitreya Bodhisattva of the monastery in which he was staying, he prayed for a man who might guide him through the pass. That night a monk of the Hu tribe, named Dharma, of that monastery dreamed that the Master was sitting on a lotus flower going west. Dharma felt it strange and in the following morning he came to tell his dream to the Master, who was delighted in his mind, knowing that this was a good omen indicating the possibility of continuing his journey. But he said to Dharma, "A dream is but a fancy and is not worth mentioning."

He again entered the shrine hall to pray. Before long a man of the Hu tribe came to pay homage to the image of the Buddha. He worshipped the Master by circumambulating him two or three times. Being asked his name, the man said that he was named Pantuo with the surname of Shi. He begged for the conferment of the Precepts and was given the Five Precepts. Greatly delighted, the Hu man went away and returned in a moment with cakes and fruits. Seeing that the man was intelligent and strong with a reverential manner, the Master told him about his intention of taking the journey. The Hu man consented to send him across the five watchtowers, and this greatly pleased the Master. He bought some clothes and a horse for the man and made an appointment with him.

On the following day, when the sun was about to set, the Master went to a bushland where he waited for the man. Before long he arrived together with an old man of the Hu tribe, riding on an aged lean horse of reddish color. At this sight the Master felt displeased. But the young man said, "This old man knows the route to the West perfectly well. He has travelled to and from Yiwu for more than thirty times. I have brought him along in the hope that he might give you some counsel." Then the old Hu man said, "The road to the West is perilous and the Sha River is an obstacle on the long way. There are demons and hot wind. Whoever encounters them cannot be spared from death. Even if you travel together with a large group of companions, you might go astray or be lost. How can you, reverend teacher, try to go all alone? I ask you to consider the matter carefully and not gamble with your life."

The Master replied, "I started on my journey to the West for the purpose of seeking the Great Dharma. I shall not return to the East before I reach the Brahmanic countries. I shall not regret it even if I die on the way."

The old man said, "If you insist on going, you had better ride my horse. This horse of mine has travelled to Yiwu fifteen times. It is sound and knows the way well. Yours is too young to travel such a long distance."

Then the Master recalled that when he was about to start on his journey to the West from Chang'an, there was a sorcerer, named He Hongda, whose witchcraft and divination were usually effective. The Master had asked him to foretell the events of his forthcoming journey. The sorcerer said, "You will be able to go, and it seems that you will be riding on an aged, lean horse of a reddish color, equipped with a varnished saddle with a piece of iron at the front." On seeing that the Hu man's horse was lean and reddish in color and that the varnished saddle had a piece of iron, the Master deemed it appropriate to take it, and so he changed his horse for that of the old Hu man, who was quite pleased and went away after due salutation.

After having packed his outfit, the Master started on the journey with the young Hu man. At about the third watch, they reached the river and saw the Yumen Pass at a distance. They went
223c up the stream for about ten *li* from the pass and came to a place where the banks of the river were over ten feet apart, beside which there was a wood of tamarisks. The Hu man cut some branches and built a bridge, on which he spread grass and paved it with sand. Then they drove their horses across.

The Master was glad to have crossed the river, and he unsaddled his horse to take rest at a place more than fifty paces from the Hu man. They spread their quilts on the ground to sleep. After a little while the Hu man got up, unsheathed his knife, and slowly advanced toward the Master, but he retreated at a distance of about ten paces. Not knowing what he had in his mind and suspecting that he might have an evil intent, the Master got up and recited scriptures and repeated the name of Avalokiteśvara Bodhisattva, whereupon the Hu man lay down and slept.

When it was nearly daybreak, the Master wakened the man to fetch some water for a wash. At the moment when they were about to continue the journey after having taken breakfast, the Hu man said, "Your disciple considers that the journey ahead is long and dangerous with neither water nor grass on the way. As water can be obtained only at the five towers, we have to reach them at night to steal water and pass along. But once discovered we shall be dead men. So it is safer to turn back."

But the Master was determined not to go back, and so the Hu man proceeded with reluctance. He took out his sword and drew his bow, ordering the Master to go before him, but the Master refused to precede him. When they had gone a few *li,* the man stopped and said, "Your disciple cannot go any more. I have a big family to support, and moreover I dare not trespass against the law." The Master knew his mind and let him go back. The Hu man said, "You will certainly not be able to reach your destination. What shall I do if you are arrested and I am involved in the matter?" The Master replied, "Even if I am cut to pieces, I will never implicate you in my affair." He then took a solemn oath and the man was satisfied. The Master presented him with a horse out of gratitude for his service, and they parted.

After that the Master travelled alone in the desert, proceeding slowly along the trail marked by skeletons and horse dung. Shortly afterward he suddenly saw an army of several hundred men scattered all over the desert, moving forward or halting for a while. They were dressed in furs or coarse cloth, and their camels and horses, as well as banners, flags, and spears, kept on changing their shapes every moment. They were quite clear at a distance but gradually disappeared as they approached. At first sight, the Master thought them to be bandits, but as they faded away when they came nearer, he realized that they were bogies and demons. He heard a voice in the air, saying, "Have no fear! Have no fear!" And then he felt a little better in his mind.

After travelling a distance of more than eighty *li* he came in sight of the first watchtower. Fearing that he might be seen by the watchmen, he hid himself in a sandy ditch and remained there
224a until nightfall. Then he came to the west of the tower, where he saw water. He went down to have a drink and washed his hands, and when he was about to refill his water bag, an arrow whizzed through the air and nearly hit his knee. A moment later, another arrow was shot. Realizing that he had been seen, he said aloud, "I am a monk from the capital. Don't shoot at me!"

He led his horse to the tower, where the watchmen opened the door and came out to see him. Seeing that he was really a monk, they brought him in to see the captain, Wang Xiang, who ordered a lamp to be lit so he could see the Master. He said, "He is not a monk from our region of Hexi. It seems that he really comes from the capital." Then he inquired of the Master what the purpose of his travel was. The Master said in reply, "Did not the captain hear the people of Liangzhou say that a monk named Xuanzang intended to go to the Brahmanic countries to seek the Dharma?" The captain answered, "I heard that the teacher Xuanzang has returned to the East. How is it that you have come here?" The Master took from his horse the petition he had written to the Emperor, in which his name was written, and showed it to the captain. The captain believed him but still said, "The road to the West is long and perilous, and you could never reach your destination. I shall not arrest you. But as I am a native of Dunhuang, I wish to send you back to that place. There there is a reverend teacher named Zhangjiao, who esteems wise and virtuous people. I am sure he will be delighted to meet you. Please go to his place."

The Master said in reply, "My native place is Luoyang and I have admired the Dharma since my youth. I have studied under all the learned teachers of the two capitals and the talented monks in the regions of Wu and Shu, and have mastered all their knowledge. In explaining and discussing Buddhist teachings, I had the honor to be ranked among contemporary teachers. If I were interested in gaining personal benefit and reputation, those places would not be inferior to your Dunhuang. But it was because I regretted that the Buddhist scriptures were incomplete and that the doctrines were ambiguous that I made a vow to go to the West to seek the bequeathed Dharma at the risk of my life, without fearing the hardships and dangers of the journey. Now you do not encourage me but advise me to go back. Can that be a cause for us to free ourselves from worldly sufferings and realize nirvana? If you have to detain me, I am prepared to bear whatever punishment you may mete out to me. But I shall never go back a single step toward the East against my original intention."

On hearing this, the captain Wang Xiang said with sympathy, "I am lucky to have this chance to meet you. How can I do otherwise than comply with your wishes? You must be tired now and should take rest until tomorrow. I shall send you off and show you the way personally." A bamboo mat was then spread to accommodate the

Master for the night. At dawn when the Master had taken his meal, Wang Xiang ordered his men to fill his water bag, provided him with wheat cakes, and escorted him for a distance of more than ten *li*. He said to the Master, "By this route you may go straight to the fourth watchtower. The man in charge there, by the name of Wang Bolong, is a man with a kind heart and a relative of mine. When you reach there you may say that I sent you." He took leave of the Master after paying homage to him with tears in his eyes.

After making his departure, the Master came to the fourth watchtower by nightfall. Fearing that he might be detained there, he intended to get some water and pass along silently. But before he could get down to fetch water, an arrow flew near him. So he made an announcement as before and went hurriedly to the tower, from which some men came down and took him in. In reply to the
224b inquiries of the officer in charge of the tower, the Master said, "I am on my way to India, and Captain Wang Xiang of the first watchtower has sent me to come by this way." Being pleased to hear this, the officer lodged the Master for the night. He presented to the Master a large water bag with some wheat as fodder for his horse, saying, "You need not go to the fifth watchtower. The man there is an imprudent fellow and he might give you trouble. About a hundred *li* from here, there is Wild Horse Spring, where you can replenish your water bag."

Beyond this place was the Moheyan Desert, which stretched more than eight hundred *li*. This was what the ancients called the desert river, where there was no bird flying above, nor any beast roaming below; neither was there any water or grass. Now the Master had only his lonely shadow travelling with him, and all he could do was repeat the name of Avalokiteśvara Bodhisattva and recite the *Prajñāpāramitāhṛdaya Sūtra*. Formerly, when the Master was in the region of Shu, he once saw a sick man suffering from a foul skin ulcer and dressed in rags. With a feeling of pity, he took the man to his monastery and gave him money to purchase clothes and food. Being ashamed of himself, the sick man taught the Master this sutra, which he often recited. In the desert he met various evil spirits with strange appearances that surrounded him and refused to be dispelled completely, although he repeated the name of Avalokiteśvara Bodhisattva. But as soon as he uttered this sutra, all of them disappeared immediately. It was by depending upon this sutra that he was saved from many a peril.

After having travelled for more than a hundred *li,* he lost his way and could not find Wild Horse Spring. When he took down his water bag to have a drink, it was so heavy that it slipped from his hands and the water that was to sustain him during his journey of a thousand *li* was spilled all at once. He lost his way in the winding path and did not know which direction to proceed. So he wished to return eastward to the fourth watchtower. When he had gone about ten *li,* he said to himself, "I vowed not to turn back even one step to the East before I reached India. Why am I going back now? I would rather die on my way to the West than return to the East and live." Then he reined back his horse and proceeded toward the northwest, whilst repeating the name of Avalokiteśvara Bodhisattva.

He looked around and saw nothing but the vast desert, where there was not a man or even a bird to be seen. In the night the evil spirits and demons sparkled as brightly as stars in the sky. During the daytime surprising gales blew the sand up high, and it fell down like a shower. Although he encountered such circumstances, he had no fear in his mind. The trouble was the lack of water; he was so thirsty that he could proceed no more. For four nights and five days he had not a drop of water to moisten his throat, and his mouth and stomach became dried up. Being at the brink of death, he could no longer move forward. He lay down on the sand and repeated the name of Avalokiteśvara Bodhisattva, and did not give up the repetition even in such a desperate situation. He prayed to the Bodhisattva, saying, "I am undertaking this journey not for the purpose of gaining wealth nor for winning reputation. It was simply to acquire the supreme Right Dharma that I have come here. I sincerely pray that the Bodhisattva will have mercy upon all living beings and save those who are in distress. I am now in distress indeed! Cannot you hear my prayers?"

When he prayed in this manner, his mind was concentrated without distraction. At midnight on the fifth day a cool breeze suddenly came and made him feel as chilly as if he were taking a bath in cold water. He was able to open his eyes, and his horse also found its feet. Being refreshed by the cool air, he fell asleep for a
224c while and dreamed that he saw a giant deity several tens of feet tall, holding a spear and a flag in his hands. The deity said to him, "Why are you sleeping here instead of forging ahead?"

The Master was startled and awakened from his sleep, and then he proceeded on his journey. Having gone for about ten *li,* his horse suddenly changed its course and would not turn back, though he pulled hard at the reins. A few *li* further on, he caught sight of a stretch of pasture several *mou* wide, and dismounted to graze his horse. When he had gone ten paces beyond the pasture and was about to turn back, he came to a pond of clean and sweet water. He went down to drink, and thus his life was preserved and both he and his horse were invigorated. One conjectures that this pasture and the water pond had not been there before but were produced out of compassion by the Bodhisattva. His sincerity of mind communicated with the divinities. This was one of many such instances. He rested for one day at the pasture and the pond, and after refilling his water bag and gathering some grass he continued his journey on the following day. Travelling for two more days, he came out of the desert and reached the country of Yiwu. The hardships he experienced were numerous and cannot be related in full detail.

Upon his arrival in Yiwu, he stayed in a monastery in which lived three monks of Han descent. The senior one was so excited that he forgot to dress himself properly and came out barefooted to receive the Master, whom he embraced while crying piteously without restraint. He said, "I never expected to have this opportunity to see a countryman again!" The Master also shed tears of sympathy for him. The monks and the king of the Hu tribe came to pay their respects, and the king invited him to his residence and entertained him with all kinds of offerings.

An envoy had been sent previously to Yiwu by Qu Wentai, the king of Gaochang. On that day he was to go back and had the chance to meet the Master. On his return the envoy reported this to the king. Upon hearing this news, the king immediately dispatched an envoy to request that the king of Yiwu send the Master to him. At the same time he selected several tens of his best horses and appointed a high ranking minister provided with a herd of camels to set up rest houses along the way for the reception of the Master. After about ten days the envoy arrived and conveyed the king's invitation with salutation and much sincerity.

Originally the Master had planned to go by way of the Khan Stupa. But now that he was invited by the king of Gaochang and could not decline the invitation, he travelled across the South Desert. After spending six days on the way he reached the city of Paili in the domain of Gaochang.

As the sun had already set, the Master wished to halt for the night. The officials of the city and the envoy said, "The royal city is near. Please proceed ahead." The Master changed good horses several times on the way, leaving behind the reddish horse which he had ridden before to be sent to him later. At midnight he arrived at the royal city. The gatekeeper reported it to the king, who ordered him to open the gate, and the Master entered the city. The king and his attendants, with candles in their hands and walking in a line, came out of the palace to receive the Master and ushered him to sit behind a precious curtain in a storeyed pavilion in the inner court. The king worshipped him and asked him about his journey in a very cordial manner, saying, "Since I, your disciple, heard the name of the Master, I have been so happy that I have forgotten to sleep and take food. Computing the distance of the way, I guessed that you would arrive tonight, and so my wife and I did not sleep but waited for your arrival while we recited scriptures." In a moment the royal consort and several tens of her attending maids came to pay homage to the Master. When it was
225a nearly daybreak, he felt tired after so much talking and wished to retire. Then the king returned to his palace, leaving some eunuches behind to attend the Master.

Early next morning before the Master had arisen, the king and the queen together with those below them in rank came to the door of his chamber to pay their respects to him. The king said, "Considering that the way through the desert is hard to travel, I deem it a great wonder that you could have come all alone!" He praised the Master with tears of emotion and could not restrain himself. Food was then served. When the Master had taken his breakfast, the king personally led him to a monastery situated by the side of the palace, and appointed eunuches to serve him. In that monastery there was a reverend teacher Tuan, who had studied at Chang'an and understood well all aspects of the Dharma. The king esteemed him and invited him to come to see the Master, and he came out in a moment. The king also ordered the royal teacher, who was over eighty years old, to live with the Master in order to persuade him to stay and give up his westward journey. But the Master did not consent.

After staying there for more than ten days, the Master wished to take his leave. The king said, "I have asked the royal teacher to extend my invitation. What do you think of it?" The Master said in reply, "It is really a great favor from the king that I have been asked to remain here. But in consideration of my intention of taking the journey, I must not do that." The king said, "I have travelled to the Great Country with the late king and have visited together with the Emperor of the Sui dynasty both the east and the west capitals, as well as the regions of Yan, Dai, Fen, and Jin. There I met many monks of high reputation, but none of them won my admiration. When I heard your name, I was so glad that I danced with delight. I planned that when you came here you should stay here and receive my offerings for the rest of your life. I will order all the people of my country to be your disciples and receive your instructions. Though we may not have many monks here, they still amount to several thousand. I will ask them to hold the scriptures and be your audience. I sincerely pray that you will consider and accept my humble suggestion, and give up the idea of travelling to the West."

The Master declined the invitation, saying, "How can a man poor in virtue such as I be worthy to accept the king's kind hospitality? The purpose of my journey is not to obtain offerings. [I undertook it] because I regretted that the teachings of the Dharma were not complete and the scriptures deficient in my own country. I have doubts and have puzzled my mind, but I could find no one to solve them. That was why I decided to travel to the West at the risk of my life in order to seek the teachings that I have not heard before, so that not only will the Sweet Dew of the Vaipulya scriptures have been sprinkled at Kapilavastu but also the sublime truth of discrimination may be known in the eastern country. The aspiration of Sadāpralāpa inquiring after the Way and the wish of Sudhana looking for friends should be strengthened day after day and must not be abandoned halfway. I hope Your Majesty will recall your words and not bother about my personal welfare."

The king said, "As I, your disciple, have a great adoration for the Master, I will decidedly invite you to stay here so that I may make offerings to you. Even if the Pamir Range could be moved, my mind would not be changed. Please believe in my sincerity and do not doubt my earnestness."

To this the Master responded, "It needs no repeated explanation to understand Your Majesty's deep kindness. But as I have come here on my way to the West to seek the Dharma, I must not stop halfway before I have found it. That is why I respectfully decline your kind offer, and I hope that Your Majesty will have
225b sympathy with me. Moreover, it was due to the superior blessedness that Your Majesty had cultivated in previous lives that you became a lord of men, upon whom not only your subjects but also the religion of Buddhism rely for support. It befits you to help its spreading. Is it appropriate for you to be a hindrance to its propagation?"

The king said, "I dare not obstruct the propagation of Buddhism. It is only because we have no teacher in our country to guide us that I wish to keep you here to enlighten the deluded and the ignorant."

The Master would not consent to stay in spite of the king's entreaties. Thus the king changed his countenance and rolled up his sleeves, while shouting, "Your disciple has other ways to deal with the Master. How can you go by yourself? Either you must stay, or I shall send you back to your country. Please consider the matter well. I think it is better for you to comply with my wish."

The Master said in reply, "I have come on my way to seek the Great Dharma, and now I encounter an obstacle. Only my physical body may be detained by Your Majesty; my mind can never be withheld." He was then choked by sobs and could speak no more. Even so, the king did not allow him to go, but increased the amount of offerings presented to him. Every day at mealtime the king held a tray of food with both hands to serve the Master. Having been detained against his own wish, the Master refused to take any food in the hope that the king would change his mind. He sat erect and did not drink even a drop of water for three days. On the fourth day the king found that his breath had become very feeble, and, feeling deeply ashamed of himself and afraid, the king worshipped him and apologized, saying, "I will allow you to go to the West. Please take food immediately."

Fearing that the king's words were untrue, the Master asked him to take an oath with his finger pointing at the sun. The king said, "If you wish me to do that, we had better strengthen our relationship before the image of the Buddha." So they went together to the temple to worship the Buddha, and in the presence of the Queen Mother, Zhang, the king acknowledged the Master to be his brother and said to him, "I will let you go to seek the Dharma. But on your return journey you must come to stay in this country for three years to receive my offerings. When you become a Buddha in the future, let me be your patron and supporter just as the two kings Prasenajit and Bimbisāra were to the Buddha."

The Master was still pressed to stay for another month to preach on the *Prajñāpāramitā Sūtra of the Benevolent King*. Meanwhile preparations were to be made for his journey. The Master consented to this request, to the great delight of the Queen Mother, who wished to be always related with the Master so that they could help one another in all future lives. Then the Master began to take food again. This was an instance of his firmness of resolution.

Two days later the king pitched a special big tent, large enough to accommodate three hundred persons, for the Master to preach in. The Queen Mother and those below her in rank, including the king, the royal teacher, and the ministers, sat on different seats to listen to the sermon. At each time of preaching, the king, holding a thurible in hand, ushered the Master to the tent. When the Master was ascending the pulpit, the king knelt down to serve as a stool for him to step up to the high seat, and this he did every day.

After the conclusion of the preaching, the king gave permission for the ordination of four *śrāmaṇera*s to serve the Master as his attendants. Thirty suits of religious garments were made, and as the climate in the lands of the West was mostly cold, some face covers, gloves, boots, and stockings were also prepared. One hundred taels of gold, thirty thousand silver coins, and five hundred rolls of silk and satin were provided for the Master as funds to last
225c him twenty years on his journey to and from the West. Thirty horses and twenty-five carriers were allotted to him. Huanxin, the palace attendant and royal secretary, was ordered to escort him to the yamen of Shehu Khan. The king also wrote twenty-four letters to Kucha, etc., twenty-four countries, and to each letter was attached one roll of fine silk as a sign of credence. Five hundred rolls of silk and two cartloads of fruits and edibles were presented to Shehu Khan with a letter, in which the king said, "The Master, who is my younger brother, wishes to seek the Dharma in the Brahmanic countries. May the Khan treat him with kindness, as he would treat me. I would also request that you issue orders to the countries in the West to send the Master out of their domains from stage to stage by corvée horses."

Upon seeing that the king sent him the *śrāmaṇera*s and provided him with credentials and rolls of silk, the Master felt thankful for the rich farewell gifts and wrote a letter to the king to express his gratitude:

> I, Xuanzang, have heard that one has to depend upon a boat with oars to cross deep and far-stretching rivers and seas. Just in the same way one has to depend on the holy teachings to guide one out of the doubts that puzzle the minds of living beings. Therefore the Tathāgata was born into this

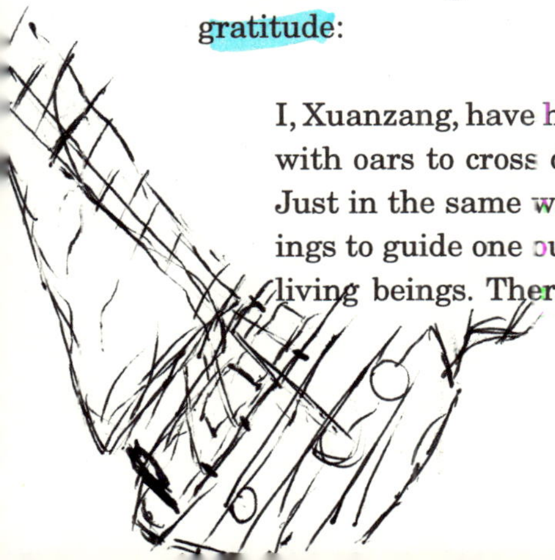

world of impurity with a mind of great compassion like a mother's love of her only son, and he illuminated this world of darkness with the Sun of Wisdom of the Three Clear Insights. The clouds of compassion covered the top of the sky, and the rain of the Dharma moistened the Three Thousand Worlds. After having accomplished his task of giving benefit and peace to living beings, he abandoned what was merely a transformation and returned to Eternal Truth. His bequeathed teachings have been spread to the East for more than six hundred years. Kāśyapa-Mātaṅga and Saṅghavarman glorified the Dharma in the regions of Wu and Luo, while Dharmarakṣa and Kumārajīva embellished it in the districts of Qin and Liang, upholding the mystic teachings and helping to maintain superior deeds. But as the translators came from distant lands, their interpretations differed, and as the time of the Buddha has gone far, his doctrines have been misinterpreted. Thus the unique teaching that he left at the twin śāla trees has been divided into the two views of substantial ego and substantial dharma, and the unequalled doctrine of the Mahayana has been split into the Southern and Northern Schools. Dissensions and disputes have lasted for several hundred years, and doubts have prevailed in the whole country without anybody to provide a solution.

By the lucky causes of my previous lives, I have been able to enter the Order at an early age and have studied under various teachers for nearly twenty years. I have consulted with many well-known scholars and learned friends, and thus I have had a glimpse of the texts of both the Mahayana and the Hinayana schools. But whenever I held a book to study it I was perplexed and felt at a loss to understand the meanings of the scripture I was holding in hand. I always longed to visit the Jetavana Garden and cherished a feeling of respect for the Vulture Peak, where I wished to go to solve the doubts accumulated in my mind. Although I knew that one could not examine the sky through a small tube, or measure the sea with a calabash shell, I still could not abandon my humble idea. Thus I made preparations and started on my journey, and with the passage of time on my way, I gradually reached Yiwu.

Being endowed with the pure harmony of Heaven and earth and gifted with the good spirit of the cosmos, Your Majesty reigns in prosperity and rules over his subjects as if they were his sons. You follow the manners of the Great Country in the East and observe the customs of the hundred tribes in the West. The lands of Loulan and Yuezhi and the countries of Cheshi and Langwang are all under the influence of your deep kindness and great virtue. Moreover, you esteem sages and love scholars, and you like what is good and treat people with benevolence. For those who come
226a from afar, you show sympathy and consideration and extend a hospitable reception. Since my arrival you have favored me with deep kindness and granted me the honor of expounding the Dharma. You have also condescended to be related to me as a brother and promoted the sentiment of fraternity. You have provided me with letters of introduction written in warm and enthusiastic terms to more than twenty states in the Western Region, requesting them to send me out of their domains stage by stage. Considering that I shall have to travel alone on my way to the West through snowy roads in cold climates, you have issued an explicit order for the ordination of four *śrāmaṇeras* to be my attendants and companions and provided me with more than fifty articles such as religious robes, cotton hats, fur blankets, and boots and stockings, as well as rolls of silk and satin, and gold and silver money for my travelling expenses, enough to sustain me for twenty years on my outward and homebound journeys.

For all these favors I feel both amazed and ashamed of myself and do not know how to express my gratitude. The outflow of the Jiao River is comparable to the amount of your kindness, and the mountains of the Pamir Range are not weightier than the favors you have shown me. Now I

> have no more worry about crossing the suspension bridge over the perilous icy river, and it is now the right time for me to visit the country of the Heavenly Ladder and the Bodhi tree. If I may, with your permission, realize my wishes, to whom shall I owe my achievement? To no one but the king's favor! I shall then visit various teachers and receive the Right Dharma from them. After returning home I shall translate the texts to spread what was not known before, so as to clear the intricacies of wrong views and to refute the misinterpretations of heretical theories, as well as to supplement the unknown part of the Buddha's teachings and to set a compass for entering the Gate of Truth. With this humble service, I shall repay you for your exceptional kindness.
>
> As the way that lies ahead is far, I cannot afford to stay here any longer. I shall take leave of you tomorrow and this makes me feel all the more sorrowful. With many thanks engraved on my memory, I am writing this letter to express my deep gratitude.

The king said in reply, "Since you have consented to be my brother, whatever we have in the country is our common property. There is no cause for you to thank me."

On the day of departure, the king and the monks, together with the ministers and people, all came out of the capital to send the Master off to the western suburbs of the city. The king embraced him and cried piteously, while the monks and lay people were all sorrowful, and the voices bidding farewell resounded in the suburbs. The king ordered his queen and the people to go back, while he, accompanied by the monks each riding on a horse, escorted the Master for several tens of *li* before he returned to the city.

The kings and nobles of the countries through which the Master passed all honored him in the same manner.

From here proceeding westward, he crossed the towns of Wuban and Dujin and entered the country of Agni, which was wrongly called Wuqi in olden times.

Fascicle II

Beginning with the Country of Agni and Ending with the Country of Kanyākubja

226b Proceeding westward from here, the Master reached the Teacher's Spring in the country of Agni. The spring was on a sandy rock by the south side of the road, which was several tens of feet high; and water flowed out halfway up the rock. It was said by tradition that once several hundred merchants ran out of water on the way and were quite exhausted when they reached here and did not know what to do. In the group there was a monk, who had no travelling money but lived on alms given by the merchants. The merchants discussed the situation and said, "As this monk serves the Buddha, we offered alms to him, so he could travel a long distance without carrying any sustenance with him. Now we are in a desperate situation, though he has shown no worry. Let us go and tell him about it." The monk said, "If you wish to get water, each of you should worship the Buddha, take the Three Refuges, and observe the Five Precepts. I shall then climb up the rock to get water for you." As the merchants were in distress, they all followed the monk's advice. When they had accepted the Precepts, the monk said to them, "When I have climbed up the rock, you should call out: 'Teacher, bring down water for us!' And tell me whatever amount of water you wish to have." A few moments later, when he had gone up, the merchants did as he had told them, and water flowed down profusely in an instant. All the merchants were delighted and grateful, but the teacher did not come down. They went up to see and found that he was dead. All of them, old and young, lamented sorrowfully, and cremated the remains according to the custom of the Western Region. At the spot where he had sat, they piled up bricks and stones to make a stupa, which was still there, and the water was also still flowing, sometimes in big quantities and sometimes less profusely, according to the number of travellers that passed by. When there was no wayfarer, it dwindled to a mere dripping.

The Master and his companions spent the night beside the spring. On the following day they resumed the journey and crossed the Silver Mountain, which was very tall and wide and rich in silver mines. This was the place where silver for making coins used in the western countries was produced. On the west side of the mountain they encountered a group of bandits; but when they had given them some valuables, the bandits went away. Then they proceeded to the place where the royal city was situated, and spent one night on the bank of a river. At that time several tens of Hu merchants who were fellow travellers, being eager to do business before others, secretly continued the journey at midnight. After having gone about ten *li,* they met robbers who killed them all; not a single one escaped the disaster. When the Master and his companions came to the spot, they saw the corpses of the merchants, and saw that all their property was gone. They were deeply grieved and sighed sorrowfully.

They proceeded gradually and saw the royal capital in the distance. The king of Agni and his ministers came to receive them and invited them to the city so as to make offerings to them. But as his country had previously been invaded and harassed by Gaochang, he bore a grudge against that country and refused to
226c provide horses for the Master. The Master spent one night there and passed on.

Proceeding forward he crossed two big rivers; and walking several hundred *li* through a plain toward the West, he crossed the boundary of the country of Kucha (in old times wrongly called Qiuci). When he was approaching the royal capital, the king and his ministers, as well as the virtuous monk Mokṣagupta and others, came to receive him. Besides them, several thousand monks pitched tents outside the eastern gate of the city, under which portable images of the Buddha were installed, and the monks stayed there performing music. On the arrival of the Master, the monks rose and greeted him, and then they returned to their seats. One monk held a tray of fresh flowers and handed it to the Master, who received it and scattered the flowers in front of the image of the Buddha. Having worshipped the image, he sat down beside Mokṣagupta. After he had taken his seat, flowers were offered to him and then he was entertained with grape juice. At the first monastery he received flowers and fruit juice, and he was treated in the same manner at the other monasteries one by one until sunset, when the monks began to disperse.

There were several tens of people from Gaochang, who had become monks in Kucha and lived in a separate monastery in the southeast part of the city. As the Master came from their home country, they invited him to spend the first night in their monastery, and he accepted their invitation, while the king and the monks returned to their respective places.

On the following day, the king invited the Master to the palace and offered him various kinds of food, among which were the three kinds of "clean meat." These the Master refused to take. The king was quite amazed by it, and so the Master said in explanation, "It is permissible to take meat in the gradual teaching of Buddhism, but I follow the Mahayana teaching, which prohibits the eating of meat." Thus he took some other kind of food.

After the meal he went to Āścarya (meaning "extraordinary") Monastery in the northwest of the city, which was the residence of Mokṣagupta. Mokṣagupta was a man of learning with elegance and intelligence, respected as the teacher of the people of that country. He had travelled in India and studied there for more than twenty years. Although he had learned various scriptures, he was most conversant with the Śabdhavidyā. The king and the people venerated him and regarded him as a unique person. Upon the arrival of the Master, Mokṣagupta merely treated him with the rites of hospitality due to a guest and did not take him to be a man knowing the Dharma. He said to the Master, "We have in this country the *Saṃyuktābhidharmahṛdaya Śāstra,* the *Abhidharmakośa Śāstra,* and the *Vibhāṣā Śāstra,* which are good enough for you to study. You need not bother to suffer the hardships of travelling to the West."

In reply, the Master inquired, "Do you have the *Yogācārabhūmi Śāstra* in this country?"

Mokṣagupta said, "Why do you ask about that heretical book, which no true Buddhist would care to learn?"

At first the Master had deeply venerated him, but upon hearing these words, he despised him as dust, saying, "We already have in our county the *Vibhāṣā Śāstra* and the *Abhidharmakośa Śāstra,* but I found to my disappointment that the theories contained in them were superficial and the sayings shallow, being not ultimate teachings. That is why I have come with the intention of learning the Mahayana *Yogācārabhūmi Śāstra.* As this *śāstra* was composed by Maitreya, a Bodhisattva in his final incarnation, how can you say that it is a heretical work? Are you not afraid of falling into the bottomless hell?"

That monk said, "You do not understand the *Vibhāṣā Śāstra* and the other works. How can you say that they are not profound?"

227a The Master said in retort, "Does the teacher understand those works?"

"I understand all of them," was the reply.

Then the Master quoted the first passage of the *Abhidharmakośa Śāstra,* but in explaining it the monk committed a blunder at the beginning. When he was unable to give adequate answers to further questions put to him, his face changed color, and he said, "You may ask me about other passages." Another passage was then put to him, but he was also unable to give a correct explanation. He said, "This passage is not found in the *śāstra.*" At that moment, the king's uncle Jñānacandra, who had become a monk and was well versed in the scriptures and commentaries, was sitting with them. He testified that there was such a passage in the *śāstra* and produced a copy of the work, from which he read out the passage. Being extremely ashamed of himself, Mokṣagupta said, "Due to my senility, I have forgotten it." He was also asked about the other works, but he could not give good explanations of them either.

As the snowy path through the Ice Mountains was not yet open, the Master could not proceed on his journey and stayed in this country for more than sixty days. Besides sightseeing, he often went to have a chat with Mokṣagupta, who would no longer sit in his chair when he saw the Master coming, but would stand up or go away to shun him. He said privately to his people, "It is not easy to answer the queries raised by this Chinese monk. If he goes to India, perhaps no young man in that country could surpass him." This showed how he respected and praised the Master.

On the day of departure, the king provided him with carriers and packhorses, and together with the monks and lay people he came out of the capital city to see the Master off.

Proceeding westward from here for two days, the Master met some two thousand Turkish bandits riding on horses. They were trying to divide the spoils pillaged from wayfarers. As they could not share the loot equally, they fought among themselves and dispersed.

Again proceeding for six hundred *li* and crossing a small desert, he reached the country of Bālukā (known as Gumo in olden times), where he spent one night. Again proceeding northwest for three hundred *li* and crossing a desert, he reached the Ice Mountains at the northern part of the Pamir Range. The mountains were dangerously steep and so tall that they seemed to touch the sky. Since the creation of the world, they had been covered with ice and snow, which had accumulated and turned into icicles and never melted in spring or summer. Cold mist mingled extensively with the clouds, and when one looked up one could see only a vast whiteness without limit. Ice peaks a hundred feet high, or tens of feet in breadth, broke down and lay across the road, rendering the rugged mountain path difficult to climb. Moreover, as the blasts sent the snowflakes flying, one would tremble in the flurry, though one had put on double shoes and heavy fur coats. At the time of sleeping or eating, there was no dry place to stop. One could only hang the pot to cook food and sleep on the ice. After seven days he came out of the mountainous region. Three or four men out of every ten fellow travellers died of hunger and cold, and the bulls and horses suffered even more.

When he had come out of the mountainous region, he reached a lake of pure water (which was called the Hot Sea, because the water, in contrast with the Ice Mountains, did not freeze; hence the name, but the water was not necessarily warm). The lake was fourteen hundred or fifteen hundred *li* in circumference, long from east to west and narrow from south to north: a vast expanse of water with waves several tens of feet high without the agitation of a big wind.

Proceeding along the lake toward the northwest for over five hundred *li,* he reached the city of Sūyāb at a time when the Turkish Yehu Khan was conducting a hunting expedition with a large troop of soldiers and horses. The khan was dressed in a green silk robe, with his hair exposed, and wearing a turban of white silk about ten feet long that wrapped his forehead and hung behind his
227b back. More than two hundred attendant officials, all with plaited hair and dressed in brocade robes, surrounded him. All his soldiers wore furs, felt, or fine woolen clothes; carried spears and large army banners; or held bows in their hands. So many were his cavalry of packhorses that they stretched out of sight. The khan was pleased to meet the Master and said, "I am going away for a short time and will return in two or three days. The teacher may proceed to my official residence." Then he ordered an attendant official named Dharmaja to escort and lodge the Master at his official residence.

After three days the khan returned and received the Master. The khan stayed in a big tent decorated with dazzling golden flowers. All the attendant officials, dressed in magnificent brocade garments, sat on mats in two long rows in front of the khan to attend upon him, while armed guards stood at his back. The sight was quite dignified and pompous, though he was merely a lord living in a felt tent.

When the Master was about thirty paces away from the tent, the khan came out to worship and receive him, and after having exchanged greetings, they entered the tent to take seats. Being fire worshippers, the Turks did not use wooden beds, as wood contained the element of fire. Out of respect they would not sit on wooden beds, but simply sat on double mats spread on the ground. They prepared a folding chair with an iron frame and a cushion on it for the Master to sit on.

In a moment an envoy from the court of Han and a messenger of Gaochang were ushered in. They presented their credentials and other authenticating objects, and the khan personally viewed them with much pleasure. He asked the messengers to take seats and ordered wine to be served and music performed. The khan drank with his ministers and the messengers, while grape juice was separately prepared and offered to the Master. Then they freely offered wine to one another and repeatedly exchanged cups, goblets, and other drinking vessels. The music of the alien tribes tinkled and clanged in symphony, and although the melodies were foreign and lacked refinement, they were quite amusing to the ear and delightful to the mind. A moment later, food was served, consisting of cooked fish, lamb, veal, and the like, piled in front of them. For the Master pure food was separately prepared, including pancakes, rice, butter, milk, sugar, honey, grapes, and other viands. After the meal, grape juice was offered, and the Master was then asked to preach the Dharma. Thus he taught them the Ten Good Deeds, and to be kind to living beings, as well as the *pāramitās* (spiritual perfections), which are the Way leading to emancipation. The khan bowed down and delightedly accepted the teachings with faith.

When the Master had stayed there a few days, the khan urged him to remain in his country, saying, "The teacher need not go to the country of Indica (meaning India), where the climate is mostly hot. The weather there in the tenth month is about the same as in the fifth month here in this country. Judging from your appearance, I fear that you would melt in the hot temperatures. The people there are dark in color and have no manners, and it is not worthwhile for you to see them."

The Master said in reply, "My intention in going there is to visit the holy sites and acquire the Dharma with a mind of adoration."

Thus the khan issued an order to find among his army men someone who could speak the Han language and the dialects of different countries. A young man who had stayed in Chang'an for several years and understood the Han language was found and appointed official translator. He was asked to write letters of
227c introduction to various countries and to escort the Master to the country of Kapiśā. The khan also presented the Master with a suit of religious robes made of red damask silk and fifty bolts of fine silk; and, together with his ministers, he went more than ten *li* to see the Master off.

From here proceeding westward for more than four hundred *li,* the Master reached Bingyul, meaning Thousand Springs. The place was several hundred *li* in circumference, with many lakes and ponds and abundant trees of rare species. The dense forests made the place cool and moist; it was the summer resort of the khan.

From Bingyul going westward for one hundred fifty *li,* he reached the city of Taras. Then, going southwest for two hundred *li,* he came to the city of White Water; two hundred *li* further to the southwest, to the city of Gongyu; and fifty more *li* to the south, to the country of Nujkend. Another two hundred *li* toward the west, he came to the country of Shash (meaning Stone country), which bordered on the Yaxartes in the west. Another thousand *li* or so to the west, he reached the country of Sutṛṣṇa, which bordered on the Yaxartes in the east. This river had its source in the northern plateau of the Pamir Range and flowed toward the northwest. Proceeding northwest, he entered a great desert, where there was neither water nor grass, and he pushed on past the skeletons that marked the way.

After travelling for more than five hundred *li,* he reached the country of Samarkand (known as the Kingdom of Kang), where the king and the people did not believe in Buddhism but worshipped fire as their path. There were two monasteries, but no monks lived in them. If a guest monk came to take lodging in them, the Hu people would drive him out with fire and would not allow him to stay. When the Master first arrived, the king received him with arrogance. After staying for one night, the Master told the king about the law of cause and effect among human and heavenly beings and about the blessedness and advantages of worshipping the Buddha and praising his merits. Being delighted, the king asked to observe the Precepts and treated the Master with hospitality and respect. When the two attendant *śrāmaṇeras* went to the monasteries to worship the Buddha, they were driven out with fire by the Hu people. The *śrāmaṇeras* returned and informed the king about it. Upon hearing this, the king ordered the arrest of the people who had attempted to burn them. After the culprits were arrested, the king ordered that their hands be cut off in an assembly of his people. The Master, who always desired to admonish others to do good, could not bear to see them mutilated and rescued them. The king then had them heavily flogged and driven out of the capital. Since then all the people, high and low, reverentially believed in Buddhism, and a great meeting was held to ordain some men to be monks and live in the monasteries. In this manner the Master reformed the wicked and enlightened the ignorant wherever he went.

Going further west for more than three hundred *li,* he reached the country of Kusānika; going further west for more than two hundred *li,* he reached the country of Kharghan (known as the Eastern An Country); going further west for four hundred *li,* he reached the country of Bukhārā (known as the Middle An Country); going further west for over one hundred *li,* he reached the country of Vadi (known as the Western An Country); going further west for five hundred *li,* he reached the country of Horiṣmīka, which bordered on the Oxus in the east; going further southwest for more than three hundred *li,* he reached the country of Kuśāna (known as the Shi Country); and going southwest for another two hundred *li,* he entered a mountainous region. The path among the mountains was long and dangerous, passable by only one person, and there was neither water nor grass. Going among the mountains for more than three hundred *li,* he entered the Iron Gate, of which the peaks were narrow and precipitous, and the rocks rich
228a in iron ore. A door was made upon the rocks, and on the door leaves

were suspended many iron bells; hence its name. This was a frontier fortress of the Turks. Going out of the Iron Gate, he reached the country of Tukhāra (wrongly called Tuhuoluo in olden times).

Proceeding from here for several hundred *li,* he crossed the Oxus and reached the country of Ghūr, which was the residence of the Tardu Shad (Shad being an official title), the eldest son of Yehu Khan and the husband of the younger sister of the king of Gaochang. The king of Gaochang had sent him a letter, but when the Master arrived, the Khatun who was the princess of Gaochang was dead and the Tardu Shad was ill. Upon hearing that the Master had arrived from Gaochang, from whence he had already received a letter, he could not refrain from sobbing with the male and female members of his family. He granted an interview to the Master and said to him, "This disciple's eyes are opened upon seeing the teacher. I wish you would stay here and take rest for some time. When I am recovered I will personally escort you to the Brahmanic countries." At the same time an Indian monk arrived and cured him gradually by reciting incantations. The Khatun whom the Shad married later was a young woman, and she poisoned her husband at the instigation of the son of a former queen. Since the Shad was dead and the son of the Princess of Gaochang was under age, the Tagin prince who was the son of the former queen usurped the position of the Shad and married his stepmother. Because of the funeral services, the Master sojourned there for more than a month.

In that country there was a monk named Dharmasaṃgha, who had studied in India and was regarded as a teacher of the Dharma by the people west of the Pamir Range. None of the monks of Kashgar and Khotan were competent to discuss the Dharma with him. Wishing to know the profundity of his knowledge, the Master sent a man to ask him how many scriptures and commentaries he could understand. Upon hearing this question, the monk's disciples were enraged; but he said with a smile, "I understand everything, and you may ask me any question as you wish." Knowing that he had not learned about Mahayana Buddhism, the Master queried him about a few points concerning the Hinayana *Vibhāṣā Śāstra,* but the monk was not well versed in that treatise. Thus he apologized and admitted his incompetence in learning, and all his disciples felt abashed. Since then he was pleased each time he met the Master, and praised him in all places, saying that he was inferior to the Master in learning.

When the new Shad had been installed, the Master asked him to provide a guide and corvée horses, as he wished to proceed southward to the Brahmanic countries. The Shad said, "In your disciple's domain there is the country of Balkh, bordering on the Oxus in the north. People say that it is the city of Small Rājagṛha, where there are many holy sites. I wish the Master would visit that place for some time and then take horses to go southward."

There were then several tens of monks coming from Balkh to express condolence on the death of the late Shad, as well as to offer congratulations upon the installation of his son. When the Master met them, he told them his intention. They said, "You may come straight with us. There is a good road. If you come here again, you would go a roundabout way to no purpose." The Master accepted their advice, and after taking leave of the Shad, he took horses and went away with the monks.

When the Master arrived there, he saw that the city was prominent and the suburbs spacious with rich and fertile fields. It was indeed a superb land. There were a hundred monasteries with some three thousand monks, all of whom studied Hinayana
228b Buddhism. Outside the city to the southwest was the Navasaṃghārāma (meaning New Monastery), which was very beautifully decorated. In the Buddha hall of the monastery there was a bathing jug used by the Buddha, more than one *dou* in capacity. There was also a Buddha tooth, one inch long and eight or nine *fen* in breadth, of a yellowish white color, and it often issued an auspicious light. There was also a broom made of *kuśa* grass that had been used by the Buddha. It was over three feet long and about seven inches round, and its handle was adorned with various kinds of gems. These three objects were always exhibited on festival days for the monks and laity to see and worship. Those who had a sincere mind

might cause them to issue a divine light. To the north of the monastery there stood a stupa more than two hundred feet high. To the southwest of the monastery there was a hermitage built many years ago. Those who lived there to practise the Way and attain the four fruitions never ceased from generation to generation. After their nirvanas, stupas were built in memory of them, and the foundations of the stupas, several hundred in number, touched one another.

Going northwest from the great city for fifty *li,* the Master reached the city of Trapuṣa; and forty *li* to the north of this city was the city of Bhallika, in which there were two stupas thirty feet in height. Formerly, when the Buddha had just attained enlightenment, he received parched flour and honey from two Elders, who were the first to hear about the Five Precepts and the Ten Good Deeds. As they requested something for them to worship, the Tathāgata gave them some of his hair and nail parings for them to build stupas around, and he also told them how to construct stupas. The two Elders brought the relics back to their own countries and built these *caitya*s.

Over seventy *li* to the west of the city was a stupa more than twenty feet high which was built at the time of Kāśyapa Buddha in the past.

In the Navasaṃghārāma there lived a Hinayana Tripiṭaka teacher named Prajñākara (meaning Wisdom-nature). Upon hearing that Balkh had an abundance of holy sites, he had come here to pay homage to them. Young and brilliant, he was an intelligent and well-learned man. He studied well the scriptures of the Nine Sections and thoroughly mastered the *Four Āgama*s. His reputation for elucidating Buddhist theories was widely known throughout India, and he was learned in the Hinayana Abhidharma works such as Kātyāyana's *Abhidharmajñānaprasthāna Śāstra,* the *Abhidharmakośa Śāstra,* and the *Ṣaṭpādābhidharma Śāstra.* On hearing that the Master had come from a distant land to seek the Dharma, he was delighted to meet him. Thus the Master inquired of him about the dubious points he had found in the *Abhidharmakośa Śāstra,* the *Vibhāṣā Śāstra,* and some other works, and the answers were very accurate and proficient. So the Master stayed there for more than one month to study the *Vibhāṣā Śāstra* with him.

In this monastery there were also two other Hinayana Tripiṭaka teachers, Dharmapriya (meaning Affection for the Dharma) and Dharmākara (meaning Virtue of the Dharma), who were highly respected by the people of that country. On seeing the Master's brilliant and elegant manners, they held him in great esteem.

To the southwest of Balkh were the countries of Zumathān and Gūzgānān. When the kings of these countries heard that the Master had come from a distant land, both of them dispatched illustrious ministers to invite him to their countries to receive offerings; but he declined to go. Then the envoys came again and again, so that he could not but accept the invitation. The kings were overjoyed and offered him gold, gems, food, and drink. But he returned without accepting anything.

Going south from Balkh, the Master entered the country of
228c Gaz together with the Dharma teacher Prajñākara, and they entered the Great Snow Mountains in the southeast. After travelling for more than six hundred *li,* they came out of the territory of Tukhāra and entered the country of Bāmīyān, which was two thousand *li* from east to west and was situated in the Snow Mountains. The path was rough and dangerous, much more so than in the Ice Mountains and the desert. The frozen clouds and flying snowflakes never cleared up for a moment, and in the worst places the flat path was only a few score feet in length. Thus when Song Yu had said that the way to the West was so difficult that one had to pass over ice piled up high one layer upon another, and pass through flying flakes of snow for a thousand *li,* this was the place he was referring to. Ah! Who would travel in this place at the risk of losing one's body which one had inherited from one's parents, if it were not for acquiring the supreme Right Dharma for the benefit of all living beings? Formerly, when Wang Zun climbed up the Nine-winding Slope, he claimed to be a loyal minister of the royal house of Han. Now, as the Master set foot in the Snow Mountains for the purpose of acquiring the scriptures, he might well be called a true son of the Tathāgata.

Going gradually on, the Master reached the capital of Bāmīyān, where there were more than ten monasteries with several thousand monks who were followers of the Hinayana Lokottaravāda school. The king of Bāmīyān came out to receive him, invited him to his palace, and entertained him for several days before he left the palace. There were two learned monks, Āryadāsa (meaning Holy Servant) and Āryasena (meaning Holy Army) of the Mahāsāṃghika school, who were well versed in the theories of the Dharmalakṣaṇa sect. When they saw the Master, they were amazed to know that there was such a monk as the Master in a country so far away as China. They guided him with much hospitality, so that he could see and worship all places.

To the northeast of the royal city, at the foot of a hill, there was a standing rock statue one hundred fifty feet in height. To the east of the statue there was a monastery, and east of the monastery there was a standing bronze image of Śākyamuni Buddha, a hundred feet tall. Inside the monastery there was a recumbent image of the Buddha, a thousand feet in length, in the posture of entering nirvana. All these images were magnificently adorned.

From here going southeast for over two hundred *li,* he crossed the Great Snow Mountain and reached a small river, where there was a monastery in which there were preserved a Buddha's tooth; a tooth of a *Pratyekabuddha* who lived at the beginning of the present *kalpa,* five inches long and less than four inches wide; a tooth of a Golden Wheel King, three inches long and two inches wide; an iron alms bowl used by Śāṇakavāsa (wrongly given as Śaṇavāsa in old times) with a capacity of eight or nine *sheng;* and his *saṃghāṭi* robe of a deep red color. For five hundred lives this person always wore this robe whether he was in the intermediate state or in the corporal form of existence, and he was always born with it. Later, it became the *kāṣāya* robe of which the story is related in detail in another work.

After travelling for fifteen days, the Master came out of Bāmīyān. Encountering a snowstorm for two days, he lost his way and came to a small sandy ridge, where he met a hunter who showed him the way. Thus he crossed the Black Mountain and reached the domain

of Kapiśā. This country was more than four thousand *li* in circumference, with the Snow Mountains at its back in the north. The king was of the *kṣatriya* caste and was a resourceful and influential person ruling over more than ten countries. When the Master was approaching the capital, the king and the monks came out of the city to welcome him. There were more than a hundred monasteries,
229a and the monks vied with one another in inviting him to stay with them. There was a Hinayana monastery with the name of Śālāka. According to tradition, it was built at the time when a prince of the Chinese Emperor was staying here as a hostage. The monks of this monastery said, "Our monastery was built by a son of the Chinese Emperor, and now as you have come from that country, you should first come and stay in our monastery." Because of their deep hospitality and because his companion, the Dharma teacher Prajñākara, a Hinayana monk, did not wish to live in a Mahayana monastery, the Master accepted the invitation and stayed in their monastery.

When the hostage prince built this monastery, he buried a large amount of valuables under the feet of the South Devarāja at the eastern gate of the Buddha courtyard, as a fund reserved to defray the cost of repairing the monastery in the future. Out of gratitude, the monks painted portraits of the hostage prince everywhere on the walls of the monastery; and they also preached and recited the scriptures for his benefit at the inception and conclusion of each rainy season. This had been done generation after generation without cease until the present time.

Recently an evil king who was covetous and cruel intended to seize the treasures of the monks; but when he ordered his men to dig at the feet of the deity, the earth quaked severely. The figure of a parrot on the top of the deity flapped its wings and screamed in alarm when it saw the men digging in the ground. The king and his soldiers lost consciousness and fell to the ground, and at last they retreated in fear.

As the wheel signs of the stupa in the monastery were dilapidated, the monks wished to take out the valuables to pay for the reconstruction of the stupa. The earth quaked again with roars, and none dared to approach the hidden treasure. When the Master arrived, the monks assembled and told him about this event that had occurred before. The Master went with them to the place of the deity and prayed to him with the burning of incense, saying, "When the hostage prince reserved this treasure, he meant to spend it for performing meritorious deeds. It is now the right time to open it and put it to use. I hope you will realize our sincerity of intention and relax just a bit the virtue of your might and dignity. If I can obtain your permission, I shall personally see to the treasure and open it and find out the exact amount to be handed over to the authorities to repair the stupa properly, and nothing will be wasted. May the deity in his spirituality understand us and sympathize with us."

After saying so, the Master asked the people to dig for the treasure, and they did so safely and without trouble. When they had dug the ground to the depth of seven or eight feet, they found a big bronze vessel, containing several hundred catties of gold and tens of bright pearls. The monks were delighted and all of them gratefully praised the Master. Then the Master spent the summer retreat in this monastery.

The king neglected the arts, but he believed in Mahayana Buddhism with respect and took delight in attending preaching and recitation functions. So he invited the Master and the Tripiṭaka teacher Prajñākara to hold a Dharma gathering in a Mahayana monastery. There were a Mahayana Tripiṭaka Master named Manojñaghoṣa (meaning Voice-at-Will), a monk of the Sarvāstivāda school named Āryavarman (meaning Holy Armor), and a monk of the Mahīśāsaka school named Guṇabhadra (meaning Virtuous Sage), all leading figures in that monastery. But they were not comprehensively learned in both Mahayana and Hinayana teachings. Although they were well versed in the theories of one or another school, each of them had his strong point in only one school. The Master alone understood all the different theories perfectly and could answer in accordance with the teachings of different schools whatever questions were put to him, to the satis-
229b faction of them all and winning their admiration. The gathering

dispersed after lasting five days. Greatly delighted, the king separately offered five bolts of pure brocade to the Master and various gifts to the other monks. After spending the summer retreat at the Śālāka Monastery, the Dharma teacher Prajñākara, being invited again by the king of Tukhāra, returned to that country, and the Master parted company with him.

Proceeding eastward for more than six hundred *li* and after crossing a black range, he entered the territory of northern India and reached the country of Lampāka, which was more than a thousand *li* in circumference and had ten monasteries, all the monks of which studied Mahayana Buddhism. After staying there for three days, he went south to a small range on which there was a stupa. Once the Buddha walked from the south to this place and stood there. In memory of the event, people of later times constructed this stupa with a mind of respect. All the lands to the north of this place were known as *mleccha* (meaning "frontier lands").

When the Tathāgata wished to go about teaching the people, he used to come and go by air and would not walk on the ground. If he walked, the earth would quake and tremble.

Going from here southward for more than twenty *li*, he came down from the range and crossed a river, after which he reached the country of Nagarahāra (in the domain of northern India). At a distance of two *li* to the southeast of the capital city, there was a stupa over three hundred feet high, built by King Aśoka. This was the place where the Śākya Bodhisattva met Dīpaṃkara Buddha in the second *asaṃkhyeya kalpa* and spread his deerskin garment as well as his hair over the muddy earth to receive a prediction from that Buddha. Although it had passed through the Kalpa of Destruction, this spot had continued to exist, and heavenly beings often scattered flowers as offerings to it.

When the Master came to this place he worshipped and circumambulated it. An old monk beside him told him the story of the construction of this stupa. The Master inquired of him, saying, "Since it was in the second *asaṃkhyeya kalpa* that the Bodhisattva spread his hair over the ground, innumerable *kalpa*s had passed between the second and the third circles. In each *kalpa* the world has been constructed and destroyed many times, as in the period of conflagration, when even Mount Sumeru was reduced to ashes. How could this spot alone have been preserved intact?" The monk said in reply, "When the world was destroyed, this spot was also destroyed, but when the world was reconstructed, the spot also reappeared at its original place where it was before, just like Mount Sumeru, which exists again after it has been destroyed. As this is a holy place, why should it not have the potency to emerge again? From this comparison, we may not bother ourselves with doubt." This was a well-spoken reply.

More than ten *li* further to the southwest was a stupa that marked a place where the Buddha had bought flowers. Again going further to the southeast and crossing a sandy ridge for more than ten *li,* the Master reached the city of the Buddha's parietal bone. In the city there was a storeyed pavilion; and on the second storey there was a small stupa, made of the seven precious substances, in which the Tathāgata's parietal bone was preserved. The circumference of the bone was twelve inches. It was of a yellowish white color with distinct hair pores and was stored in a precious casket. If anyone wished to forecast his fortune, he could grind some incense into powder, wrap it in a piece of white silk, and press it on the bone to make an impression from which to foresee whether it
229c was auspicious or inauspicious. The Master obtained an impression like the Bodhi tree. Of the two *śrāmaṇeras* whom he had brought along with him, the older got an impression resembling a Buddha image while the younger got one like a lotus flower. The Brahman in charge of the bone was delighted, and he said to the Master while snapping his fingers and scattering flowers toward him, "You have gotten a very rare impression, which indicates that you will have the opportunity to realize Bodhi!"

There was another stupa containing a piece of a skull bone in the shape of a lotus leaf. Here was also a Buddha's eye relic, as large as an apple, with a brilliant light that shone out of the casket. Here, too, was the Buddha's *saṃghāṭi* robe, made of the finest felt. There was also preserved the Buddha's religious staff with pewter rings, of which the handle was made of sandalwood. The Master paid homage to all these objects with sad memories and reverence, and then offered fifty golden coins and one thousand silver coins, together with four gorgeous pennants, two pieces of brocade, and two suits of religious robes. After scattering various kinds of flowers, he took his leave and went out.

Then he heard that at a distance of more than twenty *li* to the southwest of the city of Dīpaṃkara, there was a cave that was once the residence of the Dragon King Gopāla, whom the Tathāgata subdued, thus leaving his shadow in the cave. The Master wished to worship the shadow, but the road was deserted, blocked, and infested with robbers. Moreover, in the last two or three years people who went there could not see the shadow in most cases; and so very few people visited the place. When the Master desired to worship the shadow, the envoys who escorted him from Kapiśā advised him not to go, as they wanted to return home quickly and did not wish to linger too long. The Master said to them, "The shadow of the Tathāgata's true body is seen once in countless *kalpa*s. Now as I have come to this place, why should I not go to worship it? You may proceed slowly, and I will go and come back soon."

Thus he went alone to the city of Dīpaṃkara and entered a monastery to ask the way and find someone to be his guide. None was willing to go with him. Then he saw a child, who said, "The manor of the monastery is nearby. I will send you there." So he went with the lad to the manor, where he spent the night and found an old man who knew the place and went there with him as his guide. After going a few *li,* they met five robbers who came to them with knives in hand. The Master took off his hat and showed them his religious attire. The robbers said, "Where does the teacher wish to go?" The Master said in reply, "I wish to worship the Buddha's shadow." The robbers said, "Did you not hear that there were robbers here?" The Master said, "Robbers are also human beings. Now I am going to worship the Buddha. I would not be frightened even if the road were haunted by beasts of prey. What am I afraid of since you benefactors are human beings?" Thus the robbers also wished to go with him to worship the Buddha's shadow.

Upon arriving at the cave, which was on the eastern precipice of a stony brook with an opening facing the west, he peeped into it but could see nothing, as it was completely dark inside. The old man said, "You should go straight in. After walking for about fifty paces you will touch the eastern wall. Then gaze due east. The shadow is there." The Master entered the cave, and, having walked about
230a fifty paces, actually touched the eastern wall. He stood there as he was told and worshipped with sincerity. But he did not see anything after having made more than a hundred prostrations on the ground. He blamed himself for his own spiritual obstacles that prevented him from seeing the shadow, and wept with regret and repentance. Then he recited with a sincere mind the stanzas in praise of the Buddha in the *Śrīmālādevīsiṃhanāda Sūtra* and other scriptures. As he recited the stanzas, he made prostrations over a hundred times. Then he saw a bright light the size of an alms bowl appear on the eastern wall, but it disappeared in an instant. With a mixed feeling of grief and joy, he worshipped again and saw a light as large as a tray, but it also faded out soon. This increased his faith and adoration, and he vowed that he would not leave the cave if he did not see the shadow of the World-honored One. When he had prostrated himself again more than two hundred times, the whole cave became brightly illumined and the Tathāgata's shadow was clearly seen on the wall, just like a golden mountain becoming visible when the clouds and mist disperse. Its wonderful features were lustrous with a divine and brilliant appearance. He was so delighted to have seen the shadow that his happiness was beyond comparison. Both the Buddha's body and his robe were of a reddish yellow color. The figure was perfectly clear above the knees, but below the lotus seat it was a little blurred. It was complete with the shadows of all the Bodhisattvas and holy monks who stood at the left and right sides of his knees and behind his back.

Having seen this shadow, the Master asked the six men who were outside the entrance to bring in a fire to light incense. But when the fire was brought in, the Buddha's shadow disappeared all of a sudden. He hastily asked them to put out the fire and prayed again, and then the shadow reappeared. Among the six men, five saw the shadow and one did not see anything at all. It was distinctly visible for about half a meal's time. When they had paid homage, chanted praise, offered incense, and scattered flowers, the light faded away, and then they took their leave and came out of the cave. The Brahman who led the way was happy. He proclaimed that this was something that never occurred before, saying, "If it were not for the teacher's sincerity and great will power, this could not have happened."

Outside the cave there were many more holy sites, as is related in other works. They returned together, and all five of the robbers destroyed their weapons and received the Precepts before they went away.

The Master then rejoined his companions, and going southeast for more than five hundred *li* among mountains, he reached the country of Gandhāra (in olden times wrongly called Jiantuowei, in the domain of northern India). This country bordered on the Indus in the east and its capital was called Puruṣapura. In this country there were many sages and holy persons, and the *śāstra* writers of ancient times, such as Nārāyaṇadeva, Asaṅga Bodhisattva, Vasubandhu Bodhisattva, Dharmatrāta, Manoratha, and the Venerable Pārśva were all born in this country. To the northeast of the royal city there was a precious terrace for keeping the Buddha's alms bowl, which had been shifted to various countries and was then kept in the country of Vārāṇasī. Eight or nine *li* to the southeast of the city there was a *pippala* tree more than a hundred feet tall. The four past Buddhas had sat under it and there were now images of these four Tathāgatas. All of the 996 Buddhas of the future will also sit under it. By the side of the tree there was a stupa, constructed by King Kaniṣka, four hundred feet in height, of which the base was one and one-half *li* in circumference and one hundred fifty feet high.
230b On the top of the stupa were Diamond Wheels in twenty-five layers, and inside it one *hu* of the Tathāgata's relic bones was preserved. About a hundred paces to the southwest of the great stupa, there was a white stone statue, eighteen feet in height, standing facing north. It had manifested many divine and auspicious signs, and people often saw it circumambulating the great stupa at night.

Over a hundred *li* to the northeast of the monastery built by King Kaniṣka, the Master crossed a great river and reached the city of Puṣkalāvatī. In the east of the city there was a stupa built by King Aśoka; this was the place where the four past Buddhas had preached the Dharma. In a monastery four or five *li* to the north of the city, there was another stupa, more than two hundred feet high, also erected by King Aśoka; this was the place where Śākyamuni Buddha performed almsgiving with a happy mind when he was practising the Way of a Bodhisattva in the past. He was born as the king of this country a thousand times, and at this place he gave away his eyes as alms in a thousand lives. There were many such holy sites, and the Master visited and worshipped them all. He distributed all the gold, silver, satin, silk, and garments presented to him by the king of Gaochang to the great stupas and large monasteries that he visited, as offerings to express his devotion before he left.

From here he went to the city of Uḍakhāṇḍa. Travelling for more than six hundred *li* over mountains and rivers to the north of the city, he entered the country of Udyāna (meaning "garden," for it was a garden of King Aśoka in olden times; formerly it was wrongly called Wuchang). On both banks of the Śubhavastu River there were formerly fourteen hundred monasteries with eighteen thousand monks, but now the monasteries were in desolation and the number of monks had decreased. The disciplinary rules of the Sangha were handed down by five different schools, namely, (1) the Dharmagupta, (2) the Mahīśāsaka, (3) the Kāśyapīya, (4) the Sarvāstivāda, and (5) the Mahāsāṃghika.

The king mostly lived in the city of Maṅgala, which was rich and well-populated. Four or five *li* to the east of the city, there was a great stupa that showed many miraculous signs and was the place where the Buddha, as Kṣānti Ṛṣi in one of his previous lives, was dismembered by King Kali (meaning Combat, formerly known as Geli by mistake).

At a place two hundred fifty *li* to the northeast of the city, the Master entered a great mountain and reached the Apalāla Dragon Spring, which was the source of the Swat River, which flowed toward the southwest. It was a cold place, and it froze in the spring and summer seasons. In the evenings the snow began to fall and the flakes were of varied colors, dancing in the air like different kinds of flowers.

More than thirty *li* to the southwest of the Dragon Spring, on a huge rock on the northern bank of the river, there was a Buddha's footprint that varied in size according to the good fortune and volition of the person who measured it. It was left by the Buddha before going away, in former times when he came here to subdue the Apalāla dragon. More than thirty *li* down the river was the washing stone of the Tathāgata, and the stripes of his robe were still visible, impressed on the rock. Going south from the city for more than four hundred *li*, the Master reached Hiḍḍa Mountain, which was the place where the Tathāgata in one of his former lives jumped down to give up his body to repay the kindness of a *yakṣa* (demon) from whom he had learned half a *gāthā* (formerly known as ji, this being an abbreviation of the Sanskrit word, or jituo, a mispronunciation of the Sanskrit, of which the correct reading is
230c *gāthā,* meaning a stanza with thirty-two syllables). At a place fifty *li* to the west of the city of Maṅgala, he crossed a big river and reached the Rohitaka (meaning Red) Stupa, which was more than a hundred feet high and constructed by King Aśoka. This was the place where the Tathāgata, when he was King Maitrībala in one of his previous lives, pricked his body to feed five *yakṣas* (formerly called yecha by mistake) with his blood. More than thirty *li* to the northeast of the city, he came to the Adbhuta (meaning Marvellous) stone stupa, which was thirty feet high. Once the Buddha preached the Dharma at this place to men and heavenly beings; and after the Buddha had gone away, this stupa emerged spontaneously. To the west of the stupa, the Master crossed a big river. After going for three or four *li* he reached a *vihāra* in which there was an image of Avalokiteśvara Bodhisattva well-known for its miraculous manifestations. (The name of this Bodhisattva is a compound word: *avalokita* and *īśvara,* meaning *observe* and *supreme being.* Formerly it was wrongly translated as Light World Voice, Observing the Voice of the World, or Observing World Voice Supreme

Being.) The Master heard the people say that from the northeast of the city one might climb a mountain and cross a gully, go up the Indus River by a dangerous path, climb up a rope chain, walk over a suspension bridge, and proceed for about a thousand *li* to reach the valley of Darada, which was the old capital of Udyāna. Beside a big monastery in the valley there was a wooden statue of Maitreya Bodhisattva, painted a golden color and more than a hundred feet tall. It was made by the Arhat Madhyāntika (erroneously transliterated Motiandi in old times). By his supernatural power, he sent a craftsman up to the Tuṣita Heaven (formerly known as Dushuaituo by mistake) to observe with his own eyes the fine features of the Bodhisattva; and he went up and down three times before he completed the task.

From the city of Uḍakhāṇḍa, the Master crossed the Indus to the south. The river was three or four *li* wide, and the water was very clear and flowed rapidly. Many venomous dragons and evil animals dwelt in it. Anyone crossing the river with Indian precious gems, rare flowers, or relic bones would often have his boat overturned. After crossing this river, the Master reached the country of Takṣaśilā (in the domain of northern India). About twelve or thirteen *li* to the north of the city, there was a stupa built by King Aśoka; it often issued a divine light. This was the place where the Tathāgata, in previous lives, as a great king with the name of Candraprabha (meaning Moonlight), sacrificed his head one thousand times in order to acquire Buddhahood when he was practising the Bodhisattva path. Beside the stupa there was a monastery, in which Kumāralāta (meaning Youth's Life), a teacher of the Sautrāntika school, composed various *śāstras*. The Master heard
231a that more than seven hundred *li* from here to the southeast was the country of Siṃhapura (in the domain of northern India). Again crossing the Indus River at the northern frontier of Takṣaśilā and going southeast for more than two hundred *li,* he crossed the Great Rocky Pass. This was the place where Prince Mahāsattva had formerly sacrificed his body to feed a starving tigress and her seven cubs. As the ground had been stained by the Prince's blood, it was still of a deep red color and the plants there were also deep red.

From here again going southeast for over five hundred *li* among mountains, he reached the country of Urasā.

Again climbing dangerous defiles toward the southeast and crossing an iron bridge, he travelled for more than a thousand *li* and reached the country of Kaśmīra (wrongly called Jibin in olden times). Its capital city was beside a big river on the west, with a hundred monasteries and some five thousand monks. There were four stupas, high and splendid, built by King Aśoka, and each containing over a *sheng* of the Tathāgata's relic bones. When the Master first entered its territory, he came to Rocky Pass, which was the western gate of the country, and the king sent his maternal uncle to welcome him with carriages and horses. After entering Rocky Pass, the Master worshipped in various monasteries he had passed by and reached a temple named Huśkara, where he spent the night. During that night all the monks of the monastery had a dream in which a divine being told them, "This guest monk coming from Mahācīna wishes to study the scriptures in India, to visit and worship the holy sites, and to learn from teachers what he has not heard before. Since he has come for the sake of the Dharma, countless good deities are following him and they are all here now. Due to your good deeds done in the past, you are adored by this person from a distant land. You should recite and study the scriptures with diligence, so as to win his praise and respect. Why are you so indolent and indulging in sleeping?" The monks were startled on hearing this admonition in the dream. They walked up and down, sat in meditation, or recited the scriptures until dawn. Then they came to tell the story to the Master and treated him with greater reverence.

After staying there for a few days, he proceeded gradually to the royal city. At a place about one *yojana* from the city, he reached the *Dharmaśāla* (meaning house of benefaction, established by order of the king for entertaining travellers and looking after the poor and needy). The king, his ministers, and the monks in the capital city came to the house of benefaction to welcome the Master. The king was attended by more than a thousand body-guards, holding banners and canopies that filled the road, burning incense, and scattering flowers all over the way. Upon his arrival, the king met the Master with much ceremony and extolment. After offering him a large quantity of flowers with his own hands, he invited the Master to ride on a great elephant and proceed together with him to the capital. After arriving in the capital, the Master lodged at the Jayendra Monastery (which was built by the king's maternal uncle). On the following day he was invited to the palace to receive offerings; and a score of virtuous monks, Saṃghakīrti and others, were also invited. After the meal the king requested that the Master preach the Dharma and invited him to carry on a discussion on certain dubious questions. The king was highly pleased to observe the event. Knowing that the Master had come from a distant land to acquire knowledge, and that there was no written book for him to study, the king ordered twenty copyists to transcribe scriptures and commentaries for his use, and also gave him five persons to be his servants. Whatever was needed for his sustenance and entertainment was provided at public expense.

231b The Dharma teacher Saṃghakīrti, being a person of lofty character, observed the disciplinary rules in a strict and pure manner. He was a deep thinker, well versed in the Dharma in a comprehensive way. Possessing brilliant talents and outstanding intelligence, he inherently loved virtuous scholars. As the Master was a distinguished guest, he received him with so much delight that he opened his eyes wide and raised his eyebrows high. The Master also wholeheartedly studied under him day and night without feeling tired, and asked him to expound and teach him the various *śāstra*s. The venerable teacher was then nearly seventy and was feeble in physical strength. But as he was glad to have met an intelligent person, he exerted himself to the utmost to teach him by lecturing on the *Abhidharmakośa Śāstra* before noon, the *Nyāyānusāra Śāstra* in the afternoon, and the *Hetuvidyā Śāstra* and the *Śabdavidyā Śāstra* after the first part of the night. Thus all the scholars in the locality assembled to attend the lectures. The Master comprehended whatever was spoken by the teacher without missing anything. He studied the subtle teachings with appreciation and thoroughly mastered the mysteries. The venerable teacher was pleased with him and praised him appreciatively to the utmost, saying to the people, "This Chinese monk possesses such great and substantial wisdom that none among this congregation could exceed him. With his intelligence and virtue he could have been a worthy successor to Vasubandhu and his brother; the pity is that he was born in a distant land and could not come in contact early with the bequeathed teachings of the saints and sages."

Among the congregation there were two Mahayana scholar monks, named Viśuddhasiṃha (meaning Pure Lion) and Jinabandhu (meaning Victorious Kinsman), two Sarvāstivāda scholar-monks, named Sugatamitra (meaning Tathāgata's Friend) and Vasumitra (meaning Friend of the World), and two Mahāsāṃghika scholar-monks, named Sūryadeva (meaning Sun-god) and Jinatrāta (meaning Victorious Protector). These monks had come to this country to pursue knowledge prior to the Master. They were men firm and faithful to the Way and had great talent and profound understanding. Although they were not comparable to Saṃghakīrti in learning, they were far more learned than the rest of the monks. When they saw that the Master was praised by their great teacher, they felt so bad about it that they tried to interrogate him with difficult questions. But the Master gave them perspicuous replies fluently and without hesitation, and then the scholars felt ashamed and were convinced of his erudition.

This country was formerly the lake of a dragon. In the fiftieth year after the Buddha's nirvana, Ānanda's disciple, Arhat Madhyāntika, converted the dragon king and asked him to relinquish his lake to construct five hundred monasteries, in which various saints and sages were invited to live upon the offerings of the dragon. Later, in the four hundredth year after the Buddha's nirvana, King Kaniṣka of the country of Gandhāra invited, at the request of the Venerable Pārśva, various holy monks who were thoroughly versed in the Tripiṭaka of the inner learning and learned in the Five Sciences of the outer knowledge. They came to 499 persons, and, including the Venerable Vasumitra, there were altogether five hundred holy monks to recite and collect the Tripiṭaka. At first,

they composed the *Upadeśa Śāstra* (formerly erroneously known as the *Youbotishe*) in 100,000 stanzas for the exposition of the Sutra *Piṭaka* (formerly erroneously known as the *Xiuduoluo*), then the *Vinayavibhāṣā Śāstra* in 100,000 stanzas for the exposition of the Vinaya *Piṭaka* (formerly erroneously known as the *Pinaye*), and thirdly the *Abhidharmavibhāṣa Śāstra* in 100,000
231c stanzas for the exposition of the Abhidharma *Piṭaka* (or erroneously known as the *Apitan*), a total number of 300,000 stanzas in 960,000 syllables. The king made red copper plates to incise these treatises on and kept them in stone cases, which were sealed up and stored in a great stupa specially constructed for the purpose; he also ordered *yakṣas* to safeguard them. It was due to this effort that the abstruse teachings could be known once more in the world.

Thus the Master stayed in this country for two years to study various scriptures and commentaries and to worship the holy sites before he took his departure.

Going southwest for seven hundred *li* and wading across a ravine, he reached the country of Parṇotsa; and going further southeast for more than four hundred *li,* he reached the country of Rājapura (in the domain of northern India). After going southeast from here for more than seven hundred *li,* descending the mountains, and crossing a river, he reached the country of Ṭakka (in the domain of northern India). From Lampāka to this land, as the lay people lived in frontier and desolate countries, their costume and language were somewhat different from those in India, and their manners were vulgar and uncouth. After leaving the country of Rājapura and traveling for three days, he crossed the Candrabhāgā (meaning Moon Division) River and reached the city of Jayapura, where he lodged at a heretical monastery outside the western gate of the city, in which there were at the moment over twenty disciples. Two days later he entered the city of Śākala, where there was a monastery with more than a hundred monks. Formerly Vasubandhu Bodhisattva composed the *Paramārthasatya Śāstra* in this monastery. Beside it there was a stupa two hundred feet high that marked the place where the four past

Buddhas had preached the Dharma. The footprints of their walking up and down were still there.

From here he came out of the city of Nārasiṃha and reached a big *palāśa* wood in the east, where he encountered a band of about fifty brigands. When they had stolen all the clothes and money of the Master and his companions, they brandished their knives and drove them to a dry pond by the southern side of the road, intending to slaughter them all. In the pond there were many thorny bushes and creepers, and through the bushes the *śrāmaṇera* whom the Master had brought along with him saw a water drain at the southern bank of the pond, large enough for one man to pass through. He secretly told the Master, and the two of them slipped away through it. They ran rapidly toward the southeast for two or three *li* and met a Brahman who was tilling the land. When they told him that they had been robbed by brigands, he was astounded to hear about it. After unbridling his bull and handing it over to the Master, he blew a conch and beat a drum to sound an alarm toward the village. More than eighty men armed with weapons hurriedly rushed to the scene of the robbery. On seeing the group of people, the thugs escaped and vanished into the wood.

The Master then went back to the pond and released the captives from their bonds. Having distributed his clothes to them, he went with them to the village to spend the night. Everybody wept piteously, except the Master who alone smiled without any feeling of grief. His fellow travellers asked him, "All our clothes and travelling money have been stolen, and all that we have in our possession is our lives. As we are now in the most wretched and
232a difficult condition, we cannot but feel sorrowful when we think of what happened in the wood. How is it that you do not share our feeling of misery but smile and are in a happy mood?" The Master said in reply, "What is most precious in existence is life. Since we still have our lives, what else should we worry about? In my country we have a popular saying: 'The greatest treasure between Heaven and earth is life.' As we still possess our lives, we did not lose the Great Treasure. There is no need to grieve over such trifling matters as clothes and travelling money." Thus his

companions were convinced of the truth. This showed the Master's magnanimous quality and his ability to remain calm under adverse circumstances.

On the following day he reached the eastern part of the country of Ṭakka and arrived at a big city. In a large mango grove to the west of the city and by the northern side of the road, there lived a Brahman seven hundred years old, who looked like a man about the age of thirty, with a stalwart build and a clear mind of deep discernment. He was well versed in the *Mādhyamika Śāstra,* the *Śata Śāstra,* and other treatises, as well as in the Vedas and other books. He had two attendants, both of whom were over a hundred years old. When he saw the Master, he received him with great pleasure. Upon hearing that the Master had been robbed, the old teacher sent one of his attendants to ask the Buddhist followers in the city to prepare food for the Master. In the city there were several thousand families, of whom only a few were Buddhists, the great majority being heretical followers. When the Master was in Kaśmīra his fame had already spread far and he was known to various countries. The messenger went throughout the city and announced, "The Chinese monk has arrived and he has been robbed of all his garments at a nearby place. It befits you all to know that this is the right time to do good deeds."

Under the influence of the Master's power of blessedness, the heretics reformed their minds. Upon hearing the announcement, more than three hundred prominent people, each bringing a piece of motley felt together with food and drinks, came to offer them to the Master. They piled up the gifts before him and knelt down to worship and extend greetings to him. The Master blessed them and preached the doctrine of retribution and causality, asking them to cherish the mind of the Way, to give up heretical ideas, and to return to the Right Path. They talked to one another in exhilaration and returned home dancing with delight. The old teacher remarked with admiration that this was an event that had never occurred before.

The Master distributed the felt cloth to his fellow travellers, and each of them received a portion sufficient to make a few suits of garments. As there was more than enough cloth, fifty pieces were offered to the old teacher. The Master stayed there for one month to study the *Sūtraśata Śāstra* and the *Śataśāstravaipulya* with him. This person was a disciple of Nāgārjuna and had received in person his teacher's tradition, of which his expositions were clear and lucid.

Going eastward from here for more than five hundred *li,* he reached the country of Cīnabhukti and repaired to Toṣasana Monastery, where lived a virtuous monk named Vinītaprabha (meaning Light of Subjugation, he being a prince of northern India). He had refined manners and was well versed in the Tripiṭaka, having composed the *Exposition of the Pañcaskandha Śāstra* and the *Exposition of the Vidyāmātrasiddhitridaśakārikā Śāstra.* Thus the Master stayed there for fourteen months to study the *Abhidharmasamudāyavyākhyā Śāstra,* the *Abhidharmaprakaraṇaśāsana Śāstra,* the *Nyāyadvāratāraka Śāstra,* etc.

Going southeast from the great city for more than fifty *li,* he
232b reached Tamasāvana (meaning Dark Wood) Monastery, in which lived more than three hundred monks who studied the teachings of the Sarvāstivāda school. The one thousand Buddhas of the Bhadrakalpa will all come here to preach the Dharma to gatherings of men and heavenly beings. In the three hundredth year after the nirvana of Śākyamuni Tathāgata, the *śāstra* master Kātyāyana (erroneously given as Jiazhanyan in olden times) composed the *Abhidharmajñānaprasthāna Śāstra* at this place.

Going northeast from here for one hundred forty or one hundred fifty *li,* the Master reached the country of Jālaṃdhara (in the domain of northern India). In this country he went to Nagaradhana Monastery, where lived the virtuous monk Candravarman (meaning Moon Protection), who was well versed in the Tripiṭaka. Thus the Master stayed there for four months to study the *Vibhāṣāprakaraṇapāda Śāstra.*

From here he climbed over steep mountains and proceeded northeast for more than seven hundred *li* to reach the country of Kulūta (in the domain of northern India). From Kulūta going southward for more than seven hundred *li,* he climbed over a mountain and crossed a river to reach the country of Śatadru (in the domain of northern India). From here proceeding southwest for more than eight hundred *li,* he reached the country of Pāriyātra (in the domain of Central India). From here going eastward for more than five hundred *li,* he reached the country of Mathurā (in the domain of Central India). The relic stupas of the holy disciples of Śākya Tathāgata, such as Śāriputra (in former times wrongly given as Shelizi or Shelifu) and Maudgalaputra (wrongly given as Mujianlian in former times), were still in existence there. To the stupas of Pūrṇamaitrāyaṇīputra (meaning Full Compassion Son, formerly known as Miduoluonizi, which was an erroneous abbreviation), Upāli, Ānanda, Rāhula (formerly erroneously known as Luohouluo or Luoyun), and Mañjuśrī (meaning Wonderfully Auspicious; in old times erroneously known as Rushou, Wenshushili, or Manshushili or translated as Wonderful Virtue) the monks came on festival days each year to make offerings separately according to their different circumstances. The Abhidharma monks made offerings to Śāriputra; those who practised meditation, to Maudgalaputra; the sutra-reciters, to Pūrnamaitrāyaṇīputra; the monks who studied the Vinaya, to Upāli; the *bhikṣuṇīs*, to Ānanda; those who had not received full ordination, to Rāhula; and the Mahayana students, to various Bodhisattvas.

Five or six *li* to the east of the city, the Master came to a monastery built on a hill by the Venerable Upagupta (meaning Near Protection), in which were preserved the hair and nail relics. On the rock to the north of the monastery there was a cave more than twenty feet high and over thirty feet wide, filled with small tallies four inches long. When the Venerable Upagupta was preaching the Dharma, if a married couple became enlightened and both of them attained Arhatship, he would put in one tally, but if only one of the couple or people of separate families had attained Arhatship, he would not count it.

From here going northeast for more than five hundred *li,* he
232c reached the country of Sthāneśvara (in the domain of Central India). Going again to the east for more than four hundred *li,* he reached the country of Śrughna (in the domain of Central India),

which bordered on the Ganges in the east, with big mountains at its back in the north and the Jumna River flowing through the middle of its territory.

Again going east from the river for more than eight hundred *li,* he reached the source of the Ganges, which was three or four *li* wide, flowing toward the southeast; and it was more than ten *li* broad at the place where it entered the sea. The water was sweet and refreshing, and fine sand drifted down the river. In [Indian] popular books it was called the "water of happiness." If one bathed in it, one would be absolved of one's sins; if one sipped its water or rinsed one's mouth with it, one would be saved from calamities; and if one were drowned in it, one would be reborn in the heavens to enjoy happiness. Thus ignorant men and women often flocked to the riverside. But this was all the sayings of the heretics without any reality. Afterward, Deva Bodhisattva showed them the right truth, and then they totally relinquished their practices.

In this country there lived a virtuous monk named Jayagupta, who was well versed in the Tripiṭaka. So the Master stayed there during the winter and half of the following spring season to listen to his lectures on the *Sautrāntikavibhāṣā Śāstra* until the course was concluded.

Crossing the river to the eastern bank, he reached the country of Matipura, the king of which was of the *śūdra* caste. There were more than ten monasteries with over eight hundred monks who studied the Hinayana teachings of the Sarvāstivāda school.

Four or five *li* to the south of the big city there was a small monastery with more than fifty monks. Formerly the *śāstra* master Guṇaprabha (meaning Virtue Light) composed in this monastery the *Tattvasatya Śāstra* and over a hundred other treatises. This *śāstra* master, a native of the country of Parvata, originally studied Mahayana teachings but later degraded himself to learn Hinayana doctrines. At that time Arhat Devasena (meaning Celestial Host) often went up to the Tuṣita Heaven. Guṇaprabha, wishing to see Maitreya to solve all the dubious and ambiguous points he had in his mind, asked Devasena to bring him up by divine power to the heavenly palace. When he saw Maitreya, he just bowed slightly down without paying homage to him in the proper way, and he said, "As I am an ordained monk, while Maitreya is living as a layman in Heaven, it is improper for me to worship him." He went up to Heaven three times but never worshipped the Bodhisattva once. Owing to his arrogance and self-conceit, his doubts were not cleared.

Three or four *li* to the south of Guṇaprabha's monastery was another monastery with more than two hundred monks of the Hinayana school. This was the place where the *śāstra* master Saṃghabhadra passed away. This *śāstra* master, a native of Kaśmīra, was an erudite and highly talented person, well versed in the *Vibhāṣā Śāstra* of the Sarvāstivāda school. At that time Vasubandhu Bodhisattva, who was also a man of great wisdom and good learning, had formerly composed the *Abhidharmakośa Śāstra* in refutation of the theories held by the Vibhāṣā teachers. The tenets expounded in this work were so abstruse and the style of writing so florid that none of the students of the Western Region did not praise it with admiration, and even the spirits and deities also discussed and studied it. When Saṃghabhadra had read the treatise he felt indignant over it, and after twelve years of profound thinking, he composed the *Kośakarakā Śāstra* in twenty-five thousand stanzas with eight hundred thousand syllables. After having composed this treatise, he intended to settle his disputes with Vasubandhu face to face, but he died before he could carry out his
233a intention. Later, when Vasubandhu read the treatise, he praised the work, saying that it was a book of comprehensive understanding and that its author was no less intelligent than any of the other Vibhāṣā teachers. He also remarked that as it coincided with his own views, it should be given the title of *Nyāyānusāra Śāstra;* thus it was so named.

After the death of Saṃghabhadra, a stupa was built in a mango grove; it was still in existence. Beside the grove there was another stupa built on the spot where the *śāstra* master Vimalamitra (meaning Pure Friend) passed away. This *śāstra* master was a native of the country of Kaśmīra, who, having become a monk in the Sarvāstivāda school, travelled in the five parts of India and thoroughly mastered the Tripiṭaka. On his way back to his homeland, he came to the stupa of Saṃghabhadra and felt sorry that he should have died before his writings were popularized. So he vowed to compose more treatises to refute Mahayana teachings and efface Vasubandhu's name, so that the tenets of the *śāstra* master Saṃghabhadra might be handed down from generation to generation far into the future. When he had just uttered these words, he became demented and five tongues grew out of his mouth, with blood bleeding all over his body. He realized that this pain was caused by his evil views, and so he wrote a letter of penitence to admonish his friends never to slander Mahayana teachings. After having said so, he expired. At the place of his death, the earth sank into a pit.

In that country there was a virtuous monk named Mitrasena, who was then ninety years old. He was a disciple of the *śāstra* master Guṇaprabha and was well versed in the Tripiṭaka. The Master stayed there for half a spring and a summer to study with him the *Tattvasandeśa Śāstra* (i.e., the *Tattvasatya Śāstra* in twenty-five thousand stanzas, composed by Guṇaprabha), the *Anujñānaprasthāna Śāstra,* and other treatises of the Sarvāstivāda school.

Again going from here northward for more than three hundred *li,* he reached the country of Brahmapura (in Central India). Going further southeast for more than four hundred *li,* he reached the country of Ahicchattra (in the domain of Central India). Again going southward for more than two hundred *li,* he crossed the Ganges and turned southwest to the country of Vilaśāṇa (in the domain of Central India). Again going eastward for more than two hundred *li,* he reached the country of Kapitha (in the domain of Central India). More than twenty *li* to the east of the city, there was a large monastery; in its courtyard there were three stairways made of precious substances, standing in a row from south to north, facing the east and sloping down to the west. This was the place where the Buddha descended to Jambudvīpa when he returned from the Trayastriṃśa Heaven after having preached the Dharma to Mahāmāyā. The stairway in the middle was made of

gold, the left one of crystal, and the right one of white silver. The Tathāgata started from the Hall of the Good Dharma and walked slowly down the middle stairway with many heavenly beings following him, while Mahābrahmā, holding a white chowry, walked down the silver stairway on the right, and Indra, holding a precious canopy, came down by the crystal stairway on the left. At that time hundreds and thousands of celestial beings and great Bodhisattvas came down with the Buddha. A few hundred years before, the stairways had still been there, but now they had collapsed and were no more in existence. In memory of the stairways a king at a later time built imitations of the original ones out of brick and stone to the height of more than seventy feet, and adorned them with various precious substances. On the top of the stairways there
233b was a *vihāra* in which was enshrined a stone image of the Buddha with statues of Indra and Brahmā on its left and right after the original fashion, presenting a lively scene. Beside the stairways there was a stone column seventy feet high, erected by King Aśoka. Beside the column was a stone platform more than fifty paces long and seven feet high, which was the place where the Buddha had walked up and down in olden times.

From here going northwest for two hundred *li,* [the Master] reached the country of Kanyākubja (meaning the City of Hunchbacked Maidens, in Central India), which was four thousand *li* in circumference. Bordering on the Ganges in the west, the capital city was more than twenty *li* in length and five or six *li* in width. There were more than a hundred monasteries with over ten thousand monks who studied both Mahayana and Hinayana teachings. The king, who was of the *vaiṣya* caste, was named Harṣavardhana (meaning Joy-increasing). His father was named Prabhākaravardhana (meaning Light-increasing), and his elder brother, Rājyavardhana (meaning Kingdom-increasing). Harṣavardhana was a benign ruler and won the praise and acclaim of his people. At that time King Śaśāṅka (meaning Moon) of the country of Karṇasuvarṇa (meaning Golden Ear) in eastern India hated him for his clever strategies and, considering him a dangerous neighbor, had him killed through trickery. The chief minister Vāṇi (meaning

Eloquent Speech) and his colleagues lamented the loss of their lord and enthroned the king's younger brother Śīlāditya (meaning Morality Sun) to succeed in the royal lineage. The new king had a heroic appearance with outstanding intelligence, and, being a far-sighted man, was skilled in strategy. As his virtue moved Heaven and earth, and his righteousness influenced men and divine beings, he was able to avenge his elder brother and put India under his control. Wherever his prestige reached and his moral influence functioned, the people submitted to his rule of virtue.

When order was restored in the country and the people lived in peace, military strength was no more displayed, and weapons were stored away. Deeds of blessedness were performed, and a royal decree was issued to the effect that within the domain no slaughter of animals was allowed and all subjects were universally prohibited from eating meat. Monasteries were constructed at all holy places, every year gifts were offered to all monks for twenty-one days, and the Unlimited Congregation was held once every five years. Whatever was stored in the royal treasure house was given away as alms. In consideration of his deeds, [King Śīlāditya] might well be compared with Sudāna.

In the northwest of the city there was a stupa more than two hundred feet high; and six or seven *li* away to the southeast and on the southern bank of the Ganges there was another stupa, also more than two hundred feet high. Both were constructed by King Aśoka at places where the Buddha had formerly preached the Dharma.

The Master entered this country, stayed at the Bhadra Vihāra for three months, and completed his studies of Buddhadāsa's *Vibhāṣā Śāstra* and Sūryavarman's *Vibhāṣā Śāstra* under the tutelage of the Tripiṭaka Master Vīryasena.

Fascicle III

Beginning with the Country of Ayodhyā and Ending with the Country of Īraṇaparvata

233c From here the Master proceeded southeast for more than six hundred *li* and crossed the Ganges to the south to reach the country of Ayodhyā (in Central India). There were over a hundred monasteries with several thousand monks, who studied both Mahayana and Hinayana teachings. In the great city there was an old monastery that was the place where Vasubandhu (meaning World Kinsman, formerly incorrectly transliterated Posoupandou and mistranslated Celestial Kinsman) Bodhisattva composed Mahayana and Hinayana treatises and lectured the monks. Four or five *li* to the northwest of the city, on the bank of the Ganges, there was a big stupa more than two hundred feet high and constructed by King Aśoka at the place where the Buddha once preached the Dharma for three months. Beside the stupa was the place where the four past Buddhas had walked up and down. Five or six *li* to the southwest of the city, there was an old monastery that was the place where Asaṅga Bodhisattva had preached the Dharma. At night the Bodhisattva ascended to the Tuṣita Heaven to hear the *Yogācārabhūmi Śāstra*, the *Mahāyānasūtrālaṃkāra Śāstra,* and the *Madhyāntavibhāga Śāstra* at the place of Maitreya Bodhisattva. In the daytime he came down from the Heaven to preach the Dharma for the monks. Asaṅga, also named No Attachment, was a native of Gandhāra. He appeared in the world one thousand years after the nirvana of the Buddha and became a monk in the Mahīśāsaka school but later believed in Mahayana teachings. His younger brother Vasubandhu became a monk in the Sarvāstivāda school but also believed in Mahayana teachings afterward. Both brothers were men endowed with a genius for understanding the holy teachings and possessed a talent for writing. They composed a large number of treatises for the exposition of Mahayana theories and were great masters of Buddhism in India. Such works as the *Mahāyānasaṃparigraha Śāstra,* the *Prakaraṇāryavācā Śāstra,* the *Abhidharmasamudāya Prakaraṇa Śāstra,* the *Vijñaptimātratāsiddhi Śāstra,* and the *Abhidharmakośa Śāstra* were products of their pens.

After having paid homage to the sacred sites in the country of Ayodhyā, the Master sailed down the Ganges eastward with more than eighty persons in the same boat, intending to go to the country of Hayamukha. When they had sailed for about a hundred *li,* they came to a place where there were dense and exuberant woods of aśoka trees on both banks of the river; and from the woods on each side of the river more than ten boatloads of pirates suddenly emerged at the same time and rowed against the current toward them. The people in the boat were terrified, and in confusion several men jumped into the river. The pirates compelled the boat to sail to the bank and ordered the people to take off their clothes in order to search for gems and jewels. Being worshippers
234a of the goddess Durgā, the pirates used to find a handsome man of good quality in each autumn season to be killed as a sacrifice to the deity so they could pray for happiness and blessedness. Upon seeing that the Master was grand and handsome in appearance with proper bodily form, they looked at each other with pleased expressions and said among themselves, "The season for us to make a sacrifice to the deity is drawing near to the end, but we could not find a suitable man. Now this *śramaṇa* has a nice and refined appearance. Isn't it auspicious for us to kill him as a sacrifice?" The Master said in reply, "I would not dare begrudge this filthy and ugly body of mine as a sacrifice to the deity. But I have come from a far distance with the intention of worshipping the Bodhi tree and the Buddha's image at Gṛdhrakūṭa Mountain, as well as seeking scriptures of the Dharma. If you donors kill me while my intention has not been fulfilled, it will, I am afraid, be inauspicious for you."

All the people in the boat begged for mercy on behalf of the Master. Some of them even volunteered to substitute for him; but the pirates would not consent. The ringleader sent his men to fetch water and clear the ground in the flowery wood to prepare an altar and plaster it with clay. He ordered two men with their scimitars unsheathed to lead the Master to the altar, and they were ready to kill him by wielding their weapons. The Master showed no expression of fear, and all the pirates were amazed at this. With a feeling that he would not be spared, the Master said to the pirates, "Please grant me a little time and do not press me too hard, so that I may die happily and with an easy mind." The Master then concentrated his mind on the Tuṣita Palace and meditated on Maitreya Bodhisattva, with the desire to be born in that place, pay homage and make offerings to the Bodhisattva, and receive the *Yogācārabhūmi Śāstra* from him. After hearing the wonderful Dharma and achieving supernatural powers and wisdom, he would be reborn down in this world again to edify these people and make them practise superior deeds and abandon all evil actions. He would also widely propagate all the Dharmas for the benefit and happiness of all beings. Then he worshipped the Buddhas of the ten quarters and sat in meditation, concentrating his mind on Maitreya Bodhisattva without any distracting thoughts. While he was in contemplation, he seemed to have ascended Mount Sumeru and transcended the first, the second, and the third heavens, and to have seen Maitreya Bodhisattva at the Wonderful and Precious Terrace in the Tuṣita Palace, surrounded by a multitude of heavenly beings. At that moment the Master was so overjoyed both physically and mentally that he became unaware that he was on the sacrificial altar and also forgot about the pirates.

All his fellow travellers wailed and wept aloud. In a moment a gale of black wind rose from the four quarters, breaking down the trees and blowing sand high into the air. Waves rose in the river and the boats were overturned. The pirates, being greatly frightened, inquired of the travellers, "Where does this *śramaṇa* come from, and what is his name?" They replied, "He is the monk from China seeking the Dharma. If you gentlemen kill him, you will commit a deadly sin. In view of the windstorm, we know that the deity has been enraged. It befits you to make a quick repentance." The pirates were fearful and begged for pardon with remorse one after another. They prostrated themselves before the Master to take refuge under him, but he was unconscious of them. When the pirates touched him with their hands, he opened his eyes and said to them, "Is it time now?" The pirates said, "We dare not harm the teacher. May you accept our repentance."

The Master accepted their worship and apology, and told them that such evil deeds as killing, theft, and worshipping improper
234b deities would cause one to suffer pains in the Avīci Hell in the future. "Why should you sow the seeds of suffering for an unlimited long time just for the sake of a corporeal body which lasts only for a short time like lightning or morning dew?" The pirates prostrated themselves and apologized, saying, "Our thoughts were erroneous and upside-down. We did what we should not do and served the deity whom we should not serve. If we did not meet the teacher, whose blessedness and virtue moved the mysterious gods, how could we have heard such inspiring instructions? From today onward we shall stop practising this career. May the teacher be our witness!"

Then they admonished one another, collected their weapons, and threw them all into the river. They returned the clothes and money they had seized in pillage to the original owners. After they had received the Five Precepts, the windstorm ceased. Being delighted, the pirates worshipped the Master and went away. The fellow travellers praised the Master with amazement in an unusual manner. All the people far and near who heard about it remarked that it was an extraordinary occurrence. If it were not for his sincerity in seeking the Dharma, how could this miraculous incident have happened?

From here going eastward for more than three hundred *li,* the Master crossed the Ganges and reached the country of Ayamukha in the north (in Central India). From here going southeast for more than seven hundred *li,* he crossed the Ganges to the south; and north of the Jumna River he reached the country of Prayāga (in

Central India). In a wood of *campaka* flowers to the southwest of the city, there was a stupa built by King Aśoka at the spot where the Buddha had formerly subdued heretics. A monastery beside the stupa was the place where Deva Bodhisattva composed the *Vaipulyaśata Śāstra* to defeat Hinayana followers and heretics in argument.

West of the confluence of the two rivers to the east of the big city, there was a tableland, fourteen or fifteen *li* in circuit, which was flat and regular in shape, being the place where the kings and noblemen used to distribute alms philanthropically since ancient times; hence it was named the Great Place for Almsgiving. The present King Śīlāditya continued this practice, and he distributed all the wealth he had accumulated in five years as offerings to the Triple Gem and as alms to all poor and lonely people without exception for seventy-five days.

From here going southwest the Master entered a big forest in which he met with many fierce animals and wild elephants. After covering more than five hundred *li,* he reached the country of Kauśāmbī (formerly erroneously known as Jushanmi, in Central India). There were over ten monasteries with more than three hundred monks. Within the old palace in the city there was a big *vihāra,* more than sixty feet high, enshrining a Buddha image carved out of sandalwood with a stone canopy suspended over it. It was made by King Udayana (meaning Issuing Affection, formerly inaccurately known as Youtianwang). When the Tathāgata was preaching the Dharma to his mother in the Trayastriṃśa Heaven during the summer season, the king, longing to see the Buddha, asked Maudgalyāyana to bring a skillful craftsman up to the Heaven to observe the Buddha's features and demeanor. After returning to earth he carved a statue of the Buddha out of red sandalwood. It was this statue that went to welcome the World-honored One when he came down from the Heaven.

In the south of the city there was an old house that was the old residence of the Elder Ghoṣila (formerly incorrectly known as Qushiluo). Not far to the south of the city there was an old monastery that had been the garden of the Elder, in which there

234c was a stupa more than two hundred feet high and built by King Aśoka. Again, the storeyed pavilion in the southeast was the place where Vasubandhu composed the *Vijñānamātratā Śāstra*. Further to the east the ruins of a house in a mango grove marked the place where Asaṅga Bodhisattva composed the *Prakaraṇāryavācā Śāstra*.

From here going eastward for more than five hundred *li,* the Master reached the country of Viṣaka, where there were more than twenty monasteries with some three thousand monks, followers of the Saṃmitīya school of Hinayana Buddhism. Toward the southeast, on the left side of the road, there was a big monastery where the Arhat Devaśarman composed the *Vijñānakāyapāda Śāstra,* in which he advocated the theory of Non-ego. Meanwhile the Arhat Gopa wrote the *Treatise on the Essential Realities of the Holy Teaching* to affirm the existence of the ego, and these different views of the Dharma caused serious controversies. It was also the place where Dharmapāla Bodhisattva confuted in argument one hundred Hinayana *śāstra* masters in seven days. Beside it was a place where the Tathāgata had preached the Dharma for six years. There was a tree more than seventy feet high. Once in the past when the Buddha had cleansed his teeth with a twig, he threw away the used twig, which took root in the ground and grew into a tree that had flourished until that time. Heretics often came to cut the tree; but as soon as it had been cut, it grew up again and thrived as before.

From here going northeast for more than five hundred *li,* the Master reached the country of Śrāvastī (formerly erroneously known as Shewei), which was over six thousand *li* in circumference with several hundred monasteries and several thousand monks, all of whom were adherents of Saṃmitīya school. During the Buddha's lifetime, this was the capital of King Prasenajit (meaning Victorious Army, and formerly inaccurately known as Bosini). In the city were the foundations of the royal palace; and not far away to the east, a stupa was built on the old foundations of the great preaching hall constructed by King Prasenajit for the Buddha. There was another stupa built to mark the *vihāra* of the Buddha's aunt, Bhikṣuṇī Prajāpatī (meaning Mistress of Creatures, formerly inaccurately known as Bosheboti). Further to the east a stupa was built as the old residence of Sudatta (meaning Well-Given, erroneously known as Xuda in olden times). Beside the old residence was a stupa built at the place where Aṅgulimāla (formerly erroneously known as Yangjuemoluo) abandoned his evil behavior.

Five or six *li* to the south of the city was the Jetavana Wood (meaning Victor's Wood, formerly erroneously known as Qituo), which was the garden of Anāthapiṇḍika. Formerly it had been a monastery, but it was now in ruins. On the left and right sides of the eastern gate there were two stone pillars, seventy feet high, erected by King Aśoka. All the buildings were dilapidated, except one brick room with a golden image of the Buddha in it. Formerly when the Buddha ascended to Heaven to preach the Dharma to his mother, King Prasenajit longed to see him; and when he heard that King Udayana had a statue of the Buddha carved out of sandalwood, he also made such an image. Not far behind the monastery was the place where a heretical Brahman slew a woman to calumniate the Buddha. Over a hundred paces to the east of the monastery was a big and deep pit, which was the place where Devadatta attempted to poison the Buddha and fell into hell
235a alive. In the south there was another big pit, which was the place where Bhikṣu Kokālika slandered the Buddha and fell into hell alive. More than eight hundred paces to the south of this pit was the place where the Brahmin woman Ciñcā slandered the Buddha and fell into hell alive. These three pits were so deep that their bottoms were invisible.

Over seventy paces to the east of the monastery, there was a *vihāra* that was tall and big; and in it there was a statue of the Buddha, seated facing the east. This was the place where the Tathāgata had once debated with some heretics. Further to the east was a *deva* temple, which was the same in proportions as the *vihāra*. When the sunlight shifted, the shadow of the *deva* temple never reached the *vihāra,* but the shadow of the *vihāra* always overcast the *deva* temple. Three or four *li* further to the east, there was a stupa built at the place where Śāriputra had debated with some heretics. More than sixty *li* to the northwest of the big city there was an old city, which was the city of Kāśyapa Buddha's father at the time in the Bhadrakalpa when the life span of human beings was twenty thousand years. In the south of the city was the place where the Buddha saw his father for the first time after he had attained enlightenment. In the north of the city was a stupa containing the relics of the whole body of Kāśyapa Buddha. Both stupas were erected by King Aśoka.

From here proceeding southeast for more than eight hundred *li,* the Master reached the country of Kapilavastu (formerly known as the country of Jiapiluowei). The circumference of the country was more than four thousand *li* and that of the capital city more than ten *li.* Both the country and its capital were deserted and in ruins. The palace city was fifteen *li* in circumference, and, being constructed with bricks, it was very firm and strong. Inside it were the old foundations of King Śuddhodana's main palace hall, on which a temple was built with a statue of the king enshrined in it. Further to the north were the old foundations of the royal bedchamber of Lady Māyā, on which a temple was built with a statue of the lady kept in it. Beside it was a temple built at the place where the spirit of Śākya Bodhisattva entered his mother's womb. In this temple an image of the Bodhisattva being born in the world was enshrined. According to the tradition of the Sthavira school, the spirit of the Bodhisattva entered his mother's womb on the night of the thirtieth day of the month of Uttarāṣāḍhā, corresponding to the fifteenth day of the fifth month of our calendar, while other schools held that it was on the twenty-third day of that month, corresponding to the eighth day of the fifth month of our calendar. In the northwest was a stupa built at the place where the Ṛṣi Asita read the physiognomy of the Prince. On the left and right sides of the city were the places where the Prince competed with other Śākya youths in physical strength; where he went over the city wall on a horse; and where he returned to the palace, abhorring the world and wishing to abandon it, after having seen an old man, a sick person, a corpse, and a *śramaṇa* (mendicant) at the four gates of the city.

Travelling eastward from here through a wild forest for more than five hundred *li,* the Master reached the country of Rāmagrāma (in the domain of Central India), which was sparsely inhabited. To the east of the old city, there was a brick stupa more than fifty feet high. After the nirvana of the Tathāgata, the then king of this country obtained a share of the relics, and when he returned home he built this stupa for the preservation of the relics. It often issued a bright light. Beside the stupa was a dragon's pond. The dragon frequently took the form of a human being to circumambulate the stupa; and wild elephants always came with flowers to offer to it.

235b Not far from the stupa there was a monastery with a *śrāmaṇera* (novice) as its abbot. According to a legend, once a *bhikṣu* (monk) invited some of his fellow monks to come here from a far distance to worship the stupa. They saw that wild elephants placed flowers in front of the stupa, removed the weeds with their tusks, and sprayed water with their trunks. At this sight the monks were quite moved. One of them gave up the major rules observed by a fully ordained *bhikṣu* and volunteered to stay there as a novice to serve at the place. He said to the other monks, "The elephants are animals and yet they know to pay respect to the stupa by offering flowers to it and by spraying water and sweeping the ground clean. I am a human being and have renounced my home to become a monk under the Buddha. How could I not engage myself to serve at this place when I see with my own eyes that it is in such a desolate and neglected condition?" Thus he took leave of the other monks and stayed behind. He built a house, dredged the pond, planted flowers, and grew fruits through the cold and hot seasons without feeling tired. When the people of the neighboring countries heard about this, they donated money and valuables for the construction of a monastery through collective effort, and also invited the *śrāmaṇera* to be the abbot and take charge of the monastery's affairs. Since then the abbots had always been succeeded by *śrāmaṇera*s as a tradition.

In a big forest to the east of the Śrāmaṇera Monastery, the Master travelled for more than a hundred *li*. There was a stupa built by King Aśoka at the place where the Prince, after having come out of the city, doffed his precious robe, took off his royal crown, untied the pearl from his topknot, and handed them all to Chandaka (formerly incorrectly known as Cheni) to be taken back home. A stupa was also built to mark the place where the Prince had cut off his hair.

Coming out of the forest, the Master reached the country of Kuśinagara, which was in an extremely deserted and isolated condition. At the northeast corner of the city was a stupa built by King Aśoka to mark the old house of Cunda (formerly inaccurately known as Chuntuo), where a well was dug at a time when offerings were prepared for the Buddha. The water was still clear and fresh.

Three or four *li* to the northwest of the city, the Master crossed the Ajitavatī River (meaning the Invincible River, formerly incorrectly known as the Alibati River). Not far from the river, he came to the Śāla Grove, where the trees were similar to oak with greenish bark and very glossy white leaves. Four pairs of trees of the same height grew at the place where the Tathāgata entered nirvana. In a large brick temple there was an image of the Tathāgata in the posture of entering nirvana, lying with its head toward the north. Beside it was a great stupa more than two hundred feet high built by King Aśoka. He also erected a stone pillar to record the event of the Buddha's nirvana, but no date was inscribed on it. It was said by tradition that the Buddha lived for eighty years and entered nirvana on the fifteenth day of the second half of the month Vaiśākha, corresponding to the fifteenth day of the second month of our calendar. But the Sarvāstivāda school said that the Buddha entered nirvana in the second half of the month Kārttika, corresponding to the eighth day of the ninth month of our calendar. Since the time of the nirvana, some said it had been twelve hundred years, or thirteen hundred years, or fifteen hundred years. Others said that it had been over nine hundred but less than a thousand years. Other stupas were also built to mark the places where the Tathāgata, sitting in a golden coffin, preached the Dharma to his mother; where he stretched his arm to ask Ānanda a question; where he showed his feet to Kāśyapa; where his remains were cremated with fragrant wood; and where eight kings shared his relics.

Going on from here through a big forest for more than five
235c hundred *li,* the Master reached the country of Vārāṇasī, the circumference of which was more than four thousand *li.* Its capital, bordering on the Ganges in the west, was more than ten *li* long and five or six *li* wide, with more than thirty monasteries and over two thousand monks who were adherents of the Hinayana Sarvāstivāda school.

After crossing the river at Vārāṇasī and proceeding northeast for more than ten *li,* he reached the monastery at the Deer Park. The lofty terraces and pavilions, connected by long corridors on four sides, were so tall that they touched the clouds. There were fifteen hundred monks who were followers of the Hinayana Saṃmitīya school. Inside the large enclosure there was a temple, more than a hundred feet high, with stone steps and brick niches arranged in about a hundred tiers, each containing a golden image of the Buddha carved in intaglio. In the chamber there was a life-size bronze statue of the Buddha turning the Wheel of the Dharma. To the southeast of the temple was a stone stupa more than a hundred feet high, built by King Aśoka. In front of the stupa there was a stone pillar, more than seventy feet high, erected at the place where the Buddha first turned the Wheel of the Dharma. Beside it was the place where Maitreya (meaning the Compassionate One, formerly inexactly known as Mile) Bodhisattva received his prediction. Further to the west was a stupa that marked the place where the Buddha, as Prabhāpāla Bodhisattva in a previous life, at the time during the Bhadrakalpa when the life span of human beings was twenty thousand years, received his prediction from Kāśyapa Buddha. To the south of the place where Śākyamuni Buddha received his prediction was a place where the four past Buddhas had walked up and down. Being more than fifty paces long and seven feet in height, it was built by laying greenish slabs, upon which were images of the four Buddhas walking. To the west of the monastery was the bathing pool of the Tathāgata, and there was also a pond in which he washed his alms bowl, and another one for washing his robes. All these ponds were guarded by divine dragons and nobody contaminated them. Beside the ponds was a stupa built at the spot where the Buddha as a six-tusked white elephant, while he was practising the deeds of a Bodhisattva, gave his tusks as alms to a hunter. There was also the place where he as a bird fixed the order of seniority of a monkey and a white elephant under a banyan tree in order to teach the people to observe proprieties. There were also the places where he was once a deer king, and where he converted the five disciples, Kauṇḍinya and the others.

From here going down the Ganges eastward for more than three hundred *li,* the Master reached the country of Yuddhapati, from whence he proceeded northeast to cross the Ganges. After travelling for one hundred forty or one hundred fifty *li,* he reached the country of Vaiśālī (formerly inaccurately known as Pisheli), which was more than five thousand *li* in circumference. The soil was good and fertile, abounding in mangoes and plantains. The capital city was in ruins; and its old foundations were sixty or seventy *li* in circumference, with very few inhabitants. Five or six *li* to the northwest of the palace city was a monastery, beside which was a stupa to mark the place where the Buddha had preached the *Vimalakīrtinirdeśa Sūtra.* Three or four *li* further to the northeast there was a stupa, built at the old site of Vimalakīrti's residence, that still manifested many miraculous signs. Not far from there was a chamber, built by piling up stones, in which Vimalakīrti pretended
236a to be ill and preached the Dharma. Beside it were the old residence of Ratnākāra and that of the woman Āmrapālī. Three or four *li* further to the north was a stupa that marked the place where the Buddha, followed by heavenly beings and men, had halted while he was on his way to Kuśinagara to enter *parinirvāṇa.* Further to the west was the place where the Buddha looked at Vaiśālī for the last time. Further to the south were Āmrapālī's garden, which she offered to the Buddha, and the place where the Buddha consented to enter nirvana at the suggestion of the King of Māras.

From the southern part of Vaiśālī, the Master travelled for more than a hundred *li* to the Ganges and reached the city of Śvetapura, where he obtained a copy of the *Bodhisattvapiṭaka Sūtra.*

Once again he crossed the Ganges, went south, and reached the country of Magadha (formerly inaccurately known as Moqietuo), which was more than five thousand *li* in circumference. It was the custom of this country to advocate learning and respect men of virtue and ability. There were more than fifty monasteries with over ten thousand monks, most of whom studied Mahayana teachings. On the southern side of the river was the old city with a circumference of more than seventy *li*. Although it was deserted and dilapidated, the crenellations on the city wall were still intact. Formerly, when human life was innumerable years long, this city was called Kusumapura (meaning the Palace City of Fragrant Flowers) because the royal palace had abundant flowers. Afterward, when human life was a few thousand years long, the name was changed to the country of Pāṭaliputra (formerly incorrectly known as Xilianfuyi), being adopted from the name of the *pāṭalī* tree.

In the one hundredth year after the Buddha's nirvana, King Aśoka (meaning the King without Sorrow, formerly inaccurately known as Ayuwang), a great grandson of King Bimbisāra (meaning Stone Shadow), moved his capital from Rājagṛha to this city. As a long time had elapsed, only the old foundations of the city remained. There had been several hundred monasteries, out of which only two or three survived. To the north of the old palace and bordering on the Ganges was a small town in which lived more than a thousand families. To the north of the palace was a stone pillar, several tens of feet high, erected at the place where King Aśoka had built a hell. The Master sojourned in the small town for seven days, going around to pay homage to the holy sites. A stupa standing to the south of the hell was one of the eighty-four thousand stupas constructed by the king with human labor. In this one was preserved one *sheng* of the Tathāgata's relic bones, which often issued a divine light. Next to the stupa was a temple, in which was kept a slab on which the Tathāgata had once stood. On the slab were two footprints of the Buddha, one foot eight inches long and six inches wide. On both soles there were the signs of the Thousand-spoked Wheel; and the tips of the ten toes had the lineations of a swastika and the shapes of vases, fishes, and other things, all clearly discernable. When the Tathāgata was going to enter nirvana, he left Vaiśālī and came to this place. Standing on a big square rock on the southern bank of the river, he looked at Ānanda and said to him, "These are my footprints, left here while I have a last look at the Diamond Seat and at Rājagṛha."

To the north of the temple there was a stone pillar, more than thirty feet high, on which was recorded that King Aśoka had thrice presented Jambudvīpa as alms to the Buddha, the Dharma, and the Sangha and thrice redeemed it with precious gems and jewels.
236b To the southeast of the old city were the old foundations of the Kukkuṭārāma (meaning Cock Garden), on which there was a monastery built by King Aśoka. It was the place where he invited a thousand monks and offered them the four requisites needed by a monk. The Master spent seven days there to worship all these holy sites.

Again proceeding southwest for six or seven *yojana*s, the Master reached Telāḍhaka Monastery, in which lived several tens of Tripiṭaka Masters. Upon hearing that the Master had arrived, all of them came out to welcome and take him into the monastery.

From here travelling southward for more than a hundred *li,* he came to the Bodhi tree. The enclosure of the tree was built of brick. It was very high and strong, long from east to west and slightly narrower from south to north. The main gate faced the Nairañjanā River in the east, the southern gate connected with a large flower pond, the west side bordered on a precipitous slope, and the northern gate joined with a big monastery. Inside the enclosure the holy sites were connected together. They were temples and stupas built by kings, ministers, and wealthy Elders in memory of the Buddha. In the middle was the Diamond Seat, which was created at the beginning of the Bhadrakalpa together with the world. It was in the center of the Three Thousand Great Chiliocosm and stretched from the surface of the earth down to the Diamond Wheel at the bottom of it. It was made of diamond and its circumference was more than a hundred paces. It was called the Diamond Seat to indicate that it was strong and indestructible but was able to destroy all other things. If it were not located at this spot, the earth would quake without cease; and if there were no seat made of diamond, there would be no suitable place for the Buddha to manifest the Diamond Samādhi. In order to subdue Māra and attain enlightenment, he had to stay at this place. If he had stayed elsewhere, the earth would have been overturned. Therefore all one thousand Buddhas of the Bhadrakalpa will come here to achieve Buddhahood. The place for the achievement of Buddhahood was also known as Bodhimaṇḍa. When the world tilted and quaked, this place alone remained still.

During the last one or two hundred years, the people, being less blessed, could not see the Diamond Seat when they went to the Bodhi tree. After the nirvana of the Buddha, the kings of various countries set up two images of Avalokiteśvara Bodhisattva, sitting facing the east, to mark the southern and northern limits. It was said by tradition that when these images of the Bodhisattva sank and disappeared, the Buddha Dharma would come to its end. The Bodhisattva on the southern side had then sunken down up to its chest. The Bodhi tree was a *pippala* tree. When the Buddha was living in the world, it was several hundred feet tall; but as it had been cut down repeatedly by evil kings, it was now about fifty feet high. Because the Buddha had sat under it and achieved Supreme Perfect Enlightenment, it was known as the Bodhi tree. The trunk of the tree was yellowish white in color and the branches and leaves were green and sleek, never withering in the autumn and winter seasons. But on the day of the Tathāgata's nirvana, the leaves would all fall suddenly; and after one night new buds would burgeon as before. On this day each year the kings of different countries and their ministers always assembled under the tree to sprinkle and wash it with milk. After having lit lamps and scattered flowers, they collected the withered leaves and went away.

Upon his arrival there, the Master worshipped the Bodhi tree and the image of the Buddha attaining enlightenment made by Maitreya Bodhisattva. After having looked at the image with deep sincerity, he prostrated himself before it and deplored sadly, saying
236c with self-reproach, "I do not know where I was born in the course

of transmigration at the time when the Buddha attained enlightenment. I could only come here at this time, the end of the Image Period. It makes me think that my karmic hindrances must have been very heavy!" While he was saying so, his eyes brimmed with sorrowful tears. As that was the time when the monks dismissed the summer retreat, several thousand people forgathered from far and near. Those who saw the Master were choked by sobs in sympathy with him. For one *yojana* around, the place was full of holy sites, and the Master stayed there for eight or nine days to worship them all.

On the tenth day, the Sangha of Nālandā Monastery dispatched four virtuous monks to welcome the Master, and he went with them. After going for about seven *yojana*s, they reached the manor of the monastery, which was the village in which the Venerable Maudgalyāyana was born. Shortly after they had taken their meal at the manor, more than two hundred monks and over a thousand lay supporters, holding banners, canopies, flowers, and incense, came to greet the Master. They praised him all around and ushered him into Nālandā Monastery. Upon his arrival, all the monks assembled. When the Master had met them all, a special seat was prepared for him to sit beside the abbot. Then all the other monks also took their seats. When they had sat down, the Director of Duties was asked to strike a bell to make an announcement that the Master was to reside in the monastery with permission to use in common with all the other monks all the religious utensils and implements possessed by the Sangha. Then a group of twenty monks, neither too old nor too young, who were well versed in the scriptures and disciplinary rules, with neat appearance and good deportment, were assigned to bring the Master to see the Right Dharma Store, i.e., the Venerable Śīlabhadra. Out of respect for him, the monks did not use his name but called him the Right Dharma Store. So the Master went with the monks to have an audience with the teacher; and upon seeing him, the Master respected him as his personal tutor with uttermost veneration. In accordance with local rites, he crawled on his knees and elbows, kissed the teacher's feet, and prostrated himself to pay homage to him. When the greetings and compliments were over, the Dharma Store ordered a large number of seats to be prepared and invited the Master and the other monks to sit down. After they had taken their seats, he asked the Master where he had come from. In reply, the Master said, "I came from China with the wish to study the *Yogācārabhūmi Śāstra* under the instruction of the teacher."

Upon hearing these words, the teacher shed tears and called for his disciple Buddhabhadra (meaning Enlightened Sage), who was the Dharma Store's nephew, over seventy years old, well versed in the scriptures and commentaries and eloquent in discussion. The Dharma Store said to him, "You may tell the monks here how I suffered from illness three years ago."

On hearing this, Buddhabhadra wept and wiped his tears, while relating the event that had happened before, saying, "The *upādhyāya* (teacher) used to suffer from gout. Each time he had an attack of it, his hands and feet were convulsed as painfully as if they were burned by fire or pricked by a knife. His illness was sometimes better and sometimes worse for more than twenty years. Three years ago the pain was aggravated to such an extent that he became disgusted with his body and wished to put an end to his life by starvation. One night he saw in a dream three celestial beings. One was golden yellow, another one purplish blue, and the third one silvery white in color. All of them had regular features and were dressed in light and brilliant garments. They came and asked the *upādhyāya,* 'Do you intend to get rid of this body of yours? It is said in the scriptures that the corporeal body is a cause of suffering, but it is not said that one should discard
237a one's body with a feeling of abhorrence. You were once a king in a past life and caused much trouble to the people; so you incurred your present retribution. It befits you to meditate on your past misdeeds and repent with sincerity. Bear the pain with patience, preach the scriptures and commentaries diligently, and then it will disappear by itself. Even if you do away with your body, you can never terminate your suffering.'

"Having heard this admonition, the *upādhyāya* worshipped the divine beings. The golden one, pointing at the blue one, said to the *upādhyāya,* 'Do you recognize him? He is Avalokiteśvara Bodhisattva.' He also pointed at the silvery one and said, 'This is Maitreya Bodhisattva.' The *upādhyāya* immediately worshipped Maitreya Bodhisattva and inquired of him, 'Śīlabhadra has always wished to be reborn in your respectable palace, but I do not know whether I can realize my wish.' In reply, the Bodhisattva said, 'If you widely spread the Right Dharma, you will be able to be reborn there.' Then the golden figure introduced himself, saying, 'I am Mañjuśrī Bodhisattva. As we saw that you intended to relinquish your body without any beneficial result, we have come to advise you not to do so. You should act according to my words to propagate the Right Dharma and preach the *Yogācārabhūmi Śāstra* and other texts to all those who have not yet heard about them. Your body will then gradually regain peace and health, and you need not worry about it. A Chinese monk who takes delight in understanding the Great Dharma will come to study under you. You may wait for his arrival and teach him.' After having heard these words, the Dharma Store worshipped the Bodhisattvas and promised them, 'I shall act according to your instructions.' When he had said so, the Bodhisattvas vanished. Since then the *upādhyāya* has been cured of his painful disease." All the monks who had heard about this account remarked with praise that it was an unusual event.

Having personally heard this account, the Master could not refrain from feeling both excited and happy. He again worshipped the teacher with gratitude, saying, "If it is just as you have said, I shall study with the utmost effort. May the teacher be compassionate and accept me as his pupil to receive his instructions."

The Dharma Store asked again, "How many years have you spent on the way?"

"Three years," was the reply. Since the time coincided with the dream, the teacher, expressing the fraternity of a tutor with a pupil, gave the Master various advice and counsels, to his delight.

After the conversation, the Master took his leave. He was lodged on the fourth storey of the house of Buddhabhadra in the courtyard of King Bālāditya. When the seven days' entertainment was over, he was again lodged in the main chamber to the north of

the house of Dharmapāla Bodhisattva with an increase in provisions. He was provided daily with one hundred twenty betel leaves, twenty areca nuts, twenty nutmegs, one tael of borneol incense, and one *sheng* of *mahāśāli* rice. A grain of this rice was bigger than a black bean, and when it was cooked it had a fragrance and delicious taste that no other kind of rice possessed. This kind of nonglutinous rice was produced only in Magadha and was not found elsewhere. As it was supplied only to kings and learned monks of virtue, it was called "rice supplied to great persons." He was also given a monthly supply of three *sheng* of oil; and as regards butter and milk, he took as much as he needed every day. He had a servant and a Brahman to serve him and was exempted from monastic duties; and when he went out he had an elephant to carry him. Among the ten thousand host and guest monks of Nālandā Monastery, only ten persons, including the Master, enjoyed
237b such provisions. Wherever the Master travelled, he was always treated in such a courteous manner.

Nālandā Monastery means the monastery of Insatiability in Almsgiving. It was said by old tradition that to the south of the monastery there had been a pond in a mango grove in which lived a dragon named Nālanda. As the monastery was built beside the pond, it was named so. It was also said that when the Tathāgata was practising the Bodhisattva path in one of his former lives, he was a great king and founded his capital at this place. As he had pity on the poor and the lonely, he often gave alms to them; and in memory of his beneficence the people called the place Insatiability in Almsgiving. This place was originally a garden of the Elder Āmra. Five hundred merchants purchased it with ten *koṭi* of golden coins and offered it to the Buddha, who preached the Dharma at this place for three months. Most of the merchants attained sainthood.

After the Buddha's nirvana, Śakrāditya (meaning Indra Sun), a former king of this country, built this monastery in respectful memory of the Buddha. After the demise of the king, his son, King Buddhagupta (meaning Enlightenment Protection), repeated his great deed and built another monastery to the south. His son, King

Tathāgata (meaning Thus Come) also built a monastery to the east. His son, Bālāditya (meaning Morning Sun), built another monastery to the northeast. Afterward, when he saw a holy monk coming from China to receive his offerings, he was so pleased that he abdicated and became a monk himself. His son, Vajra (meaning Diamond), succeeded to the Throne and also built a monastery to the north. Later a king of Central India built another monastery beside it. Thus six kings built as many monasteries one after the other, and an enclosure was made with bricks to merge them all into one monastery with one common entrance.

There were separate courtyards divided into eight departments. Precious terraces ranged like stars in the sky and jade storeyed pavilions spired like lofty peaks. The temples stood high in the mist, and the shrines hovered over the rosy clouds. Breeze and fog rose from the doors and windows, and the sun and moon shone alternately at the eaves of the buildings. Moreover, brooks of clear water meandered through the compounds, with blue lotuses and water lilies growing in them. The flowers of sandalwood trees glowed inside the enclosure, and outside it there was a dense mango grove. All the monks' chambers in the different departments had four storeys. The ridgepoles were carved with little dragons, the beams were painted all the colors of the rainbow, and green beam-supporters contrasted with crimson pillars. The frontal columns and railings had ornamental engravings and hollowed-out carvings. The plinths were made of jade, and the tips of the rafters were adorned with drawings. The ridges of the roofs stood high in the sunlight, and the eaves were connected with ropes from which hung colored silk pendants. In India there were thousands of monasteries, but this was the most magnificent and sublime of them all.

Ten thousand monks always lived there, both hosts and guests. They studied Mahayana teachings and the doctrines of the eighteen schools, as well as worldly books such as the Vedas. They also learned about works on logic, grammar, medicine, and divination. Those who could understand twenty scriptures and commentaries amounted to over a thousand persons. More than five hundred

persons had mastered thirty works, while ten persons, including the Master, were experts on fifty works. The Venerable Śīlabhadra was the only person who had thoroughly mastered all the texts; and being a scholar of advanced age and unusual virtue, he was a great teacher of all the monks. Lectures were given at more than
237c a hundred places in the monastery every day, and the students studied diligently without wasting a single moment. As all the monks who lived there were men of virtue, the atmosphere in the monastery was naturally solemn and dignified. For more than seven hundred years since its establishment, none of the monks had committed any offence. Out of respect for them, the king gave more than a hundred villages for their sustenance. Each village had two hundred families, who daily provided several hundred *shi* of polished nonglutinous rice, butter, and milk. Thus the students could enjoy sufficient supplies of the four requisites without the trouble of going to beg for them. It was because of this effort of their supporters that the scholars could gain achievements in learning.

Having been properly lodged in Nālandā Monastery, the Master repaired to the city of Rājagṛha to see and worship the holy sites. The old city of Rājagṛha, [then] called the city of Kuśāgrapura (meaning the Palace City of Pointed Cogon Grass), was located at the center of Magadha; and most of the ancient kings lived in it. As the place produced good fragrant cogon grass, it was named after it. It was surrounded on all sides by high and precipitous hills with a footpath leading to the west and a main gate in the north. It was long from east to west and narrow from south to north, its circumference being more than one hundred fifty *li*. Within it was a smaller city, the foundations of which were more than thirty *li* in circumference. Sandalwood trees throve in groves everywhere, with calyxes sprouting and flowers blooming in all four seasons without intermission, and the leaves were golden in color.

To the north, outside the palace city, there was a stupa built at the place where Devadatta and Ajātaśatru released an intoxicated elephant named Dhanapāla in an attempt to injure the Buddha. To the northeast of this place was another stupa marking the spot where Śāriputra attained sainthood after hearing the Dharma from the *bhikṣu* Aśvajit. Not far away to the north there was a large and deep pitfall, which was the place where Śrīgupta (meaning Superior Secret), being instigated by the evil advice of some heretics, attempted to harm the Buddha with a fire pit and poisoned rice. To the northeast of the big pitfall a stupa was built at a bend of the hill-city, which was the place where Jīvaka (formerly inaccurately known as Qipo), the great physician, constructed a preaching hall for the Buddha. Beside the stupa the old residence of Jīvaka was still there.

Travelling northeast from the palace city for fourteen or fifteen *li,* the Master reached Gṛdhrakūṭa Mountain (meaning Vulture Peak or Vulture Terrace, formerly inaccurately known as Qidujueshan). This mountain was connected with the range of mountains in the north and stood out specially high in the shape of a vulture or a tall terrace; hence the name. There were streams of clear water with rocks of strange shapes, and the trees in the wood were dense and luxuriant. When the Tathāgata was living in the world, he spent most of his time on this mountain, preaching on the *Saddharmapuṇḍarīka Sūtra,* the *Mahāprajñāpāramitā Sūtra,* and a large number of other sutras.

Going from the northern gate of the hill city for about one *li,* he reached the Karaṇḍa Bamboo Grove, where there was still a brick chamber in which the Tathāgata had lived many times in the old days and laid down the disciplinary rules. The owner of the grove was named Karaṇḍa, and he had formerly offered it to some heretics. But when he saw the Buddha and heard the profound Dharma, he regretted that he did not offer it to the Tathāgata. When the Goddess of Earth came to know his mind, she worked disastrous and uncanny phenomena to frighten the heretics in
238a order to drive them out of the grove. Then the goddess told the owner, "Elder, if you wish to offer your grove to the Buddha, you may quickly go there now." The heretics moved out indignantly, while the Elder was happy. After having constructed a *vihāra* in the grove, he went personally to invite the Buddha, who accepted his invitation.

To the east of the Bamboo Grove, there was another stupa built by King Ajātaśatru (meaning Enemy before Birth, formerly known incorrectly as Asheshi). After the nirvana of the Tathāgata, various kings shared his relic bones. King Ajātaśatru obtained his portion, which he brought back home, and built this stupa for its enshrinement. When King Aśoka desired to construct many stupas at different places, he opened this stupa and took out the relics, leaving only a small portion in it, which now often emitted a light.

At a distance of five or six *li* to the southwest of the Bamboo Grove there was another bamboo wood by the side of a hill, in which was a large rock chamber. This was the place where the Venerable Mahākāśyapa and 999 great arhats assembled to collect the Tripiṭaka after the nirvana of the Tathāgata. At the time of the assemblage, innumerable holy monks gathered together; and Kāśyapa said to them, "Those among the assembly who know themselves to possess the three knowledges and the six supernatural powers, and who comprehend the whole Dharma *Piṭaka* of the Tathāgata without error and misunderstanding, may stay here, while the rest may go anywhere they please." Thus 999 persons were selected.

As Ānanda was still at the stage of learning, Kāśyapa said to him, "As you are not completely free from passions, you should not defile this pure assembly." Being ashamed of himself, Ānanda went away. After practising the Way earnestly for one night, he cut off the bondage of the Three Worlds and attained Arhatship. Then he came back and knocked at the door. Kāśyapa asked him, "Have you cut off bondage completely?"

"Yes," was the reply.

Kāśyapa said again, "If you have completely cut off bondage, you need not trouble me to open the door for you; you should be able to enter at will."

And so Ānanda entered the chamber through a crack in the door and worshipped at the monks' feet. Kāśyapa, holding his hands, said to him, "It was because I wished you to clear away all your passions and realize sainthood that I compelled you to go out. You should understand this and bear no grudge against me."

Ānanda said, "If I bear a grudge against anybody, how can I be said to have completely cut off bondage?" After saying so, he worshipped Kāśyapa and took his seat. This occurred on the fifteenth day of the month at the beginning of the summer retreat.

Kāśyapa said to Ānanda, "The Tathāgata used to praise you among the monks, saying that you were the most learned disciple and grasped all of the Dharma. Now you may ascend the pulpit and recite the Sutra *Piṭaka*, namely, all the scriptures, for the assembly of monks." At this order, Ānanda rose to his feet. After worshipping toward the hill where the Buddha had entered nirvana, he ascended the pulpit and recited the scriptures, while the monks recorded what he was reciting. After the recital of the scriptures, Upāli was told to recite the Vinaya *Piṭaka,* namely, all the disciplinary rules. When this recital was over, Kāśyapa himself recited the Abhidharma *Piṭaka,* namely, all the commentaries and expositions of the scriptures. During the three months of summer retreat, the Tripiṭaka was collected and inscribed on palm leaves for widespread circulation. The holy monks said among
238b themselves, "Our collection of the Tripiṭaka is an act to repay the kindness of the Buddha; and it is due to his spiritual power that we have listened to it today." As Mahākāśyapa was the Elder of the assembly of monks, they were named the school of Elders.

At a distance of twenty *li* west of this place, there was a stupa built by King Aśoka at the place where the Mahāsāṃghika school had held their assembly. Several thousand persons, including monks who were still in the stages of learning and arhats who had nothing more to learn, gathered together at this place when they were not permitted to take part in the congregation held by Mahākāśyapa. They said among themselves, "When the Tathāgata was alive, we all studied under one teacher. Now that the World-honored One has passed away, they dismiss us. But can we not also collect the Dharma *Piṭaka* to requite the Buddha for his kindness?" Thus they also collected the Sutra *Piṭaka,* the Vinaya *Piṭaka,* the Abhidharma *Piṭaka,* the Miscellaneous *Piṭaka,* and the *Dhāraṇī Piṭaka,* for a total number of five collections. As both ordinary and holy monks took part in this assembly, it was known as the Mahāsāṃghika school.

Going further northeast for three or four *li,* the Master reached the city of Rājagṛha (meaning King's House). The outer wall of the city had broken down; but the inner wall, more than twenty *li* in circumference, still remained high, with a gate on each side. Formerly, when King Bimbisāra was living in his palace at Kuśāgrapura, it was densely populated, and the houses of the inhabitants were built closely together. As they suffered frequently from fire disasters, a strict law was enforced that whoever carelessly caused a fire should be sent to live in the Cold Forest, which was a dire place where the people of that country disposed of corpses. Shortly afterward a fire broke out in the palace. The king said, "I am the king of the people. If I violate the law or do not observe it, I will be in no position to punish my subjects." Ordering the Crown Prince to stay behind, the king moved to live in the Cold Forest.

Upon hearing that King Bimbisāra was living in the wilds, the king of Vaiśālī intended to dispatch his troops to attack him. Scouts got news of it and reported to King Bimbisāra, who then built a city at the place. As it had been the abode of the king, it was named the City of the King's House; and this was the New City. Afterward, when King Ajātaśatru succeeded to the Throne, he made it the capital until King Aśoka shifted the capital to Pāṭaliputra; the city was then given to the Brahmans. Now there were no other inhabitants in the city except more than a thousand families of Brahmans.

In the southwest corner of the palace city there was a stupa, built at the site of the old residence of the Elder Jyotiṣka (meaning Luminary, formerly inaccurately known as Shutiqie). Beside it was the place where Rāhula (the Buddha's son) was converted.

To the northwest of Nālandā Monastery, there was a large temple more than three hundred feet high, built by King Bālāditya. It was magnificent and very beautiful; and the Buddha's image in it looked the same as the one at the Bodhi tree. To the northeast of the temple was a stupa built at a place where the Tathāgata had once preached the Dharma for seven days. Further to the northwest were places where the four past Buddhas had sat. To the

south was the bronze temple built by King Śīlāditya, but the construction was unfinished. Otherwise it would have been more than a hundred feet in height, according to a careful study of its design. More than two hundred paces to the east of the city was a
238c bronze standing image of the Buddha, more than eighty feet high, which could be housed only in a multilayer pavilion six storeys tall, built by King Pūrṇavarman in olden times. A few *li* toward the east was a stupa, built at the place where King Bimbisāra, together with hundreds and thousands of his people, welcomed and greeted the Buddha when he came here on his way to Rājagṛha after he had just achieved the Way.

Again travelling eastward for more than thirty *li,* the Master reached Indraśailaguhā Mountain. In front of the monastery on the east peak of the mountain, there was a stupa named Haṃsa (meaning Wild Goose). Formerly, in accordance with the gradual teaching of the Hinayana school, the three kinds of pure meat were eaten in this monastery. Once it was in short supply and unobtainable. When the supervisor was at a loss what to do, he saw a flock of wild geese flying in the air. He looked up and said jokingly, "Today the monks are running short of food. The *Mahāsattva* (great being) should know that this is the right time to make a sacrifice!" When he had just said so, the leading goose in the flight flew back, deplumed itself high in the clouds, and dropped to the ground. On seeing this the monk was both ashamed and frightened; and he told the incident to all the other monks, who were astonished upon hearing it and sighed with sorrow. All of them shed tears of regret over the matter. They said among themselves, "This is a Bodhisattva. Who are we to venture to eat his flesh? The Tathāgata taught us to prevent evils in a gradual way. But we grasped what he taught us at the inceptive stage as his ultimate teaching. It is because we stick to ignorance without trying to correct it that we have caused this disaster. From now onward we should follow the Mahayana teaching and never eat the three kinds of pure meat again."

Thereupon they built a stupa for the burial of the dead goose, with an inscription relating its good intentions, so that its good name might be transmitted to posterity for ever. That was why this stupa was constructed.

All these holy sites the Master visited and worshipped all around.

It was not until returning to Nālandā Monastery that the Master asked the Dharma teacher Śīlabhadra to expound the *Yogācārabhūmi Śāstra.* Several thousand men attended the lectures together with him. After a moment when the subject of the work had just been explained, a Brahman was heard wailing and also laughing and talking outside the monastery. Being asked why, he said in reply, "I am from eastern India. Once I made a vow before the image of Avalokiteśvara Bodhisattva at Potalaka Mountain that I would become a king. The Bodhisattva appeared in person before me and reproached me, saying, 'Do not make such a vow! Later, on a certain day of such and such a month in the year so and so, the Dharma teacher Śīlabhadra of Nālandā Monastery will expound the *Yogācārabhūmi Śāstra* for a Chinese monk. You should go to attend the lectures. As you will be able to see the Buddha after hearing the Dharma, what is the use of becoming a king?' Now I see that a Chinese monk has come and the teacher is preaching for him just as I was told before. That is why I feel both excited and exhilarated." Thus the Dharma teacher Śīlabhadra allowed him to stay and attend the lectures. After fifteen months, when the lectures were concluded, someone was dispatched to send the Brahman to see King Śīlāditya, who bestowed on him a fief of three villages.

In this monastery the Master listened to the exposition of the *Yogācārabhūmi Śāstra* three times; to that of the *Nyāyānusāra Śāstra,* the *Prakaraṇāryavācā Śāstra,* and the *Abhidharmasamu-*
239a *dāya Prakaraṇa,* one time each; to that of the *Hetuvidyā Śāstra,* the *Sabdavidyā Śāstra,* the *Samuccayapramāṇa Śāstra,* etc., two times each; as well as to that of the *Mādhyamika Śāstra* and the *Śata Śāstra* three times each. As regards the *Abhidharmakośa Śāstra,* the *Vibhāṣā Śāstra,* the *Jñānaprasthānaṣaṭpādābhidharma,* etc., which he had already studied in Kaśmīra and other countries, he merely read through them and clarified some dubious points he had found in them.

He also studied at the same time some Brahmanic books. The Indian Sanskrit book that he studied was entitled *Analytical Exposition of Grammar,* of which the origin and author were unknown. At the beginning of each *kalpa,* Brahmā transmitted it to the heavenly beings; and as it was transmitted by Brahmā, it was called the Brahmanic Book. Being a very voluminous work, it consisted of one million stanzas; and it was the work formerly translated as the *Pijialuolun.* But it was mispronounced, and the correct name is *Vyākaraṇa,* meaning *Analytical Exposition of Grammar.* It was so called because it gives a full grammatical analysis of words, by which all dharmas are explained.

Formerly, at the beginning of the Kalpa of Formation, Brahmā first taught it in one million stanzas. Later, at the beginning of the Kalpa of Existence, Indra abridged it to a hundred thousand stanzas. Still later the Ṛṣi Pāṇini, a Brahman of the city of Śalātura in the country of Gandhāra of northern India, again condensed it to eight thousand stanzas, and this was the version prevalent in India then. Recently a Brahman of southern India again shortened it to twenty-five hundred stanzas for the king of South India; but this version, though very popular in frontier and uncultivated countries, was never studied by the erudite scholars of India.

All these were fundamental texts dealing with the sounds and words of the Western Region. An auxiliary work that was lucid and helpful was the *Concise Analytical Exposition of Grammar* in a thousand stanzas. There was another book in three hundred stanzas dealing with the vowels. Of the two books that dealt with the consonants, one was named the *Maṇṭhaka,* in three thousand stanzas, and one was named the *Uṇādi,* in twenty-five hundred stanzas. They differentiated vowels and consonants. The *Aṣṭadhātu Śāstra,* in eight hundred stanzas, briefly dealt with the combining of vowels and consonants.

In all these grammatical works the active and passive voices are treated with clarity. There are two paradigms. One is the paradigm of the *tiṅanta,* with eighteen verbal inflections; and the second is the paradigm of the *subanta,* with twenty-four nominal inflections. The *tiṅanta* paradigm is used for writing elegant and graceful compositions, but seldom for ordinary writings; while the twenty-four inflections are used for all styles of writing.

The eighteen inflections of the *tiṅanta* paradigm comprise two groups, namely the *parasmai* and the *ātmane*. Each group has nine inflections, constituting a total of eighteen. Of the first nine inflections, three are for the subject of a statement, three are for transitive verbs, and three are for intransitive verbs. The three terminations of each of the three groups indicate the three numbers: the singular, the dual, and the plural. Thus it is said that each of the three groups has three terminations. Both voices, *parasmai* and *ātmane*,
239b are inflected similarly but they differ in that each of them has nine separate terminations.

In the *parasmai* voice, we may make a statement in either the positive or the negative manner. Take the root *bhū* for example. We may say in three numbers: *bhavati* (one thing exists), *bhavatas* (two things exist), and *bhavanti* (many things exist). In the second person we may say it in three ways: *bhavasi* (thou dost exist), *bhavathas* (you two exist), and *bhavatha* (you all exist). In the first person we may also say it in three ways: *bhavāmi* (I exist), *bhavāvas* (we two exist), and *bhavāmas* (we all exist).

For the nine verb forms of the *atmane* voice, we just add the suffix *vyati* to the above nine terminations; otherwise they are the same as the above endings. Those who were proficient in these rules could write excellent compositions without ambiguity and express themselves in an extremely elegant style.

The twenty-four noun forms of the *subanta* voice are made up of eight principal cases, each of which has three numbers, namely, the singular, the dual, and the plural. Thus there are altogether twenty-four forms. And each of the twenty-four forms has three genders, namely, the masculine, the feminine, and the neuter.

The eight cases are as follows: the first is the nominative, which indicates the subject; the second is the accusative, which indicates what is acted upon; the third is the instrumental, which denotes the doer and the instrument by which something is done; the fourth is the dative, which indicates for whom a thing is done; the fifth is the ablative, which denotes the cause of a thing; the sixth is the genitive, which shows to whom a thing belongs; the seventh is the locative, which shows the location in which a thing is done; and the eighth is the vocative, which implies addressing or calling a thing.

Now let us take the word for "man" of the masculine gender and go through the declension of the three numbers of the eight cases. The Indian word for "man" being *puruṣa,* we have:

1. *puruṣas, puruṣau, puruṣās* for the nominative case
2. *puruṣam, puruṣau, puruṣān* for the accusative case
3. *puruṣeṇa, puruṣābhyām, puruṣavya* [*sic*] or *puruṣais* for the instrumental case
4. *puruṣāya, puruṣābhyām, puruṣebhyas* for the dative case
5. *puruṣāt, puruṣābhyām, puruṣebhyas* for the ablative case
6. *puruṣasya, puruṣābhyām* [*sic*], *puruṣāṇām* for the genitive case
7. *puruṣe, puruṣayos, puruṣeṣu* for the locative case
8. *hi* [*sic*] *puruṣa, hi puruṣau, hi puruṣās* for the vocative case.

From these few examples, the other declensions may be understood. It would be difficult to make a full statement of the endings of all the words. The Master was thoroughly versed in this language and could talk with the people of that country in a scholarly manner with great elegance. Thus he made profound studies of the teachings of various schools and studied Sanskrit books for five years.

239c From here the Master continued his journey to the country of Īraṇaparvata. On the way he reached Kapotaka Monastery. Two or three *li* to the south of this monastery, there was an isolated hill, the peaks of which were lofty and precipitous with gloomy and desolate woods. The water in the streams and ponds was clean and lucid; and the bright flowers were sweet and fragrant. Since it was a place of beautiful scenery, there were quite a number of temples with many kinds of wonderful and miraculous manifestations. In the central temple there was an image of Avalokiteśvara Bodhisattva carved in sandalwood, which possessed spiritual power and was specially honored by the people. There were always tens of people fasting for seven days or a fortnight and praying for the fulfillment of their wishes. Those who were most pious in their minds might behold the Bodhisattva emerging from the sandalwood image as a stately figure with a majestic light shining brightly, to comfort them and grant them their wishes. Such a spiritual vision had been witnessed time and again by the people, and thus more and more devotees turned to him in adoration.

Fearing that the visitors might defile the holy image, the temple-keepers had made wooden railings around the statue at a distance of about seven paces from it. Those who came to worship the image did so outside the railings and were not allowed to go near it. The incense and flowers that they offered were flung to the image from a distance. When the flowers rested on the hands or hung upon the arms of the Bodhisattva's statue, it was considered a good omen to augur that one's wishes could be fulfilled.

With the desire to say prayers, the Master purchased different kinds of flowers and strung them into garlands, which he brought to the image. After having paid homage and said praises with a sincere mind to the Bodhisattva, he knelt before the image and made three wishes, saying, "First, may the flowers fall on your hands if I can return home safely without any trouble after I have completed my studies here. Second, may a garland hang upon your arm if I can be reborn as I wish in the Tuṣita Palace, to serve Maitreya Bodhisattva through the merit and wisdom that I have cultivated. Thirdly, as it is expounded in the holy teachings that some sentient beings possess no Buddha nature, I am in doubt as to whether I possess it or not. May a garland hang on your neck if I am endowed with the Buddha nature and can become a Buddha through spiritual cultivation."

After saying so, he scattered the flowers from a distance. All of them fell in the places he had prayed for. Since he was satisfied about his wishes, his happiness knew no bounds. On seeing this event, the other worshippers and the temple-keepers snapped their fingers and kissed his feet in delight, saying that it was an unprecedented thing. They wished that when the Master became a Buddha in the future, he would remember this occurrence on that day and save them first.

From here the Master proceeded gradually and reached the
240a country of Īraṇaparvata. There were ten monasteries with more than four thousand monks, most of whom studied the Hinayana teachings of the Sarvāstivāda school. Recently the king of a neighboring kingdom had deposed the monarch of this country, presented the capital city to the monks, and also constructed two monasteries there with a thousand monks living in each of them. There were two teachers of great virtue, both of whom were well versed in the teachings of the Sarvāstivāda school. One was named Tathāgatagupta (meaning the Secret of the Tathāgata) and the other Kṣāntisiṃha (meaning Forbearance Lion). The Master stayed there for one year to study the *Vibhāṣā Śāstra,* the *Nyāyānusāra Śāstra,* and other texts with them.

To the south of the capital city there was a stupa built at a place where the Buddha had formerly preached the Dharma to heavenly and human beings for three months. Beside it were traces left by the four past Buddhas. The country bordered on the Ganges in the west. In the south it reached the Small Isolated Hill, where the Buddha had formerly spent three months during the summer retreat and subdued the *yakṣa* Vakula. On a big rock below the peak at the southeast of the hill, there was a trace of where the Buddha had sat. It was more than one inch deep in the rock, five feet two inches long, and four feet one inch wide. There was also a trace where the Buddha had placed his *kuṇḍikā* (a bathing pot, formerly incorrectly transliterated junchi). It was over one inch thick, with decorative designs of eight-petalled flowers. On the south border of the country there was a desolate forest in which were many elephants, strong and enormous in size.

Fascicle IV

Beginning with the Country of Campā and Ending with the Invitation of the King of Kāmarūpa

Going eastward from here along the southern bank of the Ganges for more than three hundred *li,* the Master reached the country of Campā (in the domain of Central India). There were ten monasteries with more than two hundred monks who studied the Hinayana teachings. The city wall, several tens of feet high, was built with bricks. Its foundation and moat were deep and wide, rendering the city very sublime and impregnable. Formerly, at the beginning of the *kalpa,* all the people lived in caves. Afterward a celestial maiden came down to the human world, and while she was bathing in the Ganges, the water spirit touched her body. Thus she gave birth to four sons who divided and ruled over Jambudvīpa as kings. They demarcated the boundaries and built villages and towns, and this place was the capital of one of her sons.

Several tens of *yojanas* away from the southern boundary of this country there was a big mountain with a forest of dense and exuberant trees, stretching for more than two hundred *li,* in which there were numerous wild elephants, several hundred in a herd. That was why the two countries of Īraṇaparvata and Campā had
240b the largest number of elephant troops. Elephant catchers were often ordered to catch and tame elephants in this forest for the purposes of riding and replenishing the need of the state. It was also infested with jackals, rhinoceros, and black leopards; nobody dared to travel in it.

It was said by tradition that before the Buddha was born, once a cowherd who was tending several hundred cows drove the cattle into this forest. One of the cows went away from the herd by itself and repeatedly disappeared to an unknown place. In the evenings when the cattle were to go back, it returned to the herd with a brilliant and pleasant luster, and lowed in such an unusual manner that all the other cows feared it and none dared to be in front of it. This happened for many days. Feeling strange about it, the cowherd secretly watched the cow. In a moment the cow went away as usual, and he followed it to see what would happen. When he saw that the cow entered an aperture in the rocks, he also followed it in. After walking for four or five *li,* he suddenly came to a bright place with trees and beautiful flowers and many strange blossoms and fruits, so replendent to the eye that they were not found in the ordinary world. He saw that the cow grazed at a place where the color of the grass and its fragrance and gloss were also not to be seen in the human world. The man saw that the fruits were golden in color, sweet, and big in size. He plucked one, but dared not eat it, though he longed to taste it. After a while the cow came out and the cowherd followed it to return. But when he reached the aperture in the rocks and had not yet come out of it, an evil demon snatched the fruit away, not allowing him to take it out. The cowherd inquired of a great physician about this matter and told him the shape of the fruit. The physician said that he must not be so careless as to eat it but should try to bring one out.

The next day he again entered the place with the cow and picked one fruit, which he kept in his bosom with the intention of bringing it back. When the demon again tried to snatch it away, the man hid the fruit inside his mouth; but the demon gripped his throat, so he swallowed the fruit. Once it was in his stomach, his body swelled to such a big size that he could not get out of the aperture, though his head stuck out of it; thus he could not return home. When the people of his family came in search of him, they were surprised to see that he had been deformed. Being still able to speak, he told them what had happened. The people of his family went back and employed many strong men, trying to pull him out of the aperture, but they failed to move him.

When the king heard about this matter, he came to see it for himself. Fearing that it might cause future trouble, he ordered men to dig him out but they also failed to move him. In the long run that man was gradually lapidified but still retained the shape of a man. Afterward another king, knowing that this was the transformation by a fruit of immortality, said to his attending minister, "Since that man was transformed by the effect of the drug, his body itself must have become that drug too. Although it looks like a rock, the body has eventually become a divine object. Send a man to cut a few pieces of it with a hammer and a chisel and bring them to me." Under the orders of the king, the minister went to the place with a workman, who chopped with maximum effort at the rock for fully ten days but could not get a single piece of the stone. The rocky figure was still there in existence.

Travelling eastward from here for more than four hundred *li,* the Master reached the country of Kajuṅghira (in the domain of Central India) to seek and worship holy sites. There were six or
240c seven monasteries with more than three hundred monks. From here he crossed the Ganges to the east, and after going for more than six hundred *li* he reached the country of Puṇḍravardhana (in the domain of southern India) to seek and worship holy sites. There were more than twenty monasteries with over three thousand monks who studied both Mahayana and Hinayana teachings. More than twenty *li* to the west of the city was Vāśibhā Monastery, with lofty and magnificent terraces and pavilions, in which lived seven hundred monks. Beside it was a stupa built by King Aśoka at a place where the Buddha had once preached the Dharma for three months. It often issued a brilliant light. There were also traces left by the four past Buddhas when they walked up and down. Standing nearby was a temple enshrining an image of Avalokiteśvara Bodhisattva that answered without fail all prayers of those who pleaded earnestly.

From here travelling southeast for more than nine hundred *li,* the Master reached the country of Karṇasuvarṇa (in the domain of eastern India). There were more than ten monasteries with over three hundred monks who studied the teaching of the Hinayana Saṃmitīya school. In three other monasteries milk and yoghurt were not eaten; this was a tradition handed down by Devadatta.

Beside the big city was Raktamṛttikā (meaning Red Clay) Monastery, built by the king of this country when a *śramaṇa* of southern India visited this country at the time when Buddhism was not known here and subdued a heretic who wore a metal sheet over his stomach by refuting his erroneous views. Beside it was a stupa built by King Aśoka at a place where the Buddha had once preached the Dharma for seven days.

Going out from here to the southeast, the Master reached the country of Samataṭa (in the domain of eastern India), which bordered on the great sea. Its climate was temperate and pleasant. There were more than thirty monasteries with over two thousand monks who studied the doctrines of the Sthavira school. The heretical followers who worshipped in *deva* temples were also numerous. Not far from the city was a stupa built by King Aśoka at a place where the Buddha had once preached the Dharma for men and heavenly beings for seven days. Not far from here was another monastery in which there was a Buddha image made of blue jade. It was eight feet tall with a fine and dignified appearance. It often had a natural fragrance, the aroma of which pervaded the whole courtyard; and its multicolored light always lit up the sky. All those who witnessed the sight or heard about it would deeply cherish the mind of the Way.

In the valley to the northeast by the seaside was the country of Śrīkṣetra. Further to the southeast by the gulf was the country of Kāmalāṅkā. Further east was the country of Dvārapatī. Still further east was the country of Īśānapura. Again further east was the country of Mahācampā (meaning the City of Forest). And further to the west was the country of Yamanadvīpa. All these six countries were located far beyond high mountains and deep seas. Though the Master did not go into these lands, he was able to obtain information about their customs and habits.

Going westward from the country of Samataṭa for more than nine hundred *li,* the Master reached the country of Tāmralipti (in
241a the domain of eastern India), which was located near a bay of the sea. There were more than ten monasteries with over a thousand monks. Beside the city was a stupa more than two hundred feet

high, built by King Aśoka. Close to it were traces left by the four past Buddhas when they walked up and down.

At that time the Master heard that in the sea there was the country of Siṃhala (meaning Held by Lions) and that there were people there well versed in the Tripiṭaka of the Sthavira school and people knowing the *Yogācārabhūmi Śāstra* well. Going by sea one had to sail for seven hundred *yojanas* to reach there. Before he started the voyage, he met a monk from southern India, who advised him, "You need not take the sea route to go to the Kingdom of Lions, as the problems of adverse wind, *yakṣas*, and tempests often occur in the sea. You may go from the southeast cape of southern India and reach that country after a voyage of only three days. Although you will have to climb mountains and cross rivers, it will be safer for you; and by the way you may visit the holy sites in Uḍra and other countries."

The Master then proceeded southwest to the country of Uḍra (in the domain of eastern India). There were more than a hundred monasteries with over ten thousand monks who studied the Dharma of Mahayana teachings. There were also heretics who worshipped in *deva* temples, and the wrong and right believers lived together. More than ten stupas, all built by King Aśoka, often manifested miraculous signs. By the great sea in the southeast of the country was the city of Caritra (meaning Start Going), a port where seagoing merchants and travellers from distant lands came and went away or took rest. The distance to the country of Siṃhala in the south was more than twenty thousand *li.* On a calm and cloudless night, one might see at a distance the gleam of the gems and pearls on the stupa of the Buddha's tooth relic in that country, shining as brightly as stars in the sky.

Going southwest from here through a big forest for over twelve hundred *li,* the Master reached the country of Koṅgoda (in the domain of eastern India).

Going further southwest from here through a big desolate forest for fourteen hundred or fifteen hundred *li,* he reached the country of Kaliṅga (in the domain of southern India). There were more than ten monasteries with over five hundred monks who studied the Dharma of the Sthavira school. Formerly this country was very densely populated. But once the people offended a *ṛṣi* (hermit) possessing the five supernatural powers, who, out of anger and resentment, killed all the people, old and young, by malignant incantation. Afterward, people from other places gradually migrated to this country; but it was still not fully inhabited.

Going northwest from here for more than eighteen hundred *li,* the Master reached the country of South Kosala (in the domain of Central India). The king, who was a *kṣatriya* by caste, esteemed Buddhism with deference and loved the arts and learning. There were a hundred monasteries with ten thousand monks. Heretics who worshipped in *deva* temples were also numerous and of varying types. Not far to the south of the city there was an old monastery, beside which was a stupa built by King Aśoka. Formerly the Tathāgata once subdued heretics at this place with his supernatural powers, and later Nāgārjuna Bodhisattva stayed in this monastery. By that time the king was named Sātavāha (meaning
241b Correct-guiding). He venerated Nāgārjuna and provided him with rich sustenance.

At that time, Deva Bodhisattva came from the country of Siṃhala and sought to hold a debate with Nāgārjuna. He approached the door and asked for admittance, and the doorkeeper announced the guest. Having already heard about the name of the visitor, Nāgārjuna filled a bowl with water and asked a disciple to show it to the guest. On seeing the water, Deva silently dropped a needle into it; and the disciple brought the bowl back to his teacher. Nāgārjuna was greatly delighted to see it, and he said, "The bowl filled with water signifies the fullness of my virtue. He indicated by dropping the needle into the bowl that he could fathom the depth of my learning. Such is the person with whom I could discuss the mysterious Way and to whom I may transmit the Lamp of Learning!" Then he asked the guest to be ushered in. When they had taken their seats, they talked and had a discussion with each other to their mutual delight, as happy as fish put into water. Nāgārjuna said, "As I am getting old and feeble, it will depend upon you to make the Sun of Wisdom shine brightly!" Deva stood up and worshipped at Nāgārjuna's feet, saying, "Stupid as I am, I venture to say that I shall follow your kind instructions."

In that country there was a Brahman who was well versed in Hetuvidyā; and the Master stayed there for more than a month to study the *Samuccayapramāṇa Śāstra* with him.

Going southeast from a big forest in the south of this country for more than nine hundred *li,* the Master reached the country of Andhra (in the domain of southern India). Beside the city there was a large monastery, constructed magnificently with a beautiful and solemn appearance. In front of it was a stone stupa several hundred feet high built by the Arhat Ācāra (meaning Behavior). More than twenty *li* to the southwest of the arhat's monastery was an isolated hill on which was a stone stupa. This was the place where Dignāga (meaning Giving) Bodhisattva composed the *Hetuvidyā Śāstra.*

Going southward from here for more than a thousand *li,* the Master reached the country of Dhānakaṭaka (in the domain of southern India). On a hill to the east of the city was Pūrvaśaila (Eastern Hill) Monastery; and on a hill to the west of the city was Avaraśaila (Western Hill) Monastery, built by a former king of this country for the Buddha. The construction of these monasteries had all the specifications and structural styles of great mansions, and possessed all the elegance and beauties of woods and springs. Deities protected these monasteries, and saints and sages lived in them. Within a thousand years after the Buddha's nirvana, there a thousand ordinary monks often came to spend the summer retreat together in these monasteries. After the conclusion of the retreat, they all attained Arhatship and went away by flying through the air. After the lapse of a thousand years, both saintly and ordinary monks lived together in them; but during the last one hundred years or so the deities of the hills changed their temperament and molested and disturbed wayfarers. Thus the people were fearful of them and none dared go there. So the monasteries were now left empty and desolate, having become deserted; no monks lived in them.

Not far to the south of the city there was a big rocky hill, which was the place where the Śāstrin Bhāvaviveka (meaning Clear Distinction) went into the *Asura*'s palace to wait for Maitreya Bodhisattva to become a Buddha so as to solve his doubts.

In this country the Master met two monks. One was named Subhūti and the other Sūrya. Both of them were conversant with the Tripiṭaka of the Mahāsāṃghika school. He stayed there for several months to study the *Mūlābhidharma Śāstra* and other
241c treatises with them, and they also learned various Mahayana *śāstra*s from him. Then they travelled together to visit and worship the holy sites.

Going westward from here for more than a thousand *li,* the Master reached the country of Colya (in the domain of southern India). To the southeast of the city there was a stupa built by King Aśoka at a place where the Buddha had formerly displayed great supernatural powers to subdue heretics and preached the Dharma for the salvation of men and heavenly beings. To the west of the city was an old monastery, which was the place where Deva Bodhisattva had a discussion with the Arhat Uttara (meaning Upper) of this monastery. After the seventh round of disputation, the arhat was unable to say anything in retort. So he secretly went by supernatural power to the Tuṣita Palace to ask for advice from Maitreya Bodhisattva, who gave him a solution and told him, "That Deva has long been cultivating his merits, and he will achieve the perfect enlightenment of Buddhahood in the Bhadrakalpa. You must not underestimate him."

After coming back, the arhat solved the question that had been put to him. Deva said, "This is the theory of Maitreya Bodhisattva, and the solution was not found through your own wisdom." Being convinced and feeling ashamed, the arhat stood up and worshipped Deva with an apology.

From here going south through a big forest for fifteen or sixteen hundred *li,* the Master reached the country Draviḍa (in the domain of southern India). The capital of this country was Kāñcīpura, which was the birthplace of Dharmapāla (meaning Dharma-Protector) Bodhisattva. The Bodhisattva was the son of a minister of this country and was a brilliant and intelligent person since his youth. When he had come of age, the king, admiring his talents, wished to marry the princess to him. But as the Bodhisattva had been practising celibacy for a long time, he had no mind for carnal desire. Being greatly annoyed with worry on the night of his wedding, he prayed for protection before an image of the Buddha, wishing to free himself from the trouble. Moved by his sincerity, a great king of the deities carried him out and sent him into the Buddha hall of a monastery on a hill several hundred *li* away from the capital. When the monks came and saw him, they took him to be a thief. Then the Bodhisattva gave them an account of his troublesome situation. Those who heard about it were amazed and sympathetic and respected him for his high aim. So he renounced his home and became a monk. Afterward he devoted himself to the study of the Right Dharma and was able to understand the theories of various schools. Thus he became a skilled writer. He composed the *Śabdavidyāsaṃyukta Śāstra* in twenty-five thousand stanzas and also wrote several tens of books in exposition of the *Śataśāstravaipulya,* the *Vijñaptimātratāsiddhi Śāstra,* and the *Hetuvidyā Śāstra,* all of which were popular works that were widely read. As regards his rich virtues and high talents, they are related in a separate biography.

The city of Kāñcīpura was a seaport of southern India; from there one could reach the country of Siṃhala after three days' voyage. Before the Master started the voyage, the king of that country died, and the country suffered from famine and disturbance. The learned monks named Bodhimegheśvara (meaning Lord of the Cloud of Enlightenment) and Abhayadaṃṣṭra (meaning Fearless Tooth), together with more than three hundred other monks, fled to India and arrived at Kāñcīpura. Having met the
242a monks, the Master asked them, "As I have heard that the learned monks of your country are conversant with the Tripiṭaka of the Sthavira school and well versed in the *Yogācārabhūmi Śāstra,* I am desirous of going there to pursue my studies. Why have you teachers come to this place?" They said in reply, "Our king has passed away and the people are suffering from famine, so we have

nobody to depend upon. We have heard that Jambudvīpa is a rich and happy land of peace and security, being the birthplace of the Buddha and having many holy sites. That is why we have come here. As regards those who know the Dharma, none could surpass us in our country. If Your Reverence has any doubtful points, you may inquire of us just as you please." The Master then quoted some important passages of the *Yogācārabhūmi Śāstra* to seek their elucidation, but they could not exceed the scope of the explanation given by Śīlabhadra.

The Master heard that at a distance of more than three thousand *li* from the boundary of this country was the country of Malakūṭa (in the domain of southern India). It was located by the seaside and was extremely rich in unusual precious things. To the east of the city was a stupa built by King Aśoka at the place where the Buddha once preached the Dharma and displayed great supernatural powers for the salvation of numerous people. By the seaside in the south of the country, there was Malaya Mountain with its precipitous peaks and deep valleys, in which there were white sandal trees and serpent sandal trees. The latter resembled the former, but their wood was cool by nature, and so serpents mostly attached to them until the winter when they went into hibernation. By their presence the serpent sandals were differentiated from the white sandals. There were also fragrant *karpūra* trees, of which the trunk was like a pine, but the leaves were different, and the flowers and fruits were also not the same. When the wood was sappy, it had no fragrance; but after it had been cut down and dried, a scented substance like mica with the color of ice and snow was produced from the grain of the wood. This is what we call camphor.

The Master also heard that by the side of the sea in the northeast there was a city from which, by travelling southeast for more than three thousand *li,* one could reach the country of Siṃhala (meaning Held by Lions, not in the domain of India). The circumference of this country was more than seven thousand *li,* and its capital city was over forty *li* in circumference. It was thickly inhabited and had plenty of cereal products. The people were dark-complected and of mean stature with an impetuous and irascible temperament. Such was the general condition of that country. Being an island of gems, this country produced many rare and precious things.

Once in southern India a girl was sent in marriage to a neighboring country, and on the way she encountered a king of lions. The people who escorted her fled away in fear, leaving the girl alone in her carriage. The lion came, saw the girl, and carried her far and deep into the mountains, where he gathered fruits and caught fowls for her subsistence. Through the passage of time, she gave birth to a son and a daughter who were, though human in shape, cruel and brutal in nature. When the son had grown up, he inquired of his mother, "What sort of creature am I, with an animal as a father and a human being as a mother?" So his mother told him the events that had occurred in the past. The son said, "Since human beings and animals are different creatures, why do you not go away but stick to this place?" His mother said, "It is not that I have no mind to go but that I have no means of escape."

The son then followed his father, the lion, climbing up mountains and crossing over valleys in order observe his route. One day when his father had gone far away, he brought his mother and sister down to a village and proceeded to the home country of his mother to visit the family of his maternal uncle. When they found that the family had no more offspring, they took up their lodgings in a village.

When the king of lions returned, he found that his wife and children were gone. Being violently enraged, he came out of the
242b mountains, entered the villages with roars, and killed many of the villagers, both men and women. The people reported the case to the king, who commanded his four divisions of troops and specially conscripted warriors to surround and shoot the lion. On seeing them, the lion roared with such vehemence that both the men and their horses tumbled to the ground, and none dared to approach the animal. After many days they could not succeed in their attack and so the king posted a public notice, announcing that a reward of one *koṭi* of golden coins would be paid to anyone

who could kill the lion. The lion's son said to his mother, "As we are in such unbearable hunger and cold, I wish to answer the king's call. What do you think of it?"

His mother said, "No, you must not do that! Although he is an animal, he is still your father. If you committed patricide, how could you be called a human being?" But the son said, "If I do not kill him, he will never go away; and he will probably come to this village in pursuit of us. Once the king comes to know about it, we also shall die and not be spared. Why? It is because of us that the lion has become furious. How can we give trouble to many people just for the sake of one life? After careful consideration, I think it is better for me to respond to the king's call." Thus he went away.

On seeing his son, the lion became gentle and was glad, and had no harmful intention. His son then cut his throat and split his abdomen. In spite of the pain, the lion suffered the affliction motionless and died with kind feelings and deep affection for his son. The king was pleased to hear about the event, and inquired about it with amazement, "How did you do it?" At first the son refused to tell the truth, but under the pressure of interrogation he related the whole story.

The king said, "Alas! Nobody except the offspring of an animal could have such an inhuman mind. But as I have promised a reward, I will not go back on my word. Yet, since you are a patricide, a man behaving against morality, you are no longer allowed to live in my country." The king then ordered the authorities to give him a large amount of gold and gems and banished him to a wilderness. Two ships laden with big quantities of gold and provisions were put to drift aimlessly on the sea. The ship of the son sailed to this Island of Gems. Seeing that it was rich in rare valuables, he settled down on the island. Afterward some merchants came here with their families to procure gems. He killed the merchants but kept their women, by whom he had offspring. Over many generations, the population gradually multiplied; and then they established a monarchical state. As their distant progenitor had conquered a lion, they named their country the Lion Country. Meanwhile the daughter's ship sailed to the west of Pārasī, where she was caught by a demon. She gave birth to a group of daughters and founded what we now call the West Great Women's Country.

It was also said that Siṃhala was the name of a merchant's son, who, being a man of quick wits, escaped from the danger of *rākṣasīs* (ogresses). Later, when he had become a king, he came to this Island of Gems and slew all the *rākṣasīs*. He built up the capital of this country, which was then called after his name. This legend is found in the *Record of the Western Regions*.

Formerly Buddhism was not known in this country. One hundred years after the nirvana of the Tathāgata, King Aśoka's younger brother Mahendra relinquished his desire and passion and achieved
242c the fourth state of sainthood of a *śramaṇa*. He could come and go by air and visited this country to reveal and advocate the Buddha Dharma and display his supernatural powers. The people of the country had faith in him, admired him, and built monasteries. There were now more than a hundred monasteries with ten thousand monks who followed the teachings of the Mahayana and Sthavira schools. They were solemn in appearance, observed the Vinaya rules strictly without ambiguity, and admonished one another not to be idle. Beside the king's palace was the Buddha Tooth Temple, which was several hundred feet high and decorated with various valuable objects. On the temple was erected an ornamental post with a big *padmarāga* ruby set on its spire, which shone brilliantly in the air and could be seen at a distance of ten thousand *li* on a calm and cloudless night.

By the side of this temple there was another shrine, also decorated with different kinds of precious things, in which was enshrined a golden image of a Buddha whose topknot was adorned with a precious pearl, of which nobody knew the price. Once a man intended to steal this pearl; but as the temple was strongly guarded, he had no way to get to it. So he dug a tunnel under the ground, through which he entered the chamber to take the pearl. But the image rose higher and higher, so that the thief could not reach it. He gave up his attempt and said, "Formerly when the Tathāgata was practising the Bodhisattva path, he never spared his life and was not niggard in giving up his country or his capital city for the benefit of all living beings. Why is he so parsimonious today? In view of this, I fear that what was said of him might be untrue." Then the image stooped down to give the pearl to the man.

Having obtained the pearl, the man took it out to sell it. Someone who recognized the pearl caught hold of him and sent him to the king. The king asked him where he had obtained the pearl, and the thief said, "The Buddha himself gave it to me." And then he told the whole story. The king went personally to see it and saw that the head of the image was still bent down. On seeing this holy spirituality, the king deepened his faith and gave a large amount of gems and jewels to the thief to redeem the pearl, which he replaced on the topknot of the image. It was still in existence.

At the southeast corner of the country was Laṅkā Mountain, which was inhabited mostly by spirits and demons. Formerly the Tathāgata had preached the *Laṅkāvatāra Sūtra* (formerly incorrectly known as *Lengqie*) on this mountain.

Several thousand *li* over the sea to the south of this country was Nārikeladvīpa. The people of this island were dwarfish, little more than three feet high, and had human bodies with the beaks of birds. They raised no crops but lived on coconuts. As that country was far away beyond rough seas, one could not go there in person; and this brief information was heard from the people.

From Draviḍa the Master turned back to the northwest and travelled together with more than seventy Siṃhala monks to visit and pay homage to holy sites. After going for more than two thousand *li* he reached the country of Koṅkaṇapura (in the domain of southern India). There were more than a hundred monasteries with over ten thousand monks who studied the teachings of both Mahayana and Hinayana schools; and there were also numerous *deva* temples and heretics. Beside the king's palace city was a large monastery with more than three hundred monks who were all well-read scholars. In this monastery there was a precious crown of Prince Sarvasiddhārtha (formerly incorrectly known as Prince Xida), which was less than two feet high and preserved in a valuable casket. On festival days it was always displayed on a high
243a terrace, and those who worshipped it with utter sincerity might

cause it to emit a wonderful light. A monastery beside the city had a shrine hall in which was an image of Maitreya Bodhisattva carved in sandalwood. It was more than ten feet high and also often effused an auspicious light. It was made by the Arhat Śrotakoṭīviṃśa. To the north of the city was a wood of *tāla* trees, more than thirty *li* in circumference. The leaves of these trees were oblong with a glossy color and they were the best material used for writing in various countries.

Travelling northwest from here through a big forest infested with ferocious beasts for twenty-four hundred or twenty-five hundred *li,* the Master reached the country of Mahārāṣṭra (in the domain of southern India). It was the custom of the people of this country that they would rather die than lose their moral integrity. The king, a *kṣatriya* by birth, was bellicose and fond of martial arts. Thus the military forces of this country were well equipped and trained under strict and impartial discipline. When his generals were defeated in battle with enemies, he would not mete out punishments for them but simply ordered them to wear women's dress in order to humiliate them. In most cases they were shamed into committing suicide. He maintained several thousand warriors and several hundred fierce elephants. In time of war he gave them wine to drink to make them half-intoxicated and then waved his flag to order them to fight. Stimulated by the effect of alcohol, they would charge forward and shatter the enemy lines without fail. Depending on his military strength, the king was arrogant and disregarded his enemies in neighboring countries. Even King Śīlāditya, who was confident of his own great and farsighted strategic wisdom and had a strong army under his command, could not subjugate and control this country when he marched personally to attack it.

There were more than a hundred monasteries with over five thousand monks who studied Mahayana as well as Hinayana teachings. There were also *deva* temples of the heretics who smeared ashes on their bodies. Located inside and outside the capital city there were five stupas, all several hundred feet high, built by King Aśoka at places which the four past Buddhas had visited.

From here going northwest for more than a thousand *li,* the Master crossed the Narmadā River and reached the country of Bharukacchapa (in the domain of southern India). Proceeding from here to the northwest for more than two thousand *li,* he reached the country of Mālava (i.e., the Southern Lāṭa country in the domain of southern India). The people of this country were mild and gentle by custom, and they loved art and learning. In all the Five Indias, Mālava in the southwest and Magadha in the northeast were the only two countries where the people loved learning and honored sages and were eloquent in discussion as well as graceful in manners. In this country there were more than a hundred monasteries with over twenty thousand monks who studied the Hinayana teachings of the Saṃmitīya school. There were also many heretics who smeared themselves with ashes and worshipped the *deva*s.

According to tradition, sixty years ago there was a king named Śīlāditya who was highly talented and learned. Being a kind and benign ruler, he loved and took care of his subjects and respected the Triple Gem. From the time he became king until his demise, he never spoke a harsh word, nor did he show an angry face to anybody. He never hurt the feelings of his ministers and people, and would not injure the lives of such insects as mosquitoes and ants. Water was filtered before it was given to elephants and horses to drink, lest the aquatic microbes be killed. He also ordered the people in his country not to kill living creatures, so that wild animals were domesticated and jackals and wolves ceased to injure men. Peace and security prevailed in his domain, and the welfare and prosperity of his people increased day by day. He
243b constructed an extremely magnificent monastery in which images of the seven Buddhas were enshrined, and he also convened the great quinquennial assembly. During his reign of more than fifty years he performed such superior deeds without intermission, and the multitude remembered him with adoration even at this time.

Over twenty *li* to the northwest of the capital city and beside a Brahmin village, there was a pit where an arrogant Brahman, having calumniated Mahayana teachings, fell into hell alive. This event is related in the *Record of the Western Regions.*

Proceeding northwest from here for twenty-four hundred or twenty-five hundred *li,* the Master reached the country of Aṭali (in the domain of southern India). This land produced pepper trees whose leaves resembled those of the pepper grown in the region of Shu in China; and it also produced olibanum trees whose leaves were like those of our birch-leaf pear.

Going northwest from here for three days, the Master reached the country of Kheḍa (in the domain of southern India), and going further north from here for more than a thousand *li,* he reached the country of Valabhi (in the domain of southern India). There were more than a hundred monasteries with over six thousand monks who studied the teachings of the Hinayana Saṃmitīya school. When the Tathāgata was living, he visited this country several times. Monuments were erected by King Aśoka at all the places the Buddha had visited. The reigning king was a *kṣatriya* by caste, being a son-in-law of King Śīlāditya of the country of Kanyākubja; and his name was Dhruvabhaṭa (meaning Eternal Lord). He was a man of impetuous disposition with imprudent manners; but he esteemed virtue, loved learning, and also believed in the Triple Gem with veneration. Every year he held a great assembly for seven days; invited monks from different countries; and offered them the best food and delicacies, as well as bedding, garments, and everything else, including medicine, that was necessary for their maintenance.

Travelling northwest from here for more than seven hundred *li,* the Master reached the country of Ānandapura (in the domain of western India). Going further northwest for more than five hundred *li,* he reached the country of Suraṭṭha (in the domain of western India). Proceeding northeast from here for eighteen hundred *li,* he reached the country of Gūrjara. Going southeast again for more than twenty-eight hundred *li,* he reached the country of Ujjayanī (in the domain of southern India). Not far from the city was a stupa, built at the place where King Aśoka had made a hell. Going northeast from here for more than a thousand *li,* he reached the country of Jajhoti (in the domain of southern India). Going further northeast from here for more than nine hundred *li,* he reached the country of Maheśvarapura (in the domain of Central India). From here he returned westward to the country of Surāṣṭra. Proceeding further west, he reached the country of Audumbatira (in the domain of western India). When the Tathāgata was living, he visited this land frequently, and King Aśoka built stupas at all the sacred traces. These stupas were still in existence.

Going west from here for more than two thousand *li,* the Master reached the country of Laṅgala (in the domain of western India), which was close by the great sea and was the passage to the West Women's Country. By travelling northwest from here one could reach the country of Pārsa (in the domain of northern India). It was said that the land abounded in pearls, gems, thick
243c brocade, fine linen, good horses, and camels, which were the products of the country. There were two or three monasteries with several hundred monks who studied the Hinayana teachings of the Sarvāstivādan school. The alms bowl of Śākyamuni Buddha was kept in the royal palace of this country. On the eastern frontier of the country was the city of Ormus, and the northwest part bordered on the country of Hrom. An island to the southwest was the West Women's Country, in which there were only women without any men. It had many precious products. As it was a dependency of the country of Hrom, the king of Hrom sent men to mate with them once a year. It was their custom that when male babies were born, they were as a rule not brought up.

Going from the country of Laṅgala to the northeast for more than seven hundred *li,* the Master reached the country of Pāṭāsila (in the domain of western India). There there was a stupa several hundred feet high built by King Aśoka in which there were *śarīra*s (relics) that often issued a bright light. This was the place where the Tathāgata, as a *ṛṣi* (hermit) in a former life, was once killed by a king.

Going northeast from here for more than three hundred *li,* the Master reached the country of Avaṇḍa (in the domain of western India). In a big forest to the northeast of the capital city, there were the old foundations of a monastery in which the Buddha had formerly permitted the monks to wear *jifu* footgear (meaning boots). Beside a stupa built by King Aśoka was a temple that housed a standing statue of the Buddha carved in blue stone. It often emitted a bright light. In a big forest about eight hundred paces further to the south was another stupa, built by King Aśoka at a place where the Tathāgata had once spent a night and, as it was cold, covered himself with three robes one over the other. The following morning he gave his *bhikṣus* permission to wear double robes.

Going east from here for more than seven hundred *li,* the Master reached the country of Sindhu (in the domain of western India). This land produced gold, silver, brass, cattle, sheep, and camels, as well as red, white, and black salt which was taken as medicine in other places. When the Tathāgata was living, he visited this country several times. At all the holy traces stupas were built by King Aśoka to mark the spots. There were also the traces left by the great Arhat Upagupta when he travelled in this country.

Going further east from here for nine hundred *li,* the Master crossed the river to the eastern bank and reached the country of Mūlasthānapura (in the domain of western India). It was the custom of this country to worship the *devas* in a lofty and magnificent temple. The image of the sun god was cast in gold and adorned with various kinds of jewels. Many people of different countries came to pray before it. In the temple there were flowers, trees, pools, and ponds, with winding stepways paved with bricks. All those who visited the temple loved and enjoyed the place without exception.

Going northeast from here for more than seven hundred *li,* the Master reached the country of Parvata (in the domain of northern India). Beside the city there was a big monastery with more than a hundred monks, all of whom studied Mahayana teachings. This was the place where the Śāstrin Jinaputra (meaning Victorious Son) composed the *Yogācārabhūmi Śāstra Kārikā,* and it was also the place where the Śāstrins Bhadraruci and Guṇaprabha renounced their homes to become monks. As there were in this

country two or three virtuous teachers under whom one might
244a pursue learning, the Master sojourned there for two years to study with them the *Mūlābhidharma Śāstra,* the *Saddharmasaṃparigraha Śāstra,* the *Satyaśāsana Śāstra,* etc., of the Saṃmitīya school.

From here the Master turned toward the southeast and returned to Nālandā Monastery in Magadha. After having paid homage to the Right Dharma Store, he heard that three *yojanas* to the west of the monastery was Tiladhāka Monastery, in which lived a virtuous monk named Prajñābhadra, a native of the country of Balapati, who had become a monk of the Sarvāstivāda school and was well versed in the Tripiṭaka of his own school, as well as in Śabdavidyā and Hetuvidyā. The Master went to stay with him for two months to seek his advice about the solution to some doubtful points the Master had in his mind.

From here the Master again went to an *upāsaka* (layman), the Śāstrin Jayasena, at Stickwood Hill. Jayasena was a native of the country of Surāṣṭra and a *kṣatriya* by birth. Since his youth he loved learning, and at first he studied Hetuvidyā with the Śāstrin Bhadraruci. Then he learned Śabdavidyā and the treatises of both Mahayana and Hinayana schools from Sthiramati Bodhisattva. He also studied the *Yogācārabhūmi Śāstra* with the Dharma teacher Śīlabhadra. As regards various non-Buddhist books, such as the Four Vedas, astronomy, geography, medicine, and the art of divination, he thoroughly mastered all their fundamental sources as well as the subjects that branched from them. Since his learning included both Buddhist and non-Buddhist lore and his virtue was esteemed by the people of the time, King Pūrṇavarman, the lord of Magadha, who revered sages and respected scholars, was pleased to hear about his reputation. He sent a messenger to invite him to be the royal preceptor with a conferment of twenty large villages as his fief. But the Śāstrin did not accept the invitation. After the demise of Pūrṇavarman, King Śīlāditya again asked the Śāstrin to be his teacher offering eighty large villages in the country of Uḍra as his fief; and the Śāstrin again declined. The king invited him insistently time and again, but each time the Śāstrin was resolute in declining the proffered honor. He said to the king, "I, Jayasena, have heard that one who accepts the emolument given by a person has to share his responsibilities. Now since I am urgently engaged in trying to save myself from the bondage of rebirth, how can I have the leisure to attend to the king's affairs?" Having said so, he saluted the king and went away; and thus the king could not retain him any more.

Since then he often stayed at Stickwood Hill, training and educating his disciples, and he always lectured on Buddhist scriptures. The number of monks and laymen who came to study under him always exceeded several hundred. The Master stayed with him for two years to learn the *Vijñānamātraparikalpana Śāstra,* the *Manasabhidheyatā Śāstra,* the *Abhayasiddhi Śāstra,* the *Asaṃgamanirvāṇa Śāstra,* the *Dvādaśāṅgapratītyasamutpāda Śāstra,* and the *Sūtrālaṃkāra Śāstra.* He also resolved some dubious points in the *Yogācārabhūmi Śāstra,* the *Hetuvidyā Śāstra,* and some other works.

One night the Master dreamed that the buildings of Nālandā Monastery were in a deserted and filthy condition with some buffaloes tied therein and had no more monks. He entered the monastery through the western gate of the Court of King Balāditya and saw a golden figure on the fourth story of the pavilion with a dignified appearance and a brilliant light that illuminated the whole room. With a happy mind, he wished to go up, but there was no way. So he requested that the golden figure to take him up. The figure said, "I am Mañjuśrī Bodhisattva. Because of your karmic condition, you cannot come up here." And then he pointed at the outside of the monastery and said, "Look there!" Looking at the
244b place indicated, the Master saw that the villages and towns outside the monastery were all burned to ashes. The golden figure said, "You may return home soon. Ten years from now King Śīlāditya of this place will pass away and India will fall into a state of great turmoil. Then evil people may do you harm. You should be aware of this." After saying so, the golden figure vanished.

When the Master awoke from the dream, he felt it very strange and told it to Jayasena, who said, "As the Three Worlds are devoid of security, such things might well happen. Since you have been told so, it is up to you to make your own decision."

From this we may know that wherever the Master went, he was always protected by the Bodhisattva. When he was about to start his journey to India, Śīlabhadra was exhorted to wait for his arrival. When he lingered too long, he was reminded of the principle of transitoriness of life and was advised to return home. If what he was doing was inconsistent with the Holy Mind, who else could have aroused such spiritual aid? By the end of the Yonghui period (650–55) Sīlāditya actually died and India fell into a condition of great turmoil, just as had been foretold. The Chinese envoy Wang Xuance witnessed all the events.

It was at the beginning of the first month of our calendar, when it was the custom of the western country to display during this month the Buddha's relic bones preserved in the Bodhi Temple. All the monks and lay people of different countries came to see and worship the holy relics. The Master then went there with Jayasena, and saw that some of the relics were large and some small. The large ones were the size of pearls with a reddish white hue; and the flesh relics, as large as peas, had a glossy red color. When innumerable devotees had offered incense and flowers and worshipped them with praise, the relics were put back in the stupa.

Just after the first watch in the night, Jayasena discussed with the Master the different sizes of the relic bones, and said, "I, your disciple, have seen at other places that the relics were as big as grains of rice. Why are the ones we have seen here so big? Don't you, teacher, have any doubt about it?" The Master said in reply, "I also have the same doubt about it."

A moment later, the lamp in the room suddenly became dim; but it was very bright inside and outside the house. Being amazed, they went out to see and saw that the relic stupa was issuing a brilliant light, the rays of which flew high up to the sky. It was a multicolored light, shining so brightly upon the sky and the earth that the moon and stars were overshadowed. They also smelt an unusual fragrance that pervaded the courtyard. Thus the people told one another that the relics were showing a great miracle.

Upon hearing this, the multitude reassembled to worship the relics and praised it as a rare occurrence. After about the time required for taking a meal, the light gradually diminished. When it was about to disappear, it encircled the bowl that covered the relics several times and finally entered it. Then the sky and earth became dark again, and the stars reappeared. Having witnessed this sight, the people were freed from the net of doubt.

After having worshipped the Bodhi tree and other holy sites for eight days, the Master returned to Nālandā Monastery.

The Śāstrin Śīlabhadra asked the Master to lecture on the *Mahāyānasaṃparigraha Śāstra* and the *Vijñānamātraparikalpana Śāstra* for the monks. At that time the learned teacher Siṃhaprabha had already expounded the *Mādhyamika Śāstra* and the *Śata Śāstra* for the four groups of Buddhist followers on a previous occasion, in refutation of the theories of the *Yogācārabhūmi Śāstra*. Being learned in the *Mādhyamika Śāstra* and the *Śata Śāstra* as
244c well as proficient in the *Yogācārabhūmi Śāstra,* the Master considered that the saints founded each of their theories for a particular purpose without obstruction or contradiction between them, and that [only] deluded ones who could not understand them thoroughly thought them to be contradictory. It was but the fault of the transmitters and had nothing to do with the Dharma. Out of pity for his narrow-mindedness, the Master went to interrogate the lecturer several times; but the man could not give adequate replies. Thus his disciples gradually dispersed and came to study under the Master.

Considering that the purpose of the *Mādhyamika Śāstra* and the *Śata Śāstra* was mainly to refute of the view that grasped the false to be true, the Master did not mention that things depend upon conditions for their arising, nor did he mention the idea of seeing things in their perfect true nature, and so Siṃhaprabha could not well understand the truth. As he saw that the *Yogācārabhūmi Śāstra* asserted that all things are void and that nothing can be obtained from them, he held the opinion that the view of seeing things in their perfect true nature, etc., as advocated in the *śāstra,* should also be discarded. Thus he often expressed this idea in words.

In order to harmonize the teachings of the two schools without incongruity, the Master wrote the *Nikāyasaṃgraha Śāstra* in three thousand stanzas. When the treatise was completed, he presented it to Śīlabhadra and all the monks, who praised it as a good work and propagated it as well as put it into practice.

Feeling ashamed of himself, Siṃhaprabha went away to the Bodhi Temple, where he asked his schoolmate, one Candrasiṃha of eastern India, to come and start a debate with the Master in order to erase his humiliation. But when that person came he was awed into silence in the presence of the Master and dared not speak a word. Thus the Master's reputation became still greater.

Before Siṃhaprabha went away, King Śīlāditya had constructed a bronze temple over a hundred feet high beside Nālandā Monastery. It was well known in various countries. Afterward the king went personally to conquer Koṅgoda and crossed the country of Uḍra, where all the monks were Hinayana adherents and did not believe in Mahayana teachings, saying that they were the views of the Śūnyapuṣpa heretics and were not taught by the Buddha. When they saw the king, they sneered at him, saying, "We have heard that Your Majesty has constructed a bronze temple beside Nālandā Monastery. It is indeed a magnificent work of great merit, but why did you build it there and not near some heretical temple of the Kāpālikas?" The king said, "What do you mean by saying so?" The monks said in reply, "Because the friars of Nālandā Monastery being Śūnyapuṣpa heretics, they are not different from the Kāpālikas!"

There was formerly an old Brahmin teacher by the name of Prajñāgupta, who had consecrated the king of southern India by sprinkling water on his head and was learned in the theories of the Saṃmitīya school. He composed the *Mahāyānabheda Śāstra* in seven hundred stanzas, which won the admiration and respect of all Hinayana teachers. So the monks showed this work to the king (Śīlāditya) and said to him, "This is our teaching. Could there be any Mahayana follower who could refute a single word of it?"

The king said, "I, your disciple, have heard that some wild foxes and small mice claimed to be more powerful than a lion; but when they actually saw a lion, they were scared out of their wits. Because you teachers have never seen Mahayana teachers of great virtue, you persist in your erroneous views. Once you see them, I am afraid you will be just the same as the foxes and mice!"

They said, "If Your Majesty is in doubt about it, why do you not hold a meeting to decide the right and wrong?"

The king said, "There is no difficulty in doing that." And on the
245a following day, he wrote a letter and dispatched a messenger to send it to the Venerable Śīlabhadra, the Right Dharma Store, of Nālandā Monastery. In the letter he said:

> I, your disciple, am now in the country of Uḍra in the course of travelling. I see that the Hinayana teachers here, depending upon their Hinayana views, have composed a treatise in sneering language and using vicious reasoning to calumniate the Mahayana doctrines unreasonably. Yet they are so arrogant as to wish to hold a debate with you teachers. Knowing that the virtuous monks of the monastery possess both talent and wisdom in abundance and understand whatever they have learned, I, your disciple, took the liberty of granting them their request. I am ordering my messenger to submit this report to you, and I would like you to dispatch four virtuous monks well versed in both Mahayana and Hinayana teachings, as well as knowing both the inner and the outer learning, to come to my temporary residence in the country of Uḍra.

Upon receiving this letter, the Right Dharma Store assembled the monks to select the proper persons; and he appointed Sāgaramati, Jñānaprabha, Siṃhaprabha, and the Master as the four persons in compliance with the king's order. Sāgaramati and the other two monks were worried, but the Master said to them, "I have studied the Tripiṭaka of the various Hinayana schools and completely mastered their theories while I was in my own country and during my stay in Kaśmīra. It is impossible for them to refute the Mahayana teachings with their own theories. Although my learning is shallow and my intellect weak, I have the confidence to deal with the matter. I hope you teachers will not worry about it. In case I am defeated in the debate, I am a monk from China and you will not be involved in the matter." The other monks were pleased to hear it.

But later King Śīlāditya sent another letter, in which he said that the monks he had invited in his previous letter need not start the journey immediately but should wait for further notification as to whether they should go or not.

At that time a heretic of the Lokāyatika school came to seek a debate and wrote his argument in fourteen points, which he hung on the door of the monastery, while he announced, "If anybody is able to refute any one point of my argument, I shall cut off my head to apologize!"

After the passage of several days, nobody came out to accept the challenge. The Master then asked his personal servant to take down the poster, destroy it, and trample the broken pieces under his feet. Being greatly enraged, the Brahman asked, "Who are you?" The servant said in reply, "I am a servant of the Mahayana-deva." The Brahman, who had already heard of the fame of the Master, was ashamed of himself and did not say anything more. The Master sent for him and brought him to the presence of the Venerable Śīlabhadra, with various virtuous monks as witnesses, to start a debate with him about the principles of his school and the theories founded by other heretical sects as well. The Master said, "Such heretics as the Bhūtas, the Nirgranthas, the Kāpālikas, and the Jūṭakas are clad in four different ways with different appearances, while the theories established by the Sāṃkhyas (formerly known as Sengqia) and the Vaiśeṣikas (formerly known as Weishishi) are different from each other. The Bhūtas smear their bodies with ash as a means of spiritual cultivation, rendering themselves as pale in color as a dusty cat that has slept on a kitchen range. The Nirgranthas make themselves look strange by practising nudism, and they pluck their hair as a deed of virtue. With broken skin and chapped feet, they resemble rotten trees
245b beside a river. The Kāpālikas make chaplets of skulls to adorn their heads or hang them on their necks, and the sunken and dried-up

sockets in a crooked form make them appear just like *yakṣas* in a cemetery. And the Jūṭakas wear dirty clothes, drink urine, and eat filth, with a stinking and foul smell, like a mad pig wallowing in a latrine. Are you not stupid to regard these practices as the Way?

"As regards the Sāṃkhya heretics, they hold the theory of twenty-five True Entities (*tattvas*), viz., from Self-nature (*prakṛti*) comes the Great Source of Intellect (*mahat*), which gives rise to Self-consciousness (*Ahaṃkāra*), and this again causes the Five Subtle Elements (*tanmātras*), the Five Gross Elements (*mahābhūtas*), and the Eleven Organs (*indriyas*). These twenty-four entities are provided for and enjoyed by the Spirit (*puruṣa*), and when the Spirit is free and disjoined from them it gains purity. Meanwhile the Vaiśeṣikas hold the theory of the Six Categories of Cognition (*padārthas*), viz., substance (*dravya*), quality (*guṇa*), action (*karma*), generality (*sāmānya*), particularity (*viśeṣa*), and correlation (*samavāya*), which are possessed by the Spirit). When the Spirit is not emancipated, it has always been using the abovementioned Six Categories; and when it is liberated, having separated itself from the Six Categories, it is the same as the state of nirvana.

"Now let me refute the theories established by the Sāṃkhyas. Among the twenty-five entities, as you hold, the entity of *puruṣa* is of a particular nature, while the other twenty-four entities are interrelated into one substance; and the entity of Self-nature is composed of the three qualities, viz., *sattva* (virtue), *rajas* (foulness), and *tamas* (ignorance). These three qualities also extend and constitute the other twenty-three entities of *mahat,* etc., each of these twenty-three entities having the three qualities as its substance. Now if *mahat* and the rest are all constituted by the three qualities, they should then be the same as an assembly or a forest, which are merely unsubstantial false conceptions. How can you say that they are True Entities? Again, if *mahat* and the rest are all composed of the three qualities, then [any] one of them should be the same as [all] the others. And if one is the same as the others, then any one of them should have the same functions as all the others. But since this is not the case, why should you hold the view that the three qualities are the substantial nature of all the entities? Again, if one entity is just the same as the other entities, then the organs of mouth and eye, etc., should have the same function as the excretory organs. And if each organ has the functions of all the other organs, then the organ of the mouth ought to smell odors and the ear see colors. If it is not so, how can you hold the view that the three qualities are the substance of all things? How could a wise man have formulated such theories? Moreover, if Self-nature is unchangeable, it should be like the substance of *puruṣa*. How can it be transformed into *mahat* and the other things? Again, if the *puruṣa* as you conceive it is unchangeable by nature, then it ought to be the same as Self-nature and should not be the *puruṣa*. And if it is the same as Self-nature, then its substance is not that of the *puruṣa* and ought not to enjoy the other twenty-four entities. In such a case, *puruṣa* is not the subject that is able to enjoy, nor are the twenty-four entities the objects to be enjoyed. Since there is neither subjectivity nor objectivity in the proposition, your theory of the True Entities cannot be established."

In this manner the argument was carried on with repeated refutations; and the Brahman remained silent and said nothing. Then he rose to his feet and said with an apology, "I am defeated, and I am ready to keep my word." The Master said, "We Buddhists do not take any man's life. I now make you my slave, and you
245c should work according to my orders." The Brahman was glad to obey the Master's orders with reverence, and was brought to his living quarters. All those who heard about this event praised it with delight.

At that time when the Master intended to go to Uḍra, he obtained a treatise in seven hundred stanzas, composed by the Hinayanists in refutation of Mahayana teachings. He read through it and found several doubtful points in it. He asked the Brahman whom he had subdued in debate, "Have you attended lectures on this treatise?" The Brahman replied, "I have attended lectures on it five times." When the Master wished him to give an explanation of the treatise, he said, "As I am your slave, how can I explain anything to Your Reverence?" The Master said, "As this is a work of another school, I have not seen it before. There is no harm in you giving me an explanation of it." The Brahman said, "If so, please wait until midnight, lest people hear that you are studying the Dharma with a slave and defile your good name."

Thus in the night the Master sent away all other people and asked the Brahman to expound the treatise. When he had just gone through it once, the Master completely grasped its gist. He found out the erroneous points and refuted them with Mahayana teachings in a treatise he wrote in sixteen hundred stanzas, entitled the *Aghadarśanabheda Śāstra*. He presented the work to the Venerable Śīlabhadra and showed it to his disciples, who all praised it with appreciation and said, "With such all-comprehensive scrutiny, there is no opponent he could not vanquish!" The treatise is to be found elsewhere.

Then the Master said to the Brahman, "You have been my slave since you were defeated in the debate. The humiliation is long enough for you. Now I set you free and you are at liberty to go anywhere you wish." Being delighted, the Brahman took his leave and went to the country of Kāmarūpa in eastern India, where he informed King Kumāra about the Master's virtue and righteousness. The king was pleased to hear it and immediately sent an envoy to invite the Master.

Fascicle V

Beginning with the Prediction of a Nirgrantha about His Homeward Journey and Ending with His Arrival at the Western Canal in the Imperial Capital

Before the arrival of the envoy sent by King Kumāra, a naked Nirgrantha named Vajra unexpectedly came to the Master's room. Hearing that the Nirgrantha was good at divining, the Master invited him to take a seat and asked him to resolve his doubts, saying, "I am a Chinese monk and have come here to study for quite a number of years. Now I intend to return home, but I am not sure whether I shall be able to reach my home or not. As regards my going back or staying here, which is more auspicious for me? And how long shall I live? Will you please predict these matters for
246a me?" Then the Nirgrantha asked for a piece of chalk and drew lines on the ground to make a forecast by divination. He told the Master, "It is good for you to stay, as you will enjoy the respect of the monks and lay people of the Five Indias. If you go back, you will be able to reach home and will also enjoy respect, but it will not be as good as staying here. As regards the length of your life, you will live for another ten years from now. If you perform more meritorious deeds, your life may be prolonged, but that is beyond my knowledge." The Master then said that though he desired to go back, he did not know how he could carry back a large amount of scriptures and images. The Nirgrantha said, "Do not worry. King Śīlāditya and King Kumāra will dispatch men to escort you on the way. You will surely get back without trouble." The Master said in reply, "I have never seen these two kings. How would they grant me such

favors?" The Nirgrantha said, "King Kumāra has already sent a messenger to invite you, and he will be here in two or three days. After having seen Kumāra, you will also see Śīlāditya." Having said so the Nirgrantha went away.

The Master then made preparations for his return journey and packed up his scriptures and images. When the monks heard about it, they all came to persuade him to stay, saying, "India being the birthplace of the Buddha, the traces and tracks left by him are still here though the Great Saint has passed away. To wander around worshipping them with praises would be a great pleasure in anyone's life. Why do you wish to leave after having come here? China is a borderland where the common people are slighted and the Dharma despised; the Buddhas are never born in that country. As the people are narrow-minded, with deep moral impurity, saints and sages do not go there. The climate is cold and the land is full of dangerous mountains. What is there for you to be nostalgic about?" The Master said in reply, "The King of the Dharma has founded his teachings and it is proper for us to propagate them. How can we forget about those who are not yet enlightened while we have gained the benefit in our own minds? Moreover, that country is highly civilized and the people have a code of conduct to observe. The Emperor is sagacious and his ministers are loyal. The father treats his son with benignity, and the son is filial to his father. Kindness and righteousness are esteemed, and the aged and virtuous respected. The people are, moreover, able to discern what is subtle and profound, and their wisdom coincides with that of the gods. They behave according to the law of nature, and the Seven Planets cannot overshadow their culture. They invented the device for the division of time and made the flute to produce the six masculine notes of music. Thus they have the capability to enslave birds and beasts, inspire the spirits and deities, adapt themselves to positive and negative circumstances, and benefit as well as pacify all things between Heaven and earth. Since the Buddha's bequeathed Dharma was spread to the East, they have laid importance on Mahayana teachings, practised meditation in a tranquil state like a pond of clear water, and observed the Vinaya rules as a pervading influence like that of fragrant incense. They have cherished the mind to practise Bodhisattva deeds and wished to attain to the level of the Tenth Stage of Bodhisattvahood. They put their hands palm to palm for mental cultivation with the realization of the Three Bodies of a Buddha as their ultimate goal. Great saints, who heard the wonderful teachings with their own ears and saw golden figures with their own eyes, have always shown the spirituality to edify the people personally with the Dharma. They may be compared to a carriage drawn by two horses; no one knows how far it can travel. How can you despise that land simply because the Buddha was not born there?"

But the monks said, "It is said in the scriptures that according to different meritorious deeds, heavenly beings have different kinds of food, though they eat together. We are, however, living together in Jambudvīpa; but the Buddha was born here in this country and did not go there to your land, because it is a vicious
246b borderland. As that land is devoid of felicities, we advise you not to go back." The Master said in reply, "Once Vimalakīrti remarked: 'Why does the sun go across Jambudvīpa? The answer is to dispel darkness.' It is because I wish to follow the suggestion of this metaphor that I intend to return home."

When the monks saw that the Master would not listen to them, they asked him to go with them to the Venerable Śīlabhadra to state his wishes. Śīlabhadra asked the Master, "What is your final decision?" The Master said in reply, "This being the country where the Buddha was born, I certainly do not dislike it. But my intention in coming here was to acquire the Great Dharma in order to benefit all living beings. Since my arrival at this place, I have had the honor to attend your lectures on the *Yogācārabhūmi Śāstra,* whereby my net of doubts has been resolved. I have worshipped the holy sites and studied the very profound teachings of various schools. I am glad in my heart that my journey has not been fruitless. I wish to return home to translate into Chinese the texts I have learned here, so that those who have the good opportunity may also learn them as I did. In this way I may repay the kindness of my teachers. That is why I have no leisure to linger here any longer."

Śīlabhadra was pleased to hear this, and said, "This is the wish of a Bodhisattva, and it is also what I expected of you. Let him pack up his luggage; you people need not try to detain him any more." After having said so, he returned to his chamber.

Two days later, the envoy sent by King Kumāra of East India arrived with a letter for the Venerable Śīlabhadra, in which the king said:

> Your disciple wishes to see the virtuous monk from China. May the teacher kindly send him here so as to satisfy my wish.

After receiving this letter, Śīlabhadra told all the monks, "King Kumāra desires to invite Xuanzang to his country; but he has already been appointed by the assembly of the monks to proceed to the place of King Śīlāditya to hold a debate with the Hinayana adherents. If he goes now, what shall we do when King Śīlāditya needs him? It is inappropriate for us to let him go."

So he said to the envoy, "As the Chinese monk wishes to return to his own country, he has no time to comply with the king's order to visit him."

When the envoy had returned home, the king sent him to come again with a message of invitation, saying:

> Even if the Master desires to return home, it will not be difficult for him to come across my place and stay for a short time before he departs for home. I hope you will condescend to do me the favor and will not act contrary to my request.

As Śīlabhadra did not send the Master, the king became greatly enraged and dispatched another envoy to send him a letter in which the king said:

> Your disciple, being an ordinary person, is addicted to worldly pleasures and does not know how to turn his mind toward the Buddha Dharma. Now I am truly delighted to have heard the name of the foreign monk, and it seems that

the sprout of faith has burst in me. But the teacher does not allow him to come, wishing to keep all living beings enshrouded in eternal darkness. Is this the way for a virtuous monk to glorify the bequeathed Dharma to lead the people? As I am longing to meet him with a mind of respect, I am sending this second letter to you with sincerity. If he is not coming, then I am bound to be a wicked person. Recently King Śaśāṅka had the power to defame the Dharma and destroy the Bodhi tree. Do you think that I do not possess the same power? I will certainly array my troop of elephants and concentrate them to trample on and break Nālandā Monastery to dust! My words are as clear as the sun, and the teacher may wait and see!

246c Upon receiving this letter, Śīlabhadra said to the Master, "Usually that king's good mind is shallow, and the Buddha Dharma is not very popular in his domain. It seems that he has fostered a deep mind for spiritual achievements since he heard your name. You may have been a good friend of his in a previous life. You had better try to go, as our aim in becoming monks is to benefit others, and this is now the right time to do so. It is like felling a tree. When the root is cut off the long branches will become dried up by themselves. If you go there and arouse the king's mind of spirituality, his people will follow his example. If you refuse to accept his invitation, something devilish might happen. Do not hesitate to take this small trouble."

After taking leave of the teacher, the Master went away with the envoy. Upon his arrival in that country, the king was very much pleased. Leading his ministers, he welcomed the Master with salutation and praise, and invited him to his palace. Every day the king entertained him with music and offered him food, drink, flowers, incense, and all kinds of offerings. He also asked to observe the Precepts. In this manner the Master stayed there for more than a month.

When King Śīlāditya returned from his campaign in Konyodha, he heard that the Master was at Kumāra's place and said with amazement, "I have repeatedly invited him, but he did not come. Why is he now in that country?" He dispatched an envoy to tell King Kumāra, "Send the Chinese monk to me immediately!" As King Kumāra respected the Master and had such great adoration for him, he was unwilling to part with him, and said to the envoy, "You may have my head, but the Master cannot go right now!" The envoy returned and reported this to King Śīlāditya, who was greatly enraged, and said to his attending ministers, "King Kumāra despises me. Why should he speak such rough language just because of a monk?" Then he sent another envoy to reproach him, saying, "Since you said that I could have your head, now hand your head to my envoy so he can bring it back to me!"

Deeply fearing that he had made an indiscreet remark, Kumāra at once ordered the arraying of twenty thousand elephant troops and the preparation of thirty thousand boats, and then sailed together with the Master along the Ganges to the place of the king (Śīlāditya). When they reached the country of Kajuṅghira, they had an audience with the king.

Before he started the voyage, King Kumāra had ordered his men to prepare a temporary palace north of the Ganges. After having lodged the Master properly on the day he arrived at his temporary palace, he and his ministers went to see King Śīlāditya south of the river. King Śīlāditya was glad to see him. Knowing that Kumāra respected and adored the Master, he did not blame him for what he had said before, but simply asked, "Where is the Chinese monk?" "He is at my temporary palace," was the reply. The king asked, "Why does he not come?" "Since Your Majesty reveres the sages and takes an interest in the Way, it is inappropriate to send for him to come and see Your Majesty," replied Kumāra. The king said, "Very well. You may go now, and I shall come tomorrow."

Kumāra returned and said to the Master, "Although the king said that he would come tomorrow, I am afraid he might come tonight. We should wait and see. In case he comes, you need not move yourself." The Master said, "I shall certainly behave myself in accordance with Buddhist manners."

At about the first watch of the night, the king actually came.
247a Someone reported, "Several thousand torches and candles are burning on the river and the noise of the pacing drums is heard." The king said, "This must be King Śīlāditya coming!" Then he ordered that candles be lit and went personally with his ministers for a great distance to bid welcome.

Whenever King Śīlāditya went out, he always had several hundred metal drums beaten once for every step he walked. This was known as beating the rhythmic pacing drums. King Śīlāditya alone had this privilege; no other king enjoyed the same honor. Upon his arrival, he worshipped at the Master's feet, scattered flowers, and looked at him with reverence. After having eulogized the Master with many poetic expressions, he said to him, "Why did you not come when I previously invited you?" The Master replied, "I came from afar to seek the Buddha Dharma and to learn the *Yogācārabhūmi Śāstra*. When I received your order I was just in the midst of attending lectures on the *śāstra,* and that was why I could not come to have an audience with Your Majesty." The king inquired again, "You come from China; I have heard that in your country you have a dancing melody known as 'The Triumph of the Prince of Qin.' But I do not know who this person the Prince of Qin is or what meritorious deeds he has done to earn such praises."

The Master said in reply, "When the people of my country see anybody possessing the virtues of saints and sages and capable of wiping out the ferocious and brutal for the protection and advantage of the masses, they sing his praises as part of the music performed in ancestral temples above and as folk songs sung by the common people below. The Prince of Qin is now the reigning Emperor of China; before he ascended the Throne, he had been made the Prince of Qin. At that time the country was in a condition of disorder without a lord to rule over the people. Human corpses piled up in the wilderness, and human blood flowed in the rivers and valleys. Evil stars gathered together at night, and ominous vapors condensed in the morning. The regions of the Three Rivers suffered from the avarice of those who were as greedy as giant pigs, and the Four Seas were troubled as if by the poison of huge snakes.

Being a son of the former Emperor, the Prince, in compliance with the good order of Heaven, summoned up all the courage and energy of his army to suppress the rebels, who were as unrighteous as whales swallowing small fishes; holding his battle-ax and brandishing his spear, he pacified the land as far as the sea. Thus he restored tranquillity in the land and made the Three Luminaries shine brightly again. As the people in the whole country were grateful to him, they composed that music to sing his praises."

The king said, "Such a person is really sent by Heaven to be a lord of men!" And he also said to the Master, "I am going back now, and I shall welcome you tomorrow. I hope you will kindly accept my invitation." After saying so, he took his leave and departed.

The following morning the king's envoy came, and the Master went in company with Kumāra. When they arrived at the side of the palace of King Śīlāditya, the king and more than twenty of his personal teachers came out to greet the Master and invited him to take a seat in the palace. Different kinds of delicious food were spread on the table, and after having made offerings to him with the performance of music and the scattering of flowers, the king said, "I have heard that you have composed the *Aghadarśanabheda Śāstra.* Where is it?" The Master replied, "Here it is." And then he presented the work to the king, who was delighted after having read it through, and said to his personal teachers, "I have heard that when the sun is shining, the glimmering of a firefly and the light of a candle are dimmed. When it is thundering with a vibrating sound in the sky, the noise of a hammer striking a chisel is muffled. Now all the theories advocated by you teachers have been refuted by him. Would you try to offer a counter reply?" All
247b the monks dared not speak a word. The king said, "Your teacher Devasena claims to be the most learned among all scholars and is well versed in various systems of philosophy. He originated variant views and always defamed Mahayana teachings. But when he heard that this guest monk of great virtue was coming, he went away to Vaiśālī to worship the holy sites as an excuse to avoid meeting the guest. From this I sensed your incapability."

The king had a younger sister who was clever and intelligent and was well versed in the theories of the Saṃmitīya school. She was sitting behind the king. When she heard the Master explaining the profundity of Mahayana teachings and pointing out the shallowness of Hinayana doctrines, she was so glad and happy that she could not refrain from praising the Master.

The king said, "The teacher's treatise is most excellent and I, your disciple, as well as all the other teachers here are convinced of it. But as I fear that the Hinayana adherents and heretics of other countries may still stick to their ignorance and delusion, I wish to convene an assembly on your behalf at the city of Kanyākubja and ask all the *śramaṇa*s, Brahmans, and other heretics of the Five Indias to take part in the gathering, so that you may show them the subtle principles of the Mahayana doctrines and stop their minds of calumniation as well as manifest your high virtue and smash their sense of arrogance." On that day the king issued an edict to different countries, inviting the theoreticians to assemble at the city of Kanyākubja to read the treatise composed by the Master from China.

At the beginning of the eleventh month, the Master sailed together with the king up the Ganges. They reached the venue of the assembly in the twelfth month. Among those who were present at the gathering were eighteen kings from the Five Indias; more than three thousand monks well versed in both Mahayana and Hinayana teachings; and more than two thousand Brahmans, Nirgranthas, and other heretics, as well as more than a thousand monks from Nālandā Monastery. All these wise people well understood the meanings of literature and were highly talented in argumentation. As they wished to listen to the voice of the Dharma, they came to attend the meeting. They had attendants and came either by elephant or by carriage. Each of them was surrounded by pennants or streamers in a grand and lofty manner, like rising clouds and mist emerging in an area of several tens of square *li*. It was said that the region of the Six Princes of Qi was so thickly inhabited that when the people raised their sleeves they might form curtains, and that in the area of the Three Wus when the people wiped their sweat, it would rain like a shower. But even such big crowds were still inadequate to compare with this grand assembly.

The king had beforehand ordered that two thatched halls be built at the place of the gathering, [one] in which to install the Buddha's image and [another] to accommodate the monks. When he arrived there both halls had been completed; they were high and broad, and each was capable of seating more than a thousand persons. The king's temporary palace was located five *li* west of the venue of the meeting. Every day an image was cast in gold in the palace and a big elephant was caparisoned and carried a precious enclosure wherein the Buddha's image was placed. King Śīlāditya dressed himself as Indra, holding a white chowry in his hand and attending at the right side; while King Kumāra, attired as Brahmā, held a precious canopy and attended at the left side. Both of them wore celestial crowns and garlands and were adorned with pearl necklaces and jade pendants. Two more caparisoned elephants carried precious flowers and followed behind the Buddha's image; flowers were scattered as the elephants proceeded along the way. The Master and the king's personal teachers were asked to ride on different elephants that followed behind the king in the procession. Three hundred more elephants were arranged for the kings of
247c different countries, the ministers, and the monks of great virtue to ride on; they walked by the side of the road one after another, like a shoal of fish swimming in an orderly line, while praises were chanted as they proceeded along. Starting in the morning, people dressed themselves and set out from the temporary palace to the meeting place. Upon arriving at the gate of the courtyard, [riders] were asked to alight from the elephants. Then they carried the Buddha image to the hall and placed it on a precious pedestal. The king and the Master, together with some others, made offerings to the image in proper order, and then the eighteen kings were ushered in. Next came in more than a thousand of the most reputable and widely learned monks from various countries. After them came in more than five hundred Brahmans, heretics, and well-known ascetics, followed by over two hundred ministers of

different countries. It was arranged that the other monks and lay people stay outside the courtyard in an orderly way. The king ordered that food be served to all within and without the courtyard. When the meal was over, one golden tray, seven golden bowls, one golden bathing jug, one golden staff, three thousand golden coins, and three thousand robes made of the best felt were offered to the Buddha, while the Master and the other monks also received different gifts.

When the almsgiving was completed, a separate precious seat was prepared. The Master was invited to take the chair in the assembly to extol Mahayana teachings and to explain his intent of composing the treatise. The Venerable Vidyābhadra, a *śramaṇa* of Nālandā Monastery, was asked to read it to the congregation, while a written copy was hung outside the gate of the meeting place for everybody to read. If one word was found illogical or refutable in the treatise, the writer would cut off his head in apology. But until nightfall, nobody raised a word of objection. King Śīlāditya was glad of it, and after adjourning the meeting, he returned to his palace. The other kings and monks also returned to their respective lodgings. Then the Master and King Kumāra returned to their own palace. On the following morning they came again, carrying the Buddha image and entering the assembly hall just as on the previous day.

After the elapse of five days, the Hinayana adherents and the heretics, seeing that the Master had crushed their theories, felt hatred and intended to murder him. The king got wind of it and issued an order, saying:

> Since a long time ago, the heterodox schools have always tried to corrupt the truth in order to bury the right teachings in oblivion and to delude and lead the people astray. If there were no man of superior wisdom, who could discern what is untrue? The Chinese Master is a man of profound and broad mind, whose knowledge and practice are very deep. He came to tour this country in order to reveal and propagate the Great Dharma and to lead the ignorant to enlightenment.

> Some evil and presumptuous people who are not ashamed of themselves are trying to hatch a sinister plot against him with a mischievous intention. If this is tolerable, what else is unforgivable? Anybody in the assembly daring to injure the Master will be beheaded, and anyone who insults or abuses him will have his tongue cut out. But no limit is set on the argumentation of those who wish to make a statement in defence of their own doctrines.

After that the evil people withdrew from their malignant attempt, and for eighteen days nobody started a debate.

In the evening when the congregation was about to disperse, the Master once more extolled Mahayana teachings, eulogized the merits of the Buddha, and caused numerous people to return from the wrong to the right and to discard Hinayana theories and embrace Mahayana teachings. King Śīlāditya respected him all the more and offered him as alms ten thousand golden coins, thirty
248a thousand silver coins, and a hundred robes made of high-quality felt. Each of the eighteen kings also offered him rare and precious things. But the Master did not accept any of the gifts.

The king ordered his attending ministers to caparison a large elephant with a canopy on it for the Master to ride. He also asked his noble ministers to accompany and safeguard him when passing through crowds of people and announcing that the Master had established his theories unchallenged. It was the custom of the western countries that the winner in debate be honored in this way. The Master declined to accept the honor and would not go; but the king said, "Such has been done since ancient times, and we must not do things against it." Then the Master's robe was taken to the people with the announcement:

> The venerable teacher from China has established the Mahayana teachings and refuted various heterodox views. During the last eighteen days nobody dared to hold a debate with him. It befits you all to know this fact.

All the people were delighted, and they vied with one another in giving him honorary titles. The Mahayana believers called him

Mahāyānadeva, meaning Divine Being of the Mahayana, while the Hinayana adherents named him Mokṣa-deva, meaning Divine Being of Emancipation. They burned incense, scattered flowers, and paid homage to him before they dispersed. After that the Master's reputation for virtue reached still farther.

To the west of the king's temporary palace, there was a monastery supported by the king. In it was a Buddha's tooth relic, about one and one half inches long with a yellowish white color. It often issued a bright light.

Once in olden times the Krīta caste in the country of Kaśmīra destroyed the Buddha Dharma, and the monks dispersed. One *bhikṣu* travelled far away to India. Afterward the king of Himatala in the country of Tukhāra felt indignant that the king of a slavish caste should have destroyed the Buddha Dharma. So he disguised himself as a merchant, bringing with him three thousand warriors and a large amount of rare and valuable things which he pretended to offer [to the king of Kaśmīra]. That king, being an avaricious man, was pleased to hear about this, and he sent an envoy to welcome the guests. But the king of Himatala was a person of a heroic and brave nature, as dignified and austere as a deity. When he approached the Throne, he removed his hat and reprimanded the king of the Krītas, who was struck with awe at the sight of the king in disguise and fell to the ground. Then the king of Himatala strangled his neck and killed him. He said to the ministers, "I am the king of Himatala. Because you slaves have destroyed the Buddha Dharma, I have come to punish you. But as it is the fault of one man, it has nothing to do with you, and so you may feel at ease. Only those who instigated their king to commit such an atrocity will be banished to other countries, while the rest of you will not be questioned." After having suppressed the wicked evildoers, he founded a monastery; summoned back the monks, to whom he made offerings; and then returned to his own country.

On hearing that peace had been restored in his country, the *bhikṣu* who had previously fled to India took up his mendicant staff and returned home. On the way he met with a herd of elephants that came trumpeting toward him. When he saw the animals, he

climbed up a tree to hide himself. But the elephants sprayed water on the tree with their trunks and dug at the root with their tusks. In a moment the tree was pushed down. One of the elephants put the *bhikṣu* on its back with its trunk and carried him to a big forest, where a sick elephant suffering from a wound was lying on the ground. The elephant placed the *bhikṣu*'s hand on its painful sore,
248b and he saw a bamboo splinter in the wound. So he plucked the splinter out, squeezed the pus and blood, and tore a piece of his robe to dress the wound. Thus the elephant was gradually cured. On the following day the elephants busied themselves in gathering fruits to offer to the *bhikṣu*. When he had taken the fruits, one elephant brought a golden casket and gave it to the sick one, who in turn handed it to the *bhikṣu*. When the *bhikṣu* had received the casket, the elephants carried him out of the forest to the place where they had found him. They placed him on the ground and knelt down to worship him before they went away. The *bhikṣu* opened the casket and found in it a Buddha's tooth relic, which he brought back to worship.

Recently King Śīlāditya heard that there was a Buddha's tooth relic in Kaśmīra, and he went personally to the borderland to see and worship it. But the monks were so illiberal that they would not allow it to be taken out and concealed it at some other place. Their king, however, feared the power and influence of Śīlāditya and so dug in the ground everywhere to search for the holy relic. When he had found it, he presented it to Śīlāditya, who had deep respect for it when he saw it. Depending upon his mighty power, he snatched the tooth relic and took it home and made offerings to it. This was the tooth relic just mentioned above.

After the assembly was dissolved, the king put the golden image he had made, together with the robes and money, in that monastery in the custody of the monks.

As the Master had already taken his leave of the virtuous monks of Nālandā and obtained scriptures and images, he desired to take leave of the king and return home on the nineteenth day when the assembly was over. The king said, "It has been more than thirty years since I, your disciple, succeeded to the Throne of the lord of the state. I always worried that my felicity and virtue were not on the increase and that my good causes of the past might not continue. Therefore I accumulated wealth and valuables and founded a great meeting place between the two rivers in the country of Prayāga, where every five years I invited the *śramaṇas*, the Brahmans, and the poor and desolate people of the Five Indias to attend an unlimited gathering to receive alms for seventy-five days. I have convened such gatherings five times, and I am now going to hold the sixth one. Would you not like to see the gathering and share the happiness of the people?" The Master said in reply, "In the course of practising the Way, a Bodhisattva cultivates both worldly welfare and spiritual wisdom. When a wise man has obtained the fruit, he will not forget the tree. If Your Majesty is not parsimonious in giving valuables and wealth to others, why should I refuse to stay a little longer? Please allow me to go with Your Majesty." The king was greatly delighted.

On the twenty-first day they started for the site of the grand almsgiving in the country of Prayāga, with the Ganges in the north and the Jumna in the south, both flowing from the northwest to the east and joining in this country. To the west of the confluence of the two rivers, there was a great tableland, about fourteen or fifteen *li* in circumference and as flat as a mirror. Since olden times all the kings came to this place to give alms; hence it was called the Site of Almsgiving. It was said by tradition that the merit of giving one coin here was greater than that of giving a hundred or a thousand coins at other places. Thus it had been held in esteem since ancient times. The king issued a decree that a site of almsgiving be built at the tableland, surrounded by a fence of reeds, one thousand paces long on each side. Several tens of thatched halls were built inside the fence to store various precious things, such as
248c gold, silver, pearls, red crystals, precious emeralds, and sapphires. Beside the halls were several hundred storerooms to keep silk robes and robes made of spotted felt, as well as gold and silver coins, etc. Kitchens were built separately outside the fence. In front of the treasure storerooms were built more than a hundred rows

of long houses, resembling the streets in the markets of our capital, each of them capable of accommodating over a thousand men.

Before the congregation the king had issued an edict inviting the monks, the heretics, the Nirgranthas, and the poor and desolate people of the Five Indias to assemble at the site of almsgiving to receive gifts. Some of those who had attended the meeting of the Master held in the city of Kanyākubja did not go back home but went directly to the place of almsgiving. The eighteen kings also followed the king to that place. When they reached the site of the meeting, more than five hundred thousand monks and lay people had already arrived there. King Śīlāditya encamped on the northern bank of the Ganges, King Dhruvabhaṭa of South India encamped west of the confluence, King Kumāra encamped beside a flowery wood south of the Jumna, and all the almsmen encamped west of King Dhruvabhaṭa's lodgment.

On the following morning, King Śīlāditya and King Kumāra sailed on board warships, while King Dhruvabhaṭa went with his elephant troops in an orderly and well-guarded array to assemble at the place of meeting. The eighteen kings and those below them in rank accompanied them in an orderly manner. On the first day the Buddha's image was installed in the thatched hall at the site of almsgiving, and the best valuables and robes as well as delicious food were offered to it. Music was performed and flowers scattered until nightfall when the devotees returned to their encampments. On the second day the image of the God of the Sun was installed, and half the amount of valuables and garments offered on the first day was presented to this image. On the third day the image of Īśvaradeva was installed, and the offerings presented to it were the same as those offered to the God of the Sun. On the fourth day alms were given to more than ten thousand monks, seated in a hundred rows, to each of whom were given one hundred golden coins, one pearl, and one felt robe. After food, drink, incense, and flowers had been offered to them, they left the place. The fifth group of alms receivers were the Brahmans, and it took more than twenty days to distribute gifts to them all. The sixth group of alms receivers were the heretics, and it took ten days to give alms to every one of them. The seventh group of alms receivers were people coming from afar to seek alms, and it took ten days to present gifts to all of them. The eighth group of alms receivers were poor and desolate people, and the distribution of gifts to them all took one month.

Then the king exhausted all that he had accumulated in his treasure house during the past five years, except his elephants, horses, and weapons, which he kept for the suppression of rebellions and the defence of the state. All other valuables including his own garments, gems, earrings, bracelets, precious headdress, necklaces, and the lustrous pearl in his topknot, were given away as alms, without sparing a single one.

When everything had been given out, he asked his younger sister to give him a coarse suit to wear and worshipped the Buddhas of the ten quarters with great delight. He joined his palms and said, "Since I accumulated these valuables I always feared that I could not store them in a strong treasure house. Now I have stored them in the Field of Blessedness, and they are really well stored. I hope I can always possess wealth and the Dharma to give them as alms to all living beings in all my future lives, so that I may achieve the Ten Capabilities and realize the Two Adornments."

249a After the conclusion of the meeting, the various kings gave their valuables and money to the people to redeem the necklace of gems, the topknot pearl, the royal garments, etc., which King Śīlāditya had given away as alms, and returned them to the king as gifts to him. In a few days the king wore his royal garments and his best jewels as usual.

Then the Master desired to take his leave and return home, but the king said, "I, your disciple, am only intending to spread the bequeathed Dharma together with Your Reverence. Why do you wish to return home so soon?" So he tarried for another ten days or so. King Kumāra was also solicitous to detain him and said to the Master, "If the teacher can come to stay in my country and live on my offerings, I will build one hundred monasteries for you."

Upon seeing that the kings were so earnest in their intention, the Master appealed to them sincerely, saying, "China is a country far away from here, and the Buddha Dharma became known there at a very late time. Although we know the main ideas, we are not able to understand the teachings in a perfect manner. That is why I came here to search for what was unknown to us. It is owing to the sincerity of the sages of my homeland who are eager to study the Dharma that I have been able to realize my wishes. Therefore I can never forget them even for a moment. It is said in a scripture, 'Those who impede others from studying the Dharma will be born without eyes for many lives in the future.' If you keep me here, you would deprive many monks of the advantage of learning the Dharma in that land. Wouldn't you fear the retribution of being born without eyes?" The king said, "As I admire and respect your virtues, I wish I could always support you. Since it would spoil benefits to many people, I am really afraid of doing so. Now I shall let you go or stay as you see fit. But I do not know which route you will take for your homeward journey. If you go by way of the South Sea, I shall send an envoy to escort you." The Master said in reply, "When I came from China, I reached the western border of my country, where there is a country by the name of Gaochang, the king of which is an intelligent, brilliant person who takes delight in the Dharma. On seeing that I was coming here to seek the Way, he was deeply pleased and provided me with abundant supplies for my journey. He asked me to visit him again on my way home, and I must not act against his feelings; I should go back by the northern route." The king asked, "How much provision do you need?" The Master said in reply, "I need nothing." The king said, "How can that be so?" And then he ordered that money and other things be offered to him. King Kumāra also offered him various valuables, but the Master did not accept anything except an *aurṇika* cape (made of the finest wool), presented by King Kumāra to be used in case of rain during the journey. Then he took his leave, and the kings and monks escorted him for a distance of several tens of *li* before they turned back. At the moment of parting, none of them could refrain from sobbing.

The Master, bringing his scriptures, images, etc., with him, travelled in company with the army of King Udita of northern

India. He rode on a horse and proceeded gradually. Later, King Śīlāditya sent an elephant, three thousand golden coins, and ten thousand silver coins to King Udita to cover the Master's travelling expenses. Three days after the parting, the king, together with
249b King Kumāra and King Dhruvabhaṭa, each bringing several hundred light cavalrymen, came up to say farewell again to the Master, so much did they accord him warm hospitality and cordiality. Four attendant officials, known as *mahātāra* (similar to our officials without portfolio), were dispatched to send the king's letters written on white kapok cloth and sealed with red wax to the various countries through which the Master would pass on his way, requesting that the authorities supply him with horses and escort him stage by stage until he reached the land of Han.

Starting from the country of Prayāga and travelling through the wilderness of a big forest toward the southwest for seven days, the Master reached the country of Kauśāmbī. To the south of the city was the garden presented to the Buddha by the Elder Ghoṣila. After having worshipped the holy site, he proceeded again with King Udita to the northwest. In more than a month he passed through several countries and revisited the holy site of the Heavenly Ladders.

Proceeding further northwest for three *yojana*s, he came to the capital city of the country of Vilaśāṇa, where he stayed for two months and met two schoolmates, Siṃhaprabha and Siṃhacandra, who were then lecturing on the *Abhidharmakośa Śāstra,* the *Mahāyānasaṃparigraha Śāstra,* the *Vijñaptimātratāsiddhi Śāstra,* etc. They were very happy to greet him. After his arrival, the Master also lectured on the *Yogaparikalpana Śāstra* and the *Abhidharmasamuccayavyākhyā Śāstra* for two months, after which he took his leave and continued his return journey.

Going northwest again for more than a month and passing through several countries, the Master reached the country of Jālandhara, the capital of the king of North India, where he sojourned for another month. King Udita then appointed a guide to escort him. Going westward for more than twenty days, he reached the country of Siṃhapura. There were then more than a hundred monks, all northerners, who carried scriptures and images and travelled with the Master on their way home. After more than twenty days, they came to a mountain stream that was infested with bandits. Fearing that he might be robbed by them, he always sent a monk to precede the others and asked him to tell the bandits, in case he should encounter them, "A monk has come from a distant country to seek the Dharma. What he has with him are scriptures and Buddha's images and relic bones. May you almsgivers protect him and not cherish any ill intention." The Master leading, the other monks followed behind. He actually met with some bandits on several occasions, but they did not do him any harm.

After travelling for more than twenty days, he reached the country of Takṣaśilā and revisited the place where King Candraprabha had sacrificed his head a thousand times in his previous lives. Fifty *yojanas* to the northeast of this country was the country of Kaśmīra. The king sent an envoy to invite the Master; but as he was riding on an elephant and had luggage with him, he was unable to go. After staying there for seven days, he proceeded northwest again for three days and reached the great Sindhu River, which was five or six *li* broad. His scriptures and images were loaded in a boat with his companions to sail across the river, while the Master waded through the river on his elephant. He had appointed a man in the boat to take care of the scriptures and some seeds of different kinds of rare Indian flowers. When the boat sailed to midstream, a turbulent gale suddenly arose. The waves tossed the boat and almost overturned it. The man who was asked to look after the scriptures was so frightened that he fell overboard, but was rescued by the other passengers. Fifty bundles of scriptures and flower seeds were lost, while his other property narrowly escaped damage.

249c At that time the king of Kapiśā who was already in the city of Uḍakhāṇḍa heard that the Master was arriving and went personally to the riverside to greet him. He inquired, "I heard that you lost your scriptures in the river. Did you bring any seeds of Indian flowers and fruits with you?" "Yes, I did," was the reply. The king said, "That was the cause of the gale that stirred up the waves and almost overturned your boat. Since ancient times, those who brought flower seeds to cross this river have always had the same trouble." Then he returned to the city with the Master, who lodged in a monastery for more than fifty days. As he had lost some of his scriptures, he sent a man to the country of Udyāna to copy the Tripiṭaka of the Kāśyapīya school. On hearing that the Master was approaching, the king of Kaśmīra, disregarding the long distance, also came personally to pay his respects to him and spent one whole day before he returned home.

The Master travelled with the king of Kapiśā toward the northwest for more than a month and reached the domain of the country of Lampāka. The king sent his prince to go beforehand to instruct the people and monks in the capital to prepare pennants and streamers to greet the Master outside the city, while the king and the Master proceeded slowly. When they reached the capital, they were greeted by several thousand monks and lay people holding pennants and streamers in a grand and spectacular manner. Upon seeing the Master, the people were very happy. After worshipping him they surrounded him and proceeded with him while chanting praise. In the capital the Master stayed in a Mahayana monastery, and the king also convened a great and unlimited almsgiving meeting for seventy-five days.

From here the Master proceeded again due south for fifteen days and went to the country of Varaṇa to worship the holy sites. Again going northwest, he went to the country of Avakan and also to the country of Jāguḍa. Again going north for more than five hundred *li,* he reached the country of Vṛjisthāna. Going out eastward from here he reached the domain of the country of Kapiśā, where the king once more held a great almsgiving meeting for seven days. Then the Master took his leave and continued his journey. Going northwest for one *yojana,* he reached the city of Grosapam, where he parted with the king and proceeded northward.

The king dispatched a minister commanding more than a hundred men, carrying fodder and food supplies, to escort the Master across the Snow Mountains. After a journey of seven days,

they reached the summit of the great mountain, which had peaks rising one higher than another and dangerous cliffs of different shapes. Some were flat and some steep with irregular features. It is difficult to describe in full the hardships and difficulties of climbing this mountain. After that the Master could not ride on a horse and had to walk with a cane in hand. Travelling for seven days more, he came to a high range, below which was a village of about one hundred families. The villagers reared goats as large as donkeys. He lodged at this village. At midnight he resumed his journey with a villager riding on a mountain camel to lead the way. That place was full of snow gullies and ice-covered streams; without a villager as guide, all the travellers feared they might fall into them. The following day he crossed this dangerous icy place. By then there were only seven monks with some twenty hired men and one elephant, ten mules, and four horses. On the next day he reached the bottom of the range. Going by a winding path, he
250a climbed up to another range, which looked to be snow clad; but when he approached it, he saw it was all white rocks. This was the highest range, and not even clouds and snowflakes could reach its top. In the evening of that day, he reached the summit of the mountain. The cold wind was so strong and piercing that none of his companions could stand erect. There was neither grass nor tree on the mountain. There were only rocks piled up high into lofty peaks, resembling a forest of stalagmites. As the mountain was high and the wind strong, no bird could fly over it; it could only stretch its wings at a distance of several hundred paces away on either the southern or the northern side of the range. None of the lofty mountains in Jambudvīpa surpassed this one in height.

The Master descended from the northwestern side of the mountain for a few *li* and came to a little piece of flat ground where he encamped for the night and resumed his journey the next morning. After five or six days, he came down from the mountain and reached the country of Andarāb, which was the old territory of Tukhāra. There were three monasteries with several tens of monks who studied the Dharma of the Mahāsāṃghika school. There was a stupa erected by King Aśoka. The Master stayed there for five days and came down the mountain on the northwest side. After proceeding for more than four hundred *li,* he reached the country of Khost, which was also the old territory of Tukhāra. Going again northwest from here in a mountainous area for more than three hundred *li,* he reached the country of Ghūr, which was situated beside the Oxus River and was the eastern boundary of Tukhāra. The capital city was on the southern bank of the river. There the Master had an interview with the grandson of Yehu Khan. As he ruled over Tukhāra, he claimed to be a *yehu.* The Master stayed in his *yamen* for a month, and then the Yehu sent guards to escort the Master on his eastward journey in the company of some merchants.

Two days later, he reached the country of Munjān. Beside it were the countries of Arini, Rohu, Kṛṣma, and Pārghar, all old territories of Tukhāra. Going again eastward from Munjān through a mountainous region for more than three hundred *li,* he reached the country of Himatala, which was also the old territory of Tukhāra. Here the customs were roughly the same as those of the Turks. What was peculiar was that the married woman wore a headdress with a wooden horn more than three feet high. It had two branches in front representing her husband's parents, with the upper one denoting her father-in-law and the lower one, her mother-in-law. On the death of one parent the corresponding branch was removed. When both parents were dead, the whole headdress was discarded.

Going again eastward from here for more than two hundred *li,* the Master reached the country of Badakshan, which was also the old territory of Tukhāra. Because of the cold weather and snow, he stopped there for more than a month.

Going southeast from here through a mountainous region for more than two hundred *li,* he reached the country of Yamgān. Again proceeding southeast by a dangerous path for more than three hundred *li,* he reached the country of Kurān. Going northeast from here over mountains for more than five hundred *li,* he reached the country of Tamasthiti (also known as *Hu-mi*). This country was located between two mountains close by the Oxus River. It produced good horses, which were small in size but of
250b sturdy build. The customs of this country lacked etiquette and

righteousness. Its people were fierce by nature, ill-looking in appearance, and different from those in other countries. Most of them had blue eyes. There were more than ten monasteries. In the city of Khamdādh, the capital of the country, there was a monastery built by a previous king. Above the stone image of the Buddha in this monastery was a canopy made of gold and copper and adorned with various gems, suspended by itself just over the Buddha's head. When anybody worshipped the image by circumambulating it, the canopy also rotated with him. When the worshipper stopped walking around, the canopy also stood still. Nobody could explain this miraculous phenomenon. (A detailed account of the establishment of this monastery is to be found elsewhere.)

Going northward from the great mountain in this country, the Master reached the country of Śikni. After traversing the country of Tamasthiti, he reached the country of Śāmbhī. Going eastward from here over mountains for seven hundred *li,* he reached the Pamir Valley, which was more than a thousand *li* from east to west and over a hundred *li* from south to north, being situated between two snowy mountains. As it was in the midst of the Pamir Ranges, flurries of wind and snow never ceased even in the spring and summer seasons. Since it was a place of piercing cold, there were scarcely any plants and no crops at all. The region was desolate and without human traces. In the middle was a large lake, three hundred *li* from east to west and over fifty *li* from south to north, situated in the center of Jambudvīpa. The terrain was high and protruding, and the lake was so vast that the eye could not reach its limit. There were hundreds and thousands of different varieties of aquatic animals, which produced a boisterous noise like the din of various craftsmen's workshops in the marketplace. There were also different kinds of birds, as tall as ten feet, with eggs as big as urns, which were perhaps what the Tajiks called huge ova in olden times. A river branched out from the west of the lake, flowing westward to the eastern boundary of the country of Tamasthiti, where it converged with the Oxus and flowed westward to the sea. All the rivers on the right side converged in the same way. Another big river branched out from the east of the lake, flowing eastward to the western boundary of the country of Kashgar, where it converged with the Sītā River and flowed eastward to the sea. All the rivers on the left side converged in the same way. Beyond the mountains to the south of the valley was the country of Balūra, which abounded in gold and silver. The gold was of a fiery color. The length of this lake from south to north corresponded to that of the Anavatapta Lake.

Exiting from this valley in the east, climbing over precipices, and walking on snowy paths for more than five hundred *li,* the Master reached the country of Kabandha. The capital city was built upon a lofty range with the Sītā River at its back in the north. This river flowed eastward into the Salt Lake (Lop Nor) and then became a subterranean current, coming out again at the Mountain of Accumulated Stones, which was the source of the rivers in this country.

The king was wise and intelligent and had been on the Throne for many years. He acknowledged himself to be a descendant of the *Cīna-deva-gotra* (the Divine Stock of Han). In the old palace of the king there was a temple of the Śāstrin Kumārajīva. This venerable teacher was a native of Takṣaśilā. Being a man of divine perception and refined manners, he recited thirty-two thousand words daily and wrote as many words in his treatises. He was so conversant with the Dharmas that they seemed to be child's play for him, and he was such a productive writer that he composed several tens of
250c treatises, all very popular works. He was the founder of the Sautrāntika school. At that time Aśvaghoṣa in the east, Deva in the south, Nāgārjuna in the west, and Kumārajīva in the north were known as the Four Suns, as they could shed light on the delusions of living beings. As Kumārajīva had a great reputation, the late king went personally to attack his homeland and brought him back in order to make offerings to him.

More than three hundred *li* to the southeast of the city, the Master went to a great precipitous rock where there were two caves. In each of them one arhat entered the Samādhi of the Cessation of Mentality, sitting erect and motionless and looking very thin and weak, but not collapsing or decaying for more than seven hundred years. The Master stayed in this country for more than twenty days.

Going northeast again for five days, he came upon a gang of robbers. His merchant fellow-travellers were so frightened that they climbed up the mountain, and his elephant was chased and drowned in a river. When the robbers had gone away, he proceeded again with the merchants, gradually descending toward the east. Braving the cold climate and travelling through dangerous ways for more than eight hundred *li,* he emerged from the Pamir Ranges and reached the country of Usar.

Two hundred *li* to the west of the city was a great mountain with very lofty ridges and peaks, on which stood a stupa. He heard an old legend that several hundred years before, the mountain had once collapsed with the shaking of thunder, and in it was found a dried-up and tall body of a *bhikṣu* sitting with closed eyes; his long beard and hair covered his face and shoulders. A woodcutter saw it and reported to the king, who came in person to see and worship the *bhikṣu.* Upon hearing about this, the common people assembled there from far and near and made offerings of flowers that were piled up in heaps. The king inquired, "Who is this person?" A *bhikṣu* said in reply, "This is an arhat monk sitting in the Samādhi of the Cessation of Mentality. He must have been here for many long years, so that his hair has grown to such a length." The king said, "How can we wake him up from his meditation?" The *bhikṣu* replied, "Once a person is out of meditation, his corporeal body that is sustained by material food will be ruined. We should first sprinkle ghee and milk over his body to moisten the skin and then strike a bell to wake him up. He might thus come out from meditation." The king said, "Excellent!" And he followed the advice of the monk, sprinkled milk over the arhat, and struck a bell. The arhat then opened his eyes and looked around, saying, "Who are you dressed in religious robes?" They replied, "We are *bhikṣu*s." The arhat asked, "Where is my teacher Kāśyapa Tathāgata now?" They replied, "He entered nirvana long ago." Upon hearing this, the arhat felt sorrowful and inquired again, "Has Śākyamuni Buddha achieved Supreme Enlightenment yet?" They replied, "He has already achieved enlightenment. After having completed his task of benefitting all living beings, he also has entered nirvana." On hearing this, the arhat lowered his eyes for a long time, and holding up his hair in his hands he rose into the air and performed a great miracle, which produced fire and cremated his body. His ashes dropped to the ground, and the king and the people collected them and built a stupa in which to bury them. This was the stupa that they built.

Going north from here for more than five hundred *li,* the Master reached the country of Kashgar (which was known in olden times as Sule after the name of its capital, but the correct pronunciation is Śrīkrītāti; the name Sule was incorrect). Again going
251a southeast from here more than five hundred *li,* he crossed the Sītā River, climbed over a large mountain, and reached the country of Chakuka (known as Juqu in olden times). In the south of the country there was a great mountain with many caves. Most of the Indians who had gained the various stages of sainthood came to live in those caves by supernatural powers, and quite a number of them entered nirvana there. There were then three arhats still living in the caves. Since they were in the Samādhi of the Cessation of Mentality, their beard and hair grew long gradually; so the monks went to shave them from time to time. In this country there were many Mahayana scriptures. Those that consisted of ten thousand stanzas each amounted to several tens of works.

Travelling eastward from here for more than eight hundred *li,* the Master reached the country of Kustana (meaning Earth Breast, that being the correct name used by the people; commonly known as the country of Hvamna; to the Huns it was known as Odun, and to the various Hu tribes, as Hotan, while the Indians called it Kustana; it was incorrect to call it Yutian in olden times). Most of the country was sandy land that was good for growing cereals and had plenty of fruits. It produced carpets and fine felt, and the felt-makers also spun coarse and fine silk. The land also had large quantities of white as well as black jade. The climate was temperate. The people knew rites and righteousness and were fond of learning and music; they deported themselves in a meticulous and correct manner, quite different from the customs of the other Hu peoples. Their system of writing was derived from the Indian language but with slight alterations. The Buddha Dharma was esteemed; there were a hundred monasteries with more than five thousand monks, most of whom studied Mahayana teachings. The king was a valorous and intelligent man with a martial spirit, and he respected and loved men of virtue. He claimed to be a descendant of the deity Vaiśravaṇa. His ancestor was a prince of King Aśoka in the country of Takṣaśilā who was later exiled to the north of Snow Mountain to be a shepherd. In the course of searching for water and grassland he came here and founded his capital. But for a long time he did not have a son, and so he prayed for one in the temple of the deity Vaiśravaṇa. A son was born to him from the forehead of the deity, and the ground in front of the temple produced something with a wonderful taste, as sweet and fragrant as milk, which was taken to feed the infant. In this way he was brought up. After the demise of the king, his son succeeded him on the Throne. The influence of his virtue spread far and wide, and he was so powerful as to have annexed many other countries. The reigning king was descendant of his. As his ancestor was nourished with milk from the earth, the country should correctly be called Kustana, meaning the Earth Breast country.

After entering this country, the Master came to the city of Bhāgya, in which there was an image of the Buddha seated, more than seven feet in height, wearing a precious crown and with dignified and perfect features. It was said by legend that this image was originally in the country of Kaśmīra and was brought to this city. Once an arhat had a novice who was afflicted with measles. At the moment of dying he wanted to eat some vinegary rice cakes. With his divine sight, the teacher saw that there were such cakes in Kustana. So he went there secretly with his power of divine feet and begged for some to give to the novice. After eating the cakes, the novice was happy and wished to be reborn in that country. By the power of his will he was reborn after his death in the family of the king. When he had succeeded to the Throne, he was brave and talented in strategy. As he was ambitious and desirous of annexing

the territory of other countries, he crossed the Snow Mountains to attack the country of his previous life. Then the king of Kaśmīra also selected his generals and drilled his troops to resist the invaders. The arhat said to him, "Do not take the trouble to raise
251b your weapons. I shall send him away." So he went to the place of the king of Kustana and told him the fault of cherishing a mind of craving and cruelty. When the novice's robe worn by him in his previous life was shown to him, the king gained the wisdom of knowing past events and felt deeply ashamed of himself. He renewed his friendship with the king of Kaśmīra and withdrew his troops, but he brought back with his army the Buddha's image which he had worshipped in his former life. When the image reached this city, it refused to be moved any further. Even when the king and his soldiers tried to move it with maximum effort, they failed to shift it. Thus a temple was constructed over the image, and monks were invited to live there. The king gave his crown, which he loved, to adorn the head of the Buddha image. The crown was still in existence with many valuable gems on it, and those who saw it praised it with admiration.

The Master sojourned there for seven days. When the king of Kustana heard that the Master had arrived in his domain, he came in person to welcome and greet him. On the day after the following day the Master continued his journey, while the king returned to the capital beforehand, leaving his son behind to attend to the Master. When the Master had proceeded for two days, the king dispatched his attending officials to meet him. He stopped for the night at a place forty *li* away from the capital. On the following day, the king together with monks and lay people received the Master on the left side of the road with music, incense, and flowers. Upon his arrival, he was invited into the city and was lodged in a Hinayana Sarvāstivāda monastery.

More than ten *li* to the south of the royal city, there was a large monastery, constructed by a previous king of this country for the Arhat Vairocana (meaning Universal Illumination). Formerly, when the teachings of the Dharma had not spread to this country, the arhat came here from Kaśmīra and sat in meditation in a wood.

When someone saw him dressed in a strange manner, he reported it to the king, who, upon hearing it, went personally to see and asked him, "Who are you staying alone in this wild wood?" The arhat said, "I am a disciple of the Tathāgata and am staying here calmly in accordance with the Dharma." The king inquired, "What is the meaning of the term Tathāgata?" The arhat said in reply, "Tathāgata is an honorable title of the Buddha, who was Prince Sarvasiddhārtha, the son of King Śuddhodana. Out of pity for all living beings submerged in the sea of suffering without salvation or rescue, the Prince abandoned all his property, all the seven kinds of jewels that were the possessions of wealthy persons, and gave up being a universal monarch ruling over the four continents to live in a quiet forest and practise the Way. After six years he achieved his fruition, gained the golden body of a Buddha, and realized the Dharma untaught by any teacher. He sprinkled the Sweet Dew at the Deer Park and let his *maṇi* pearl sparkle on Vulture Peak. For eighty years he taught his teachings for the benefit and delight of the people. When the cause of his edification had been fulfilled, he ceased to exist in his incarnate body and returned to Ultimate Reality. His bequeathed images and scriptures have been handed down until the present time. It is due to the good deeds you have done in the past that you are now a lord of men. You should assume the responsibility of turning the Wheel of the Dharma and wisely take refuge in it. But how is it that you are in such darkness as not to have heard about it?" The king said, "I was submersed in my accumulated sins, so I did not hear the name of the Buddha. It is by the benefit of the blessedness of my ancestors that today I am honored by the presence of a saint. Since there are images and scriptures bequeathed by the Buddha, I beg to have them so that I may practise the Way." The arhat said in reply, "If you have such a wish, you should build a temple first, and then a divine image will come by itself."

Thus the king turned back his royal carriage. Together with his
251c ministers, he selected a fine plot of land with discretion and ordered that good artisans be chosen. After having asked the arhat about the style of the building, they constructed a temple. When

the temple was completed, the king inquired again, "Now the temple is ready, but where is the Buddha image?" The arhat replied, "Just be utterly sincere in your mind. The image is not far from coming." The king and his ministers, together with the common people, burning incense and holding flowers in their hands, stood with concentrated minds. In a moment a Buddha image came down from the air and descended onto the precious pedestal, shining brilliantly with awe-inspiring features. The king was happy to see it and praised it without limit, and he invited the arhat to preach the Dharma to the people. Thus the king and the people of the country made profuse offerings to the temple, which was the first one ever erected in this country.

As the Master had lost some scriptures while crossing the Indus, he sent someone, after arriving in this country, to Kucha and Kashgar to seek new texts. As the king of Kustana pressed him to stay, he could not resume his homeward journey at once. Thus he wrote a letter and asked a servitor from Gaochang to go in company with some merchants to inform the court of China that he had gone to the Brahmanic countries to seek the Dharma and was now at Kustana on his return journey. In the letter he wrote:

> I, Śramaṇa Xuanzang, beg to make the following statement: I have heard that Ma Rong was a man of great erudition and Zheng Xuan went to Fufeng to study under him, and that Fu Sheng was a scholar with a bright and intelligent mind, so Chao Cuo repaired to Jinan to be his student. From this we may know that ancient people travelled far to acquire even the shallow learning of Confucianism. Needless to say, we should not be daunted by the long distance and give up the attempt to visit the mysterious traces left by the Buddha after he had benefitted living beings or to search for the wonderful teachings of the Tripiṭaka that will emancipate us from the bondage of ignorance. I undertook the journey because the Buddha flourished in the western countries. Although his bequeathed teachings had been transmitted to the East and the outstanding texts had been introduced to

our land, there were still many to seek to make them complete. So I always thought of going to undertake further studies, disregarding the safety of my life.

Thus in the fourth month of the third year of Zhenguan (629), I ventured to act against the law and the regulations, and I set out privately for India. I traversed the vast shifting desert, climbed over the lofty range of the Snow Mountains, passed through the dangerous way of the Iron Gate, and sailed across the billowy Hot Sea. I started from the divine capital of Chang'an and ended at the new city of Rājagṛha. The distance in between was more than fifty thousand *li*. Although I travelled through lands with a thousand different customs and encountered a myriad of dangers and hardships, I met no hindrance wherever I went, because I was depending upon Your Majesty's celestial prestige. I even enjoyed magnanimous hospitality, so that I did not feel fatigue or weariness and had my wishes fulfilled. Thus I could visit Gṛdhrakūṭa Mountain and worship the Bodhi tree, see the traces that I had never seen before, and read scriptures unheard-of previously. I witnessed all the divine wonders in the universe and perceived the transformation and development of the principles of *yin* and *yang* in nature. I also publicized the grace and virtue of Your Majesty so as to inspire the respect and admiration of the people in the countries with dissimilar traditions that I visited in the course of travelling around for seventeen years. Starting from the country of Prayāga, coming through the domain of Kapiśā, climbing over the Pamir Range, and crossing the Pamir Valley, I have now reached Kustana on my homeward way. As my elephant has been drowned and I have brought with me a large number of scriptures that I have not yet
252a obtained horses to carry, I have to stop on the way for some time and am unable to come by galloping steed to have an interview with Your Majesty at an earlier moment. While I stretch my neck and look up to Your Majesty with extreme respect, I am sending Ma Xuanzhi, a layman of Gaochang,

> to go with some merchants to present this letter before my arrival.

After that the Master lectured on the *Yogācārabhūmi Śāstra,* the *Abhidharmasamudāya Prakaraṇa Śāstra,* the *Abhidharmakośa Śāstra,* and the *Mahāyānasaṃparigraha Śāstra* for the monks of Kustana. In one day and one night he expounded these four treatises one after another. The king, together with the monks and lay people, took refuge in the Master and attended his lectures; and a thousand people came every day. After the lapse of seven or eight months, the messenger returned with an imperial decree from the court, promising to dispatch envoys to welcome the Master with an expression of regards. It said:

> We are extremely happy to hear that the teacher is coming back after seeking the Way in foreign lands. He may come speedily to see us. Let him bring back those foreign monks who understand the Sanskrit language and the meanings of the scriptures. We have already instructed the authorities of Kustana and other countries, asking them to escort the teacher, so that carriers and horses may not be lacking. The governor of Dunhuang has also been ordered to receive the teacher in the desert, and the governor of Shanshan, to receive him at the Jumo River.

Having received this decree, the Master immediately resumed his journey; and the king of Kustana presented him with rich farewell gifts.

After leaving the capital and travelling eastward for more than three hundred *li,* the Master reached the city of Pima, in which was a standing image of the Buddha carved in sandalwood, more than thirty feet high, that had a stately and awe-inspiring appearance and worked miracles very often. If a man was suffering from a disease, he might paste a piece of gold foil on that part of the image corresponding to his diseased part, and his illness would be cured at once. Whatever prayed for would mostly be fulfilled. It is said by tradition that this image was made when the Buddha was living in the world by King Udayana of the country of Kauśāmbī. After the nirvana of the Buddha, the image flew from there to the city of Araurak north of this country. Afterward it moved itself to its present place (the story is found elsewhere). It is also said by tradition that a prediction foretold that the image would enter a dragon's palace after the extinction of the Dharma of Śākyamuni Buddha.

From east of the city of Pima the Master entered the desert. After travelling for more than two hundred *li,* he reached the city of Nina. From here he again went eastward to the great shifting desert, in which the sand drifted with the wind and there was neither water nor grass, but many troubles from heatstroke, demons, and evil spirits. There was no path, and wayfarers had to look for human and animal skeletons as road signs when they travelled to and fro. It was difficult to cross this barren desert; one had to follow the traces and proceed from stage to stage. Going again for more than four hundred *li,* he reached the old territory of Tukhāra. Again going for more than six hundred *li,* he reached the old country of Calmadana, the land of Jumo. Again going northeast for more than a thousand *li,* he reached the old country of Navāpa, the land of Lulan, and finally the domain of his own country, after passing through many different places. Having obtained horses, he dismissed the messengers from Kustana, who returned home with their camels and horses. The local authorities wished to reward them for their services, but they departed without accepting anything.

Upon arriving at Shazhou, the Master wrote another letter to the Emperor, who was then in his palace at Louyang. When the letter arrived, the Emperor knew that the Master was approaching. He instructed Fang Xuanling, the Imperial Regent of the Western Capital and Left Premier with the title of the Duke of Liangguo, to order the authorities to wait and welcome the Master.
252b Having heard that the Emperor was about to go on a punitive expedition to the region near the Liao River, the Master feared that he would be delayed on the way and could not see the Emperor in time. Thus he proceeded with double speed and reached the canal so quickly that the authorities were at a loss how to receive him,

as they had had no time to lay out a reception in an impressive and dignified manner. But the people, who heard about his arrival, voluntarily rushed out to greet and worship the Master in the streets, which were so crowded that he was unable to move forward and was obliged to spend the night at the canal.

Fascicle VI

Beginning with His Arrival at the Western Capital in the First Month of the Spring in the Nineteenth Year and Ending with His Thanks for the Preface Written by the Emperor to the Scriptures and the Emperor's Reply in the Sixth Month of the Summer in the Twenty-Second Year

On the day of Jingzi [i.e., Bingzi, the seventh day] of the first month in the spring of the nineteenth year of Zhenguan (645), when the Master arrived with scriptures and images, Fang Xuanling, the Imperial Regent in the Capital and Left Premier with the title of the Duke of Liangguo, and some others, dispatched Houmochen Shi, the Great General of the Right Wuhou, Li Shushen, the Prefect of Yongzhou, and Li Qianyou, the Magistrate of Chang'an, to greet and welcome him. The Master entered the city by the canal and stayed at the posthouse in the capital, with a cloud of people following behind him.

On that day the authorities issued orders to various monasteries that carriages with curtains and gorgeous banners be prepared for sending the scriptures and images to Hongfu Monastery. The people were so delighted that they vied with one another to prepare the adornments. On the following day a great meeting was held south of Vermilion Bird Street, at which several hundred articles brought back from the Western Region by the Master were displayed in an orderly manner, including one hundred fifty grains of the Tathāgata's relic bones; a golden image of the Buddha's

shadow as left in the Dragon Cave at Prāgbodhi Mountain in the country of Magadha, three feet three inches in height including the halo and the pedestal; a sandalwood imitation of the image of the Buddha when he first turned the Wheel of the Dharma at the Deer Park in the country of Vārāṇasī, three feet five inches high including the halo and the pedestal; a sandalwood replica of the image of the Buddha made by King Udayana of the country of Kauśāmbī when he was desirous of seeing the Tathāgata, two feet nine inches high including the halo and the pedestal; a silver image of the Buddha, which was a copy of the statue of the Tathāgata descending from the Heavenly Palace by precious steps
252c in the country of Kapitha, four feet in height including the halo and the pedestal; a golden replica of the image of the Buddha preaching the *Saddharmapuṇḍarīka Sūtra* and other scriptures at Vulture Peak in the country of Magadha, three feet five inches in height including the halo and the pedestal; a sandalwood statue carved after the shadow image left at the place where the Buddha subjugated the venomous dragon in the country of Nagarahāra, one foot five inches high including the halo and the pedestal; a sandalwood image of the Buddha going around the city to collect alms in the country of Vaiśālī, and so on.

Displayed also were the texts brought back by the Master from the Western Region, namely, 224 Mahayana scriptures; 192 Mahayana treatises; 15 scriptures that were works on the disciplinary rules and treatises of the Sthavira school; 15 scriptures that were works on the disciplinary rules and treatises of the Mahāsāṃghika school; 15 scriptures that were works on the disciplinary rules and treatises of the Sammitīya school; 22 scriptures that were works on the disciplinary rules and treatises of the Mahīśāsaka school; 17 scriptures that were works on the disciplinary rules and treatises of the Kāśyapīya school; 42 scriptures that were works on the disciplinary rules and treatises of the Dharmagupta school; 67 scriptures that were works on the disciplinary rules and treatises of the Sarvāstivāda school; 36 texts on Hetuvidyā (logic); and 13 texts on Śabdavidyā (grammar), a total of 657 books bound in 520 bundles and carried back by 20 horses. On that day the authorities ordered all monasteries that possessed precious curtains, tapestries, banners, and other ceremonial appurtenances to assemble on the morning of the following day, the twenty-eighth day, on Vermilion Bird Street to welcome the newly arrived scriptures and images and conduct them to Hongfu Monastery.

With increasing enthusiasm and keenness, the people vied with one another in making the most splendid arrangements of banners and curtains, tapestries and canopies, as well as precious tables and carriages. These were brought out by different monasteries and were put at various places, while neatly dressed monks and nuns followed them. Court and monastic musicians played in front and thuribles were lined up at their back; several hundred such things were arrayed side by side in the street. They moved forward with the scriptures and images amid the tinkling of pearls and jade pendants, and golden flowers of various hues were scattered. None of the participants in the procession for sending the scriptures did not praise it as a rare occasion; they forgot the dust and fatigue and admired it as a rare event. Along the way, beginning from Vermilion Bird Street up to the main gate of Hongfu Monastery, a distance of several tens of *li,* the common people and scholars in the capital, as well as officials inside and outside the palace, lined up on both sides of the road, standing there to see the procession, and making the street so overcrowded that the authorities, fearing that they might tread on one another, ordered that they should burn incense and scatter flowers at the places where they were standing without moving about. Thus the fumes of incense and the sounds of praise continued from place to place.

Formerly, when the Tathāgata was born in Kapilavastu and when Maitreya first ascended to the Tuṣita Heaven, the dragons and deities made offerings to them and heavenly beings surrounded them. Although this procession was not as grand as those occasions in ancient times, it was a great event after the Dharma had been bequeathed to the world. On that day all the people
253a simultaneously saw a beautiful cloud of different colors appear north of the sun in the sky. It circled around above the scriptures and images and stretched over an area several *li* in circumference,

as if it were welcoming and escorting them. When it reached the monastery, it vanished out of sight.

> *Shi Yanzong's annotation:* By research and investigation of historical works, I found that this was what was known as the Vapor of Heaven's Jubilation. It was appreciated by learned people. Formerly, when the Tathāgata was born in Kapilavastu and when Maitreya was about to ascend to the Tuṣita Heaven, dragons and deities made offerings to them, and heavenly beings received and welcomed them. The present occasion was, however, not as grand as that in ancient times. Nothing so glorious had ever happened since the introduction of the bequeathed Dharma to the East.

On the twenty-third day the Master had an interview with Emperor Taizong at the palace in Luoyang. On the first day of the second month, he again saw the Emperor at Yiluan Hall, where the Emperor received him with great loving-kindness. After taking his seat, the Emperor said, "Why did the teacher take the journey without informing us?" The Master said in reply with an apology, "When I was about to take the journey I had repeatedly submitted petitions to Your Majesty, but as my sincere wishes were insignificant I was not favored with official permission. As I had an immense desire to seek the Way, I ventured to go in a private manner. For my guilt in taking action without authorization, I feel deeply ashamed of myself and fearful." The Emperor said, "As you are a homeless monk, you are treated in a different way than the lay people. We are glad that you could risk your life to seek the Dharma for the benefit of the common people, so you need not feel ashamed of yourself. But we wonder how you managed to reach that land at a great distance beyond the hindrances of mountains and rivers and through various places with peoples of different mentalities." The Master said in reply, "I have heard that to visit the Heavenly Lake is not far for those who can ride on a speedy wind, and it is not difficult to cross a stormy river if one sails in a dragon boat. Since Your Majesty held sway over the empire and pacified the Four Seas, your virtue prevailed in the Nine Regions and your benevolence covered the Eight Areas, with the wind of honesty blowing to the hot regions in the south and imperial prestige reaching so far as beyond the Pamirs. Therefore, whenever the rulers of foreign tribes saw a bird flying from the East, they would suspect that it started in the Superior Country and would bow to it to show their respect, not to say that I am a human being who has personally received education and edification from Your Majesty. Since I depended upon imperial prestige, I have been able to go and return without difficulty." The Emperor said, "This is but the saying of a teacher. We are not worthy of the praise."

Then he inquired in great detail about events in the lands west of the Snow Mountains and in the domain of India, such as the climate in the four seasons, the products and customs, the old traces of the eight kings, the ancient sites of the four Buddhas, and what was not mentioned in the writings of Zhang Qian or the Marquis of Bowang nor recorded in the historical works written by either Ban Gu or Sima Qian. As the Master had visited those places in person and had seen the countries and cities, he could remember all that he had heard and seen without forgetting
253b anything. He made replies in an orderly manner to whatever was asked of him. The Emperor was greatly pleased; and he said to his attending ministers, "Formerly Fu Jian praised the Venerable Dao'an as a man of divine personality who was respected by the whole court. Now we see that the Master's utterance is elegant and refined and his character and morality are pure and lofty. He is by no means inferior to the ancients but far surpasses them."

Zhangsun Wuji, the Duke of Zhaoguo, said to the Emperor, "It is as Your Majesty has remarked. I, your humble servant, have read the *Annals of the Jin Kingdom,* in which is related the life story of Dao'an, who was indeed a monk of noble deeds and erudite learning. In his time the Buddha Dharma was newly introduced, and there were not many scriptures and treatises. What he learned was but the branches and leaves of the tree. He was unlike the Master, who has been to the Land of Purity in person, done research into the origin of all the wonderful teachings, and visited the site where the Buddha entered nirvana."

The Emperor said, "What you have said is right." And he also said to the Master, "The Land of the Buddha is far away. His holy traces and the teachings of his Dharma are not fully recorded in our historical works. Since the teacher has personally visited that land, an account of it should be written to inform those who have not heard about it."

Through observation the Emperor also realized that the Master was competent to take the post of premier or minister, and so he exhorted the Master to give up the robe in order to assist him in administering secular affairs. The Master declined the offer, saying, "Since my youth I have been living a monastic life. I believe deeply in the way of the Buddha and I have studied his profound teaching, but I have learned nothing of the theories of Confucius. If Your Majesty ordered me to return to secular life, it would be like dragging a ferryboat out of water and putting it on land. Not only would it become useless but also it would get rotten for nothing. I wish to practise the Way for life in order to repay the kindness shown to me by the state. That would be very fortunate for me." In this manner he resolutely declined the offer, and so the Emperor desisted from persuasion.

At that time the Emperor was about to leave on a punitive campaign to the region of the Liao River, and the military forces were already concentrated at Luoyang. When he heard that the Master had arrived, he ordered that in spite of his busy military activities the Master should be ushered into the court just to have a brief interview with him. But he was so interested in the conversation with the Master that he was unaware that the sun had passed the meridian. So Zhangsun Wuji, the Duke of Zhaoguo, reminded the Emperor, "The Master is staying at the guesthouse of the Department of Protocol. I am afraid it is getting too late for him to return." The Emperor said, "We are in such a hurry that we have not yet fully expressed ourselves. We wish that the teacher could go with us to the East to see the place and observe the local customs, so that we could continue our conversation besides commanding the army. What does the teacher think of it?" The Master said with an apology, "As I have travelled a long way and I am

suffering from a rash, I am afraid I am unable to accompany Your Majesty." The Emperor said, "You have been able to travel alone to faraway regions; the present journey is merely a step for you. Why should you refuse to go with us?" The Master said in reply, "In the eastward expedition, Your Majesty will be protected by six armies. In punishing traitors and executing treacherous ministers, Your Majesty will surely achieve the merit of Muye (the place where King Wu of the Zhou dynasty overthrew the tyrannical King Zhou of the Shang dynasty) and enjoy the same victory as (Emperor Guangwu of the Eastern Han dynasty who defeated the troops of the usurper Wang Mang) at Kunyang. I think that my presence could render no service to the campaign but would simply make me feel shame at wasting provisions on the way. Moreover, a monk is prohibited by the disciplinary rules from beholding military operations. Since this is the teaching of the Buddha, I must report
253c it to Your Majesty. May Your Majesty show pity and compassion on me. That will be a great honor for me."

The Emperor accepted his words and ceased to invite him.

The Master said again to the Emperor, "I have obtained from the Western Region more than six hundred Sanskrit texts of which not a word has been translated into Chinese. I know that south of Song Mountain and north of Shaoshi Peak, there is Shaolin Monastery. It is located in a quiet place where there are springs and boulders, far away from noisy markets and villages, and was constructed by Emperor Xiaowen of the Later Wei dynasty. It is the place where the Tripiṭaka Master Bodhiruci translated scriptures. I wish I could stay there to translate the Sanskrit texts for the sake of the country. I am humbly waiting for the approval of the Throne."

The Emperor said, "You need not stay in the mountains. After your departure to the West, we constructed Hongfu Monastery at the Western Capital in honor of our mother, the late Empress Mu. In that monastery the courtyards set apart for meditation are quiet and peaceful. You may stay there to translate the Sanskrit texts." The Master said again to the Emperor, "As the people are curious and know that I have returned from the West, they are eager to see me and would thus turn my dwelling into a marketplace. It would not only be against the law but also impede me in my religious affairs. I hope that janitors will be appointed to prevent people from committing blunders." Being greatly pleased to hear this, the Emperor said, "What you have said is a precaution for safeguarding yourself; necessary measures will be taken. You may rest for a few days and then return to the capital to settle down at Hongfu Monastery. For whatever you need, just consult with Fang Xuanling." Then the Master took his leave and went back.

On the first day of the third month the Master returned from Luoyang to Chang'an and took up his abode at Hongfu Monastery. When he was about to undertake his translation work, he wrote a letter to Fang Xuanling, the Imperial Regent, Minister of State Affairs and Duke of Liangguo, requesting that he appoint assistants, such as theory-provers, literary composers, scribes, copyists, etc. Fang Xuanling ordered the authorities to make a report to the Emperor at Dingzhou, who issued a decree to the effect that whatever the Master needed must be adequately provided.

On the second day of the sixth month in the summer, twelve monks of great learning who were well versed in both Mahayana and Hinayana scriptures and treatises and esteemed by the people of the time arrived to be theory-provers, namely, Śramaṇas Lingrun and Weibei of Hongfu Monastery in the capital, Śramaṇa Huigui of Luohan Monastery, Śramaṇa Mingyan of Shiji Monastery, Śramaṇa Faxiang of Baochang Monastery, Śramaṇa Puxian of Jingfa Monastery, Śramaṇa Shenfang of Fahai Monastery, Śramaṇa Daoshen of Fajiang Monastery at Guozhou, Śramaṇa Xuanzhong of Yanjue Monastery at Bianzhou, Śramaṇa Shentai of Pujiu Monastery at Puzhou, Śramaṇa Jingming of Zhenxiang Monastery at Mianzhou, and Śramaṇa Daoyin of Duobao Monastery at Yizhou. There arrived also nine literary composers, namely, Śramaṇa Qixuan of Puguang Monastery in the capital, Śramaṇa Mingjun of Hongfu Monastery, Śramaṇa Bianji of Huichang Monastery, Śramaṇa Daoxuan of Fengde Monastery at Zhongnan Mountain, Śramaṇa Jingmai of
254a Fuju Monastery at Jianzhou, Śramaṇa Xingyou of Pujiu Monastery at Puzhou, Śramaṇa Daozhuo of Qiyan Monastery, Śramaṇa

Huili of Zhaoren Monastery at Youzhou, and Śramaṇa Xuanze of Tiangong Monastery at Luozhou. There arrived also one philologist, namely, Śramaṇa Xuanying of the Great Zhongchi Monastery in the capital. There arrived also one prover of the Sanskrit language and script, namely, Śramaṇa Xuanmu of the Great Xingshan Monastery in the capital. And other scribes and copyists as well as material requisites provided by the authorities also arrived at the same time.

On the first day (of the seventh month) the Master started to translate the palm leaf Sanskrit texts. He first translated four texts: the *Bodhisattvapiṭaka Sūtra,* the *Buddhabhūmi Sūtra,* the *Ṣaḍdvāradhāraṇi Sūtra,* and the *Prakaraṇāryavācā Śāstra.* Of these the translation of the *Ṣaḍdvāradhāraṇī Sūtra* was completed on that same day, and the *Buddhabhūmi Sūtra* was finished on the fifteenth day (of the seventh month), while the *Bodhisattvapiṭaka Sūtra* and the *Prakaraṇāryavācā Śāstra* were done by the end of the year.

On the first day of the first month in the spring of the twentieth year (of Zhenguan, 646), he began to translate the *Mahāyānābhidharmasaṃyuktasamudāya Śāstra,* which was completed in the second month. He also translated the *Yogācārabhūmi Śāstra.*

On the first day of the seventh month in the autumn, the Master presented the newly translated scriptures and treatises that had already been completed to the Emperor and attached a letter [that read] as follows:

> I, Śramaṇa Xuanzang, beg to submit the following words: I have heard that the teaching of the Eightfold Noble Path is a ferryboat or a bridge for crossing over the sea of suffering and that the doctrine of the Ekayāna is a ladder for ascending to the state of nirvana. But as the opportunity was not ripe (for introducing these teachings to the East), they were stored on the western side of the Pamir Range. During the reign of the ancient monarchs they were not heard of, and they did not reach us during the Zhou and Qin dynasties. It was at the time when Kāśyapa-Mātaṅga came to the region

of Luo that these teachings were spread over the area of the Three Rivers, and it was not until Senghui visited the State of Wu that the regions of Jin and Chu received their benefit. Since then the people have had cause to cultivate emancipation, and families can perform deeds of Bodhi. Thus we may know the benefit of transmitting the Dharma, of which the advantages are really great. After that Zhiyan and Faxian went abroad to seek scriptures, and Buddhatuṅga and Kumārajīva translated Buddhist texts one after another. Although they fanned the wind of abstruse teachings, both of them lived under the rule of illegitimate governments. Having risked my life to take the journey, I am the only person to have met with a noble and sagacious ruler to whom I could present all the scriptures and treatises I have brought back home. As Your Majesty esteems and respects the holy teachings, I have the honor to be ordered to translate them into Chinese. Working together with various theoretically learned monks, I have spent all my time, without wasting a single moment, with brush in hand; but I have not yet completed the translation of all the texts. What I have finished are five works in fifty-eight fascicles, namely, the *Mahābodhisattvapiṭaka Sūtra* in twenty fascicles, the *Buddhabhūmi Sūtra* in one fascicle, the *Ṣaḍdvāradhāraṇī Sūtra* in one fascicle, the *Prakaraṇāryavācā Śāstra* in twenty fascicles, and the *Mahāyānābhidharmasaṃyuktasamudāya Śāstra* in sixteen fascicles, copied separately and bound in eight bundles. These I have respectfully brought to the palace to be presented to Your Majesty. I also have the humble view that when the holy image was made in Hongfu Monastery, Your Majesty personally went there in an Imperial Carriage decorated with small tinkling bells to open the eyes of the image, which were in the shape of blue lotus flowers. So I hope that now, as the scriptures and treatises are first translated into Chinese as new literature of the
254b present glorious dynasty, Your Majesty will condescend, with the previous event as a precedent, to write a preface

> with the Divine Pen to extol the supreme teaching, so that the profound doctrine and the abstruse gists may shine as brightly as the sun and the moon. The words written by Your Majesty will last as long as Heaven and earth, to be read and sung for a hundred generations without limit and to be seen with admiration for a thousand years without end.

When the Master saw the Emperor at Luoyang on a previous occasion, he was ordered to write a *Record of the Western Regions,* which was completed by now.

On the fifth day the Master presented another letter to the Emperor, in which he said:

> I, Xuanzang, beg to make the following statement: I humbly consider that Mount Panmu and the State of You are recorded by ancient officials as having been the territory of Emperor Xuanyuan, and that according to the *History of Xia* the region from the shifting desert up to the blue sea was the domain of Emperor Yao. The white jade ring of Wangmu in the West was offered to the lord dressed in a loose garment (who governed by doing nothing against nature), and the fragile arrow made of a red vitex twig of the Yi tribe in the East was presented to the monarch who ruled over his land without resorting to punishment. These were past events of the bygone days, and the ancient classics are on the wane. I humbly consider that Your Majesty will grasp the time and make use of this opportunity to raise the level of and be an example to the people. By excavating trees into canoes and stretching strings on wood to make bows, you extended your prestige to the whole empire to succor the people. (Empress Nüwa in remote ages) cut four legs off a turtle to support the four corners of the earth, absorbed floods with the ashes of reeds, reclaimed the square land, and mended the dome of Heaven. Thus she displayed the seven military virtues and expounded the ten principles of moral culture. Her beneficence permeated all fountains and sources of rivers, and her edification benefitted mugworts and reeds (so that they

could be used to make musical instruments). (The time was so auspicious that) glossy ganoderma bloomed, and the water in natural wells had waves (a sign of good fortune). One took delight in parks with trees and ponds where musicians were trained and the notes were tuned by bamboo pitch pipes. Purple grease (as fuel to warm wine) was used in the palace, and white clouds flew over the jade covers of book containers. Thus a horse range was founded at the Ruo River, and a reservoir was constructed at the place where the sun set. A blazing fire was built to shine upon the accumulated ice, and one climbed up the slope of red clay to receive the Emperor's decrees and also sailed to the ford of the Canglang River to distribute gifts. History is devoid of such sages in the past, and such events never happened under the rule of previous governments. During the Han dynasty the government opened up Zhangye and approached only Jincheng, while the court of Qin stationed its troops at Guilin and had communication merely with Hepu, where pearls were produced.

I, Xuanzang, being fortunate enough to live at a time when the empire was under correct governance and peace prevailed in China and abroad, had deeply set my mind on the Brahmanic domains and ventured to be in keeping with good actions, although my life is as ephemeral as morning dew and my strength is comparable only with that of a katydid in the autumn season. It was depending upon the divine influence of the Emperor that I travelled with nobody but my own shadow, to worship the holy lands one after another, and wandered such a long distance that I stayed in many resthouses on the way. I saw the huge ovum of the Tajiks, which confirmed what I had heard before, and the solitary phoenix of Kaśmīra testified to its real existence in the old ways. As years passed, my wish was granted by Heaven, and thus I was able to go to the Snow Mountains and cross the Hiraṇyavatī River. I looked at Crane Grove and saw Vulture Peak. The road to Jetavana Garden seemed

to be still in existence, and the foundation of the city of Rājagṛha remained there on the slopes. I sought the holy sites and travelled to visit them. As time elapsed I spent more than twelve years before I started my homeward journey back to the imperial capital. The countries I have either heard of or visited in person amount to one hundred twenty-eight in number. In my humble opinion, Zhang Yun's book of travels only stated the extension of the places he had visited and nothing else, while Kuafu, though flying high, did not relate the natural conditions or social customs of the localities he had gone through. Ban Chao, the Marquis of Dingyuan [*yuan* means "far"], did not travel far, and Zhang Qian, the Marquis of Bowang [*bo* means "wide"], was not widely travelled, though he did see some places. What I have related now is different from what was heard before. Although I did not reach the limit of the great world, I
254c visited all the regions west of the Pamir Range and made a factual account of them without daring to add any embellishment in flowery language. With due compilation and abridgement, my work is entitled the *Great Tang Dynasty Record of the Western Regions* in twelve fascicles as copied separately. I hope that it will be publicized by your honorable pen and my incorrect wording improved, so that it may cover all the wide knowledge of the minister of Jin and enlarge the *Record of the Nine States* in the present imperial dynasty. But as my endowment is shallow and my learning short, my work must be full of omissions and defects. Moreover as I am clumsy in writing, I am afraid it is unworthy of perusal.

On the sixth day, a personal letter was written with the Divine Pen, in which it was said:

After reading your letter, we are fully aware of its meaning. You have been marked as a man of lofty deeds in your early days and were free from the secular world when you were young. You sailed in a precious boat and reached the yonder

> shore, and through seeking the wonderful Way you opened the Gate of the Dharma. You widely propagated the Great Way for cleansing and absolving people's sins. Thus when the cloud of compassion was about to roll up, you stretched it to shade the four quarters. When the Sun of Wisdom was getting dark, you made it bright to shine over the eight remotest points. Is it not the Master who rolled up the cloud and made the sun shine? Being shallowly learned and dull-minded, we are deluded even in worldly affairs. How can we fathom the mystic and subtle teachings of the Buddha? As for your request that we write an inscription for your translations of the scriptures, that is something we have not heard of. As to your new work, *The Record of the Western Regions,* we shall certainly read it through.
>
> The above is written to Monk Xuanzang.

On the seventh day, the Master wrote another letter to the Emperor which read as follows:

> I, Śramaṇa Xuanzang, beg to make the following statement: I have respectfully received Your Majesty's letter, in which I have been overpraised. Upon listening to Your Majesty's words, I shall pay more attention to my personal integrity and be more diligent than before. Having scarcely any achievement in learning, I have been excessively honored by being admitted into the Sangha. It is fortunate that the nine seas have limits and that vast space is free from obstacles. But it was by depending upon imperial blessedness that I was able to travel far, and what enabled me to seek the Way was the nation's prestige. I journeyed far through dangers because I was sincere in my undertaking. I collected exotic books and cherished the memory of distant countries in order to provide material for the court to carry out education and edification. I am honored to have been asked to translate the scriptures and treatises I have obtained. They are now bound into fascicles and scrolls, but without a preface. I

> humbly consider that Your Majesty's wise thinking is as high as a cloud spread in the air from which heavenly flowers fall splendidly. Your reasoning includes the principles of the *Book of Changes,* and whatever talented men you have selected are persons of outstanding ability. Your high repute will extend to the remote future, and your present good deeds have exceeded those of all the monarchs of the past. In my humble opinion, divine power is infinite, and without divine thinking nothing is adequate for the exposition of its truth. The Holy Teaching is profound and mysterious. How can its origin be made explicit without a preface composed by the Throne? Thus I venture to offend imperial prestige by requesting that Your Majesty write a foreword. The bounties bestowed by the Emperor are enormous, but I have not been favored with a promise. I often stroke myself with repeated sighs of regret and look at myself with disappointment. I have heard that the sun and the moon beautify the sky and also shed their light on doors and windows, and that the rivers flow on the earth but also moisten cliffs and crags. The grand music of the zither played on Mount Yunhe does not hide its melody from the deaf, and precious gold, jade, and other valuables do not conceal their brilliant luster from the blind. It is for this reason that I venture to repeat my entreaty. I humbly beg that Your Majesty will condescend with the might of thunder to grant me the favor of writing a composition that will shine like stars in the sky, last as long as Heaven and earth,
> 255a and hang in the air forever like the sun and the moon. The subtle sayings of Gṛdhrakūṭa Mountain have to depend upon the Divine Pen for their propagation, and the abstruse texts of the Kukkuṭārāma have to be expounded by sapiential language. So it is not merely for the limited number of monks to enjoy the benefit or for the multitude of ignorant beings to free themselves from worldly burdens.

Thereupon the promise was granted.

In the spring of the twenty-second year (648) the Emperor favored the Yuhua Palace with his presence. On the fourteenth day of the fifth month in the summer, the translation of the *Yogācāra-bhūmi Śāstra* was completed in a hundred fascicles.

On the first day of the sixth (seventh?) month, an imperial decree arrived, inviting the Master to go to the palace. When the Master had started on the way, imperial envoys arrived repeatedly, asking him to proceed at leisure and not to get tired. After his arrival he was very happy to see the Emperor at the Yuhua Palace. The Emperor said, "As we were troubled by the hot climate in the capital, we came to this palace in the mountains. As it is cool here amid fountains and boulders, we feel somewhat better and more energetic; thus we are able to attend to court affairs. But as we are thinking of Your Reverence, we have sent for you to take the trouble to come here. You must have been greatly fatigued on the way." The Master said gratefully in reply, "All the common people within the Four Seas depend upon Your Majesty for their lives. When you are feeling unwell the whole country is upset and anxious. Upon hearing that your Presence is here with a good appetite, whoever of the people with sentience will not dance with delight? May Your Majesty keep eternal sublimity as limitless as the sky. Being a mediocre person with meager knowledge, I feel it is a great honor to have been summoned by Your Majesty as if I were a man of talent. Filled with a sense of gratitude, I did not feel any fatigue."

Realizing that the Master was an erudite scholar with an elegant demeanor, the Emperor often considered pressing him to persuade him to give up his robe so that he could appoint him to serve in the court in managing state affairs. This he had mentioned to the Master before when he granted him an interview at the palace in Luoyang. He then repeated his request once again, saying, "Formerly the Emperors Yao, Shun, Yu, and Tang, and the lords of the prominent Zhou and the fiery Han dynasties considered that the state affairs of the empire were extensive and the duties of an Emperor were numerous. One's two eyes cannot see everything, and it is difficult to make good judgements with one mind alone. Thus the ruler of Zhou depended upon his ten good courtiers and the Emperor Shun entrusted five ministers to assist him in deliberating state affairs at the court and help him put the country in harmony. They were sagacious kings and wise lords, and yet they depended upon able and virtuous men for assistance. How can we, a man of little learning, act without the aid of sagacious people? Our desire is that you take off the dyed religious robe worn by Subhūti and put on the white dress used by Vimalakīrti, so as to ascend the path leading to the position of a minister, stating your political views and sitting in the courtyard under locust trees to discuss the Way as high-ranking officials do. What do you think of it?"

The Master said in reply, "As Your Majesty has said, the affairs of the world are extensive. Even the Three Monarchs and the Five Emperors of ancient times could not keep them in order alone, but had to depend upon various sages and wise men to achieve it. Confucius also remarked that what the monarch might lose, his ministers would gain to make it up; therefore the monarch is the head and the ministers are merely his limbs. I deem that this saying was for the admonishment of mediocre people and was not said for men of superior intelligence. If all monarchs who had ministers to serve them would always make achievements, then did the tyrannical rulers Jie and Zhou not have ministers to assist them? Drawing an inference from this fact, it is unnecessary to follow that adage. I humbly consider that when Your Majesty, as a lord of superior wisdom, holds the reins of government himself,
255b everything in the country will go smoothly by itself in good order. Moreover, since Your Majesty has possessed the empire by destiny, the whole country has been in a state of peace and happiness, and tranquillity and felicity have prevailed in and outside the country. This is but the result of Your Majesty's non-negligence of state affairs and non-extravagance in private life, and of your never indulging in sumptuousness and wastefulness but being cautious and conscientious, not forgiving even what is forgivable, thinking of danger while living in safety, and doing good deeds in accordance with the order of Heaven. Who else has done anything for it?

"Please allow me to cite two or three instances to clarify my point. Your Majesty's strategy of ruling over the whole empire within the eight directions in an orderly manner, your talent for employing and managing outstanding personages, your repression of rebellions and disorders, your upholding of peace and happiness, your intelligence and adroitness in managing state affairs, and your physical form, which is the embodiment of goodness and befits the supreme position, are all endowed by Heaven and not inherited from man. This is the first point. You promote what is fundamental and disregard the incidental, uphold kindness and advocate etiquette; you have removed frivolous habits from the customs of this decadent age and restored the natural political principles of the foremost ancient Emperor. In levying taxes the system of collecting a small amount of duties has been adopted, and for punishment light criminal codes are followed. All living beings that possess consciousness in the Nine States and the Four Seas are bathing in the waves of your beneficence and are living in safety and happiness. All this is done out of the sacred edification of your sacred mind; it is not inspired by any other man. This is the second point. The ultimate Way is connected with other bypaths. Your deep kindness reaches far to benefit the peoples beyond the region of the sun in the east, over the Kunlun Range in the west, to the edge of the Fiery Island in the south, and to the Great Wall in the north. Those who have the custom of tattooing their feet and drinking through their noses, and those who wear clothes made of *ko* hemp with lappets buttoned on the left side, all come, while forecasting the wind and rain, to kowtow and kneel down, offering precious treasure as tribute. They filled the guest house for receiving foreigners. This is effected by imperial prestige and not by any other man. This is the third point. The troubles caused by the tribe of Xian-yun started a long time ago. The Five Emperors could not subjugate them, nor could the Three Kings suppress them. Thus the region between the Yellow River and the Luo River became a wild place inhabited by uncivilized people with dishevelled hair, and the areas of Feng and Hao were turned into battlefields with the shooting of whistling arrows. The Middle Kingdom was on the

decline and the Huns enjoyed success; since the time of the Yin and Zhou dynasties they could not be pushed back or subjugated. Emperor Wu of the Han dynasty mobilized his troops, and the famous generals Wei Qing and Huo Qubing exerted themselves to the utmost. However, though the branches were cut off, the root still remained intact. Since then no more good strategy was heard of. But when Your Majesty ruled over the empire, just one campaign extirpated them all and overthrew their nests and lairs, without a single one left behind. The regions of the Mongolian Desert and Yanran Mountain were included in the empire as feudal lands; and the Chanyu with his tribespeople, who were good archers and riders, came to be subjects and concubines. If one says that this was the achievement of the ministers, then there had been numerous sagacious assistants to rulers since the Yu and Xia dynasties. Why did they not gain such an achievement? Therefore we know that this achievement was acquired by the one who possesses the Way and not by anybody else. This is the fourth point. Korea, a small vassal state, had been discourteous to the suzerain country. The Emperor of the Sui dynasty, commanding all the troops of the whole empire, personally went on three punitive expeditions. But while he attacked the cities he did not break even half a battlement, nor did he capture a single prisoner of war. He simply lost his six armies for nothing and returned home in an awkward predicament. Your Majesty went there for a short time,
255c and commanding a few myriads of cavalrymen you destroyed the strong formation of the guards of the enemy and broke the fortified cities at Liao and Ge. After that Your Majesty returned triumphantly in a grand manner with three hundred thousand prisoners of war. Although the soldiers were employed and the generals directed in the same way, the House of Sui lost its power and the Court of Tang gained sovereignty. From this we know that it all depended on the ability of the lord, without the aid of anybody else. This is the fifth point. Moreover, when Heaven and earth are in perfect communication with each other, the sun and moon shine brightly, an atmosphere of peace prevails, the clouds of rejoicing are rich and luxuriant, the five auspicious things appear

in substantial form, the unicorn emerges as a strange sight, and white wolves and foxes as well as red phoenix and red grass are clearly seen in a mixed way. Such things are so numerous that they are counted by thousands and crores, and cannot be cited one by one. All of them come in response to your virtue and are not caused by any other man. As regards the analogy of the ancient king who depended upon his ten courtiers to gain his merits, I presume to take a different view from that of Your Majesty. Even if persons are really needed, there are now many sagacious people as good as Yi Yin and Lu Shang. How can I, Xuanzang, being a humble, mediocre man, be competent to participate in political affairs? I wish to observe the Precepts as a monk and spread the bequeathed Dharma. I crouch to plead with your Heavenly Kindness not to press me to change my mind till the end of my life."

The Emperor was very much pleased, and said to the Master, "What you have just said are the favors shown by Heaven and are the spiritual manifestation of our ancestors as well as the efforts of our civil and military officials. How can we alone achieve such merits? Since you wish to propagate the abstruse Way, we shall not act contrary to your sublime convictions. Be effortful, and from now onward we shall help you spread the Way."

> *Comment by Shi Yancong:* The Master, being learned in both Buddhist and worldly lore, could give adequate answers in accordance with different circumstances. It is difficult indeed to possess such eloquence! Formerly when Dao'an remonstrated with Fu Jian, the latter did not stop his carriage (during his military operation). When Daoheng and Daobiao boldly explained their position as monks, they could not cause Yao Xing to change his intention (of persuading them to return to secular life) until the ruler incurred the insult of being defeated in a battle and suffered the trouble of escaping from the enemy. They could by no means compare with the Master who, just by making a scholarly statement, won the Emperor's consent and permission. His pure character turned purer, and his final aspiration proved

> true. From this we may say that we need not make an appraisal to see who was superior and who was inferior.

At that time Chu Suiliang, the Chief Privy Councillor, made a statement to the Emperor, saying, "Peace now prevails in the empire within the Four Seas, and the Nine Regions enjoy comfort and tranquillity. All this is due to the sagacious virtue of Your Majesty. As the Master has truly said, your humble servants did nothing more than occupy official positions. Under the light of the sun and the moon, what merit can a glowworm or a candle achieve?"

The Emperor said with a smile, "No. It is not so. A valuable fur coat is not made with the fur of a single fox, and a large amount of timber is needed for the construction of a great mansion. How can a ruler do anything by himself alone? It is because the Master wishes to preserve his moral integrity that he extolled and glorified us so profusely."

The Emperor asked the Master, "What scriptures and commentaries are you translating now?" The Master said in reply, "I have recently completed the translation of the *Yogācārabhūmi Śāstra* in a hundred fascicles." The Emperor remarked, "This is indeed a voluminous work. By whom is it written and what theory does it elucidate?" The Master replied, saying, "It is taught by Maitreya Bodhisattva for the exposition of the Seventeen Stages of Bodhisattvahood." "What are the Seventeen Stages?" inquired the Emperor again. In reply, the Master said, "They are the stage of correlation of the five cognitions, the stage of correlation of mental functions, the stage of having both deliberation and discrimination, the stage of having no deliberation but only discrimination, the stage of having neither deliberation nor discrim-
256a ination, the stage of *samāhita* (one's body and mind both fixed in meditation), the stage of non-*samāhita,* the stage of mental activity, the stage of non-mental activity, the stage of achievement by hearing the Dharma, the stage of achievement by reflecting on the Dharma, the stage of achievement by practising the Dharma, the stage of *Śrāvaka*s (disciples), the stage of *Pratyekabuddha*s

(self-enlightened Buddhas), the stage of Bodhisattvas, the stage of incomplete nirvana, and the stage of complete nirvana." And he also gave an outline and explained the gist of the work. The Emperor was so deeply pleased with it that he dispatched a messenger to the capital to fetch the *Yogācārabhūmi Śāstra*. When the treatise arrived, he read it in detail, finding that both the theories and the language of the work were more grand and far-reaching than he had ever heard before. He remarked to his attending ministers with admiration, "We see that Buddhist scriptures are comparable with the immeasurable height of the sky or the fathomless depth of the sea. The Master has obtained the profound Dharma from foreign countries; but as we were busy in military and state affairs, we did not have time to engage ourselves in pursuing the teachings of the Buddha. Now we have come to see that the teachings have a far and profound origin. We can hardly know their limits. Compared with the Buddhist teachings, Confucianism and Taoism, including all the nine schools of thought, are merely a small pond in contrast with the great sea. It is ridiculous that the world should say that the three religions are equal in value."

Thus an imperial decree was issued to the authorities to instruct the copyists of the Imperial Secretariat to produce nine copies of each of the newly translated scriptures and treatises to be distributed to the nine states of Yong, Luo, Bing, Yan, Xiang, Jing, Yang, Liang, and Yi for circulation from place to place, so that all the people in the whole land might receive the doctrines that they had not heard before.

At that time, Zhangsun Wuji, the Minister of Education, and Duke of Zhaoguo, Chu Suiliang, the Chief Privy Councillor, and some others, presented a report to the Emperor, saying, "Your servants have heard that the Buddha's teaching is so profound and abstruse that it is beyond the comprehension of heavenly and human beings. The principles expressed by the words are very deep, and the language barrier is difficult to cross. We humbly consider that Your Majesty is as brilliant as the ultimate Way, as a flying light shining upon the sun. You grant beneficence to places far away and give ample edification to the Central Region. Your Majesty protects and advocates the Five Vehicles and establishes the Triple Gem. Therefore Your Majesty has gained the acquaintance of a Master who has an elegant demeanor in the Age of Decline, such as is born only once in a thousand years. He passed over one obstacle after another to seek the scriptures, and travelled over dangerous roads to acquire the Way. He has seen strange and peculiar customs and obtained the true texts, which he has brought back home and translated into Chinese for propagation, just as [they were] originally taught [by the Buddha] in the Āmravana Garden. The refined language and abstruse teachings are just the same as what the Golden Mouth spoke. All these are effected by the influence of Your Majesty's holy virtue. We, your humble servants, being ignorant persons deficient in judgement, have the chance to participate in this event and thus have a boat by which to cross the rolling sea of suffering. Moreover, Your Majesty's heavenly compassion extends far and wide, spreading the Buddhist texts to all the nine states, so that the uncivilized masses of common people may also enjoy the taste of the wonderful Dharma. It is indeed very lucky of us to have met with what is rarely encountered once in a hundred million *kalpas*!"

The Emperor said, "This is due to the great power of the Master's compassionate vow. It is also due to your own good deeds, done in the past, that you could meet with this occasion. It is not caused by us alone."

The Emperor had previously promised to compose a preface to the newly translated scriptures; but as he was busily engaged in state affairs, he had no time to pay attention to the matter. At this time, as the Master had made the request again, the Emperor moistened his brush with ink and completed in a short time a composition entitled the *Great Tang Dynasty Preface to the Holy Teachings of the Tripiṭaka* in 781 characters. He wrote it with his own hand and ordered it to be placed at the beginning of the
253b various scriptures. The Emperor, [who was] staying at the Qingfu Palace, attended and guarded by different officials, asked the Master to be seated and ordered Shangguan Yi, a scholar of the

Institute for the Expansion of Culture, to read aloud the preface the Emperor had composed in the presence of all the officials. It was written in a brilliant and flowery style with the highest praise and extolment. The words of the preface are as follows:

> We have heard that Heaven and earth have visible forms to cover and carry all things that possess life, and that the four seasons, though formless, may potentiate cold and hot climates for the evolution of all things. Therefore by watching Heaven and scrutinizing earth, mediocre and ignorant people may perceive their origin; but by understanding and having a keen insight into the principles of *yin* and *yang* (negativity and positivity), even sages and wise men can hardly thoroughly comprehend the fate of the world. This is because Heaven and earth have forms, so they are easily perceived even though they contain the principles of *yin* and *yang*. While the principles of *yin* and *yang* are latent in Heaven and earth, they are difficult to grasp thoroughly because they are formless. Thus we may know that what has visible form may be perceived even by the ignorant without perplexity. But even wise people may be bewildered by what is latent and invisible, let alone by the Way of the Buddha, which advocates voidness, embraces quietude, and controls serenity, extensively saves people of all grades, and holds sway over the ten quarters. When its mighty spirituality is raised it has nothing above it, and when its divine power is withdrawn it has nothing below it. When it is large it may fill the whole universe, and when small it may be contained in a hair. It neither dies out nor exists, passing through a thousand *kalpa*s without becoming ancient. It seems to be hidden away from sight, but at the same time it is apparent, carrying down an abundance of happiness for a long time up to the present. The excellent Way is so profound and mysterious that no one could know its limits in proceeding along it. The Stream of the Dharma is so pure and calm that one could not find out its origin when dipping up water from it.

Thus how can the ignorant common people and small mediocre vulgarians be without doubt and suspicion when the purports of the Way are presented to them? But the Great Teaching flourished in its base, the Western Land. It was introduced into the Court of Han as the result of a clear dream of the reigning Emperor, and so it shone upon the Eastern Region with spreading compassion. Formerly when [the Buddha] was born in his own separate form with separate traces, his edification was achieved even before his words were spread. In today's world the people respect his virtue and know enough to follow his example. When his shadow faded away and returned to ultimate truth and he shifted his appearance to another world, his golden features lost color, without the luster of his three thousand rules of deportment. His graceful appearance was then painted in pictures, but they were devoid of the thirty-two physical marks when one looks at them. Since then his subtle words have been widely spread for the salvation of living beings in the three evil states of existence, and his bequeathed instructions have been propagated extensively to guide all living beings to the Ten Stages of Bodhisattvahood. But the true teaching is difficult to appreciate, and nobody can make the ultimate purport an all-pervading unity, while crooked theories may be easily followed. Thus disputes arose between the right and the wrong. The theories of unreality and reality were either accepted as right or denied as wrong according to convention, and both the Great and the Lesser Vehicles prospered for some time and declined by turns over the passage of time.

Being a leader of the Buddhist community, the Venerable Master Xuanzang has been pure and clever since his childhood, and realized the mind of three voidnesses at an early age. When he grew up he acted in accordance with divine sentiment. First of all he conceived the practice of the Four Endurances. The wind from a pine wood and the reflection of the moon in water are not comparable to his

purity and elegance, so how can the dew of immortality and lustrous pearls be a match for his brilliance and resplendence? Thus his wisdom is perfect without bondage, and his spirituality could inquire into what is formless. He transcends the Six Defilements and is far removed from the
256c world. He has been a unique person without an equal since remote times. He concentrated his mind on the inner domain and grieved at the decline of the Right Dharma. He fixed his consideration on the Gate of the Abstruse Teaching and regretted that there were errors and mistakes in the profound texts. He desired to make a systematic analysis of all that he had learned before, in order to cut off the spurious and perpetuate the genuine for the benefit of the learners of the future. Therefore he raised his mind toward the Pure Land and travelled to the Western Region, overcoming dangers through long distances and journeying alone with a staff in his hand. Accumulated snow flew in the mornings, and the earth was lost to sight on the way. Startling sandstorms rose in the evenings, blurring the sky into outer space. Crossing a distance of ten thousand *li* over mountains and rivers, he pushed through colored mist and proceeded with nobody but his own shadow. For many years, through the cold and hot seasons, he trod on frost and dew to follow the track forward. He attached importance to sincerity and slighted toilsomeness. What he sought after was profound, and his wishes were fulfilled. He travelled in the Western World for seventeen years and visited all the states where the Way prevailed to acquire the right teaching. At the twin śāla trees and at the eight rivers he tasted the flavor of the Way and took his meals in the wind. At the Deer Park and on the Vulture Peak he saw marvellous and unusual sights, where he inherited the golden sayings of former saints and received the true teaching from superior sages. He made researches into the subtle meaning of the Wonderful Gate and thoroughly mastered the mysterious deeds. The Way of the One Vehicle and the five schools of the Vinaya were

speedily accumulated in the field of his mind, and the texts of the Eight Stores and the Three Baskets were lectured on fluently through his mouth.

Then from the countries that he had visited he collected all the important texts of the Tripiṭaka, totalling 657 works, which were translated and spread in China for the propagation of superior deeds. The cloud of compassion was ushered in from the extreme West, and the rain of the Dharma poured down over the borderland in the East. Thus the Holy Teaching, which was incomplete [in this land], was made complete, and the common people regained blessedness after the purification of their sins. The flames of the house on fire were extinguished, and all people were saved from the wrong path. The bewitching waves in the river of desire were stilled, so that everyone could reach the other shore together. From this we may know that evils diminish because of [good] deeds, and goodness arises from [good] conditions. The commencement of the rising and falling depends upon man only. When an osmanthus tree grows on a high ridge, only cloud and dew can fall on its flowers; when a lotus emerges from pure water, no flying dust can defile its leaves. It is not that the lotus is pure by nature, nor that the osmanthus is undefiled by origin. It is owing to the height at which the tree is rooted that not even a tiny thing can cling to it; and as what the flower depends on is pure, nothing of the foul sort can contaminate it. Even inanimate flowers and trees thus depend upon goodness to achieve goodness. So how can human beings not draw support from felicity to win felicity? We now hope that the circulation of these scriptures will be as everlasting as the sun and moon, and that the blessedness gained therefrom will spread far and always be as great as Heaven and earth.

When the Master received the preface composed by the Emperor, he wrote a letter to him to express his gratitude:

I, Śramaṇa Xuanzang, beg to say that I have heard that the Six *Yao* Expositions of the Hexagram (in the *Book of Changes*) probe into abstrusity, but they are limited to the scope of birth-and-death. All things are properly named, but none of them touch upon the sphere of absolute truth. Yet one still has to make a deep study of the *Book of Changes;* and even if one sees the abstrusity one does not perceive its spirit. After thinking deeply over the lofty *Hetu* (the *River Plan*), one would attribute all goodness to it through repeated selection.

I humbly think that Your Majesty, the Emperor, condescended to make inquiries of me with your jade writing brush, and that your Golden Wheel is driven across the sky. You have extended the nine states of former monarchs, and your glory outshines hundreds and thousands of suns and moons. You have enlarged the territory possessed by succes-
257a sive generations and embraced as many *Dharma-dhātu*s (domains of the Dharma) as there are grains of sand in the Ganges. Thus the Jetavana Vihāra is situated within a fief of the empire, and spiritual texts inscribed on palm leaves are included in the Imperial Library. Therefore I travelled with my religious staff in hand for a distance of ten thousand *li* to visit Gṛdhrakūta Mountain; but under imperial prestige, it was very short for me. Without riding on a thousand-petalled [lotus flower], I reached the twin śāla trees in a moment as short as the time for taking a meal. I searched for the Tripiṭaka and saw all that is stored in the Nāga Palace. I studied the Unique Vehicle and made a thorough inquiry about the bequeathed theories at Vulture Peak. These have been carried back by white horses and offered to the imperial palace. Later I have been honored to receive an imperial decree ordering me to translate the holy texts. My knowledge is not the same as that of Nāgārjuna, and yet I have the honor to transmit his Lamp of Truth. My talent is different from that of Aśvaghoṣa, whose eloquence like water pouring out of a bottle caused me deep

> humiliation. There must be many errors and mistakes in my translations of the scriptures and treatises, yet I have enjoyed the imperial favor of having a preface composed by Your Majesty with concentrated spirit. Its wording excels the exposition of the symbolism and the Great Treatise in the *Book of Changes*. Its reasoning includes all the wonderful gates of the Dharma. Now this humble person has personally heard [from Your Majesty] the voice of the Buddha, making me dance with delight as if I had heard the Buddha's prediction. As I am extremely happy and grateful, I am presenting this letter to the palace to express my gratitude.

Upon receiving the letter, the Emperor wrote a reply with his own hand, in which he said:

> Our endowment is less brilliant than jade, and we are ashamed that our words are not broad and extensive. As regards Buddhist texts, we are particularly unacquainted. The preface we composed yesterday is very awkward and unpolished, and we fear that it would defile your writing inscribed on golden plates. It is like marking a heap of pearls with a piece of rubble. I have now received your letter, in which you overpraise us with high commendation. After making retrospection and consideration of ourselves, it made us feel all the more ashamed. It is not good enough to be praised and is unworthy of your thanks.

Fascicle VII

Beginning with the Composition of the "Statement of the Sacred Preface" by the Crown Prince in the Sixth Month of the Summer in the Twenty-Second Year and Ending with a Reply by the Master in the Second Month of the Spring in the Fifth Year of Yonghui

In the sixth month of the summer in the twenty-second year (of Zhenguan, 648), when the Heavenly Lord and Great Emperor (a title adopted by the Crown Prince later in 676 after his ascension to the Throne) was living at the Spring Palace, he read the Sacred Preface with respect and composed *A Statement on the Sacred Preface,* the wording of which is as follows:

> In displaying and propagating the right teaching, if one is not a man of wisdom, his literature will not widely spread. In the advocacy and exposition of subtle sayings, their essence
> 257b cannot be ascertained by a man who is not sagacious. The Holy Teaching of *tathatā* (absolute truth) is the mysterious gist of all Dharmas and the criterion of various scriptures. Its content is great and far-reaching, and its abstruse purport is lasting and profound, explaining the theories of voidness and reality in their extreme fineness and subtlety and embodying the essence of birth-and-death. The wording is ornate and the way it expresses is broad, so much so that a seeker could not find its origin; the language is apparent but the meaning is so deep that a practiser could not fathom its bottom. Thus we know that under the cover of holy

compassion no good deeds are unattainable, and that by the influence of wonderful edification no evil conditions cannot be cut off. It unties the headrope to open the net of the Dharma in order to publicize the right teaching of the Six *Pāramitā*s, and it saves all living beings from misery and suffering and opens the secret gate of the Tripiṭaka. Therefore its name flies far though it has no wings; and the Way, although without root, is steadfast for ever. The Way and its name transmit happiness to the future, and they always have done so since remote and ancient ages. The Buddha's body that moved in response to the needs of living beings will not decay for as many *kalpa*s as an enormous number of atoms. The sound of the bell in the morning and the voice of chanting hymns in the evening mingled on Vulture Peak; the Sun of Wisdom and the Stream of the Dharma turned the Twin Wheels in the Deer Park. The precious canopy that stretched in the air fluttered with the fleeing cloud, and the exuberant grass in the wild forest in springtime added its color to the heavenly flowers.

I humbly consider that His Majesty, the Emperor, having been blessed by Heaven, governs the empire within the eight quarters without taking any action. He covers the people with his virtue, and, dressing himself properly, he meets (envoys) from all countries. His grace is extended to the dead whose bones are rotten, and in stone chambers he stores palm-leaf texts. His kindness benefits even insects, and Sanskrit stanzas are kept in golden caskets for circulation. Thus the water of Anavatapta Lake is connected with the eight rivers in the Divine Land, and Gṛdhrakūṭa Mountain is linked with the green peaks of the Song and Hua Mountains.

In my humble opinion, the nature of the Dharma is immutable and quiet, and no mind that turns toward it will not comprehend it. The stage of wisdom is mysterious and abstruse, but when moved by sincerity it will become manifest. Shall we say that it is like a torch of wisdom shining in a night of darkness and ignorance and like the rain of the Dharma pouring upon the house on fire? Thus a hundred rivers flow separately, but they all meet in the sea; a myriad of distinctive meanings aggregate to constitute reality. How can King Chengtang and King Wu compare with His Majesty as superiors or inferiors? How can Emperor Yao and Emperor Shun compete with him in holiness and virtue? Master Xuanzang is a person who has possessed intelligence and goodness since his early days and resolved to be plain and simple. He has been sober-minded since he was a child, and he has pulled himself out of the world of vanity and ostentation. He concentrated his mentality in a chamber of meditation and lived in seclusion on a peaceful rocky mountain. He dwells in the third range of *Dhyāna* (contemplation) and roams about the Ten Stages of Bodhisattvahood. He surpassed the sphere of the Six Defilements and went alone to Kapilavastu, where he grasped the gist of the Unique Vehicle and instructed others according to circumstances. As there was nowhere to make inquiries in China, he went to India to search for true texts. He travelled far to the Ganges and obtained Mahayana scriptures at last; he repeatedly climbed the Snow Mountains and also acquired Hinayana texts. He spent seventeen years on his way there and back and thoroughly mastered the Buddhist texts with a mind to benefit all living beings.

On the sixth day of the second month in the nineteenth year of Zhenguan (645), he was ordered by imperial edict to translate at Hongfu Monastery the important texts of the
257c Holy Teaching, amounting to 657 books. The current of the great sea of the Dharma is diverted, without being exhausted, to wash away defilements, and the lasting flame of the Lamp of Wisdom is transmitted to dispel darkness with constant brightness. If he had not cultivated superior conditions a long time ago, how could he have revealed and propagated such Teachings? That is why it is said that the Dharma nature is eternal and as bright as the light of the

> Three Luminaries, and that our Emperor's blessedness is as solid as Heaven and earth. Now I have the honor to read the preface written by the Throne to the various scriptures and commentaries, shining upon ancient times and illuminating the present age. Its reasoning is expressed by exquisite phrases with the melody of music, and its literary style is polished by wind and clouds. I, [Li] Zhi, ventured to add an atom of dust to supplement the big mountain, and let fall a drop of dew to replenish the flowing river in citing the outlines of the preface in this statement.

The Master submitted a letter of thanks as follows:

> I, Xuanzang, have heard that the Seven Luminaries emit light and depend upon the high sky to cast shadows, and that the nine rivers spread moisture and flow unobstructed because the earth is thick. From this we may know the beauty of interdependence. Such being the case in natural phenomena, it is also true in the propagation of the Dharma, which has to depend upon men. There is no doubt about this reasoning. Your Highness the Crown Prince has given full play to your literary talent in repeating the Heavenly Composition to commend the Mahayana doctrine and glorify the theory of reality. It is written in a fluent style, like rolling pearls and polished jade, as splendid as the evening glow and unfolded brocade, shining brilliantly like the light of the sun and moon, and rhyming with the melodies of the ancient music of *xian* and *shao.* I, Xuanzang, being a humble person but very fortunate, bathing in special privilege, beg to submit this letter of thanks to express my deep gratitude.

It was then ordered that a reply be sent to the Master, which reads as follows:

> I, [Li] Zhi, have always been a man with little talent and learning, nor am I bright and intelligent by nature. I have not read any Buddhist texts, and in the statement I wrote about the preface there must be many vulgar and awkward

expressions. I have just received your unexpected letter in which you praise and eulogize me. After introspection, I feel both ashamed and uneasy. Your Reverence and other teachers took the trouble to reach faraway lands, which makes me feel deeply abashed [at my own inability].

Shi Yancong's annotation: Since the publication of the two holy prefaces, the princes and dukes, the vassals and religious and lay persons, as well as the common people danced with delight in praise of the Voice of Virtue. Both inside and outside the palace, the people praised the two compositions, and in less than twelve days they were widely known throughout the empire. The cloud of compassion cast its shade again, and the Sun of Wisdom shone brightly once more. Those who came to embrace Buddhism rushed in like waves and mist that had accumulated together. Is this why it is said that the edification of inferiors by superiors is like wind bending the grass growing beneath it? It was for just this reason that the Tathāgata entrusted the Dharma to kings.

At that time Abbot Yuanding of Hongfu Monastery and some other monks in the capital asked permission to inscribe the two prefaces on metal vessels and stone slabs to be preserved in the monastic buildings, and the Emperor granted permission. Later, the monk Huairen and some others of the monastery collected the characters from among the calligraphies of Wang Xizhi, General of the Right Army of the Jin dynasty, and had them engraved on slabs.

On the first day (of the seventh month), the Crown Prince, whose mother, the late majestic Empress Wende, had relinquished her people and died early in life, wished to repay his mother's
258a kindness by performing posthumous religious ceremonies as good deeds for the benefit of the departed. He ordered Gao Jifu, a Great Officer of the Middle Class and Acting Director of the Crown Prince's Right Palace, to make the following announcement:

I, a man of little virtue, am unfortunate in that my evil deeds caused trouble to the person on whom my feelings were concentrated, for when I was at the age of innocence,

> my loving mother left me behind in lifelong distress, which pierced painfully into my heart; and my sorrow at being unable to be filial to my deceased parent hurt me deep in my bones. On each anniversary of the demise of the late Empress, I expressed my grief and cherished a feeling of affection for my mother in vain, simply increasing the sorrow of remembering her in my mind. Although I kept myself away from the amusement of music, I could no longer sustain my mother in a filial way. My desire to repay her kindness, which is as great as Heaven, could not be fulfilled, and now I can no longer express my filial sentiment in the way a young crow feeds its mother.
>
> I humbly consider that the Way of enlightenment is great and compassionate and may give blessedness to the deceased. With the hope of expressing the affection of a child for his parents, I take refuge in the Way. The authorities should be ordered to select a suitable site at some disused temple in the capital for constructing a monastery in the name of the late majestic Empress Wende. When the construction is completed a number of monks will be specially ordained for the occasion. Trees should be planted and fountains made amidst the monastic buildings so as to render it a place with perfect scenery. I look up to imitate the perfection of the Trāyastriṃśa Heaven (where the Buddha went up to preach the Dharma for his mother), so that I may fulfill my wish to repay the unlimited kindness of my mother.

Thus the authorities carefully chose a superior location at the Jinchang residential quarter to the south of the palace city, facing Qu Lake. There a monastery was constructed at the site of the former Jingjue Temple. After the stars were observed and the land measured, it was built to resemble the imperial palace and imitate the Jetavana Park, with ingenious workmanship like that of the famous craftsmen Lu Ban and Chui of ancient times and the best timber from the Heng and Huo Mountains. In the woods there were plenty of rocks of fine grain, catalpa and cassia trees, and camphor and palm trees, and for decoration, pearls and jade, cinnabar and blue earth, ochre and chalk, and gold and jadeite were provided. There were more than ten courtyards, comprising storeyed buildings and complex halls, together with deep chambers and pavilions that towered to the clouds, and a total number of 1,897 rooms, fully furnished with beds, quilts, utensils, and other articles.

His Majesty Emperor Wenwu also read the *Bodhisattvapiṭaka Sūtra* submitted by the Master and praised it. Thus he ordered the Crown Prince to write a postscript to the scripture, which was written in the following words:

> It is said that the essence of the abstrusity of Emperor Fuxi is preserved in the script carved on tortoise shells, and that the correct profundity of the truth of Emperor Xuanyuan that probes into what is hidden and unrevealed is fully explained in the *zhuan* script in the shapes of birds. If one wished to verify the *Red Book* by examining obscure sayings, one would be ignorant of the origin of reality. If one consulted the literature written in green ink to do research into what is subtle and mystic, that would not be the way of permanence and joy. Yet their activities still enlarged and glorified the contents of literature and history and aroused the southeast wind blowing to the eight points of the compass. Their virtue benefited living beings, and they stirred up the waves of their influence so that it rolled forward to a myriad of generations.
>
> I humbly consider that His Majesty the Emperor, ruling over the empire with ease as a *Cakravartin* King, extended his edification as far as the Kukkuṭa Garden (Kukkuṭārāma), and that although he is residing in his superior palace, wearing his crown in an august manner, he is in spiritual communication with Vulture Peak. [The Buddha] with the title of the General Guide of Men is beyond the squinting perception of intelligent men, and the words of the Emperor sum up the teaching of *prajñā,* which is not comparable to

the theories of the Great Treatise and the Symbolism in the *Book of Changes*. Thus the teaching extended far beyond boundary markers and conveyed the voice of the Eight Emancipations, and its inculcation benefitted the whole empire comprehensively so that all people could proceed along the track of the Four *Dhyānas*. Thereupon the three thousand Dharma worlds could be expected to cherish all
258b living beings, and a hundred *koṭis* of Sumeru Mountains might enter the fiefs of the feudal lords to be prominent land guardians in them. The water of virtue of the Nairañjanā River is near the Blue Lake at the Imperial Residence, and the Āmravana Garden in Śrāvastī is connected with the exuberant wood of Shangling Grove. Although the nature of the Dharma is void and tranquil, it does respond to individual requests through spiritual communication; and the vehicle of truth, being deep and wonderful, is able to shed light upon all that is dark. This is why it is said that the great power that is on the Throne may deepen the Stream of the Dharma to the utmost, and that its competent benevolence holds sway over the movement of the sun and the moon and wipes the stones of stupas without end. His body is so well-proportioned and possesses such a good shape that it is beyond conception and description, and if one compares it with the beauty of former monarchs, they certainly cannot be mentioned in the same breath.

At the time when Heaven was separated from earth, the land was limited at the drifting desert, while Cathay was not bright and the divine language was hidden and undeveloped. Through spiritual inspiration, Emperor [Ming] of the Han dynasty had a dream on a dark night; and the remarkable sincerity of Empress Jin caused Buddhist scriptures to be brought to the White Horse Monastery. But it was merely like measuring the water in the sea with a ladle; one could not reach the edges of the Four Seas by only doing this. It may also be compared to peeping through a pipe; how could one perceive the abstrusity of the seven stars through it?

When the imperial spirit spread far, its prestige reached the outside of the Iron Enclosing Mountains. When the Most Sacred One was clearly elucidated, his virtue extended to the edges of the Diamond Ranges. In as many countries as the grains of sand in the Ganges, the people wear clothes and caps properly in a civilized manner, and the Gate of Emancipation is open so that they can tread on the Path of Reality. The stanzas in Sanskrit preserved in the Dragon Palace are surely collected on the Terrace of Purity, and the Lion's Roar of the Buddha as inscribed on palm leaves is stored in the Imperial Library. This Sweet Dew is sprinkled to moisten all sprouts and stalks universally, and this cloud of wisdom is lowered to benefit all birds and beasts. Is this not a manifestation of the superior deed of taking refuge [in the Triple Gem] and the spiritual inspiration of His Majesty's sagacious administration?

The *Bodhisattvapiṭaka Sūtra* contains the gist of the teachings of Mahābodhi (great enlightenment). It was by practising this Way that the Buddha realized the wisdom of non-rebirth, and all Bodhisattvas who accept it and hold onto it will attain to the stage of non-retrogression. It is the key to the achievement of the Six *Pāramitās* and provides the roots and potencies of the Four Unlimited Mental States. It is indeed a ford to cross to the yonder shore and a guide to the attainment of perfect enlightenment. In the middle of the Zhenguan period (627–49), Sindhu came under the political influence of the Emperor, who extended the use of his calendar by which the first day of each month was fixed across the hot slope; and treasures were transported over the suspension bridge. Since the language is similar and carriages are built with axles of the same length so that they can travel along common tracks, there was no obstacle on the way. Śramaṇa Xuanzang, holding his religious staff, journeyed out of Yumen Pass to seek the truth. Proceeding straight to the park at Vārāṇasī he reached Kuśinagara in the land of the Hindus, where he obtained this sutra. After

> bringing it back home he offered it to the Emperor, by whose order the text has been translated into Chinese. The task is now completed. After paying my respects to the Emperor, I spent my leisure time in studying the precious teachings of the wonderful Dharma with a pure heart. I have the honor to relate the Emperor's edict just to express my praise in a small way. Thus I ordered the authorities to write it down and attach it to the end of the text.

After that the Emperor's faith and friendly feeling increased day by day, and he made comments on the doctrines of the Dharma. He never stopped saying things about the Field of Blessedness and merits, and he did not leave the Master even for a single moment. Orders were issued to provide more supplies to the Master, and his seasonal payments and beddings were changed for new ones from time to time.

258c After the conclusion of the summer retreat on the seventeenth day of the seventh month in the autumn, a religious robe worth a hundred gold coins was presented as alms to the Master. It was so dexterously made that the stitches left no trace of sewing. In the palace storehouse there were many religious robes made at previous times, but none of them were good enough. So the Emperor ordered the ladies in the harem to make this one to his satisfaction, and several years were spent completing the needlework. Wherever the Emperor went in his carriage on inspection tours to the four quarters, he always brought [the Master] along with him.

In the twenty-second year (648) the Emperor favored Luoyang Palace with his presence. There then were the Ven. Daogong of Suzhou and the Ven. Huixuan of Changzhou, both persons of high character and learned in both Buddhist and worldly lore, who had won the praise of the court as well as of the common people. The Emperor summoned them, and after their arrival they were ushered in to take seats and exchanged greetings. Each of the two monks was wearing a religious robe presented by Emperor Wu of the Liang dynasty to their teachers. They had inherited the robes as treasures. As they came to visit the Emperor, they took them out and wore them. Smiling at the poor quality of the robes, the Emperor produced the robe [made for the Master] and showed it to the two monks, asking them to write poems in praise of it. The Ven. Daogong's poem reads:

> The Field of Blessedness provides a symbol of virtue;
> The seeds of the Holy Teaching are deeply perfumed.
> No gold is used as thread for sewing,
> But colors are employed to form patterns.
> Crimson and blue are mixed together;
> Emerald green gleams with the hue of silk.
> The separate stripes and pieces
> Resemble the patches of rice fields.

The last two lines of Ven. Huixuan's verse are as follows:

> If I may put it on for a moment,
> A Field of Blessedness it is to my content.

By this verse he indicated that he wished to have the robe, but the Emperor gave it to neither of them. However, he presented fifty rolls of silk to each of them. This was the robe mentioned above, and considering its exquisiteness, it was not for an ordinary person to wear, except for the Master, whose high virtue qualified him to use it. A razor was also presented to him at the same time. The Master expressed his thanks in the following letter to the Emperor:

> I, Śramaṇa Xuanzang, have respectfully received the gifts of a religious robe and a razor granted by Your Majesty. Special favors have been bestowed on me repeatedly and the good graces I have received from Your Majesty are great and conspicuous. Facing this kindness with sense of awe and uneasiness, I feel as if I were walking over ice in springtime. I am fortunate to have met with peaceful edification and joined the company of monks at an early age. But my three activities have not been brought under control, and the benefits I received from the four sources have not been requited. I do not deserve the kind consideration of Your

> Majesty, and I unduly enjoy your beneficence. In this robe of endurance the colors resemble the glow of sunset, and the knife of wisdom is sharp enough to cut jade. I shall protect myself with this robe against the evil spirit of defilement and carry the razor to break the entanglement of trouble in the mundane world. I am afraid I shall arouse more sneers from other people, and I fear that my shallowness of learning is unworthy of the glory that I venture to enjoy. I feel ashamed that I rushed about from place to place without any achievement. I hasten forward to bow with respect, and while I cultivate my mind with an uneasy feeling, my spirit soars high. With a feeling of great trepidation and gratitude, I am writing this letter of thanks to Your Majesty while I crouch and tremble with fear lest it disturb your serene mind.

The Emperor had toiled at military affairs since his youth. After succeeding to the Throne in accordance with the order of Heaven he always kept in mind the welfare of his myriads of subjects. During his punitive expedition to Liaodong, he suffered from the vile weather, the rain and frost. After he returned with his troops, his strength became much less vigorous than before; thus he worried about his life. When he met the Master he paid attention
259a to the Eightfold Path and protected the Five Vehicles, and then he recuperated and regained his health. So the Emperor asked the Master, "We intend to perform meritorious deeds, but which is most beneficial?" The Master said in reply, "Living beings lie in delusion, and without wisdom they cannot be enlightened. If you would foster the sprout of wisdom, the Dharma is conducive to its growth. As the propagation of the Dharma depends upon men, the most beneficial deed is the ordination of monks." The Emperor was thus highly pleased.

On the first day of the ninth month in the autumn, a decree was issued, saying:

> When the former Sui dynasty lost its power of governance, the empire was shattered to pieces. The people within the

> Four Seas suffered great misery, with all the eight quarters in turmoil and confusion like a seething cauldron. It befitted us to suppress the turbulence, and we had to go in person with our troops. We were frequently attacked by wind and frost and spent the night on horseback. In spite of taking medicine, we were not completely cured of illness. Only recently have we recovered health. Is it not a symbol of good fortune effected by good and beneficial deeds? Each of the monasteries in the capital and the various states of the empire should ordain five monks, with the exception of Hongfu Monastery, which should ordain fifty.

There were altogether 3,716 monasteries in the whole empire, and a total number of over 18,500 monks and nuns were ordained. Before then the monasteries in the empire had suffered destruction during the Sui dynasty and Buddhist monks had become almost extinct. After ordination was performed once again, Buddhist disciples were multiplied. How splendid that gentlemen of virtue should attach importance to right sayings!

The Emperor again inquired, "The *Vajracchedikāprajñāpāramitā Sūtra* is the source from which all Buddhas are born. The merit of hearing it without calumniation surpasses that of surrendering one's body in almsgiving and cannot be overtaken by offering as many gems and jewels as the grains of sand in the Ganges. Moreover, as its teaching is subtle and its wording concise, most virtuous and prominent gentlemen love to hold onto it. We are not sure whether the meaning of the previously translated text is fully expressed or not." The Master said in reply, "The merit of this sutra is really as Your Majesty has remarked. All the people in the West hold it dear and respect it. Now I see that in the old translation of this sutra there are a few omissions. The full title of the text in Sanskrit is *Vajracchedikāprajñāpāramitā Sūtra,* but the old version simply entitled it the *Vajraprajñā Sūtra*. It is intended to explain that for a Bodhisattva discrimination is regarded as affliction, and the delusion of discrimination is as strong as diamond. Only by the wisdom of nondiscrimination that is explained in this sutra can it be cut off; thus it is known as the *Vajracchedikāprajñā-pāramitā Sūtra*. From this we may know that the component part *cchedikā* (able to cut) has been omitted from the title of the old translation. And in the ensuing text one of the three inquiries and also one of the two verses are missing. Out of the nine parables three are wanting, etc. The teacher Kumārajīva's translation of *śrāvastī* and Bodhiruci's translation of *bhagavat* are more or less acceptable." The Emperor said, "Since the teacher is in possession of the Sanskrit text, we entrust Your Reverence with producing a new version, so that living beings may read a full text."

Since what is valuable in a scripture is its teaching, it is unnecessary to use polished language in contradiction to its doctrine. Thus the new version of the *Vajracchedikāprajñāpāramitā Sūtra* was translated according to the Sanskrit text. It was presented to the Emperor, who was very much pleased with it.

In the tenth month in the winter, the Imperial Carriage returned to the capital, and the Master also returned with it. The Emperor
259b had previously ordered the authorities to construct a separate house known as Hongfa-yuan (House for the Propagation of the Dharma) to the west of Ziwei Hall in the northern part of the imperial palace. After his arrival, the Master was lodged in it. In the daytime the Emperor invited him to stay to engage in conversation with him, and at night he went back to his house to translate scriptures. He translated Asvabhāva Bodhisattva's *Exposition of the Mahāyānasaṃgraha Śāstra* in ten fascicles and Vasubandhu's *Exposition* of the same work in ten fascicles, as well as the *Pratītya-samutpāda Sūtra* and the *Śatadharmavidyānikāya Śāstra,* each in one fascicle.

On the first day (of the tenth month) the Crown Prince again announced an imperial decree, saying:

> The construction of the Ci'en Monastery is nearly completed with all its lofty splendor, but there are no monks to live in it. An imperial edict has been issued to ordain three hundred monks and invite a separate group of fifty monks of great virtue to live and practise the Way at the divine abode.

> This newly built monastery should be named the Great Ci'en Monastery, and a separate house for the translation of scriptures should be constructed. The beams and ceilings should be painted in colors with decorative patterns of cloud, and the plinths made of jady stone. The steps of bronze, as well as the golden knockers in the shape of animal heads with rings in their mouths, should all be made especially resplendent. The Master is required to move into it to do his translation work and at the same time take charge of the monastic affairs.

Upon receiving the decree, ordering him to be the Chief Monk of the monastery, the Master wrote a letter to the Emperor to decline the appointment:

> I, Śramaṇa Xuanzang, beg to submit the following statement: I have respectfully received the imperial edict ordering me to be the Chief Monk of the Ci'en Monastery. Upon hearing this honorable order with a feeling of deference, my mind is so upset that I walked to and fro and held my breath, trembling with deep fear. My learning of the art of the Way is unsystematic, and my moral activities are scanty and unsubstantial. I ventured to take the vow to give up all I had in the hope that I might gain the Great Assistance. It was depending upon the spirituality of the Emperor that I travelled far to seek the Way, and what scriptures and commentaries I have obtained are to be translated under imperial order in the sincere hope that the Stream of the Dharma will gradually bring in moisture able to benefit the Throne, and that the Holy Teaching will continue to spread and glorify history.
>
> Formerly, when I was undertaking the dangerous journey, I was suffering from a rash for a long time, rendering me as weak and exhausted as a lame jade. I feared that I would not be able to fulfill my task, would fail to live up to the goodness shown to me by my country, and would be punished without pardon. The order that I should take

> charge of the monastic affairs would put me in a position of incurring reprimand, just as when fish and birds changed their nature and the flying and submerging ones lost their way. I humbly consider that His Highness the Crown Prince is kind and filial with talents endowed by Heaven. His love and respect come from his mind of intimacy. He is grieved at the loss of his mother and suffers from the sorrow of remembering his deceased parent. He has constructed a monastery to increase the Great Blessedness. To help and take care of the monks an able man must be appointed. If the wrong man is employed, things would become topsy-turvy. I humbly wish that the farsighted wisdom of Your Majesty will attend to the blessed cause of spreading the Dharma, and that Your Majesty will be kind enough to stoop to consider my foolish but loyal sincerity, so that this monk of the Dharma will not have to repent the fault of declining the appointment, and the fish and birds may each enjoy their own pleasures of flying or sinking under water. With utmost loyalty and sincerity, I am submitting this letter to express my circumstances while feeling a sense of shame, increased awe, and trepidation.

On the twenty-second day of the twelfth month, an imperial edict was issued that [Li] Daozong, the Prince of Jiangxia and Director of Ceremonies, should command the nine palace bands, and that Song Xingzhi, the Magistrate of Wannian, and Pei Fangyan, the Magistrate of Chang'an, should lead the musicians of their respective prefectures as well as the religious banners and canopies of various monasteries, which should be arranged in an extremely grand and solemn manner. On the morning of the twenty-third day
259c they assembled at the street of the Anfu Gate to welcome the Buddha's images and send the monks to the Great Ci'en Monastery. The procession was then arrayed in the thoroughfare. It consisted of over fifteen hundred carriages with handrails decorated with variegated silk and more than three hundred curtains and canopies, as well as magicians performing jugglery amidst

pendent streamers. On the previous day more than two hundred pieces of embroidery and paintings of the Buddha's image, two golden and silver statues of the Buddha, and five hundred banners made of satin and silk gauze sewn with gold thread were brought out from the palace and sent to Hongfu Monastery for the night. The scriptures, images, and relics of the Buddha that the Master had brought back from the western countries were then taken out of Hongfu Monastery and placed on curtained seats in various carriages that proceeded in the middle of the procession. On both sides in front of the images there were big carts moving along on which were erected long poles hanging banners. Behind the banners were the Divine King of Lions, etc., set as vanguards of the procession. There were also fifty precious carriages to carry various monks of great virtue, while the other monks in the capital, holding incense and flowers and chanting praise, followed behind. Next came the civil and military officials accompanied by their attendants and bodyguards arranged in rows. The nine bands of the Board of Ceremonies flanked both sides, and the musicians of the two prefectures followed behind them. The pendent streamers and banners and the bells and drums presented a riot of color in the air that dazzled the eye and produced loud noise resounding throughout the capital. When one looked as far as the eye could see, one could find neither the beginning nor the end of the procession. The Crown Prince dispatched his chief Guard Yuchi Shaozong and Deputy Chief Guard Wang Wenxun to command more than one thousand bodyguards to act as carriers. The Emperor also ordered Li Qianyou, the Imperial Inspector, to be Grand Astrologer and assist the Marquis of Wu in supervising the procession. The Emperor, attended by the Crown Prince and the ladies of the harem, stayed on the tower-arch of the Anfu Gate with a thurible in his hand, watching the procession passing by him with great delight. Tens of thousands of people on the street looked on the procession. When the scriptures and the Buddha images reached the gate of the monastery, the Duke of Zhao and the Duke of Ying, together with Chu Suiliang, Chief of the Imperial Secretariat, were ordered by the Emperor to receive and place them in the main hall while holding censers in their hands. The nine bands played music, and dancers performed the Dance of Triumph and other acrobatic feats in the courtyard. When this was over they returned home.

On the twenty-sixth day (of the twelfth month), the ceremony for the ordination of monks was ready to be performed. On the twenty-fifth day the Crown Prince left his palace and spent the night at his old residence. On the morning of the following day he came from south of the monastery with his guard of honor lined up in rows, holding flags decorated with feathers fixed on poles. When he reached the gate he alighted from his carriage and walked into the monastery with all his officials following him in attendance. After worshipping the Buddha's image, he had an interview with fifty monks of great virtue, to whom he related his purpose in building the monastery, with sobs as he spoke, and his sentiment affected those who were beside him. None of the attending ministers and monks did not shed tears of sympathy. Considering his emotion of filial piety he might be regarded as an Emperor Shun of his time.

Having finished his talk with the monks, he ascended the eastern pavilion of the main hall and ordered Zhang Xingcheng, Deputy Manager of General Affairs to the Crown Prince, to proclaim an imperial decree of amnesty to all prisoners then confined in the capital, and he had [the new monks'] hair shaved. Then he watched them having their midday meal. After presenting gifts of rolls of silk to the princes and dukes and those below them in rank, the Crown Prince had the people cleared away and descended from the pavilion to worship the Buddha image. He then went to have a look through the buildings of the monastery with his wife and others. When he came to the chamber of the Master, he composed a poem with five characters to a line and pasted it on the door,
260a reading:

> Halting my carriage to see the Hall of Bliss,
> I looked at the imperial capital in the far distance.
> Around the sun the Dharma Wheel is turning;
> Touching the clouds, the gorgeous canopy is fluttering.

The emerald mist renders the splendid pavilion fragrant;
Red sunset shines upon my precious raiment.
The colors of the rainbow on the banners are mixed far
away,
Beyond space the hues stay separately.
To the Tenth Stage I have serenely attained,
As in myself the Triple Gem I comprehend.

After visiting the monastery, the Crown Prince returned to his palace. Both the monks and the laymen of the time felt glad and happy and congratulated one another. All of them sang his praises, saying that the abstruse Way was revived, that the Buddha's bequeathed Dharma would prosper again, and that such an affair had never happened in ancient days or in recent times.

On that day an imperial decree was issued asking the Master to return to the northern palace.

In the fourth month of the summer in the twenty-third year (649) the Emperor favored the Cuiwei Palace with his presence, and both the Crown Prince and the Master accompanied him. After his arrival, the Emperor, besides attending to state affairs, only discussed metaphysics and the Way with the Master. He asked him about the law of causation and retribution, as well as about the holy traces left by former sages in the Western Region. The Master answered all the questions with quotations from scriptures, which the Emperor accepted with deep faith; he often pushed up his sleeves and remarked with a sigh, "We met the teacher too late, so that we did not perform Buddhist affairs more extensively."

When the Emperor left the capital he was, though slightly indisposed, still filled with divine dignity and wise discernment as usual. On the twenty-sixth day of the fifth month, he suffered a slight headache and kept the Master to spend the night in the palace. On the twenty-seventh day he died at Hanfeng Hall, but his demise was kept a secret and was not announced until his remains were brought back to the capital, where his coffin was laid at the Taiji Hall. On that day the ascension of the Crown Prince to the Throne took place beside the coffin; his reign title was changed to Yonghui in the following year. The people in the whole empire wailed grievously as if their parents were dead.

The Master returned to Ci'en Monastery and engaged exclusively in his translation work without wasting a single moment. He made a timetable for himself; and if he did not complete his work because of the interference of some business or other in the daytime, he would finish it at night. He put down his pen only after the second watch. When he had laid aside the scriptures, he would worship the Buddha's image as a means of practising the Way until the third watch and then go to sleep for some time. In the fifth watch he would get up to read the Sanskrit texts and mark out with red ink the paragraphs he would translate the following day. After the midday meal and for two divisions of time in the evening every day, he would lecture on the newly translated scriptures and commentaries. The student monks and others from various regions always came at this time to solve their doubts and ask for elucidation. Since he was abbot of the monastery, monastic affairs were also brought up for his attention. Palace envoys were sent to perform meritorious deeds. They made altogether ten complete sets of all scriptures, as well as producing more than two hundred images of the Buddha made of double ramie and decorated with gems. In the performance of all these works, they solicited the Master's advice. When the sun had set in the evenings, more than a hundred disciples in the monastery would all flock into the corridors and side rooms to seek his admonitions. He would answer their questions and handle their dubious points without missing a single person. Although he had to attend to the various duties that were focused on him, he coped with them in a leisurely manner without confusion. He also talked with the virtuous monks about the theories established by the saints and sages of the West and about the heterodox views of different schools as well as
260b how he attended lectures at various learning centers in the capital when he was young. He was so unusually energetic and full of vigor that he often talked eloquently in high spirits without feeling tired. Several princes and ministers often came to worship the Buddha and repented of their faults. Through the reception and

inducement of the Master, they cherished the mind to attain enlightenment. They all gave up their supercilious and ostentatious manners and praised the Master with reverence.

On the eighth day of the first month in the spring of the second year (651), Jia Dunze, the governor of Yingzhou; Li Daoyu, the governor of Puzhou; Du Shenglun, the governor of Cuzhou; and Xiao Rui, the governor of Hengzhou, who were in the capital to attend a court assembly, made an appointment to visit the Master when they were free from public affairs and asked to receive the Bodhisattva Precepts. The Master granted their request accordingly. He explained to them in detail the practices of a Bodhisattva, and exhorted them to serve their monarch with loyalty and treat those below them with love and kindness. The governors took leave of the Master and went away. They offered their well-earned money and dispatched a messenger to take a letter to the Master to express their gratitude for having received the Bodhisattva Precepts. The letter reads:

> We presume that it was not to satisfy his physical desire for food that the Tathāgata accepted the meal offered by Cunda, and that the Dharma was in need of nothing but was taught by Vimalakīrti at the request of Mañjuśrī. These things were done for the purpose of showing the immutable constancy of ultimate truth and manifesting the identity of ordinary and saintly persons. They were also done for the sake of receiving the people according to their capacity of understanding, and propagating the Way by means of phenomena. The one who does the deed expresses his sincere respect for the Dharma, and the one who receives the deed gains the blessedness of practising almsgiving. How can we say that their mind is attached to this or that, or that their intention is stained by [the desire for] fame and profit? We respectfully believe that you have planted the root of virtue in the past not merely at the time of one, two, or three Buddhas, and that you deeply understand the aspects of the Dharma, being learned in the scriptures of the Twelve

Divisions. You realized the true teaching by yourself and travelled far to look for holy sites, visiting the pure land of Gṛdhrakūṭa Mountain and bathing in the limpid water of the Ganges. You went deep into the world of the Dharma to seek good advisors, collected the most excellent texts to be handed down for a hundred generations in the future, and also probed into the abstruse doctrine that was advocated a thousand years ago. You received officials of all grades, disregarding whether they were brilliant or unintelligent, and treated them all equally without giving priority to anyone.

As we are unaware of the two categories of voidness, we are submerged through our own deeds in the three spheres of the world, just like a silkworm bound by its own silk, or the winch over a well that keeps on turning without cease. However, we have faith in the teaching of which we have acquired comprehension and understanding, take refuge in it with homage, and adhere to the theory expounded by the Four Propositions. We engage ourselves in meditation at secluded places, while abhorring suffering and seeking permanent happiness. But we were obstructed by ignorance for a long time in the past; and at the present time we are in the dark about the ultimate truth, not knowing that the Buddha nature is within ourselves and that external environments are but the reflection of consciousness. Our minds are not free from grasping at theories concerning existence and nonexistence. It is impossible to enter the Eightfold Noble Path by going through the Eight Erroneous Practices or to reach the Way of the Buddha by travelling on the wrong path. We are like [people] wishing to cross the sea without a boat, or facing a wall that obstructs our sight. Yesterday, as we had some spare time, we were able to pay you a visit, and you condescended to receive us and granted us the Bodhisattva Precepts. You gave us the Dharma that we had never heard before and aroused in us the supreme mind of the Way. One thought may break through the infinite, and
260c the four boundless mental states will pass into the future.

> The seed of Bodhi arises from passions, and a lotus flower growing out of fire is inadequate to compare to it. Thus we begin to know that the nature of the Tathāgata is none other than that of the world, and that nirvana is not different from birth-and-death. The practice of *prajñā* (wisdom) is the nonpractice of it, and the attainment of Bodhi is on the contrary non-attainment. Being persons of little intelligence, we have heard the Great Teaching all of a sudden, accepted it reverentially, and pondered on it with unlimited delight. The action of *dāna* (almsgiving) has six meanings, of which the *dāna* of the Dharma excels all the others. There are three positions of honor, and the teacher occupies one of them. With great compassion he benefits all living beings, but he does so like the sun and moon shedding light upon all without intention. We turn up to the light with a feeling of gratitude, resembling the sunflower and the bishop-wort that are sensitive to sunlight. Once when the Bodhisattva heard the Dharma, he sacrificed his body; we can never hope to do this. At the sight of the Buddha the young prince [Aśoka] offered him a handful of earth; this is an example we may venture to follow. We are sending you a small gift, as stated separately, to express our minds of respect. We hope that in accordance with our sincerity, this will produce a good result in the Field of Blessedness. After accepting this small gift you may spend it as you wish, just as a drop of dew added to the sea may deepen the Bohai Sea, and flying dust may accumulate into a mountain as lasting and strong as Mount Sumeru is durable and enlargeable. That will be very, very fortunate indeed! As it is still rather cold in the spring season, we hope you will take proper care of yourself. We are submitting this letter to you to express our respect and for no other reason. With homage from Jia Dunze and others.

He was adored like this by the worthy personages at the Imperial Court.

In the third month in the spring of the third year (652) the Master intended to build a stone pagoda south of the main gate of the monastery, because he feared that as human affairs were inconstant the scriptures might be lost in the course of successive changes, and also as a means for preventing fire disaster. The pagoda was designed to be thirty *zhang* in height, with the intention of showing the magnificent foundation of the great country and in imitation of the ancient sites of Śākyamuni Buddha. When the construction was about to start, a report was submitted to the Emperor, who ordered Li Yifu, an imperial secretary, to inform the Master:

> The pagoda to be built is such a great undertaking that we are afraid it cannot be completed in a short time, so it should be constructed with bricks. As we also do not wish the Master to labor for it, we have ordered the contribution of all the garments and other properties left by the deceased members of the imperial household, including the Eastern Palace, the harem, and other chambers, seven in all, in the palace, toward the construction of the pagoda. That will be sufficient to defray the cost of the completion of the work.

Thus bricks were used for the construction, and the site was shifted to the west courtyard of the monastery. Each side of the base of the pagoda was 140 feet in length after the style of the Western Region, not following the old Chinese fashion. The pagoda had five storeys, and including the Wheel Sign and the Dew Basin it was 180 feet in height. At the center of each storey there were relic bones, as many as a thousand or two thousand, amounting to more than ten thousand grains. On the top storey was a stone chamber with two slabs on the southern side, one inscribed with the *Preface to the Holy Teachings of the Tripiṭaka* composed by the late Emperor, and the other one with the *Postscript* written by the reigning Emperor. The inscriptions were engraved in the calligraphy of Right Premier Chu Suiliang, the Duke of Henan.

On the day of laying the foundation stone of the pagoda, the Master related his own sincere wishes briefly as follows:

261a I, Xuanzang, considered that I was unfortunate to have been born at a time when I could not meet the Buddha. But by the effect of some small good deed of mine, I was able to hear the teaching of Buddhism taught by symbols. Having been born in the Final Period of the Dharma, where could I take refuge? I was happy, however, that I could become a monk while I was young, and see with my own eyes the divine image of the Buddha. I have admired the Dharma ever since I was a youth and have listened attentively to the words that conveyed the truth left behind by the Buddha. When I heard about the religious practices of the Bodhisattva, I thought of equalling him even though I am an inferior person, and when I heard about the Dharma realized by the Tathāgata, I looked up to it both physically and mentally. Thus I always esteemed what my teachers taught me and made extensive inquiries of advanced scholars.

It is true that envoys were sent to the West because of a dream of an Emperor of the Han dynasty, and consequently the Right Dharma was transmitted to the East. But as the road was obstructed and long, the transmission was incomplete. Thus there arose particular controversies, most of which stuck to the theories of the two categories of permanence, causing suspicion and dissidence among different parties, contrary to the teaching of One Taste. This made the students of later times look at one another, not knowing which way to follow. That was why the sight of Gṛdhrakūṭa Mountain made me feel all the more grieved, and as I admired Sadāpralāpa Bodhisattva (who wept while searching for truth), I fell into a catnap. While I secretly prayed for spiritual protection and openly depended upon the prestige of my country, I made up my mind to travel out of the land where I was born and threw myself into the regions at the risk of almost certain death. As I stayed at holy sites, I paid visits to all the spiritual spots of the Buddha, and wherever there were people who propagated the Dharma, I would go to all of them to seek the right theories. When I passed through a place I would be deeply moved to see what I had never seen before. When I came across a word I would be happy to learn it, if I had not learned it previously. So I spent all my resources, saving a portion required to sustain my life, to copy texts that were missing at home. After having fulfilled my sincere wish, I returned to the court of my own country, where I was lucky enough to meet with a wise and virtuous ruler who permitted me to translate the texts into Chinese. His Majesty the late Emperor rode on the Golden Wheel to rule over his domain with the sounding of the Jade Drum. He glorified the Dharma in the Image Period and was competent to bear the responsibility for its propagation. He also had the mind to write a preface to the Tripiṭaka personally. Now the reigning Emperor has lectured on the Way in the Spring Palace and has also composed a postscript to the holy scriptures. These two compositions may well be regarded as the sun and moon, appearing at the same time and emitting light simultaneously with beautiful hues blended together. These compositions, shining upon the world like the Seven Luminaries, are similar to irrevocable decrees that will be handed down to posterity. The rhymes of the sentences have the effect of the nine musical variations performed with bells and drums. How can the great events of the translation of Buddhist scriptures at White Horse Monastery in the eastern capital and at Caotang Monastery in the western capital be mentioned in the same breath with the present occasion? But as living beings are shallow in fortune and have lost the one whom they venerated, it is feared that the Sanskrit texts of the Tripiṭaka might be scattered and sink into oblivion, and that the celestial compositions written by these two saintly Emperors might be left unknown without a record. Therefore I formed the intention of constructing this pagoda with veneration in order to store the Sanskrit texts as well as to erect steles engraved with the inscriptions of the Preface and the Postscript, so that they may stand loftily forever and all the

> thousand Buddhas may see them as we do. May the two sacred monuments standing high in the mist last as long and be as firm as the sun and moon!

The Master personally carried baskets or crates to fetch bricks and stones for the construction, which was completed in two years' time.

On the twenty-third day of the fifth month in the summer, the most virtuous monks Jñānaprabha and Prajñādeva of Mahābodhi Monastery in Central India sent a letter to the Master. Jñānaprabha thoroughly understood the teachings of both the Mahayana and Hinayana schools, as well as such heretical works as the Four Vedas and the treatises of the five branches of learning. Being the chief disciple of the Venerable Śīlabhadra, he was held in esteem
261b by all scholars in the five regions of India. Prajñādeva was erudite and well versed in the theories of the eighteen Hinayana sects, and he was also respected for his virtue in giving instructions as a teacher. While the Master was touring the Western Region they often exchanged views to promote learning. However he gained merits in studying Hinayana theories and did not set his mind on Vaipulya (extensive Mahayana) texts. For his obstinacy in sticking to biased views, the Master always berated and denounced him. At the religious assembly convened in the city of Kanyākubja he was completely frustrated in debate and admitted defeat with a sense of shame.

Since the Master had departed from them, [Jñānaprabha and Prajñādeva] always cherished a feeling of respect for him and never forgot about him. So they asked Dharmadīrgha, a *śramaṇa* in the same monastery, to send a letter together with eulogistic verses and two rolls of cotton cloth to the Master, singing his praises with minds of deep veneration. The letter said:

> The abbot Prajñādeva, of Mahābodhi Monastery at the Diamond Seat of the mysterious and auspicious World-honored One, surrounded by a multitude of learned monks, begs to send this letter to the Mokṣācārya of the country of Mahācīna, who is most learned in the subtle teachings of many

> scriptures, disciplinary texts, and treatises, extending to him unlimited respect and wishing that he may live in good health with the least ailment and trouble. I, *bhikṣu* Prajñādeva, have composed verses in praise of the Buddha's great supernatural powers as well as the wisdom of inference from the various scriptures and commentaries, etc., which I have handed to the *bhikṣu* Dharmadīrgha to deliver to you. The old virtuous *ācārya* Jñānaprabha of this place, whose learning is unlimited, also sends his greetings to you just as I said above, and the *upāsaka* Sūryalabdha also prostrates himself to pay homage to you. We are now sending you two rolls of white cotton cloth to indicate our remembrance of you. As the way is long, we hope you will not deem it a small gift but will accept it. Whatever scriptures and commentaries are needed over there, just give us a list and we shall make copies of the same and send them to you. May the Mokṣācārya take notice of the above.

This shows how the Master was admired by scholars of distant lands.

In the second month of the spring of the fifth year (654) Dharmadīrgha took his leave to return home and asked the Master to write a reply. The Master wrote a reply and prepared some tokens. He made a copy of the letter and submitted it to the Emperor before he handed it to the messenger. In the letter he said:

> Bhikṣu Xuanzang of the great empire of Tang begs to send this letter to the presence of the Tripiṭaka Master Venerable Jñānaprabha of the Kingdom of Magadha in Central India. As time passes so quickly, it has been over ten years since I took leave of you. Being separated from you by a long distance, I have scarcely heard any news of you. My remembrance of you often increases my prolonged concern about you. When Bhikṣu Dharmadīrgha arrived he conveyed your kind regards to me and informed me that you are living happily in good health. My eyes suddenly became bright at

this news, as if I could see your respected countenance in person, and my pleasure was beyond description by brush and ink. As the season is becoming warmer, I wonder how you are getting on since you wrote your letter. Some years back when our envoy returned home, he informed me that the great teacher of the Law, the Right Dharma Store, had passed away to verify the Principle of Impermanence. When I was told of this sad news, I could not refrain from feeling heartbroken. Alas! It may be said that the ferryboat on the sea of suffering has sunk and the eyes of heavenly beings and men are closed. The pain of his passing away befell us so soon! The Right Dharma Store had cultivated bliss long in the past and performed meritorious deeds for many *kalpa*s;
261c thus he was endowed with an excellent nature that engendered the qualities of simplicity and tranquillity as well as great talent that symbolized perfection and prominence. He succeeded to the virtue of Āryadeva and continued the splendor of Nāgārjuna, and he also rekindled the torch of wisdom and raised once again the Banner of the Dharma. He extinguished the fire on the mountain of heterodoxy and dammed up the torrential current in the sea of suffering, and he also urged those who were fatigued to proceed on the way to the place of treasure and showed the Great Path to those who lost their way. So great and lofty, he was indeed a pillar of the Dharma Gate! He also comprehensively stored in his bosom and thoroughly understood by heart such teachings as the doctrines of both the Great and the Lesser Vehicles of the Three Vehicles, as well as the books of the heretics advocating the theories of annihilation or permanence. He could lucidly apprehend difficult and complicated literature and clarify hidden and obscure teachings. Therefore he was followed by both Buddhists and non-Buddhists, who regarded him as a religious teacher of India. He was good at teaching his pupils by an orderly method day and night without feeling tired. His knowledge was compared to a self-replenishing wine vessel placed at a crossroad; it was

inexhaustible for all who came to drink from it. When I was seeking the Way some years ago, I had the opportunity to receive his instructions; he was so kind as to enlighten me by pointing out my ignorance. Although I am a stupid ordinary person, I was benefitted by his guidance, very much as the fleabane depends upon jute to grow erect. When I was about to return home he gave me deep advice and admonitions. His solicitous words are still sounding in my ears. I hoped that he would live in good health and grow eyebrows of longevity so as to glorify the mysterious way, and I never expected that he would return to eternity so soon. It is really unbearable for me to recall what has gone forever. I humbly consider that you, having received the teacher's good instruction at an early time and being his long-standing and learned student, must have had a hard time getting rid of the emotional attachment to your teacher. We are quite at a loss as to what to do! Since this is but a phenomenal world, what can we do? I hope you will restrain your grief.

In the past, when the Great Enlightened One faded away with his brilliance, Mahākāśyapa succeeded him to spread the Great Cause. When Śāṇakavāsa passed away, Upagupta elucidated his good Way. Now that the Leader of the Dharma has returned to reality, you are the person to continue his task. I hope that your elegant language and wonderful eloquence in debate will always flow like the water in the Four Seas, and that your adornments of bliss and wisdom will last as long as the five mountains. Of the scriptures and commentaries that I have brought back, I have already translated the *Yogācārabhūmi Śāstra* and other long and short texts, making a total of over thirty works. The translation of the *Abhidharmakośa Śāstra* and the *Abhidharmanyāyānusāra Śāstra* is not yet completed, but it will be finished this year. The reigning Emperor of the Great Tang Empire is enjoying every felicity, with peace prevailing throughout his land. With the compassion of a

Cakravartin King, he has spread the edification of the Buddha, composed a preface with his Divine Pen to all the Chinese translations of the scriptures and commentaries, and also ordered the authorities to copy them for circulation in the country. Thus even neighboring states also follow and study them. Although we are now at the end of the Image Period, the brilliance of the Dharma is still as genial and as glorious as when it was taught in the Jetavana Garden in Śrāvastī. I hope you will take note of the above information. When I was crossing the Indus [on my way back home], I lost a pack of scriptures. I am now sending you herewith a list of the lost texts, of which I request that you send me new copies by some convenient messenger. Attached under separate cover is a small offering to you. I hope you will accept it without thinking it too little. As the way is far I could not send you anything more. With homage from Xuanzang.

And he also wrote a reply to the Venerable Prajñādeva as follows:

262a Bhikṣu Xuanzang of the Great Tang Empire begs to send this letter to the Tripiṭaka Master Prajñādeva of Mahābodhi Monastery. It has been a long time since we parted, and I have been thinking of you with deep respect. As no means of communication is available, I have no way to comfort myself in remembering you. When Bhikṣu Dharmadīrgha arrived, he conveyed to me, to my great delight, your kind letter in which you inquired after my health and welfare. Also received are two rolls of fine white cotton cloth and one folder of eulogistic verses as a token of deep friendship. Being a person of little virtue, I really do not deserve such gifts, and I am quite perplexed and uneasy. While the season is becoming warm, I do not know how your health is since you wrote me the letter. I presume that since you are well versed in the theories of a hundred schools, fix your mind in pondering the scriptures of the Nine Divisions, raise the Banner of the Right Dharma to guide those who have been converted to Buddhism, beat the drum of victory to vanquish the boastful heretics, feel proud in the presence of kings and nobles, and associate with people of eminent talent, your life must be quite happy and pleasant. I am an ordinary person with faults and my strength is declining. Moreover as I remember the favor and benignity I have received from the Emperor, I have to work hard constantly. When I was travelling in your country for my studies, I had the chance to meet Your Reverence. In the assembly convened at Kanyākubja we held debate in the presence of various kings and hundreds and thousands of disciples to test the depth and shallowness of our arguments. One side advocated Mahayana teachings while the other side supported the incomplete Hinayana theories. In the course of argumentation, the words and tones must have been high or low. As we were determined to defend the truth, we did not care about personal feelings, often resorting to humiliating and abusive language. But as soon as the meeting was over, all resentment was cleared up in no time. Now your messenger again conveys to me your apology in connection with that event. Why do you stick so much to scruples? Your Reverence is a scholar of rich learning and clear expression with a strong will and a noble character. The water in Anavatapta Lake is not comparable to the amount of your learning, and the stainless *maṇi* pearl cannot equal your purity. Being a criterion for those who come after you, you belong to the class of high-minded men. I hope you will strive to be a good example for the propagation of the Right Dharma. As far as the perfection of truth and the thoroughness of language are concerned, nothing exceeds the Mahayana teachings. The grudge I bore against you was that you did not have deep faith in them, like one taking pleasure in possessing a goat cart or a deer cart while discarding a cart drawn by a white bullock, or appreciating quartz instead of precious crystal. Why is a virtuous man of discernment like you so obstinate as to persist in your delusive views? As our body, which is as perishable as a utensil, is ephemeral and cannot last long, it befits you to awaken the great mind for enlightenment and entertain the Right View at an early date, so that you may not feel remorse on your deathbed.

Now the messenger is returning home and I am asking him to convey my respect to you. Also attached is a small gift for you in token of my gratitude for your good wishes to me, quite inadequate to express my deep admiration of you. This I hope you will note. Formerly when I was crossing the Indus on my return journey, I lost a pack of scriptures. I am writing separately a list of the lost texts, and I hope you will kindly send me new copies of the same at your convenience. As regards other matters, I am unable to relate them all in detail in this letter. Sent respectfully by Bhikṣu Xuanzang.

Fascicle VIII

Beginning with the Translation of the *Nyāyamukha Śāstra* in the Fifth Month of the Summer in the Sixth Year of Yonghui and Ending with the Expression of Thanks by Court Officials for the Inscription Composed by the Emperor for the Monastery in the Third Month of the Spring in the First Year of Xianqing

262b On the first day of the fifth month in the summer of the sixth year (of Yonghui, 655), the Master translated, besides his regular work of translation, the *Nyāyamukha Śāstra.* He had previously translated the *Hetuvidyā Śāstra* while he was living at Hongfu Monastery. Each of these two treatises comprises one fascicle. They are works on logic explaining the methods of argumentation or refutation by direct perception and inference. The monks at the monastery of translation competed with one another in writing commentaries on the works. The monk translator Xixuan showed the treatises to Lü Cai, the Chief of the Imperial Medical Bureau, who altered the reasoning, pointed out strong and weak points, and composed *A Diagrammatic Exposition of Proposition and Refutation in the Commentary on the Hetuvidyā Śāstra,* of which the preface reads as follows:

> It has been said that the growth and passing away of things are in concordance with the regularity of Heaven and earth, and that what is great and most profound is the order shown by the changeable and transformable lines of the

Hexagrams in the Eight Diagrams (expounded in the *Book of Changes*). However, this principle has not spread to the external world but is practised within our domain. By inferential study of the great spirit of the universe, one can never get to know of it. By penetrating into the principle of *yin* and *yang* (negativity and positivity), one cannot fathom its depths. Has anyone ever heard that the expressions of Symbolism and the Appended Judgments (in the *Book of Changes*) also opened the gate to the Eightfold Noble Path, and that before the formation of the material world the teachings of the two categories of wisdom were already propagated? That is why through the application of the theories of voidness and reality, one can gain double insight, and by meditating on truth and convention, one can realize the two tranquilities, be ferried across the sea of lust by the boat of the Six *Pāramitā*s, and escape from the burning house by riding on the three kinds of carts. From this we may know that the Dharma power of the King of the Dharma surpasses all living beings without hindrance. He enlightened himself as well as others and destroyed all evil ones, while he remained alone in Awakenment. When he started his karmic movement, it had the force of thunder and lightning. When his cause of edification had reached its limit, he vanished like fire extinguished when the fuel is consumed. In view of the traces of his incarnation, he seemed to show coming and going; but in consideration of the Eternal Truth, there is ultimately neither birth nor abiding in the world. Yet as the Way of great salvation responds to those who have the cause to be saved, and heavenly blessedness and illustrious virtue may reach all places, however far they may be, so he had his inception of life in the past with his divine light only seen in days of yore. Lucky and auspicious events had their time of returning to the Pure Land, and all people sighed with regret on such a day.

It is humbly thought that when the imperial Tang dynasty held sway over the empire, Emperors riding on Golden

Wheels reach the four quarters. Commanding supreme power, they pacified a myriad of countries. While they brightened the Six Heavens with the Sun of Wisdom, they raised the Dharma Cloud to the Tenth Stage of Bodhisattvahood. Cross-
262c ing the desert in the west, they possessed the wonderful regions of happiness. Approaching the sea in the east, they had the big cities of pleasure in their possession. They extended their prestige and influence without limitation and standardized the method of writing as well as the length of axletrees of carriages for common use in all countries under the sky. Thus they offered sacrifices to a hundred *koṭis* of Sumeru Mountains and allowed the three thousand Dharma worlds to enjoy the benefit of imperial influence. Thus people coming from the five parts of India were asked to change their simple garments in the guesthouse on Gao Street [in the capital], and the eighteen books of the Veda were translated from the Sanskrit into Chinese in the Imperial Library.

Now there is the Venerable Xuanzang, the Tripiṭaka Master, who may be said to be the Śākyamuni of our present age. Having innate intelligence and wisdom, being a learned scholar of versatility, pure in virtue and deed, and studying the disciplinary rules hard, he is indeed a pillar of the Triple Gem and a leader of the four groups of Buddhist followers. He often worried that as the teachings of Śākyamuni Buddha had been introduced to the East quite a long time ago, mistaken views might have mixed with right theories as water mingles inseparably with milk. If the real aspects were not verified at Kapilavastu and the true texts not checked at Magadha, how could one decide what was the authoritative Tripiṭaka, to be taken as the ultimate truth? It was lucky for him that Heaven and earth were in harmony and no disturbance raised dust within the Four Seas, so that he was able to start his journey to the Great Desert and reach the Pamir Ranges to shake his travelling staff with pewter rings. He did not take the route in the south where he could taste the betel leaf but went straight to the alien land. Neither did he carry with him any asarum grass (the aroma of which would speed his horse) to render the long distance short and easy to cover. Thus he reached the source of the [Yellow] River in the Western Region and crossed the Ganges east of Kapilavastu. He collected palm leaf scriptures at Gṛdhrakūṭa Mountain and got a glimpse of the texts of Golden Words at the Crane Grove. He visited the capitals of more than a hundred countries, where he obtained nearly seven hundred books of scriptures and commentaries, which were carried by relays of carriages from garrison stations and brought back to the imperial capital. Thus he was able to present the texts to His Majesty and explain the supreme doctrine to him face to face. This *Hetuvidyā Śāstra* is one of the Sanskrit texts obtained by the Tripiṭaka Master. Its principles include the teachings of all of the Three Vehicles, and the matters it cites comprise a hundred dharmas. It does research into the essence of the doctrines of voidness and reality and elaborates the teachings of both Buddhist and non-Buddhist schools. Its wording is, however, concise; its reasoning is comprehensive; and its style of writing is truly subtle, although its meanings are obvious. A student cannot grasp its abstrusity in one lifetime, and those who are interested in studying it for several years cannot fathom its origin. As it is the gate to all mystic teachings, it has been translated first.

There were then the Dharma teachers Shentai, Jingmai, Mingjue, and others, who were all men of divine intelligence, with high aspirations and noble deeds, well versed in various scriptures and having such understanding and comprehension. They were ordered by a special decree of the Emperor to take part, later than the others, in the Dharma congregation. Thus they had the opportunity to derive benefit from the Master by listening to his instructions while holding texts in their hands. Being adept at preaching the Dharma, the Tripiṭaka Master thoroughly expounded the mystic and profound teachings in a marvelous manner. Thus the Venerable Shentai and the others recorded what they had heard, each in his own way, in explanation of the lectures. When the expository comments were finalized, they were ready to be published for circulation; but most of the people did not have a good chance to read them.

Now the Dharma teacher Xixuan has been an old friend of mine since we were young. Formerly when I was living in
263a seclusion on Song Mountain, I once set foot at the outer entrance of the monastery. After coming to serve as an official in the imperial capital, I still lived in a cramped abode in a mean alley. It has been more than thirty years since I cultivated the [four] all-embracing virtues. We two, being bosom friends, are sincere in being earnest and urging each other in a perfect manner. But the Dharma teacher is refined and pure in moral integrity, and his observance of the disciplinary rules is as stainless as ice and frost. What he has learned is aimed at achieving the Ekayāna (the One Vehicle), and his actions are confined within the scope stipulated in the *Sarvāstivāda Vinaya.* On seeing that he was living a simple and ascetic life, I often urged him to change his way of living according to the principles of permission and prohibition. But as monks and laymen follow different modes of living, their actions are also dissimilar. So in the course of exchanging jesting remarks, we had a series of arguments about the right and wrong of matters. The teacher calmly said to me, "Munificent man, you have studied the *Six Classics* and probed into the abstruse theories of a hundred schools. You can prognosticate unseasonable weather by calculating the principles of *yin* and *yang* and discern the slightest deviations in music. I have also heard that you had never read the *Great Mystery Classic* (*Tai Xuan Jing*) but could explain it instantly when the Emperor inquired about it, and that you had never glanced at chess but tried to make a set of chessmen in ten days. With limited faculties, you wish to penetrate everything you meet. But as

Buddhism is mysterious and profound, I presume it is not similar to other things. Although you exert yourself to the utmost in trying to search into its truth, I am afraid it is not something for you to utilize your mentality on. Why should you now use a Buddhist text in a perverse way to sneer at me?"

Later, when the Dharma teacher met with the first publication of [the translation of] the *Hetuvidyā Śāstra,* a work of deep and abstruse meaning, he had a copy of it produced before others did so, and presented it [to me] with the following note: "It is most difficult to make a profound study of the obscure and mysterious theories of this treatise. Most clever and erudite scholars could not understand it when they heard about it. If you can thoroughly master this work, you will be regarded as knowing both Buddhist and non-Buddhist lore."

As this treatise has been recently introduced into China, I did not hear about it before. Being ashamed to try to understand what I did not know, I had to read it through under pressure. With utmost effort, I probed into its profound theories and endeavored to acquire the subtle gist through comparison and inference. After making repeated studies, I have obtained a shallow understanding of the meanings of this school. Afterward I also borrowed the theoretical commentaries of the three teachers and made further studies. Although the various teachers' explanations are deep and rich in meaning and their literary style has unity and coherence, they make contradictory remarks because they hold to different points of view. Since they all received theories from the Tripiṭaka Master, why should they be divided into two sects? But as internal conflict occurred among them, outsiders were liable to watch for a chance to make contumelious attacks. Even what the Buddha taught in his one voice was understood in different ways by various types of people, so why should a layman clad in white be excluded from the category of living beings?

In my spare time when I was free from public affairs, I wrote this commentary in which I follow the good opinions of the three teachers as explained in their works but refute their doubtful views with my own standpoint. Divided into three fascicles, it is entitled *Annotated Commentary on Theoretical Proposition and Refutation.* In it the lines written in black are the main text of the treatise, while the annotations
263b written in red preserve the old views of the three teachers. The notes written below in black are my new opinions judging more than forty of the aforementioned views of the teachers. What is after my own judgement is not fully recorded. For the elucidation of these obscure languages and of theories that are somewhat difficult to perceive, I have also drawn a theoretical diagram for the purpose of making comparative studies with the text. I have separately drawn a large diagrammatic exposition exclusively for the preservation of my recent annotations. Since the treatise is unintelligible to outsiders, nowhere could one get an interpretation on the highway. If people say that I know it inherently, that is certainly not my expectation. But in the matter of learning one who does not need a second inquiry may be considered a Transmitter of the Lamp [of the Dharma], and one who knows ten points of the subject after having heard only one may be said to be near to perfection. Not having seen the work before in my life, I took up my pen and wrote the commentary in a hasty manner. Moreover, as I did not study it with a teacher, my annotations cannot be without errors and incoherences. I have heard that when a *yakṣa* of the Snow Mountains spoke on the law of birth-and-death, the wild animals in the countryside were so delighted that they remarked that they had never heard it before. If what he said was reasonable, he would win the respect and homage of heavenly beings and immortals. I hope what I write in my annotations will be almost like that. If you teachers can forget about my mean and low position, like that of a fox fairy and a ghost, and reflect on the significance of those

> passages that are valuable, selecting the good points to follow them, disregarding whether they are written by a religious or a secular person, then the Tathāgata's Way will not fall to the ground and many people will propagate it. How can there be any immutability in this matter? If you insist on the idea of a permanent ego and your theories do not discern right from wrong, then I will still avoid the two extremities [and accept the middle point of view]. But anyhow I shall ask the opinion of the Tripiṭaka Master.

On the first day of the seventh month in the autumn, the monk translator Huili, feeling concern on hearing about this matter, wrote a letter to Left Premier Yu (Zhining), the Duke of the State of Yan, to discuss the pros and cons of the issue as follows:

> I, Huili, have heard that in establishing his teachings the Buddha used classic language with abstruse meanings to explain deep and subtle doctrines that were as expansive as the dome of the sky and similar in vastness to the blue sea. When one talks about the nature and form of *tathatā* (reality), one is bewildered even if one has attained to the Tenth Stage [of Bodhisattvahood]. When one speaks about the causation of a little grass, one is ignorant of it even if one is free from rebirth. Moreover, when one is entangled in the net of the Eight Erroneous Practices and submerged in the stream of the Four Inverted Views, is it not absurd if one should wish to penetrate syllogisms consisting of proposition, reason, [and example] and thereby distinguish similarity and dissimilarity and make them manifest? I humbly believe that the Master of Translation of the Great Ci'en Monastery built his base of wisdom at an early date and achieved his power of knowledge early in his life. His conduct is as pure as precious jade and his morality is as upright as a pine tree, so he was able to make a personal visit to the holy regions in search of the subtle teachings. Having embraced the whole Tripiṭaka in his bosom and grasped the *Four Āgamas* in his palms, he inherited the

sublime personality of the former sages and propagated in his own time the good examples of the past. He is really a boat for lay people in the Final Period of the Buddha Dharma and is truly a good model to be followed by monks.

The holy scriptures he has translated amount to more than three hundred scrolls, among which is a short treatise entitled *Hetuvidyā*, which is a guidebook to methods of argumentation and narrates the rules for refuting erroneous views. Although it is not an essential and mystic text of the profound teachings of Buddhism, it cannot be under-
263c stood in a hurry. I have recently heard that Lü Cai, Chief of the Imperial Medical Bureau, with his mediocre talent, has plagiarized the theories of various teachers and composed the *Diagram of Hetuvidyā* for the exposition of the meanings of logic. Being unable to understand it accurately, he is likely to cause heterodox views. In order to seek fame improperly, he gives strained interpretations in a wrong way. He denies the right sayings of virtuous men and allows his self-conceit to lead him to biased views. He would try to flaunt his learning in the presence of nobles and people of high rank and make a clamorous display of himself by the side of the street, brazenly and without shame, not feeling tired of it. He is experienced in the inconsistency of human relationships, but his worldly desire has not yet come to an end. As the Chief of the Imperial Medical Bureau was somewhat familiar with worldly affairs, he thought that he could also understand the truth of religion, just like a house mouse saying that it was not difficult to climb over Langfeng Peak in the Kunlun Mountains when it saw that it could ascend the cooking oven, or a spider that, seeing that it could easily make a net over a thornbush, thought that it could also enmesh the giant mulberry, not considering the limits of its ability. He is no different from the [animals in] these parables. I have also heard that ultrasound makes scarcely any noise and that a man of great eloquence is slow in speech. Thus Vimalakīrti, though conversant with

> reasoning, did not say anything in the city of Vaiśālī; and Confucius, a man of high virtue, was so sincere and respectful that he kept silence in his own village. Again, [Huang] Shudu enjoyed fame as great as the ocean and [Li] Yuanli had the reputation of being an exemplary person, yet I never heard that they praised themselves to win the commendation of government officials.

With this letter from Huili, the matter was settled.

On the first day of the tenth month in the winter, having heard that the matter was settled, Liu Xuan, an official scholar of the Board of Rites, composed *A Letter of Homage in Verse* to inspire the monks who took part in the translation of the scriptures as follows:

> Homage to all Buddhas!
> May they protect us with divine powers.
> I make this statement with sincerity,
> Not to blame or disparage anyone.
> One who sinks in darkness without awakening
> Should return to complete enlightenment.
> In the sea of desire one has long been submerged,
> There is scarcely a boat with oars for crossing.
> When variant views are in disagreement,
> One should depend upon harmonization
> And be free from existence and attachment
> In order to reason without faults and self-contradiction.
> Arrogant and perverse views of the Eightfold Noble Path
> Will lead one astray into a hundred evil ways.
> Grasping and rejecting of desire are mixed in argument,
> Defilement and purity are put in confusion.
> Gold should be picked out and rubble discarded;
> Jade needs to be carved to increase its brilliance.
> The Buddha shone universally upon all beings
> And concentrated his mind to delve into truth.
> Since he has achieved the Great Way,
> Who dares to defame him?
> Forthright words will sublimate virtue;

Sycophancy causes gradual downfall.
I hope you will listen to my words
So as to develop the meanings.
May you show sympathy with my truthfulness
And grant me in return your admonitions.

The message of homage said:

Formerly Śākyamuni appeared in physical form in his royal palace and showed the phenomenon of death between the twin [śāla] trees. When his subtle sayings were explained, the ultimate truth was propagated. His land benefited by being accepted into his fold, and all living beings enjoyed the beneficence of being enlightened as if they had been awakened at dawn. The tree of the Buddha cast its shade in the West, and the shadow of enlightenment covered the East. This happened during the Han and Wei dynasties. Under the rule of the houses of Fu and Yao, it flourished with great
264a brilliance. Since then eminent monks have emerged one after another, virtuous and sagacious people followed one another in succession, the Sun of Wisdom always hung high, and the Wheel of the Dharma rotated constantly. The merits of initiation were first due to Kāśyapa-Mātaṅga and Faxian, but propagation depended upon Kumārajīva and Dao'an. A separate branch stretched far to Luofu; and recently Buddhatuṅga appeared in the states of Zhao and Wei, where he spoke in a brief manner and behaved with uncompromising uprightness that cannot be related in detail. They debated nothing else but the theories of voidness and existence as taught by the Ekayāna; or they discussed the suffering and the cause of suffering [as explained by] the Four Noble Truths. To understand the meaning of existence through verbal exposition cannot release one from conditioned existence. One has to cease talking about the Way to comprehend it, in order to realize the state of absolute quietude. If one clings to abstrusity [as real] to seek for abstrusity, that abstrusity is not the theory of abstrusity. If one forgets about

abstrusity because it is abstrusity, that abstrusity may be the meaning of abstrusity. Although ignorance is found on the path of darkness and phenomenon and noumenon are beyond verbal description, the absorption of living beings into nirvana has to be done by means of exposition, an instrument like a fish pot or a snare for catching fish or rabbits. Once variant opinions were expressed by words, viewpoints on right and wrong rose in swarms, one party fighting against another, just as in a war in which the defeated held his breath tight while the winner voiced his first triumph. Thus we esteem the conquest of Māra and the subjugation of various heretics. If it were not for dauntless eloquence and adroit refutation of challenging questions, the heretics and the like would be noisily arrogant and put us to shame. Therefore we should fix our mind on understanding the Way and maintain absolute control over all good and evil influences, so as to raise high the Banner of the Dharma and beat loudly the drums of the Dharma. When the banner and drum are properly set up, the antagonists will be crushed, and since the Wheel of Dharma is in rotation, what force will not be subjugated? If a man lowered his banner on sight of the enemy at a distance and rebutted challenging queries with irrelevant words, it would be impossible for him to propagate the Triple Gem. Lü Cai, the Chief of the Imperial Medical Bureau, has entered the gate of the theories of voidness and existence and is galloping along the Path of Right View. What he has learned and practised is similar to that of the past sages, and his understanding of the subtle teachings is equal to that of philosophers in bygone days. He is eloquent in speech, his meaning is perspicuous, his virtue is true, and his deeds are remarkable. He has bathed in the stream of the Eight Emancipations and comprehended the Seven Links of Enlightenment. His prompt response to the teaching of perfection resembled [that shown by] the visit of Vimalakīrti to the Āmravaṇa Garden. Whenever he heard about the Way, no matter where it was, he would certainly go to seek it, just like Sādapralāpa, who went out in search of truth and never returned home. His purpose is to spread the Buddha Dharma and to approve or disapprove the *Commentary on Hetuvidyā.* One must approve the strong points of correct views, and it is reasonable to point out the shortcomings of incorrect ones. Now I see that all the monks who are assembled here are trying to derive benefit from other people's knowledge, as one gets a grindstone from another mountain to carve one's own jade into a vessel. Both the court and the commonalty have heard about Mr. Lü and asked him for detailed advice. All of them listened attentively to his words, which were as fluent as water flowing out of a bottle, with the hope wiping away the source of ambition and remorse and dissolving the accumulation of doubts and resentment.

Upon hearing about this statement, Li Chunfeng, the Court Astronomer, wrote me the following letter:

> I, your servant, cherish the Right Path in my mind. My deeds are in connection with the refuge [in the Triple Gem], regarding substantial wisdom as the mystical embodiment of the Great Enlightened One, and non-action as the Dharma-body of the Buddha, the Guide of Men. But the bright sun glorifying the sky actually aids the function of Heaven, and the sagely monks who expound the Dharma really support the wonderful Way of the Teacher of Men and Heavenly Beings. This is what I believe and accept, and it is where I rest my mind. I dare not, however, take a piece of yellow leaf for gold, or a pheasant for a phoenix. Neither dare I pass myself off as a competent player in an ensemble as the scholar Nanguo (a bogus performer of the *yu* mouth organ) did in the past, or mix the water of the Rivers
> 264b Zi and Sheng [which are of different tastes]. If I did otherwise, it was not out of my mind, certainly not out of my mind! It has been nearly two thousand years

since [the Buddha passed away] at the Crane Grove. As the Right Dharma started declining, the Final Period of the Dharma has commenced, when abstruse teaching is depressed and unmanifest and the Way of enlightenment is going to sink into oblivion.

The Master Xuanzang, who practised *dhūta* (morality) in the Dharma world, travelled far to Kapilavastu, saw the Bodhi tree as well as the Hiraṇyavatī River, beheld the seven places [where the *Avataṃsaka Sūtra* was preached] in eight assemblies, visited in person the city of Vaiśālī and Vulture Peak in that country, and testified to the authenticity of the śāla trees [where the Buddha passed away] and of the Precious Staircase [by which the Buddha once descended from the Tuṣita Heaven]. As for his journey to Rājagṛha, Dantaloka Mountain, the Ganges, etc., it is not easy to relate them all in full. All the famous monks of the Western Region discussed the theories of *prajñā* with him, and he inquired of those teachers to solve the doubts and questions he had entertained in the Eastern Land. He observed the Vinaya *Piṭaka* without negligence and always understood the full meaning of the Abhidharma [works on Buddhist philosophy] through insight. He has obtained the sutras through oral transmission and had his doubts and knotty points solved by Supreme Enlightenment. All Dharmas, whether great or small, are contained in his bosom; and all theories, deep and shallow, are comprehended by his keen deliberation. Therefore the title of Tripiṭaka Master is reverentially conferred on him in Cathay, while he is commonly known as Mahāyānadeva in Kapilavastu. His deeds are so worthy of his fame that no title is adequate to praise him. Mr. Lü, however, is a versatile scholar, who is proficient in the theoretical principles and knows well the crucial importance of words and deeds [which may produce either good or bad effects]. As regards the

> protection of the Buddha Dharma, he knew it inherently; his unhindered eloquence was not acquired by learning and practice. But as the meaning of the *Hetuvidyā* is obscure, there arose diverse interpretations, just as a group of blind men who grope at different parts of an elephant get variant ideas of the shape of the animal, or as cooked rice collected in the same alms bowl may have various colors. Since Mr. Lü persists in his own views, both monks and lay people are looking forward to a decisive opinion. When autumn frost has fallen [indicating a man's declining years], one listens attentively to the toll of a bell [to count his last days]. Since the Cloud of Dharma has spread in the sky, thunder has seldom crashed. But a donkey is incapable of being treaded on and trampled by a dragon-elephant, just as a layman is not expected to set foot in the secluded living quarters of a monk. Or it is like Mañjuśrī, the Buddha of the Superior Dragon Race, who refuted his opponent's theories, and Vimalakīrti, who solved other people's doubts. Thus the established conclusions of a *bhikṣu* in an argument may also be reached by an *upāsaka*. I venture to attach my humble note [to your letter]. Please do not feel annoyed by it. If there is any obscurity or doubt, I hope you will seek the advice of the Tripiṭaka Master to give a judgement. If you will show and transmit what teachings you have received to the four groups of Buddhist followers, then the Right Way may prosper and be free from destruction and obstruction forever. Is this not the way to make the Triple Gem thrive? [Li Chunfeng]

What exceeds this limit is beyond the scope of my knowledge. Expressed with homage from your disciple Liu Xuan.

On the fourth day (of the tenth month) the monk-translator Mingjun wrote a verse in response to the letter of the official scholar Liu Xuan, in which he pointed out the scholar's merits and demerits:

Hurray for the Great Saint
Whose omniscience is bright and round!
No obscurity does he not discern,
Just as echo follows sound.
If he induces not happiness,
Who would awake to take refuge in him?
A respectable good teacher he is,
Who actually guides all deluded beings.
A hundred rivers with mild waves flowing,
264c Being of the same taste, are swallowed at one gulp.
Some things should be accepted and others rejected,
Some are correct and some not, some complete and some imperfect.
The eightfold wrong path is spreading fast.
One strives for fame with a verse of four lines,
Distorting what is right, covering up mistakes,
And suppressing the important in favor of triviality.
But ice melts under the shining sun,
And water becomes clean when a pearl is put in.
The supreme virtue is manifested;
The embodiment of the Way rests upon moral integrity.
Even if he is praised or disparaged,
He would not be moved by derogation or sublimity.
Lofty is the sage of reverence,
The one who is abundant in sentience.
Let us wait for one who is all-knowing
To balance the right and wrong of things.
I am just submitting what I am unable to express
So as to distinguish the brilliant ones.

The responsive statement says:

Not long ago I had the opportunity to read your message of homage at the Sacrificial Marking Post. After reading the magnificent composition, I see that it is a brilliant piece of literary work written in a grand and beautiful way. When one goes into it to see its elegance, is it not truly so? What a pity the sea of desire has waves running high to the sky, and the mountain of heresy is as lofty as the sun! Those who hold the conception of an individual soul will fall and topple down without stopping, and those who rely on the bondage of pride will sink into [the sea of suffering] endlessly. Thus those who held the sixty-two views strove to find shelters in which to lodge themselves, and the ninety-five types of heretics prostrated themselves one after another and forgot to return home. With great compassion as his original vow, the Tathāgata, forgetting about secondary causes, condescended to respond to them. Internally he perfected the four wisdoms, and externally he revealed the six supernatural powers. Employing the Ten Powers he subjugated the heavenly demons. Speaking aloud in seven eloquent ways, he defeated the heretics in argument. He drained the sea of desire and saved sentient beings with the three voidnesses. He destroyed the mountain of heresy and dispelled what resembled the Eightfold Noble Path in shape. He pointed out the causes and showed the effects, reverting to the root and returning to the origin of things. So great is the function of compassion and wisdom that it is not describable by words.

Formerly when he ascended the seat under the Bodhi tree, his prestige and edification spread to over a hundred *koṭis* of people. When he ceased his activities in the grove of śāla trees, his bequeathed teachings were promoted in the Three Thousand Worlds. When the Sun of the Buddha sank in the West with its remnant radiance shining upon the East, the auspice of a bright light [indicating the existence of the Buddha] was seen on a night during the Zhou dynasty. One night an Emperor of the Han dynasty had a dream [which presaged the inception of Buddhism in China]. Kāśyapa-Mātaṅga and Dharmāraṇya lit the Lamp of Wisdom first, and Buddhasiṃha and Kumārajīva inherited the lamp and transmitted it afterward. They translated the scriptures to spread the Dharma, saved the people of their times with supernatural power, subdued heretics with their brilliant views, and rested their minds in quiet meditation. In mending decadent discipline they succeeded their predecessors and followed the example of those who refastened loose buttons. They were esteemed for their edification by people of both foreign lands and China; and they helped to teach the dull as well as the clever ones. Their flowery deeds were connected one after another without decline, but I can give only a brief account of what might be related in detail.

The present Tripiṭaka Master possesses inward intelligence and outward elegance. He has internal beauty as his substance. He taught the people as water is poured from one bottle into another, so that they might look up to the Five Vehicles. He felt pity that the time of the Saint was receding and regretted that the holy teachings that had been introduced into China were mostly deficient. While he was thinking of the complete theories, he made up his mind to risk his life for the sake of the Way. Consulting nobody but himself, accompanied by his own shadow, he shook his robe and held a religious staff in hand to start his journey to search for the origin of the Way. He went out of Yumen Pass, travelled far away, and aimed to reach the Hiraṇyavatī River before taking a rest. He solved his doubts in the monasteries of India, where he did thorough research into the profound and abstruse teachings. After returning home he instructed the people of the Divine Land, propagating truth and wiping out
265a falsehood. The defective texts of the bequeathed teachings are being made complete in his day, and the perfect theories of the Vaipulya (Mahayana) school are spread more extensively than former sages [spread them] in the past. The superior theories he has expounded are the most wonderful in the center of the world. The real nature of true voidness extends to the outside of the universe. Because one has the desire to grasp [external objects], this grasping causes one

to lose the truth. If one seeks truth from nothingness, that nothingness will spoil reality. If one removes the traces of the two extremes and forgets about the Middle Way, one cannot easily reach the depth of truth, even if one repeatedly tries to do so. If one lays emphasis on voidness, how can one attain ultimate truth? How important and wonderful it is! It is profound and great indeed! When it is engraved on the mind, then it is regarded as the Dharma. In the mind it is the Dharma, and uttered in words it is teaching. Dharma has individual as well as common aspects, and teaching is negative or positive expositions. How can one get a systematic understanding of such pure gists and abstract teachings in a hurry?

The Master concentrated his spirit and made use of his wisdom to study the root in detail in order to put right the branches. He shed light on the abstruse texts and widely opened his mind. He kept secret the rare voice, which responds in big or small volume according to the strength of the striker. He enlarged the sea of doctrines to embrace the water of all rivers long and short, just as all dukes and princes go to court to pay respect to the Emperor. Thus men of great virtue from different quarters and eminent monks of various regions were convinced of his knowledge. They came to inquire of him about the Way and solve their accumulated doubts. Since he has drunk from the river [of knowledge] until his abdomen was full, his depth of learning is unfathomable. One would be amazed to listen to his remarkable utterances, not knowing how far they could reach. As regards the small way of Hetuvidyā, its direct knowledge and inference are but a mere method to guide beginners and a standard for establishing a thesis. As for the pivot of spiritual abstrusity, the secret key to truth, and the wonderful root of achievement, they are all related in profound texts and are not to be mentioned here.

Lü Cai, Chief of the Imperial Medical Bureau, a man of magnanimous air and mentality, has been a versatile scholar since his early days. He is broad-minded and learned, always having a clear understanding of things. He acquired and studied ancient texts and made deep researches into the books that were once secretly kept inside a wall and recovered when the wall became dilapidated. In contact with people of his own kind, he increased his knowledge and became proficient in the art of divination. He raised a high wind in the garden of argumentation and displayed his glorious brilliance in the forest of eminent scholars, with his head held high, up to the clouds, as a leading figure in the capital. The Five Virtuous Elements aided him in his writings and corrections of mistakes, and all people of the six social positions stood to listen to his eloquent discussions. After having read the *Taixuan Jing* (*Scripture of Great Mystery*) once, he could respond to questions and give explanations about the text. In trying to rediscover the lost game of chess, he succeeded in doing so in an instant. He is indeed a [Zhang] Maoxian of the Jin period and a [Jun] Manqian of the Han dynasty, such people being no longer found nowadays. Having mastered all strategies, he still had ample time to pay admiring respect to Mahayana teachings, in which he had inherent and sincere faith. Once he had a jocular talk with his friends. They incidentally came to the subject of Hetuvidyā; but he disregarded what his teacher had taught him and gave strained interpretations indiscreetly, refuting all the commentaries one by one, pointing out their defects, and finding fault with them. He pronounced his views at court and rashly put them into writing. As far as his ambition is concerned, it is unsurpassed; but when his knowledge is examined, it is really doubtful.

This treatise of his is complete in one fascicle, consisting of five pieces of paper, in which all three commentaries are studied in full detail, he having read them through once. He raises forty objections without mentioning a single correct point of his own. He says nothing right himself, but he says

he is right. The commentaries have nothing wrong in them,
265b but he would say they are wrong. What he says is wrong is not wrong, and what he says is right is not right. Since what he says is right is not right, it is always wrong. Since what he says is wrong is not wrong, it is always right. As what he condemns as wrong is always right, it is right, but not because he says it is right. As what he justifies as right is always wrong, it is wrong, but not because he says it is wrong. It was because of such derogatory views that he incurred censure upon himself. Moreover, cause has two aspects, the producing cause and the illuminating cause; but he grasps one entity, forgetting about the two functions. Both the illuminator and the illuminated are given one name, which makes one perplexed about the two entities. Again, of the two component parts [the subject and predicate] of a proposition, he retains the subject, while giving up the predicate as the proposition. As for the substantial meaning of the example and the object on which the example depends, he rejects the substantial meaning, while keeping the object on which the example depends as the example. Due to these two systems of thought, there arose many doubtful views groundlessly, and the confusion of a conclusion accepted by both parties in argumentation would cause the seven confutations in a wrong way. Although he praises the two treatises to the utmost, he regards his own mind as his teacher, misunderstanding the context of the sentences and pronouncing the words in mistaken tones. He also mistakes the *Sāṃkhya Śāstra* for the *Śabda Śāstra,* and cites the City of Birth as the City of Death. This not only is contrary to the separation or combination of the proposition and the reason but also deviates from the sequence of the antecedent and the consequent [in a syllogism]. He also tries to use vulgar words and erroneous rhymes to transliterate original Sanskrit terms. Although he widely cites the seven noun cases, they are simply equal to one case in the Sanskrit language. He does not mention the eighth case,

the vocative. Where did these arbitrary errors and absurd mistakes come from?

Moreover, the Vaiśeṣika school holds that the atoms are permanent and infinite in number but infinitesimal in body. In time, they gradually amalgamated and produced many offspring atoms, the number of which decreased to half of the original atoms, while their bodies became twice as large as those of their parents. In the end their bodies pervaded the great chiliocosm, but tracing to the ultimate limit their number is only one. The revered Mr. Lü cites the Appended Judgements in the *Book of Changes:*

> The Supreme Ultimate engenders the two Primal Forces [*yin* and *yang*]. These two Primal Forces give rise to the Four Forms, which in turn give rise to the Eight Trigrams from which all things are created.

He remarks that this saying is different in language, but the same in meaning [as (the saying of) the aforesaid school]. Now we know that the Supreme Ultimate is formless and that whatever is born has a shape at its inception. The origin of all things lies in one vital force which finally turns into the myriad things. How can we make use of the production of the one from the many to exemplify the production of the many from one? If the citation of similarities is intended to show off erudition, what if the connotations are perversive? Suppose a good example is cited to exemplify a similar concept of production, but the elucidation is the same as that of heterodox views. How could one rid oneself of deep involvement [in misconceptions]? How can one mix the right with the wrong just for the sake of winning the praise of one's contemporaries? Unless one bears a personal grudge against somebody, why should one go so far as this? All of Mr. Lü's errors and confusions cannot be fully related. His awkward position is caused simply by his own imprudence. Since the roots are not upright, the branches and leaves will naturally fall to one side. From mistakes arise doubts, and

the doubts lead to perplexity. Can one expect to see a crooked object casting a straight shadow? I am just giving two or three examples, so that one may get a general idea. As the deep errors are manifold, rejoinders will be given separately. As the revered Mr. Lü is a man of sensibility and intelligence, why should he have been as reckless as this? In the manifestation of truth and convention, difficulty and ease are as different as clouds [high up in the sky] and mud [low down on the earth]. The Buddha's teachings have spread far,
265c to the prominent regions of Chu and Yue, where the Right Dharma is firmly established, like a burning furnace that cannot be quenched with a handful of snow, or like the Bohai Sea, which cannot be crossed by a boat built with glue.

Mr. Li, the Court Astronomer, has immersed his mind in what is abstruse and cherishes in his bosom what is remote and far-reaching. He is specially versed in the Nine Principles of Mathematics and has comprehensively studied divination with the six lines of a hexagram. He has made extensive researches into ancient texts and has observed the color of clouds to augur things, while despising Wei Hong for his loss of propriety and disdaining Pi Zhao for his unskillfulness. His spirit is unobstructed, and it is in this that his reputation lies. Having collected the revered Mr. Lü's discussions on other subjects, he has also made further inquiries, considering ultimate reality as the mystical embodiment of the Great Enlightened One and nonaction as the Dharmabody of the Guide of Men. This means that through faith in the unconscious impression of virtuous deeds one has cultivated, one may gain partial realization of truth; it can never be achieved spontaneously after all. I am very much afraid that your words may be seemingly good with contrary meanings, and that your expressions are Philistine with obscure purposes. As regards the mystic Way of the [Taoist] heavenly teacher, I hope you will reconsider it. Moreover, the heavenly teacher Kou [Qianzhi] was specially recommended to the court by Mr. Cui [Hao]. What more can be said to show that they caused the disaster together? Although they did not indiscriminately mix the water of the Zi and Sheng Rivers, they did confuse gold and brass.

But you alone are an outstanding person of noble character, learned in all the texts of the three ancient rules and the Classics about the Eight Diagrams. You shield yourself with benevolence and righteousness, and treat people according to the pivotal rules of conduct of a gentleman. Solemnly and magnanimously your unbending moral integrity soars high up to the clouds, and your pure and simple benefitting spirit pacifies the earth. Your good reputation has spread in literary circles, and you stand as a principal figure in the assembly of scholars. You have collected the principles of the Nine Categories of the Great Law of Governance and have made detailed researches into the theories of the two Dai's [Dai De and Dai Sheng]. As for the three hundred rules of the Regular Rites and the three thousand Minor Rules of Conduct, you can understand all of their meanings as easily as you can point to your palm; the matter is as simple as bending down to pick up a thing. Your manner of arranging wine vessels and placing sacrificial tables is regarded by all as the standard way, and all rules and regulations have to wait for your review and amendments [before enforcement]. Thus the satiric poem "Xiangshu" (criticizing improper manners) is heard no more among the people, and the eulogistic ode "Yuli" (praising propriety) is now filling the ears of the court. Your fame matches your deeds perfectly well. The sincerity of your honesty and piety is inherited from innate endowment. You have always truly cherished the mind of spreading and protecting [the Dharma], and so in this clamorous argument you also share the feeling of shame and compunction. Therefore you could have cast away your calling cards to live a retired life in seclusion and forbear erroneous views in order to glorify the Great Teaching. If you were not a talented man well versed in both Buddhist and non-Buddhist lore, illuminating the darkness of the neighboring regions, how could you dispel evil and encourage good, as well as rectify vulgarity and preserve truth?

Formerly the Venerable Kumārajīva had three thousand disciples who submitted themselves to the Way. In the present congregation there are as many men of the same virtue as people in the market. I, a poor mediocre and incompetent monk, have been privileged to take a back seat in the assembly. Although I am happy to have heard about the Way in the morning, I am ashamed that I still have to be active and vigilant up to the evening. It is well known that all three virtuous monks who wrote the commentaries were thoroughly learned in the teachings of the Five Vehicles. Their wall of knowledge was a fathom high, hard to peep over. Their words were as lofty as peaks that are difficult to look up to. If the *shang-yang* bird is dancing on one foot [indicating the advent of torrential rains], one will surely be graced by the benefit of moisture and humidity; but a sudden peal of thunder may leave one no time to cover one's ears. It is said by all that the ancients remarked that a bird may fold its wings and perch on [any] branch, so it need not confine itself in a forest created by a divine being; and that a pond is deep enough for a fish to sink down in, so it need not wait until it is in the blue sea. Therefore, without considering my stupidity and weakness, I have been obliged to examine what is false. As I am not spared the task in spite
266a of my decline, I present this statement in a rough outline. Although the style of writing is poor, the content may be readable. Looking at my own mediocrity and incompetence simply increases my trembling with shame. I am just giving a response to the sayings that have been pointed out. I have nothing more to express. Stated by Shi Mingjun.

On the seventh day (of the tenth month), when [Liu] Xuan received the letter, he again incited Lü [Cai], Chief of the Imperial Medical Bureau, who consequently reported the matter to the

Emperor. The Emperor ordered that a group of ministers and scholars be dispatched to Ci'en Monastery to invite the Tripiṭaka Master to hold a decisive debate with the revered Mr. Lü. Mr. Lü had a weak case and withdrew with an apology.

On the first day of the first month in the spring of the first year of Xianqing (656), [Li] Zhong, the Crown Prince, considering that he was not an offspring of the Empress and not daring to occupy the position of Crown Prince for long, followed the example of Taibo and submitted memorials once and again to the Emperor, asking to retire from his position. The great Emperor consented and made him the Prince of Liang with a grant of ten thousand gift articles and a magnificent mansion of the first grade. In the same month, [Li] Hong, the Prince of Dai, was appointed Heir Apparent.

On the twenty-third day, a feast to entertain five thousand monks in honor of the [new] Crown Prince was prepared in the Great Ci'en Monastery. Each of the monks was offered a gift of three pieces of linen and silk, while courtiers were dispatched by order of the Emperor to offer incense in the monastery. When Xue Yuanchao, a palace attendant, and Li Yifu, an imperial secretary, visited the Master on that occasion, they asked him, "The translation of Buddhist texts is indeed a good task for the Gate of the Dharma, but we do not know what else could be done for its glorification. We also do not know in what manner the translation work was achieved in ancient times."

The Master said in reply, "As the Dharma *Piṭaka* is abstruse and profound, it is really hard to elucidate it at full length. However, it depends upon the Śākya monks for the exposition of its inner meaning and for its safekeeping, while its external protection and establishment rest on Emperors and kings. Just as a boat that sails on the sea may travel a thousand *li,* or the kudzu vine that twines upon a pine tree may stand a myriad fathoms high, it must depend upon favorable conditions to be able to extend its benefits widely. Now as the Han and Wei dynasties have lasted a long time, we need not discuss them here in detail. But let me relate the events involved in translating and propagating Buddhist scriptures since the times of the House of Fu (350–94) and the House

of Yao (384–417). Besides the monks, the lords and ministers also supported the task. At the time of Fu Jian, Dharmanandi translated scriptures with Zhao Zheng, a palace attendant, as his amanuensis. At the time of Yao Xing, when Kumārajīva translated scriptures, both the Lord of Yao and Yao Song, the Marquis of Ancheng, served as amanuenses. During the Later Wei dynasty, when Bodhiruci translated scriptures, Cui Guang, the Premier, acted as amanuensis and composed a preface to the translated texts. Such was the case during the Qi, Liang, Zhou, and Sui dynasties. At the beginning of the Zhenguan period (627–49), when Prabhāraṇa translated scriptures, Fang Xuanling, the Left premier; Li Xiaogong, the Prince of the Prefecture of Zhao; Du Zhenglun, Chief Chamberlain to the Crown Prince; and Xiao Jing, the Imperial Treasurer, were ordered to supervise and pay scrupulous attention to the compilation. But now we do not have such a system. Moreover, this Ci'en Monastery has been constructed by order of the present Emperor in memory of his deceased mother, the Holy Empress of Cultural Virtue. Its splendor is so magnificent that it has no parallel either in the present or in the past. Yet we do not have a stele with an inscription describing the event so as
266b to transmit the glory to posterity. Nothing can surpass this way of making the event known to all. If you gentlemen would send word to the Emperor, this good idea could be realized."

The two honorable officials consented and went away. On the following day when they attended the court, they submitted a report on behalf of the Master; and the heavenly Emperor granted him all his requests.

On the twenty-seventh day, Cui Dunli, a minister without portfolio, Chief of the Imperial Secretariat and concurrently Chief Chamberlain to the Crown Prince with the rank of Imperial Inspector and Supervisor of the Compilation of National History with the honorary titles of Pillar of the Nation and State-founding Duke of Guan County, announced an imperial decree:

> Since the scriptures and commentaries rendered by the monk Xuanzang of the Great Ci'en Monastery are new

> translations, they should be well done both in literary style and in the explication of their meanings. It is befitting to appoint Yu Zhining, Grand Tutor to the Crown Prince, Cabinet Minister, Left Premier, and the Duke of the State of Yan; Lai Ji, Chief of the Imperial Secretariat, concurrently Minister of the Board of Official Personnel Affairs with the rank of Imperial Inspector and the State-founding Baron of Nanyang County; Xu Jingzong, Minister of the Board of Rites and State-founding Baron of Gaoyang County; Xue Yuanchao Acting Palace Attendant, concurrently Left Attendant to the Crown Prince with the rank of Imperial Inspector and State-founding Baron of Fenyang County; Li Yifu, Acting Deputy Chief of the Imperial Secretariat, concurrently Right Attendant [to the Crown Prince] with the rank of Imperial Inspector and State-founding Baron of Guangping County; Du Zhenglun, Deputy Chief of the Imperial Secretariat, and some others to read the translations from time to time. Should there be any unfitting or improper expressions, they should polish and improve them as required. If scholars are needed, two or three persons may be coopted to meet the requirements.

When the interview was over, the Emperor sent the eunuch Wang Junde to dispatch the message to the Master, saying, "As Your Reverence needed men of letters to assist you in translating the scriptures, we have instructed Yu Zhining and others to go to you. As regards the slab inscription, we wish to compose it with our own hands. We do not know whether this is satisfactory to you or not. We are just sending you this information."

Upon receiving this imperial decree, which satisfied the Master's long-cherished desire, he felt moved and happy in the presence of the messenger and could not refrain from shedding tears of gratitude. On the following day he went with his disciples to the court to present a letter of thanks to the Emperor. (*Original note:* the text of the letter has been lost.)

In the second month, there was a *bhikṣuṇī* named Baocheng who had been a lady official under Emperor Gaozu, posthumously honored as Emperor Shengyao. She was a daughter of Xue Daoheng, Governor of Xiangzhou and Duke of Linghe of the Sui dynasty. Being a lady of virtue and good name, she had the honor to use a writing brush with a red holder and was an outstanding beauty in the inner palace. Her father was a scholar renowned for his learning, and she did not deviate from the family tradition of education. She mastered the classics and also possessed good literary talent. When the great Emperor was young, he studied under her. When he ascended the Throne he showed his gratitude to her as his old tutoress by conferring upon her, with great respect, the title of the Lady of Medong Prefecture. As the Lady desired to become a nun, the Emperor fulfilled her wishes and specially built the Helin Nunnery in the Forbidden Palace for her residence, with a slab inscription erected to record her virtues. Several scores of people were also permitted to be her attendants. The four requisites [of a Buddhist nun] were provided for them by the government, so that they might be ready to receive full ordination.

266c On the tenth day of the second month, an imperial decree was issued to invite the Master to proceed to Helin Nunnery to ordain the Lady of Hedong Prefecture, the Xue *bhikṣuṇī,* and to bring with him nine virtuous monks, each one waited upon by an attendant. It was also ordered that ten preciously decorated carriages and ten carriages for musicians should wait inside the Jingyao Gate. Horses had previously been sent to the monastery to welcome the monks; and when they reached the city gate, they were invited to ride in the carriages to proceed forward. The carriages for the monks went in front and those for the musicians followed behind. As it was in the second month of the spring season, the scenery was beautiful and splendid with green willow leaves and pink peach flowers, as well as blue pine trees wrapped in a mist of jasper color. The carriages adorned with brocade curtains and purple canopies shone brilliantly amid the pleasant surroundings and moved in an easy and graceful manner, just like monks repairing from the Jetavana Garden to the city of Rājagṛha.

Upon their arrival the monks were lodged in a separate house. An altar was erected to ordain Baocheng and more than fifty others. The Master alone was the *ācārya* (preceptor); the other monks were merely witnesses to the ceremony, which lasted for three days. When the ordination ceremony was over, a skillful artisan, Wu Zhimin, was asked to draw portraits of the ten teachers to be kept and venerated.

Beside the Helin Nunnery, there was the Deye Nunnery, which had been built previously and had several hundred *bhikṣuṇī*s living in it. They also requested that the Master confer on them the Bodhisattva Precepts, and so he went to the Deye Nunnery. After the function was completed, he took his leave and returned to his own monastery with the rich alms that had been offered to him. The Emperor ordered the eunuch Wang Junde to lead some servants holding a gorgeous umbrella to escort the Master. The beholders along the streets were greatly inspired to be good-hearted. Later, the Helin Nunnery changed its name to the Longguo Nunnery.

Shortly afterward the Emperor completed his composition of the inscription. He ordered Zhangsun Wuji, the Lord of Military Affairs, to show it to all the noblemen. The words of the inscription read as follows:

> We have heard that at the commencement of the constitution of the universe and at the beginning of the creation of all things, nothing was not carried on the earth and covered under the dome of Heaven. But the two luminaries shining in the sky are unfathomable in their waxing and waning phases, and it is impossible to get to the limit of the billows in the Four Seas flowing over the earth. Moreover, the Gate of the Dharma is profound and quiet, and it manifests its existence before its [realization of] non-destruction. The Holy Teaching is all-embracing and shows its form beyond formlessness. Thus the light of the Way shines through *kalpa*s as numerous as atoms in the world to edify all living

beings comprehensively. We remember that when the Buddha was born in his royal palace he was clad in lotus flowers and had blossoms to receive his first steps. Light issued from the divine pond, and the trees bent their branches low in the air. He pronounced the Voice of Virtue at the Deer Park and met various men of learning in the Dragon Palace, blessing those beings who had committed sins and invigorating a generation of men that were on the decline. In order to enable the ignorant of the lowest class to imbibe the Way, he broke his bones at a cemetery in the wilderness. The respectful edification of the Superior Man of Wisdom made the Youth of the Himalayas give his life to hear a stanza of the Dharma. The silky rain of the Dharma quenched the flames of the house on fire, and the Sun of Wisdom rolled up high and illumined the deep darkness of midnight to bring in the light of day.

We have widely read histories bound with silk covers of light yellow color and made careful studies of morality and the arts, but we have found that the Śākya teaching is perhaps the only blessedness that will last for infinite *kalpas*.
267a Our mother, the late Empress Wende, depending on a helve made with the wood of a jade tree, dredged the Gu River and cleared out its springs and source. Her virtue shone upon Tu Mountain and her way [of life] illuminated the bend of the Gui River. Her fame flowed out through the writing brush with a red holder, which made her beneficial actions manifest to the eight directions of the world. Her admonitions given in the Purple Palace will spread her high reputation to all the ages. The essence of negativity, however, abruptly obscured the moon, whose light of righteousness was hidden forever. The maternal connection was cut off, with its outstanding events sunk into oblivion eternally. When her toilet mirror is stroked, our feeling of sorrow is increased, and we wish to ascend the barren hill to look around, but where could we find any trace of her? In old times, Zhong You heaved a sigh of sadness at the sight of his emolument of

one thousand *zhong* of millet [reminding him of his mother who died poor], and Yuqiu suffered grief over his three losses.

The very great indebtedness we owe to our mother is really a matter of lifelong concern to us. Therefore, we intended to construct a memorial building, and so this monastery has been established like one paved with gold on the ground. At its back is a suburb, the Bin District, where a thousand estates dot the brocade-like scenery of trees, while in the front it faces the Zhongnan Mountains with peaks spurting out like lotus flowers to the height of a hundred fathoms. On the left side are eight rivers, the waters of which formed lakes shining like mirrors scattered over the earth. On the right side it adjoins the highway that reaches nine localities, and moving along it are carriages with canopies of feathers so tall as to touch the clouds. It overbears the inner area of the Land of Heaven and is credibly [known as] a superior spot in the Upper Capital. It displays engraved long corridors winding away to a far distance, and it has gorgeous pavilions rising up high in the air. The Morning Crow emerging in the rosy clouds shines upon the Palace of the Sun with variegated hues; and the New Rabbit appearing in the clear sky illuminates the Hall of the Moon with lucid brilliance. The paths are perfumed by autumn orchids, wisteria hangs in the courtyard where trees are sparse, osmanthus renders the rocks fragrant in the winter, and the windows are closely covered with clusters of red blooms. The lamps are brightly lit, producing many puffs; and flames burn on the crane-shaped lampstands in the midst of smoke. Streamers mark the distant spires of pagodas and their colors entangle the rainbow beyond the sky. The flights of steps are irregular and moistened with dew resting on jade with a fine grain. The light curtains roll back and forth with their nets shrunk into the shape of dimples and strings of pearls. The low hills are reddened by the rosy dawn, and over the ponds floats the green of the quiet mist. The tinkling of jade pendants harmonizes with the sound of evening bells, and the gentle breeze mingles with voices chanting Sanskrit stanzas in the morning. Not only is the Heavenly Palace of Accumulated Fragrance shamefully inferior in splendor, but the abodes of the immortals on Langfeng Mountain are also regretfully less exquisite in carved ornamentation.

We have the Venerable Xuanzang, who is really the crown of understanding of the truth of Suchness. Being a man of quiet and dignified bearing, he is like a cool breeze blowing gently over a tall pine tree. His resplendent thoughts are multifarious, resembling beautiful clouds reaching as far as the Milky Way, and his wisdom that surpasses the present age and discerns ancient times is inherent, while his sincere wish to foster tranquillity and cherish truth was aroused when he was a child. An outstanding figure of his generation, he has excelled Daosheng and Huiyuan and glorified previous ages, and with intelligence exceptional in this millennium, he surpassed Buddhasiṃha and Kumārajīva of a later time. Considering that the pure and simple customs of ancient ages had been discarded and vulgar conventions had become popular in the present, he was saddened by the long pitch-dark night and felt pain that the subtle teachings were buried in eternal oblivion. Thus he journeyed to foreign lands and widely studied the secret theories. He sailed beyond the Milky Way and shook the tin rings of his mendicant staff above the clouds. On the great sea with billows dashing to the skies, he voyaged upon terrific waves. Over long stretches of land covered with heavy frost, he forged ahead against the cold atmosphere and disappeared alone. While he was travelling on the plains, his robes were in tatters. He had to stand the gale on the Snow Mountains in his unlined garment. In the wilderness the daystar lay low, and his skin was scorched by the sun in the shifting desert. Marching on a long road in the moonlight, his shadow was his temporary

companion at night. Going far over precipitous peaks, his
267b form always became solitary with the approach of dawn. He thoroughly researched the sphere of wisdom and deeply investigated the ultimate truth. His mind understood the Buddha's teachings exhaustively and knew well the gists of secret learning. He mastered what previous sages did not know and comprehended what he did not learn previously from books. Thus the golden texts were introduced to the East to maintain teachings that were on the verge of breaking up, and the precious stanzas were shifted from the West to fill in the missing words. While he was looking reminiscently at the ruins of temple foundations in that country, his mind was fixed on this land. He propagated the profound gists while the leaves were verdurous in the Jetavana Grove. When he opened his mind in a distant land, the waves in the water of meditation became quiet once again.

We are devout toward the Eightfold Noble Path and mindful of paying homage to the twin śāla trees in order that the immense bliss gained thereby may help and benefit the deceased. Let us pray that our mother, the deceased Empress, will gain liberation through the Six *Pāramitās*; that her spirit will appear in front of the red gate of the palace; and that, having rested in the four stages of *Dhyāna,* her spirit will come over the area of the imperial residence. Alas! The Jade Candle is easily gone, urging the four seasons to change from warmth to cold. The Golden Arrow is hardly detainable, driving the Six Dragons to compete with the sundial and clepsydra in speed. We fear that slopes may be removed, but the trees will be still there; that seas may turn into mulberry fields and the locality remain the same; but that landforms may be changed when high peaks have sunk into deep valleys. Hence we respectfully inscribe this everlasting slab to state and make known the true circumstances. The inscription reads as follows:

The Three Luminaries shine upon all forms;
Like water flowing, everything changes.
The human path is long and far-reaching,
And time has its waxing and waning.
Simple and honest customs have long degenerated;
Callous and unkind practices have sprung up unperceived.
The waves of passion submerge consciousness,
And the mist of [evil] deeds besmirches sentiments.
Magnificent is the Guide of Men
Who first stepped on the earth at Kapilavastu.
His wonderful Way excels in abstrusity;
His profound origin controls tranquility.
Vulture Peak stood high in the distance;
The Dragon Palace was broad and spacious,
The Sun of Wisdom issued brilliant light;
The clouds of compassion shed the rain of benevolence.
Retrospection on the holy words and teaching
Gives rise to reflection on the Voice of Virtue.
These theories were esteemed in past *kalpas*,
And the Way covers both the present and the future.
His spirit prevails throughout the Nine Regions,
And his traces vanished at the twin śāla trees.
The dream of Emperor Ming of Han seems still in existence,
But the star dropped suddenly during the [Later] Zhou dynasty.
Our sorrow is attached to our mother's toilet mirror,
And our grief is as deep as the grand mansion.
In the Zhuolong Garden the plants are moist unnoticed;
At Jiaofeng Palace our feelings are concealed.
Frost and dew infringe in the morning;
Branches are raised by wind in the evening.

Riding in a Carriage of Clouds,
She passed away forever in peace.
These magnificent buildings are thus constructed:
The solid structures are adorned with engraved flowers;
The purple ridgepoles retain the moonlight;
With the glow of sunset are the red beams embellished.
At the windows painted with clouds, leaves are scattered;
Over the pond, flowers drift up and down in the wind.
The Imperial Carriage lowers its canopy and halts;
Beside the bridge the rainbow is slanting.
With the life of wisdom the Master is endowed,
An outstanding person with a calm and peaceful mind.
A unique personality appearing once in a thousand years,
He walks alone on the Path of Three Voids.
In the Jetavana Garden he had a taste of the Way;
In the Snow Mountains he ate his meal in the gale.
The Lamp of Wisdom is rekindled,
And the true words are once again esteemed.
The four seasons flow away rapidly;
The Six Dragons fly speedily.
At midnight the evil atmosphere is dispersed,
And at dawn the Hangu Pass is opened.
His good virtue is a lasting example;
His repute is known in the world of atoms.
This inscription is engraved in praise of him;
It will remain conspicuous for many years to come.

On the sixth day of the third month, various honorable gentlemen, on receiving the Emperor's composition, went together to the court to submit a memorial to express their gratitude to the Throne. It reads:

We knelt down to see heavenly flowers blooming and witnessed the marvelous treasure of the God of the Yellow River. We piously opened the secret scriptures and listened to the sweet melody of the Fairy Lady Yunyin. The composition embraces the moral principles of a myriad of generations
267c tions and contains the unusual views of a thousand years. We hastened to impart the happy news to one another, and our delight knew no bounds. We humbly believe that the Sun of Wisdom shining from the West has illuminated midnight and dispelled the darkness, and that the River of the Dharma has flowed to the East and moistened withered roots to enable plants to grow tall and graceful again. Nowhere is the edification not one and the same, and all principles in concordance with things come to the same end. Through successive dynasties up to the present, all people have esteemed these texts. We bow down to consider that Your Majesty may cut off the sea by merely dropping a garment [without effort] and discerns affairs in the Central Region as clearly as if in a mirror. The way of having dutiful descendants from generation to generation is increasingly glorified, but the ferry to cross over the sea of rebirth is more important. A Jetavana Garden has been opened in the superior area, and eminent ascetics have been invited to live in retirement in it. The place is extremely lofty and resplendent, and the people therein are marked by moral strength as mighty as that of dragons and elephants. Thus the profound teachings, for which a grand stele has been prepared, are once again deeply explored. The thought of the inscription is wonderful with hardly any limit, and only [monks wearing] black robes can master it. The meaning is beyond the surface of the words, and the truth is hidden deeply in emptiness. We, your subjects, have always been ignorant of the teaching but are lucky to have a peep at Your Majesty's composition. It is, however, just like comparing a small amount of water in a depression on the ground with the huge pool in which the divine turtle lives, or like a group of

ephemeral mayflies discussing how they feel about the long life of the cranes on which the immortals ride. We sang and danced while we were reciting the composition by heart. Having read it completely through, we could not refrain from leaping for joy.

Fascicle IX

Beginning with a Letter of Thanks for the Completion of the Inscription of the Ci'en Monastery in the Third Month of the First Year of Xianqing and Ending with His Return to the Western Capital with the Emperor in the First Month of the Third Year

On the ninth day of the third month in the spring of the first year of Xianqing (656), the Emperor completed the composition of the slab inscription regarding the Great Ci'en Monastery. Xu Jingzong, the Minister of the Board of Ceremonies, dispatched a messenger to send the composition to the Master, while the Protocol Department also granted a tally of authentication to the monastery. On the tenth day, the Master, bringing with him the monks of the monastery, repaired to the palace to submit a letter of thanks in which he said:

> I, Śramaṇa Xuanzang, beg to state that having received the tally from the Protocol Department, I bowed to accept the imperial decree informing me that Your Majesty has personally composed with your sacred writing brush the essay to
> 268a be inscribed on a slab for the Great Ci'en Monastery. Your Majesty's favor has descended upon me, and the majestic expressions of the essay have shed light on all things universally. The Gate of Mystery has thus become loftier, and the glory of Buddhist monks is augmented. I feel ashamed to squat on this thick earth, as I am short of strength to support the high firmament. I, Xuanzang, have heard that

the function of nature is to produce things through which to effect edification, and that the Way of the saints is to express their sentiments through words and phrases. But the drawing of the Eight Diagrams to bequeath literature to posterity is merely empty talk about things possessing definite shapes, and the explanations and divisions of the strokes of the diagrams do not go beyond the world. The virtue of Emperor Fuxi was extolled in ancient times, and the morality of Empress Ji was prominently high in a later age. But how could they be compared with the development of people's aspirations for the achievement of their affairs, with the ornate writings for the exposition of the eight aspects of human relationships, or with the utterances for the explanation of the Way in order to testify to the Three Clear Insights for the guidance of ordinary people? The reasons elaborated in the essay reach the limit of what is manifested by Heaven and earth, and the sentiment expressed in it is beyond the sun and the moon. If we compare them as to superiority or inferiority, this essay is the most magnificent of all.

I humbly believe that the Golden Wheel of Your Majesty is in motion, that time is guided by the calendar, that moral edification fills the four continents, and that kindness extends to the nine states. Your Way includes the Great Saint, and your merits are as plentiful as those of the gods. Your various abilities were endowed at birth, and your talents were given by Heaven. First you were grieved at the sight of the toilet mirror [used by your mother]; and then a *caitya* (monastery) was constructed where splendid banners were hung immediately. Furthermore, a rhymed composition was published. It is like the blooming of heavenly flowers. Wise words surge forward like great waves, swallowing up a sea of fine words, including the Dragon Palace, and covering a forest of rhetorical phrases embracing the Crane Wood. It contains the internal teachings of eighty-four thousand Dharma *Piṭaka*s and investigates the external *Six Classics*.

> Although it is abstruse, it is a standard work of scholarship. It is comprehensive in content but compact in style. The ruins of the Jetavana Garden are raised higher in reputation by these precious thoughts, and the remnant fragrance of the park at Vārāṇasī is kept undispersed with the aid of this excellent composition. It does not merely defame or praise a dreamland or enlighten those who have gone into the wrong path. It is really a model for all in the four quarters under Heaven and comprehends all the Three Worlds. My words and deeds are insignificant, and I am just an ordinary person among the monks. I have enjoyed extreme kindness from the Throne and have always considered myself fortunate. I had the good opportunity to visit the city of Kanyākubja twice, and I am happy to have been born at this prosperous time during the Image Period of the Dharma. I am ashamed of my unworthiness, but I also bounce with delight and feelings of actuality are mixed in my mind. With unlimited respect and sincerity, I come to the Imperial Court to present this letter to express my thanks.

On the eleventh day, the Master again thought that the literary talent and brilliant intelligence of the Sovereign were endowed by Heaven; that he was both sagacious and versatile; and that not only were his literary works as elegant as those of the ruler of Wei but his calligraphy also surpassed the characters written by the Lord of Han. Considering that the inscription was being composed by the Emperor, the Master thought that it should also be written with the Divine Pen. Thus he went to the palace with a letter to ask the Emperor to write the inscription with his own hand, saying:

> Śramaṇa Xuanzang and others beg to say that we presume that the heavenly bodies are shown in accordance with circumstances and that their divine functions are great and comprehensive. Edification is implemented at any time that it is required, so that holy duties may be completely fulfilled. From this we may know that when both the sun and the

moon are bright, they can move through their full course across the sky, and when both grasses and trees are exuberant, they fully manifest their power of beautifying the land. We humbly believe that the wisdom of Your Majesty covers all things on earth and that your kindness benefits the Three Worlds, both glorifying the Great Teaching and eluci-
268b dating abstruse moralization. King Mu of the Zhou dynasty was disdained for his fondness for the Way simply because he appreciated the song of Lake Yao (the dwelling of the immortals) in an empty way. Emperor Ming of the Han dynasty was slighted in spite of his veneration of the Dharma, as he merely founded White Horse Monastery and did nothing more. So [Your Majesty] condescended to write a Heavenly Composition to spread the abstruse gists far and engraved a piece of splendid jade to perpetuate the excellent principles. They are similar to the melodies produced by the antique music of the Six Yings and are like the radiance issued from the five planets, spreading utmost tenderness to inspire the common people and enhancing the great oath to rectify the defects of the time. It is certainly not merely for deep praise of the Doctrine of Suchness and propagation of the mysterious and profound Teachings. Although the elegant composition is fluently accomplished and is ready to be inscribed on an emerald slab, the characters have not yet been written, and the imperial edict in red script is still unproclaimed. After the music of the *kui* has been started with the beating of drums and bells mounted on *xun* stands, no vulgar songs can be sung in harmony with it. After the rooster has crowed at daybreak, how can the flame of a torch give any more illumination? If [Bo] Ya and [Shi] Kuang did not play the seven-stringed zither in harmony with the melodious rhythm and the sun did not control all things, how could the great sound of the drum of the Dharma be spread far and the resplendent colors of the Sun of Wisdom be made more glorious? On the basis of this allusion, I venture to plead for Your Majesty's favor in rendering it a

> complete achievement by wielding the Divine Pen, so that it may be as fine and lofty as if it were above the clouds, surpassing the handwriting left by previous monarchs. Thus Your Majesty's wonderful style of calligraphy may transmit its good repute to the rulers of future generations. The sound of the bells and the vibration of the chimes may give immediate awakening to a deluded one, and the characters written in the cursive style, resembling a phoenix soaring high in the sky or a dragon lying in coils, will open the eyes of those who, like blind men, have never seen such marvellous handwriting. It will not only glorify the teachings of the Image Period but also greatly benefit sentient beings. It will really extol the present age of good polity, when both the ancestral temple and the state are enjoying unlimited blessedness. Being stupid and shallow by nature, I have spent a number of years among the monks as an unworthy man feeling shame at my lack of learning and my imperfection in observing many of the disciplinary rules, but the Throne has deigned to overpraise me with panegyrical phrases. Although I am seized with so much fear that I have no place to hide myself, I have felt eager and earnest in my sincere request for many days, and I venture to repeat my annoying entreaty with a feeling of trepidation, as if I were walking on thin ice or burning charcoal.

The petition was not accepted.

On the twelfth day, the Master submitted another request, saying:

> Yesterday I was honored to receive with great delight a letter from the Throne, not consenting to favor me with the divine handwriting, but I still hold fast to my mind of loyalty. I presume that the wonderful tree with flowers climbing upon it must be the magnolia fuscata that issues fragrance. When I kneel before the precious Jade Hill, favors are still bestowed upon me with the presentation of honors. I humbly consider that Your Majesty wrote the composition

with a balanced mind, very exquisitely, maintaining peace without exerting effort. Your sagacious thought is expressed through your gorgeous writing brush, and your versatility is manifested when you fix your mind in concentration. Your grand pattern glorifies the banks of the Luo River, and the expert cursive calligraphist acquired his talent by practising handwriting beside a pool as his inkstand. I have previously received Your Majesty's favor, which I accepted like flowers of the *ruo* tree from the Golden Mirror. I venture to anticipate a second favor, as I expect to see the shadow of the cassia in the forceful strokes of your handwriting. It is not only because the two component parts of a pair of carved jade [pieces] always match each other or because it is the joining of [solar and lunar] rays that wins our admiration, but also because it is feared that nothing but your handwriting could carry the composition, which is as brilliant as the sun and the moon. Only the combination of the two can unfold the imperceptible Way. Although I am longing for the favor with all my soul and I touch the ground with my forehead in earnest expectation, I do not dare to hope for it.
268c With great sincerity, I venture to submit this request at the risk of my life.

At the request in this petition, the Emperor wielded his divine writing brush. As the Emperor had granted his entreaty, the Master, being highly pleased and greatly delighted, wrote a letter to express his thanks, saying:

I, Śramaṇa Xuanzang, beg to say that I have deferentially received the edict granting the favor of writing with your own hand the composition for the slab inscription for the Great Ci'en Monastery. When the decree affixed with the Great Seal arrived, it brought me Your Majesty's profuse kindness, which I accepted with a sense of apprehension, feeling ashamed of my own unworthiness and embarrassed at not knowing what to do. I have heard that when a powerful crossbow is drawn to the full, a mere flying squirrel is not strong enough to pull its trigger, and that when a big bell is silent, a slender dry leaf of grass can never make it sound. I never thought that the light of the sun and the moon would cast my shadow at the Gate of Emptiness, or that the moisture of rain and the evaporation of clouds would arouse inspiration in a secluded monastery. That is what I wished for, but it is not what I aimed to acquire. I humbly think that Your Majesty, walking on the Crater and riding upon the Dubhe, wielded the scepter and succeeded to the good fortune of the Throne. You have followed after Emperor Xuanyuan and exceeded Emperor Zhuanxu of ancient times. You could comprehend the Xia and embrace the Yin dynasties, elucidating various wonderful teachings for the education of your time and assembling versatile talents to illumine the common people. All men within the Nine Regions of the empire are bathed in the wind of kindness, and even those who are outside the four quarters under the sky are also benefitted by the edification of the mysterious Teachings. But the Dharma that serves as a bridge to cross a river cannot be traced to its origin unless it is explained by a perfect saint, and how can the task of elucidating the profound teachings be widely done if it is not done by a consummate man? Although remembrance of one's departed parents to the utmost will naturally touch the feelings of Heaven, one may also pray for protection from the nether world; this may cause the Throne to think back on past events. The beautiful composition that Your Majesty has deigned to write for us is already a precious object that surpasses valuables rarely seen in the world. When the divine handwriting is made open to the public, it will exceed all priceless treasures. All living beings will be greatly delighted and respectful. Buddhist monks, however, will feel double happiness and dance with rejoicing, as if they heard in a dream the magnificent music performed at the center of Heaven, which is no more marvellous than their present exhilaration. Even if they obtained the pearl

in the topknot of a Wheel-turning King, it would not be more precious than a piece [of your calligraphy]. We shall inscribe it on a durable slab of stone and plant it in the Courtyard of Blessedness, so that ignorant and deluded people may open their ears and eyes. This blazing torch of the Dharma will be transmitted to the future to enable those who see the valuable words and appreciate the calligraphy to cherish the mind of Bodhi on that same day. By reading the impressive composition, they may seek the ultimate truth and realize *prajñā* on the very spot. For as many *kalpas* as there are innumerable mustard seeds, the brilliance of the beauty of the composition will exist eternally. Through changes in the world such that seas may turn into mulberry fields, your graceful style will never perish. Being a man of ordinary origin, I always felt uneasy about my actions and deeds. But ever since I discarded my hair ornaments after having cut off my hair to become a monk, I have thought of propagating the mysterious Way. It was depending upon imperial prestige that I was able to visit Kapilavastu. Now in my translation work I have again received encouragement from the court. During the Zhenguan period (627–49) I bathed myself, though unworthy of it, in the great compassion of the Throne. Since the commencement of the Yonghui period (650–55) I have enjoyed all the more special treatment from Your Majesty. Through the Divine Pens of these two lords I have been overpraised, and the encomiums of two Emperors have overwhelmed me with honor and glory. In view of my own stupidity and inferiority, my mind is really filled with anxiety
269a and fear. Day and night, I never forget my sincere wish to repay this kindness. But the favors are as deep as a huge abyss, and how can a drop of water replenish it? The alms given to me are as large as a lofty hill, and I cannot express my thanks for them with a grain of dust. All I should do is to depend upon the various powers of wisdom and make use of them without limit to support the Great Blessedness in the Imperial Ancestral Temple and to assist in maintaining

> the deep foundation of the empire for a long period. With extreme fear and respect, I am writing this letter, which I entrust to the Palace Attendant Wang Junde to submit with my gratitude to Your Majesty. Having offended your august prestige unscrupulously, I am crouching with trembling and deep trepidation.

On the eighth day of the fourth month in the summer, the engraving on a slab of the inscription written by the great Emperor was completed by carving artisans. When it was about to be sent to the monastery, the Master, out of respect for the Emperor, did not dare to wait and do nothing for its arrival. So he led his disciples in the Ci'en Monastery, as well as the monks and nuns in the capital, in proceeding with banners, canopies, precious curtains, streamers, and flowers, all prepared by themselves, to the Fanglin Gate to welcome the inscription. The Emperor also dispatched musicians of the nine bands of the Board of Rites and the orchestras of the two counties of Chang'an and Wanlian to send the inscription. Of the more than three hundred ceremonial articles, even the shortest banners rose above the clouds and the smallest streamers touched the firmament. There were over a hundred vehicles carrying the musicians. On the evening of the seventh day they assembled at Anfu Gate Street in the western part of the city. It rained that night, and on the eighth day the road became unfit for the procession to move on. So the Emperor ordered the suspension of the procession but still invited the Master to the palace. On the tenth day, as the weather had turned fine and sunny, the Emperor ordered the display set out as had been arranged. On the morning of the fourteenth day, the procession started with banners and streamers and other articles properly arrayed one after another, presenting a gorgeous view that filled the road for thirty *li* from the Fanglin Gate to the Ci'en Monastery. The Emperor went up to the tower of the Anfu Gate and was very much delighted to watch the procession. More than a million people in the capital witnessed the sight. On the fifteenth day seven persons were ordained to be monks, and a feast was prepared to entertain two thousand monks, with nine bands playing music in front of the Buddha hall. It was not until nightfall that they dispersed. On the sixteenth day the Master again went with his disciples to the court to express his gratitude for the arrival of the slab inscription at the monastery. In a memorial he said:

> Śramaṇa Xuanzang and others beg to state that on the fourteenth day of this month we respectfully received the imperial decree sending the inscription engraved in the pattern of Your Majesty's handwriting for the Great Ci'en Monastery, together with an offering of music performed by nine bands. The sun, shining high, shares its light, to increase the brilliance of the torch of wisdom. The great expanse of the sea stretches its waves to replenish the River of the Dharma to its fullness. The great stele stands erect as a precipice, and the Heavenly Composition is as brilliant as sunlight, resembling colorful clouds shining in the morning upon Gṛdhrakūṭa Mountain and giving the impression that an illuminant star has descended upon a divine peak. All monks and laymen have rushed to the spot like fleeing clouds stimulated by lightning to see the inscription with amazement, dancing as if they had never seen such a marvellous thing before.
>
> I humbly believe that the Eight Trigrams bequeathed the symbols of writing and that the six lines of the Hexagrams are explained by the Appended Statements [in the *Book of Changes*]. By observing the traces of birds, the principle of writing characters was formulated, and the melody of *The Weeping Kylin and the Lamenting Phoenix* evolved into an allusion quoted in literary works. This is all the sages could
> 269b do, as is seen in these examples. They set up moral standards as an example for posterity, giving instructions whenever necessary and molding the character of sentient beings so as to glorify and publicize their good demeanor and meritorious deeds. But the rock carvings of the first Emperor of Qin just exalted his performance of the ceremony of

offering sacrifices to Heaven to mark his ascension to the Throne, while the slab inscription engraved by the Empress of Wei merely recorded the merit of offering grand sacrifices at the Ancestral Temple. Even such doings were praised as estimable, as standing high to look down upon all other rulers. But they are by no means like the composition Your Majesty deigned to write, as openly shown in your divine calligraphy. It has rhymes like music performed with metal instruments, and its forceful strokes produce a bright and splendid impression. Your Majesty visited the Dragon Palace and mastered the three mysterious teachings [of Laozi, Zhuangzi, and the *Book of Changes*]. Your calligraphy surpasses the phoenix style of writing and is extremely good in all the eight types of penmanship. It raises waves in the springtime to give free play to your thoughts, while it drops autumnal dew to create a novel style. It propagates the wonderful theories of the Ekayāna (the One Vehicle) and extols the abstruse meanings of the Six *Pāramitās*. It edifies all the regions of the Three Thousand Worlds, with its fame spreading beyond a hundred *koṭi*s of Buddha lands. The subtle sayings uttered at the Deer Park are rendered more manifest by your heavenly words and phrases, and the Bodhisattvas of the Bamboo Grove Monastery are more respectful because of your Divine Pen. Thus did the Brahmanic ascetics turn their minds [to the Buddha], breaking the net of doubts under [his] great guidance. Likewise Pāpīyān, the Evil One, rectified his intrigues, crushing down the hill of wickedness to follow the Way. Not only are the people within the gate of the mundane world beginning to be aware of their wrong position but also those who are held back in this dreamlike life are also taking actions to detach themselves from the sphere of suffering. The teachings of the Image Period were introduced to the East nearly six hundred years ago, but their propagation was not so popular then as it is now. In spite of the inspiration that Emperor Ming of the Han dynasty had obtained in his dream, he still consulted with

> Fu Yi about the matter, and when the Lord of Wu adopted Buddhism, he had to inquire of Kan Ze to solve points on which he had doubts. Since then, nobody else is worth mentioning except Your Majesty, who edifies the people according to circumstances and pushes forward all alone toward the bright future of destiny. Your good deeds will certainly be rewarded, and you will be able to build a strong foundation for posterity. Your Majesty's divine merits are as uncountable as those of a King of the Golden Wheel, and your good fortune and happiness are as everlasting as those of an Emperor wearing a crown adorned with precious jade. Xuanzang and the others, unworthy of favors received from the court, are fortunate to have entered the religious establishment with the earnest expectation that the cloud of compassion will spread again and the drum of the Dharma will sound once more. While the edification of the three kinds of knowledge is successful, the Gate of the Eightfold Noble Path is always open. Although we lack purity and devoutness, we have received encouragement and guidance in spite of our unworthiness of the privilege. Looking up to the high sky, we have gained the beneficence showered upon us. Drooping down to see the deep valley, we are ashamed of ourselves. With feelings of extreme fear and gratitude, we come respectfully to the palace to express our thanks to your Presence.

When the slab inscription arrived, the authorities built a separate stele house to preserve it at the northeast corner in front of the Buddha hall. The building had double arches and overlapping beam supports, and the lintels were painted with cloud patterns. The ridgepoles were gorgeously decorated with golden flowers shining downward and precious wind-bells emitting light upward, while the dew-receiving basin supported by the palms of an immortal was the same as that of a relic stupa. The Emperor was good at writing in regular script, the clerical style, the cursive hand, and the running style of characters. He was also particularly adept at writing in the "flying white" style, in which the strokes of a character have places not fully covered with ink. The inscription was written in the running style; but the four characters *xian qing yuan nian* (first year of Xianqing) were done in the "flying white" style, both styles being written in a most marvellous and beautiful manner. Thousands of people came to see the inscription every day. Those civil and military officials above the third rank who asked to make rubbings of it were permitted to do so.

After the method of keeping records by tying knots on a rope fell into disuse, written language replaced it and became popular.
269c The greater and lesser styles of the seal script are variant in form, and regular script is different from the cursive hand in shape. The writing brush is manipulated so as to produce different styles known as "hanging needle," "dropping dew," "cloudy vapor," "tiny ripples," "style of inscription on metal vessels," and the "service style," also known as the "running clerical style," with characters eight *fen* square, for writing official documents. Some of the ancients were expert at writing one style and others at another, but none was all-round at writing all styles. For example, Emperor Yuan of the Han dynasty was good at writing the clerical style for recording history; Emperor Wu of the Wei dynasty was expert at writing the cursive and running styles; Zhong You was adept at writing the three styles, ancient script, the seal script, and the clerical style; Wang Cizhong was skilled at writing the eight *fen* square characters; Liu Shao and Zhang Hong were known for their ability to write the "flying white" style; and Zhang Boying and Cui Ziyu were well-known as "sages of cursive writing." Only Wang Xianzi, Chief of the Imperial Secretariat, and Wang Xizi, Right Army Commander, were somewhat experienced at writing more than one of these beautiful styles, but even they could not write all the types of calligraphy. Thus when Wei Wenxiu saw the handwritings of the two Wangs, he remarked, "The two Wangs may certainly be praised as good hands at handwriting, but they know nothing of the art of calligraphy." Our Emperor [is known for] the prominent gracefulness of his sharp strokes and the highly elegant and forceful structure of his characters. He [can write] the various

types of handwriting of the ancient sages, possesses the versatilities of all wise men of previous ages, is peerless among great calligraphists, and is matched by scarcely anyone in writing compositions.

As the Master attended lectures and studied hard in the days of his youth, and travelled across icy mountains and snowy ranges on his way to the West, he suffered from a kind of cold disease. Each time it relapsed his heart was infarcted, causing him much pain and trouble. For several years he depended upon medicaments to prevent recurrences of his illness and keep himself in a steady condition. During the summer of this year, in the fifth month, he went to live in a cool place to avoid the heat of the season. This caused an attack of his old illness that became almost fatal to him. Both the monks and the lay people worried about his health. When the imperial secretary heard about the matter, he reported it to the Emperor, who ordered that the experienced imperial physician Jiang Xiaozhang and the acupuncturist Shangguan Cong be sent to attend upon him exclusively. All medicines needed were sent from the palace. Messengers were dispatched from the Imperial Guards several times a day in shifts, to observe climatic conditions and send back information. Even the Master's sleeping quarters were arranged by adroit attendants sent from the inner palace. He was treated with such great care by the Emperor that it was no less than the affection of a kindly father treating his only son. Jiang Xiaozhang and others attended on the Master day and night without leaving him. After five days his recovery from illness made people within and without the palace feel relieved. Having received the beneficence of the Emperor, the Master submitted a letter of thanks to him on the following day, saying:

> I, Śramaṇa Xuanzang, beg to say that as I am inept at taking care of my health, my cold disease became so much exacerbated that I was in critical condition and was on the verge of taking my last leave of Your Majesty. Under your heavenly beneficence, however, good physicians were sent to me, and as soon as the needle and medicine were administered to me, I regained my health. My declining age was

retained when it was drawing near to its end, and my spirit was revitalized when it was about to disperse. I am not only cured of my fatal disease forever and have my poor constitution regulated at all times, but I shall be able to see once again the prosperity of the time and follow more of your instructions. I am but a humble mediocre person, yet I have repeatedly been favored with special privileges. What has been granted to me is heavy while my life is light, and I do not know how to repay the kindness. All I can do is to depend upon the Power of Wisdom to requite your deep benefaction. As I am still feeble and weary, I am unable to come in person to the palace to express my gratitude. With much fear and respect, I am sending my disciple Mahāyānaprabha to submit this letter to your Presence.

270a After reading the letter, the Emperor sent the palace attendant Wang Junde to console the Master, saying, "Since you have just taken medicine, you must still be feeble in strength. May Your Reverence take good care of yourself. It is unfitting for you to exert your mind very soon."

Having been inquired after by the Emperor, the Master was overjoyed and felt awe and respect. He wrote another letter to express his thanks, saying:

I, Śramaṇa Xuanzang, beg to say that due to my karma I suffered from the pains of disease, and in an instant of breath I was almost separated from the present age of brightness. Suddenly the Emperor and Empress favored me with a mind of compassion and worried about my life. Imperial messengers came more than ten times to console me; and I was saved by divine medicine, as if I had taken a single pill that cured my illness at once. By drinking and bathing in the kindness of Your Majesties, I have been relieved of my severe pains; and by the medical treatment I was able to get rid of my ailment. I never anticipated that my dying soul would be summoned by the Supreme Emperor and that my life, which was about to end prematurely, might

> be retempered in the great furnace of morality. When I privately examined myself and my faults, I made an introspection of my own mediocrity and insignificance and wondered why I should have enjoyed all these favors. I clapped on my chest, feeling ashamed of being overendowed with grace and of my words being unworthy of publicity. The extraordinary beneficence I have received is inexhaustible. Even if I smashed my humble body into pieces, I could not repay this kindness. I just hope that I can exert myself to the utmost of my physical and mental strength to worship the Buddha and recite the scriptures in order to requite the exceptional grace granted to me. Thus I may be spared a small portion of the blame that I should bear. With extreme gratitude and respect, I am submitting this letter of thanks to your Presence. I am feeling both joy and fear and do not know what to do. My letter is a defilement in your eyes, and this increases my trepidation and trembling.

Formerly, in the eleventh year of Zhenguan (637), an imperial decree was issued, saying:

> As Laozi was our forefather, his name, position, and titles should be placed before those of the Buddha.

At that time the virtuous monk Fachang of Puguang Monastery, the virtuous monk Puying of Zongchi Monastery, and several hundred others debated the matter at court; but no rectification was granted. After returning home, the Master sent repeated petitions about the problem to the Emperor, who promised to reconsider the matter; but before it was done Emperor Wendi passed away.

In the sixth year of Yonghui (655) an edict was issued to the effect that if Taoist priests and Buddhist monks violated the law in a case difficult to judge, they could be tried and investigated according to secular judicial procedure. As the officials at the frontier and distant places did not properly understand the intent of the edict, they unscrupulously cangued and cudgelled [priest and monk culprits], to their great grief and humiliation, disregarding whether it was a grave or a minor case. The Master often worried about the matter and became dispirited because of his anxiety. Fearing that he might not be able to see the Emperor again, he wrote a note attached to another person's letter to the Emperor, explaining that the above-mentioned two points were disadvantageous to the state:

> As I might die at any moment, I fear I shall not have another chance to speak to Your Majesty. So I am writing this note while leaning upon my pillow with a feeling of fear and trepidation.

The Emperor sent him a reply, saying:

> We have noticed what you stated in your note. As the name and position of the Buddhists and Taoists were designated by the preceding Emperor, the matter needs deliberation and clarification. As for the decree that places [priests and monks] on the same level as lay people [in juridical affairs],
> 270b it should be cancelled immediately. The Master should be at ease and try to take medicine.

On the twenty-third day, an edict was proclaimed, saying:

> The teachings of Taoism inspire purity and voidness, and the texts of Buddhism are subtle and wonderful. They constitute a bridge for the people [to cross the sea of suffering] and are followed with respect in the Three Worlds. As it is now the Final Period of termination of the Dharma, people are disposed to do evil and liable to break regulations and the law. Thus [clergymen] were put under the control of the secular legal system as a temporary expedient to punish evildoers in the hope of forbidding them to do evil and persuading them to do good. It is not out of contempt for the Dharma if monks are involved in a lawsuit. But as the homeless ones have their own disciplinary rules, it must be troublesome for them to subject themselves to another judicial system. The order issued previously that Taoist priests and priestesses as well as Buddhist monks and nuns were

> to be tried according to secular law if they committed an offence should be abolished. If they commit any offence, they should be dealt with according to their monastic rules and regulations.

Upon receiving this favor from the Throne, the Master submitted a letter to the Emperor and went to the palace to express his gratitude, saying:

> I, Śramaṇa Xuanzang, beg to state that I have respectfully seen the imperial edict abolishing the regulation that when monks and nuns commit an offence against the law, they should be punished according to the secular jurisdiction, and restoring the old institution. Unexpected grace is suddenly bestowed upon the monks and nuns dressed in dark robes, and unlimited kindness has benefitted the religious establishment, like the morning sun shedding its light upon the Way with actual glorification. I bend my back to bow down and feel more excitement and fear. I humbly believe that since the King of Dharma has passed away, the edification of the Image Period of the Dharma is transmitted in vain, and the enforcement of monastic rules depends upon the favor and help of wise monarchs. I respectfully deem that Your Majesty, the Emperor, has ascended the Throne with the precious title and is legitimately riding on the Golden Wheel. You paid attention to the religion of Śākyamuni Buddha and cherished in your mind the propagation of his Teachings. Those who have discarded their hair ornaments and entered the Gate of the Abstruse Dharma are regarded as different from the laity in outward appearance. Although their sentiments are still involved in the world of the five turbidities, and they are mostly imperfect in keeping the disciplinary rules, they are the embodiment of the Field of Blessedness because they are dressed in the three robes. The close meshes of the net of justice are cut open, and instead the principle of leniency and kindness is spread. It is true that the straight words from the Golden Mouth

> rightly transfer this merit for the good of all. This is indeed a pleasure carried by celestial gods and terrestrial deities that respond to good omens. The monks and nuns are not only grateful for the kindness, but their purity and firmness are also augmented. If anyone acts against this policy of leniency and forgiveness, he will incur calamity upon himself, and his action will be contrary to the strict teachings of the Buddha, the great teacher, and unworthy of the deep compassion of our Imperial Lord. It befits all wise deities to reprimand such a person, without waiting for the deliberation of the law to mete out punishment to the offender. I am a mediocre and stupid person, unworthily occupying a place among the monks and often enjoying undeservedly great beneficence that makes me feel ashamed and uneasy. The unusual commendations that are repeatedly bestowed on me make me tremble with more fear. As I have been ill recently, I could not come to attend regular interviews in the palace. With unlimited respect and sincerity, I am sending my disciple Mahāyānaprabha to submit this letter to express my gratitude to your Presence.

After that the monks lived in peace, engaging in meditation and recitation of scriptures. With mixed feelings of grief and joy, the Master was moved to tears, making his sleeves and the front of his garment wet, while he clapped his hands and danced merrily. He wrote another letter to the Emperor to express his thanks, saying:

> I, Śramaṇa Xuanzang, beg to say that I have been graced with the edict abolishing the statute that monks and others
> 270c were liable to be interrogated according to secular law. For this my delight and gratitude is beyond compare. In my humble opinion, the rise and fall of the Right Dharma depends upon its being uplifted or repressed by the ruling lord, and high or low ethical standards match the perfection or deficiency of an Emperor's moral influence. Since imperial destiny has empowered Your Majesty to observe, as a

Sovereign monarch, the heavenly bodies with the jade armillary sphere, you have been a brilliant Emperor able to hold to purity. You have discriminately advocated the Path [of three virtues and three acts] and the Six Arts [of Confucianism], making a distinction between the abstruse religion and Confucian theories. You possess the key. You have opened the Gate of the Truth of Nonduality and widened the Track of Oneness. You have had the scriptures, obtained from the Dragon Palace, copied at Penglai Pavilion. You have connected the land of Gṛdhrakūṭa Mountain with the divine domain, so that the sound of the bell of purity may permeate throughout the realm and the deeds of blessedness and goodness may wash away the vices of the common people. This is really an auspicious occasion for the Gate of the Dharma and a great happiness for the people in the whole empire.

Recently, monks who were imperfect and who inculcated the people in an abnormal way internally damaged the good name of Buddhism and externally violated the imperial law. When one person is guilty, the entire group is covered with blemishes. Thus imperial prestige is offended and the culprit should be dealt with according to secular law, in order to eliminate evildoers and prevent them from committing further evil deeds. At a time when the monks were shocked and terrified, feeling shame and fear day and night, the Emperor's admonishment descended from Heaven, and his gracious beneficence extended to them manifestly, showing his sincerity in his deep expectation of the abstruse and wonderful teachings and covering up trivial smirches by his virtue of magnanimity. Thus he granted unusual benevolence and abrogated the law of strict punishment, not because those men are good enough to be valued, but because the Dharma they stand for is to be respected. Therefore, the fishes caught in a net were able to swim once again in the Yangzi and Han Rivers, and the birds ensnared in a cage could fly back to the distant sky. The water of the Dharma

> turned pure once again after being turbid, and the Field of Blessedness regained fertility after being barren. Every one of the monks and others is deeply grateful. They know they must try their best to clear away evil, so as to be in concordance with the mind of the Emperor and concentrate on worshipping the Buddha and reciting scriptures in order to repay the kindness of the Great Heaven. I humbly wish that Your Majesties, the Emperor and the Empress, will achieve a hundred blessings forever by your merit of perpetuating and making prosperous the truth of Buddhism. By your deeds of compassion, you will govern the empire without effort for a myriad of springs. The region of Cathay is associated with auspiciousness and the city of Vaisālī is in possession of goodness. With extreme gratitude, while dancing in delight, I am submitting this letter to express my thanks once again. I am in great fear that it may cause annoyance and offence to the Crown.

After reading the letter, the Emperor knew that the Master had recovered from his illness and sent a messenger to invite him to the palace. He was lodged and given offerings at the western pavilion in the court of the Ningyin Palace, where he continued his translation work and came out only every twenty or thirty days.

In the tenth month, during the winter, when the Empress was about to lie in confinement, she took refuge in the Triple Gem, praying for spiritual protection. The Master said to the Emperor, "Her Majesty will certainly be safe in childbirth; but should the infant be a boy, I wish that he be allowed to become a monk after he is born in safety." The Emperor consented instantly. On the fifth day of the eleventh month, the Empress offered one religious robe and a few scores of miscellaneous articles to the Master, who wrote a letter of thanks, saying:

> I, Śramaṇa Xuanzang, beg to state that I have been favored with the gifts of a religious robe and some miscellaneous articles, which I received with a sense of fear and shame without compare. The superior robe sewn with golden thread

271a and handed down by previous sages, and the invaluable cassock that I have heard about in the sacred texts, are not so fine and exquisite as this one I see with my own eyes. As for the colors evenly spread on the silk in rich and light shades, even Jing Jun could not surpass the skill required to produce them. It is cut and sewn with such fine and minute stretches that even Li Lou with his sharp sight could not discern the space between them. Once it is put on, one feels as if mist and clouds had entered the chamber, and it seems that a bouquet of orchids is placed on one's body. When one turns around to look at oneself, the value of glory is augmented at once. In olden times, Tao'an, whose words were valued during the Qin period, did not come across such benevolence; and Zhidun, praised and venerated during the Jin dynasty, seldom heard about such grace. But I, being a mediocre and shallow-minded person, have alone enjoyed such great favors, and the kindness bestowed on me by Your Majesties in person has made me tremble and perspire more and more. I respectfully wish that the Emperor and the Empress will have a large number of offspring and enjoy limitless blessings, that you will be constantly present at the Jade Mirror [in the imperial palace] and rule with the precious title forever, so as to protect and nurse all the common people in a manner as unlimited as the sky. With a feeling of deep shame and gratitude, I am writing this letter to express my thanks. The alms given to me are heavy, while my words are light, and I am incapable of expressing myself in full.

After the time of *sheng* (3–5 P.M.) on the fifth day, a red bird came all of a sudden and alighted on the imperial tent, at which event Xuanzang rejoiced and was delighted. He wrote a letter of congratulations, saying:

I, Śramaṇa Xuanzang, beg to say that I have heard that a white turtledove augured prosperity for the Emperors of the Yin period, and that a red bird presented a good omen of happiness for the monarchs of the Zhou dynasty. From this we may know that the presage of human affairs by good omens granted by Heaven has had a long standing. After the time of *sheng* (3–5 P.M.) and before *you* (5–7 P.M.) today, I saw inside the curtain at the courtyard of Xianqing Hall a red bird, its back, abdomen, and feet covered all over with red feathers, coming flying from the south. After entering the tent, it stopped at the Throne, pacing up and down and hopping in a leisurely manner. Upon seeing this strange bird, I said to it, 'As the Empress is pregnant and the time is yet unripe for the delivery, I am deeply concerned about her safety, for which I have said prayers. If my prayer is to be answered, show me a good sign.' Apparently understanding my human mind, the bird then turned around and stepped with its feet, as a gesture of showing safety. Feeling delight deeply in my mind, I beckoned at it and moved slowly toward it. The bird showed no fear when I approached it and was not scared when I stroked it. All the people around me witnessed this scene. So in return for its good will, I tried to make it take refuge in the Triple Gem, but before I could catch it, it flew away while I was following it up and down.

I humbly believe that Your Majesties, the Emperor and the Empress, have virtues that communicate themselves to the deities, and that your benevolence is extended to the myriads of common people, with rites conducted harmoniously and music performed in a happy way. Your kindness is deep and your righteousness far-reaching. Thus it has caused the feathered tribe to present auspicious signs and the divine bird to offer nature's service, showing that your offspring will thrive and that their prosperity will last for the long period of eight hundred years. This is an indication of happiness as in olden times, and it is also a divine gift in the present age. Being a humble man, I am lucky to have seen for the first time this happy and auspicious event. My gladness is so deep that I dare not keep silent about it. So I

> write this brief report to submit to your Presence. As regards
> 271b the impressiveness of the bird's feathers and wings, the simplicity and grandness of its masculine spirit, the researches done about it in successive dynasties, and the foreign land from which it emerged, they are beyond the scope of my knowledge. Stated with respect.

Shortly after the letter had been submitted to the palace, an imperial order was issued to send a messenger to inform the Master, saying:

> The Empress has finished parturition, eventually giving birth to a boy who is unusually handsome. A divine light filled the courtyard and shone up to the sky. Our delight is without limit and the people danced in and outside the palace. We will certainly not go back on our promise. We wish the Master will protect the baby, keep him in mind, and name him Prince Buddha Light.

The Master wrote a letter of congratulation, saying:

> I, Śramaṇa Xuanzang, beg to say that I have heard that the ultimate Way keeps itself and unfolds to enlighten human and heavenly beings at the beginning of their lives. Being moved by your deep expectation, a sagely child of wisdom and discernment is born. I humbly believe that the Emperor and the Empress have realized the three subjective and objective voidnesses, as well as edified and protected all sentient beings living in the nine dwelling spheres. Thus Your Majesties could discard your crowns with jade pendants on account of the two forms of truth, and give up your riding horses to take the One Vehicle. At the first moment of jubilation in the Empress' palace, she made a crore of vows. When the sagely baby was still in the womb, it showed signs of renunciation of home, so that the Buddha with ten titles manifested spiritual power to accept the child with great compassion. A hundred deities protected good people and paid homage to the inner chamber of the palace. Therefore

disasters and evil devils were cleared away, and the child was born in peace and safety. Seven flowers raised their heads to support his first steps, and nine dragons spouted water to bathe his body. His traces will be stored in the Gate of Abstrusity, and among the trees of the Way there will be the shade of spirituality. Although the Emperors of yore saw auspicious signs that touched the sky to indicate unusual events, how can that be sufficient to compare with the present gift granted by Heaven and match this personage of outstanding resourcefulness? The whole empire is singing with delight at the imperial lineage being blessed by divinities, and the monks who are courageous and astute are happy at the arrival of a divine colt. I humbly wish that Your Majesty will not withdraw your previous favor but will give a special order that the baby should wear religious robes and always cling to their gorgeous patterns, so as to make good karma. Moreover, the sublimity of the son of an Emperor is perpetual, no matter where he is, and his duty as the King of the Dharma is more and more lofty and prominent. In addition, merits have no limit. A ferry or a bridge may help one go far, supposing that Your Majesty's kindness is faultless and that your great vow remains unchanged.

I believe that the merit of giving all the resources within the Four Seas in charity is not adequate to compare with the merit of this donation [offering the Prince to the Sangha], and the deeds of all the Ten Stages of Bodhisattvahood cannot parallel this foundation of blessedness. It befits me to wish that the Emperor and the Empress will enjoy a hundred blessings that will coagulate into flowers with a brilliance to match the North Star and live for a myriad of springs on a base as solid as South Mountain. May you enjoy all amusements in your long lives and act upon all-knowing wisdom for many *kalpa*s to come. The Crown Prince, who is honest and splendid, will steadily succeed to imperial sovereignty; the one who is still in swaddling clothes is a brilliant descendant whose good fortune and happiness will increase

> day by day. He will mark his high moral integrity to posterity and succeed his sagely predecessor on the grass seat [of a monk]. I have incidentally met with this period of great fortune and confined my shadow within the gate of the forbidden palace. My height is not due to the upgrowth of my virtue but to the favors that are heaped upon me. It is lucky that national jubilation has begun and the foundation is laid for pure deeds. I am so happy that I am dancing with
> 271c delight. Even should I be ground to dust I should have no regrets. With unlimited gladness and greetings, I respectfully submit this letter to your Presence. My imprudence in doing so may have offended your august dignity, which makes me feel more and more trepidation.

Three days after the birth of the Prince Buddha Light, the Master wrote another letter to the Emperor, saying:

> I, Śramaṇa Xuanzang, beg to say that I have heard that in the *Book of Changes,* the idea of daily renovation of one's virtue is praised, and that in the *Book of Songs,* an unlimited line of progeny is glorified. So the Throne of the Zhou dynasty, which lasted a very long time, and the calendar of the Han period, which was handed down from the distant past, were responses to this Way. I have also heard that at the Gate of the Dragon [in the Yellow River] the water whirls rapidly and that because of its long source, it flows a great distance. Osmanthus trees grow in thickets and owing to their deep roots their flowers are fragrant and exuberant. It is humbly believed that the imperial dynasties were succeeded by one sagely Emperor after another, and that all of them have repeatedly observed the rules of accumulating and cultivating kindness and righteousness for the benefit of the common people since a long time ago. Thus the two Sovereigns [of the Zhou dynasty] had the honor to accept the Throne as a base for their descendants, and this may well be called having deep roots and a remote source. After Your Majesty accepted the order of Heaven, your exploits

increased all the more. Returning to simplicity and restoring purity, Your Majesty overstepped the traces of the Three Sovereigns and the Five Emperors; you have formulated rites and composed music, surpassing the standard established during the Yin and Zhou dynasties. You do not depend on the Imperial Carriage covered with yellow silk to show your nobility, and the salvation of billions of common subjects is in your mind. Before dawn you ask for your clothes to rise, and you forget food when the sun has declined in the west. With one man ruling over the country, this vast empire ten thousand *li* in area is in peace and tranquillity. Even the prosperity of the periods of King Cheng and King Kang of the Zhou dynasty was not up to the level of the present time. Therefore, auspicious clouds scatter luxuriantly, and both the rivers and the sea are waveless. All regions under the sun follow your moral instruction, and the Country of the Dragon is bathed in your edification. How grand and lofty they are! It is difficult to relate them at full length.

Then the Way is in connection with Heaven, and the perceptive deities have granted blessings. At a propitious hour in an auspicious month, the Crown Prince was born. The branches of the imperial family are extensive and prosperous, with jadelike calyxes spreading increasingly, and none of the people in the whole country is not rejoicing with a mind of dependence. As for me, I have enjoyed a hundred times more bliss than in ordinary cases. I am not only happy at the safety of Her Majesty, the Empress, I am also glad that the Tathāgata has one more successor. I respectfully wish that Your Majesty will not recall the previous edict but will instantly allow the Prince to leave home, so that the offspring of a secular monarch may be transformed into a son of the King of the Dharma, wearing religious robes with a clerical name given to him and taking the Three Refuges among the ranks of monks. He will perpetuate the Buddha's teachings and make them prosper during the Image Period, as well as expound and

propagate the profound theories, so that the grove of meditation may flourish once again and the garden of enlightenment may shine once more. He will follow the dense traces of Vimalanetra and tread in the high steps of Candrachattra. He will cut off the two kinds of bondage and become a fully enlightened one, with a splendid physical body like the king of mountains, adorned with a net of flames that will outshine the sun and the moon. After that he will shade the domain of the great chiliocosm with the cloud of compassion, raise high the torch of wisdom to a hundred *koṭis* of continents, strike the drum of the Dharma to defeat the heavenly devils, wave the superior banners to subdue the heretics, hold the deep water of the turbulent sea, quench the blazing fire on the evil mountain, drain the profound river of passions, and break the huge egg of ignorance to be a teacher of
272a celestial and human beings and a Guide of Men. Let us pray that on account of the good fortune of their offspring, the imperial ancestors and progenitors will ascend to the other shore [across the sea of suffering], and that with the benediction of your son, the Emperor and the Empress may enjoy a myriad of years of long life, eternally holding sway over the empire and always being present in the Nine Regions of the country. Only in this way can a son be considered a person of great filial piety who glorifies his parents. It was, therefore, for this reason that Śākyamuni abandoned his kingdom and strove to gain enlightenment. How could the trivial goodness of the Prince of Dongping and the mediocre talent of Prince Si of Chen dispute with him about superiority or inferiority on the same day, or argue about who is deep or shallow in the same year? I have respectfully prepared the religious robe and an alms bowl in my hands to wait for the welcome guest. A seat has been whisked clean and the road swept clear for the arrival of the carriage that will carry the Prince from the imperial city. With great delight and respect, I am submitting this letter to your Presence. My imprudence may have offended imperial

prestige; I deeply regret this and am trembling with utmost fear.

The prince immediately took the Three Refuges and put on the religious garb. He was under the care of the Grand Tutor, but his dwelling place was always close to the Master.

On the fifth day of the twelfth month, when the Prince was a full month old, an imperial decree was issued to ordain seven persons to become monks in the name of Prince Buddha Light, and the Master was also invited to tonsure the Prince. To express his gratitude, the Master submitted a letter to the Emperor, saying:

I, Śramaṇa Xuanzang, beg to say that yesterday I received the imperial decree ordering me to shave the hair of Prince Buddha Light and to ordain seven persons to be monks. By shaving his hair the passions of the Prince are cut off, and the monks ordained are to be his attendants and guards. Thus the palace of Pāpīyān, the Evil One, is shaken, and the hearts of the dwellers in the Heaven of Pure Abode are gladdened. Since the great vow has been announced, the grand blessedness will become more splendid. It cannot be considered a humble and unskilled hand that applies the craft [of a barber] to the skin of a noble person. Common men are allowed to enter the Way on auspicious occasions, when all people high and low happily clap their hands with mixed feelings of sadness and joy. I humbly think that it is important to be given protection when one is first dressed in swaddling clothes and that to put down one's hair ornaments is the inception of the cause of emancipation.

I believe that the Way of the Emperor and the Empress is concentrated beyond material limit and that their blessedness permeates the human world. Therefore they have expanded the Gate of Mystery and cultivated the root of virtue. What I wish is that the imperial descendants will enjoy blessings and that the Emperor, sitting in front of jade screens, will live on in prolonged peace and harmony, reigning over a hundred *koṭi*s of worlds for thousands and myriads of years. Being a sublime son, Buddha Light should be breast-fed. As he is guarded and protected by benign deities, all Buddhas will lay their hands upon his head to increase the glory of his wise and sagacious countenance and place their hopes for the prosperity of the Dharma on him. The newly ordained monks, having received deep grace, should also look up to and seek to achieve deeds of the Way, and observe the disciplinary rules in a perfect manner, so as to fit in with the imperial decree. Please keep what is appropriate and mow down what is worthless as dry grass in my letter; I shall be extremely grateful for it. With respect I am submitting this letter to your Presence.

On that day the Master also celebrated the occasion of Prince Buddha Light being one full month old. He presented him with a religious robe, while writing a letter, saying:

I, Śramaṇa Xuanzang, beg to say that I have heard that a whirlwind or a quick-flying eagle takes several days to soar up to the sky, and that when one is depicting the moon or polishing a pearl not quite round, one requires more than ten days to achieve fullness and the round shape. From this we may know that that which has received its spirituality from beyond the material world and shines colorfully in the
272b middle of the sky will certainly reveal its beauty at a later time and renew what is good and fair. Prince Buddha Light, depending upon superior goodness, will create auspiciousness. By expounding the philosophy of equilibrium and harmony, he will cultivate virtue. Since the moment he was born in the exquisite garden, heavenly temples were moved to look upon him. The air of profound wisdom has made his mind pure and lofty, since he is always protected by deities whether he is sleeping or awake. His jadelike countenance has an elegant appearance, with resplendence increasing day and night. If it were not for the Sun of Wisdom shining upon the Emperor and the Empress, whose thoughts are washed in the Stream of the Dharma, so that they place the

glorious achievements they have inherited from their predecessors on a basis as solid as a huge rock and unveil the abandoned hair ornaments to heavenly beings, how could the Prince have enjoyed the bliss of his swaddling clothes and sucked milk in security, without harm or distress, to grow into an intelligent youngster? Now the new moon has been shining for its first round, and the appearance of the Prince after a full month is indeed magnificent. When the auspicious plant *mingjia* has grown new stalks during its monthly period of growth, his lotus-like eyes will turn out to be really handsome. Therefore everyone in the imperial palace is feeling pleased, and all the common people are delighted; the seven groups of Buddhist disciples will seek his protection, and at the four gates of the center of learning, scholars will stand long to wait for his instruction. How could he be merely a man making daily inquiries into backbiting, or be like a crane or a horse ready for its rider? I am lucky to have been favored with a promise to grant me protection, but it is not my hope to form the relationship of teacher and disciple with the Prince. However, to foster a feeling of fraternity in the same brotherhood would be in keeping with my mind. Thus I venture to offer a copy of the *Prajñāpāramitā Sūtra,* written in golden characters in one fascicle and kept in a case, one copy of *The Story of the Scripture of Requiting Favors,* as well as one religious robe, an incense burner together with a table to place it on for burning incense, a bathing jug, a reading shelf, a rosary, a staff with pewter rings, and a vessel containing bathing power, all articles used by a monk, to express my personal exultation. I expect that he will ride in an auxiliary carriage and play with half a piece of jade, substituting an arrow made with a stalk of bitter fleabane for a double-edged sword, so that when the good deities see it, they will dance with delight and his great vow will be strengthened. I make bold to offer these gifts of ordinary use, and for my indiscretion in doing so I really feel deep fear with trembling. I

> humbly wish that the Emperor and the Empress may be served by honored and aged men, like stars surrounding the North Star with the sun and the moon shining together at the same time. May they gain the affection of myriads of common people and enjoy long life for ten thousand springs. The prince is comparable to the Smaller Sea, which is clear and lucent and covers a vast area. From it talented men may be selected. He will bestow favors on the feudal states to rouse their moral excellence and drive his carriage from one place to another with horses galloping at full speed. I pray that a thousand Buddhas may stroke the head of Prince Buddha Light and that a hundred blessings may concentrate upon his body so that his Voice of Virtue will increase day by day and his good moral standard gives great assistance to others. With extreme gratitude, I am submitting this letter to your Presence.

In the second month, during the spring of the second year (of Xianqing, 657), the Emperor favored the palace at Luoyang with his presence. The Master also accompanied him, bringing along with him five scripture-translating monks, each attended by one disciple, with all their daily requisites provided at public expense. Prince Buddha Light set off before the Emperor, and the Master went with the Prince, while the other monks followed behind. Upon their arrival, they were lodged at Jicui Palace.

In the fourth month, during the summer, the Emperor went to Mingde Palace to avoid the heat of the season. The Master again accompanied him and was lodged at Feihua Palace. Bordered by the Zao Brook in the south and stretching over the Luo River in the north, this was known as Xianren Palace during the Sui dynasty.

In the fifth month, an edict was issued ordering that the Master return to Jicui Palace to do his translation work. Having received the imperial decree, the Master wrote a letter to take his leave of the Emperor, saying:

> I, Śramaṇa Xuanzang, beg to state that I have respect-
> 272c fully received the kind edict permitting me to translate

scriptures at Jicui Palace. I am very grateful for this munificent treatment, which I accept with a feeling of deep thanks and gladness. The thought of departure from Your Majesty instantly made me feel sorry in my heart. My service to the House of National Achievements is insignificant, and my morality simply fades to nothing in the presence of virtuous people. Yet I have always overstepped and caused confusion to the principles regarding fame and conspicuousness and have been covered with heavy favors layer upon layer. When one is proceeding on a high precipice, one has the sense of fear, while one down in a valley is in no more danger. I respectfully consider that as the Emperor and the Empress are sage, wise, and magnanimous, as well as kind and merciful in edification and moralizing, all of the people have enough and the unitary empire is at peace. Now I shall be separated from the flight of steps in front of the palace hall, where orchids are planted and from which the tinkling bells of the Imperial Carriage can be heard. This would make me feel sad and melancholy, but that at the mere sight of Cogon Grass Ridge I am glad to think that Your Majesty will stay here longer. I respectfully hope that the Imperial Residence will enjoy everlasting peace and that the immortal peach will bring long life, while Your Majesty passes a cool summer at the Sweet Spring, as one might spend a pleasant time at the Jade Pond, the dwelling place of immortals. I hope that the trees growing in the warm season will usher in the autumn, and that a cool breeze will prevail in the summer. I shall be waiting for your returning carriage at the slab-paved path amid the fields and reverentially put away my dark-colored staff in the high forest to hail long life; I shall be willing to follow Your Majesty to distant places numerous times. With a very sad feeling of reluctance to leave, I am submitting this letter to take farewell of Your Majesty. My mental confusion is shown on my face, and it causes me such uneasiness that it is as if fire and water were fighting in my mind.

When the Master was in the capital, he had already translated the *Abhidharmajñānaprasthāna Śāstra* in thirty fascicles but had not yet completed the translation of the *Mahāvibhāṣā Śāstra* into Chinese. Then an edict informed the Master:

> Among the scriptures and treatises you intend to translate into Chinese, you should first translate those that do not yet have Chinese versions, and translate those that already have Chinese versions at a later time.

The Master submitted a letter to the Emperor, saying:

> I have heard that the Crown is for the protection of the common people in competition with previous sages. Although my literary activity may have exhausted my mental abilities, it is certainly to the wise monarch's credit. With his recondite contrivances that extend far without impediments, the Emperor has created everything [needed] to guard the imperial capital city from the surrounding suburbs and to glorify the palm-leaf scriptures at Yulin. A separate cottage for the work of translation has been opened, and a grand preface has been composed as a favor from the Throne, which will shine forever and transmit the brilliance for numerous generations in the future. Your Majesty has succeeded to the Great Task, the light of which will spread far in a graceful manner. Your divine functions are renewed daily. You never neglect to praise and distinguish the people. I have undeservedly enjoyed natural endowments and have respectfully received sagacious edicts. Each time I stroke my humble self, I always feel deep fear, while panting with uneasiness. On a day last month a decree was received to the effect that among the scriptures and treatises to be translated into Chinese, those which have not been previously translated should be done first, while those which already have Chinese versions are to be translated anew at a later time. But as for the *Mahāvibhāṣā Śāstra,* a work in two hundred fascicles for the exposition of the *Abhidharmajñānaprasthāna Śāstra,* only half of it has been previously

> translated into Chinese in some one hundred fascicles, with many errors and mistakes that need to be rectified in a new translation. Since last autumn, I have been translating this text and have finished more than seventy fascicles, with some one hundred thirty fascicles remaining untranslated.
> 273a As this treatise is very important for scholars, I hope that I may be permitted to complete the translation. As for translations of other scriptures and treatises, either in full or in abridged forms, which have faulty or mistaken renderings, I also wish to retranslate them as the case may require, to make them coincide with the holy teachings.

The Emperor granted the request.

The Master left Luoyang, the capital, when he was young. As he was now among the retinue attending the Emperor on his journey, he had a chance to pay a short visit to his native place, where he went to see his old family house and inquired about his relations and old acquaintances. But all of them were deceased except his elder sister, who had married into the Zhang family at Yingzhou. He sent for her, and when they met each other they felt both grief and joy. He asked his sister where the tombs of their parents were located; then he went in person to sweep the graves and pay his respects to his deceased parents. As the graves had been neglected for many long years, they were in a state of dilapidation; thus he carefully selected another plot of good land, desiring to rebury the inner and outer coffins. Although he had this intention, he dared not take arbitrary action. So he wrote a letter to the Emperor to solicit his permission, saying:

> I, Śramaṇa Xuanzang, beg to say that I, being unblessed by Heaven, lost my parents when I was young, and as it was during the chaotic times of the Sui dynasty, the funeral ceremonies were performed in a hurry. Time has flown by. More than forty years have passed; and the graves have become dilapidated, almost disappearing completely. When I look back on past events, I cannot calm down my emotions. Together with my old only sister, I have respectfully

> collected the coffins containing the remains of our deceased parents and removed them from that narrow unsightly place to be reburied at the West Plains, so as to express in a small way our gratitude for the kindness of our parents, which is as limitless as the great heavens. Yesterday I was favored with an edict allowing me to go out on an inspection tour for two or three days. As I have neither an elder nor a younger brother, but only one old sister, I have fixed by divination a distant date, the twenty-first day of this month, to perform the reburial service. Now because the affairs of the reburial have scarcely been arranged, I am afraid that the two or three days granted to me will not be sufficient for me to make the arrangements. I beg of Your Majesty the favor of allowing me to complete the reburial affairs and then return. Moreover, an honorable Brahmanic guest is travelling with me. If the funeral functions are too brief and perfunctory, I fear he would sneer at me. For all these troubles and harassment caused by me, I am extremely sorry and fearful. I respectfully submit this letter to your Presence, begging the kindness of Your Majesty, which is like the sky covering all clouds drifting under it, to comply with the request of an orphan.

After reading the letter, the Emperor granted the request and also instructed the authorities to provide the Master with whatever he needed for the funeral service at public expense.

Having received such unusual favor, the Master wrote another letter to the Emperor to express his thanks, saying:

> I, Śramaṇa Xuanzang, beg to state that my disasters are deep and my sins have accumulated in heaps, but the deity in charge of punishment has failed to inflict the death penalty upon me, so that I have dragged out my life to this day. The seasons change quickly, and the moon keeps on waxing and waning without cease. Over the passage of time, [my parents'] tombs became weatherworn and dilapidated, with weeds and brambles growing wild all around. For some

> years I have thought of changing their graveyard, but as I was far away, separated by mountains and passes, I could not fulfill my wishes. Luckily I accompanied the Imperial Carriage. Thus I was able to come to my native place with permission to realize my long cherished wish to change the burial ground of my parents' coffins. Whatever was needed for display at the tumulus was provided through the kindness condescendingly shown by the Emperor and the Empress to help me build the graves. I did not expect that the light of
> 273b the sun and the moon would shine even upon debris or that the humidity of clouds and rain would also moisten such wild plants as erigeron and artemisia. Being deeply grateful and perplexed, I am both feeling joy and choked with sobs. With great gratitude toward the living as well as the deceased, I am writing this letter to express our thanks to the Throne. This is a matter of importance for me; and being a humble person, I am unable to express myself in full.

With the permission of the Emperor, the Master reburied the coffins of his parents in another place; and the funeral service was performed at public expense. More than ten thousand people, both monks and laymen of Luoyang, attended the ceremony.

When Emperor Xiaowen (r. 471–99) of the Later Wei dynasty moved his capital from Dai to Luoyang, he built Shaolin Monastery to the north of Shaoshi Mountain. Consisting of twelve courts built along the slope of the mountain, it has two separate parts, known as the upper and lower sections. With Mount Song on the east, the monastery faces Shao Peak in the south, while at its back in the north is a high ridge of mountains with three streams flowing down. Towering rocks and precipitous steeps are reflected in the flying waterfalls. Pine lichens twine round giant bamboos; and cassia, cypress, lycium, and catalpa trees form a dense forest, presenting a grand and lovely view of peace and purity. It is really a pleasant place. The Western Terrace, which is the most beautiful spot, is the place where Bodhiruci translated scriptures, and it is also the place where the *Dhyāna* Master Buddhabhadra used to sit in meditation. A stupa (tope) preserving his body is still there. At the end of the Daye period (605–16), a group of insurgents tried to burn it but found it incombustible. People far and near thought it was a marvelous event.

At the foot of the range of mountains to the northwest of the monastery is Chen Village, also known as Chenbu, situated in the Phoenix Valley in the southeast of Goushi County, which is the birthplace of the Master.

On the twentieth day of the ninth month in the autumn, the Master asked permission to live at Shaolin Monastery to carry on his translation work. He wrote a letter to the Emperor, saying:

> I, Śramaṇa Xuanzang, beg to say that I have heard that the road to enlightenment is long and the one who is prepared to go along it has to make use of funds and provisions, and that the river of rebirth is deep and the one who wishes to cross it has to depend on a boat or a raft. "Funds and provisions" consist of wonderful deeds of the three learnings and the three kinds of wisdom, not merely rice pounded overnight or the like. "A boat or raft" means pure deeds of the Eight Endurances and the Eight Insights and not merely a boat, a raft, or the like. Because the Buddhas possessed [such prerequisites], they were able to go to the other shore, while ordinary people lacking them have to sink into the river of rebirth. Thus the vast world of three spheres is completely flooded by the river of the seven leakings; and the multitude of beings born through the Four Modes of Birth are all submerged under the waves of the ten bondages. None of them are not tumbling in the waves or whirling in the mist of bewilderment and confusion, without remission even at the end of an infinite amount of time when the *kalpa* rock is wiped away. Their bewilderment and confusion become even stronger when as many *kalpa*s as there are mustard seeds stored in a city have been exhausted. They do not know to get out of the house on fire by riding on the Three Vehicles or how to repair to the treasure-house by

proceeding along the Eightfold Noble Path. Really pitiful they are!

It is not the atmosphere of autumn that increases sighing but rather the sentiments of Confucius [concerning gains and losses]. That is why I sometimes stop eating at the time of taking meals, or start to wake up from sleep. I have often reflected that this physical body is a temporal congregation of various conditions, and that it is impermanent
273c thought after thought. Even a tree growing by a riverside, or a cluster of liana climbing on the wall of a well, are not adequate to compare with its precariousness and fragility, and the foam on the water in a dry city is not comparable to its instability. Therefore any morning or evening may be the end of one's period of existence, and nobody can hope for a long and lasting life. The months and years elapse as fast as flowing water, and in a blast of wind I have already reached the age of sixty. Since time is passing so quickly, one should be aware of how brief the span of human life is. Moreover, as I sought after the Dharma and looked for teachers and friends when I was young, I travelled to many places at home and abroad, and these long journeys made me feel quite exhausted. In recent years I have felt all the more weak and feeble. Looking at the moving shade of the sun and my own shadow, I do not know how much longer I can live. My funds and provisions [for the journey to enlightenment] have not yet been sufficiently collected and my future is gradually shortened. Not a day passes without my feeling worry about this matter indescribable by my writing brush and ink. But my humble life has been very fortunate to have met with sagacious rulers. I enjoyed unusual privileges granted by the preceding Emperor and have also received from Your Majesty more kindness than I am entitled to accept. It has been a long time since I began to enjoy such great kindness. As regards my increment of fame and reputation and the spread of my good name and prestige, flying without having wings and ascending to the skies while I still

sit on my seat, receiving offerings of the four requisites and surpassing the glories of my contemporaries, such cases are not to be found even among the ancients. What merits have I to reach such a stage of privileges? It is all due to the extensive waves of benevolence of the Emperor, like the light of the sun and the moon shining in a curved way even upon things lying in corners, so that the worthless rocks of Mount Yan are turned into precious stones and a jade is taken as a valuable steed. With a sense of introspection, I feel deeply ashamed. Moreover, to avoid completeness and avert fullness is a good adage of former sages; to be content with few desires is also a truthful saying of all the Buddhas.

Through self-evaluation I find that I am devoid of learning and talent. Both my fame and my deeds are inconsiderable. It is not fitting for me to be so bold as to overenjoy the kindness and benignity of the Emperor for too long. I beg permission to live in the forest on a mountain for the rest of my life, so that I may worship the Buddha, recite the scriptures, and walk up and down in meditation in order to repay the support and encouragement rendered me. With the dignity of a *Cakravartin* King, and, as a monarch, to spread the edification of the Dharma, Your Majesty ordered that the texts of the scriptures obtained from the Western Region be translated into Chinese. I, an incompetent person, have been unworthily favored with an appointment to take up the task. Since I received the imperial order I have been busy without rest from morning until night every day. Up to now I have translated more than six hundred fascicles of texts, all of which are the theoretical gists of the *Four Āgamas* in the Tripiṭaka and pivotal works of both the Great and the Lesser Vehicles. They constitute a comprehensive collection of the deeds and positions of both ordinary and saintly beings, and a sea of the eighty thousand Dharma gates; they are praised and sung as texts for pacifying the country in the Western Region. None of the literary definitions one should know is not found in them. As one chooses timber in a fairy wood, one may get a big or a small tree at one's option; as one collects pearls at the seaside, one is free to take square or round pearls. They seem to be the principal gists for scholars. With these translations I wish to repay the kindness of the state. It is true that I can never do so in full, but I hope I may repay one ten-thousandth of the favors granted to me.

But to cut off and subdue passions, one needs the aid of *samādhi* (contemplation) and *prajñā,* which are like the two wheels of a cart: neither of them is dispensable. As regards study and pondering over the scriptures, it is the lore of wisdom, while sitting relaxed in meditation in a forest is the
274a lore of contemplation. Since my youth I have engaged myself mostly in theoretical studies and have had no time to set my mind on the four categories of meditation and the nine grades of contemplation. Now I wish to pay attention to the practice of meditation and tranquilize my mind in the water of contemplation, so that I may curb my sentiments from being flippant like an ape, and hamper my mind from galloping like a horse. If I do not seclude myself from the world to live in the mountains, I shall not be able to achieve my object.

I humbly admit that in this region Songgao Mountain and Shaoshi Peak have ridges and precipices overlapping one upon another with peaks and ravines in strange shapes, where wind and clouds are generated, and benevolence and intelligence are contained. Fruits and medicinal herbs are rich and plentiful, while dodders and *Ficus pumila* grow freely and elegantly. It is really a famous mountain in this country and a sacred prominence of this region. There are also the Shaolin Saṃghārāma (monks' dwelling), Xianju Monastery, etc., all of which are built on rocks or across valleys surrounded by woods and springs. Buddhist affairs are done in a stately and solemn manner in the deep and spacious rooms and halls. This is where the Tripiṭaka Master Bodhiruci of the Later Wei dynasty period translated scriptures. One may really stay here to practise meditation and contemplation. Moreover, even the two Shus, who were courtiers, understood [enough] to retire and live in seclusion after resigning their glorious posts; and the two laymen, Chao Fu and Xu You, also knew [enough] to abide in truth and preserve naturalness. I have, what is more, renounced my home for the sake of the Dharma; but on the contrary I am staying inside a city; being stimulated by a cool breeze, I feel all the more ashamed whenever I think of this matter. I respectfully believe that Your Majesty is brighter than the Seven Luminaries and illuminates down to the nether world beneath nine layers of earth. I humbly beg for your brilliant understanding of my blunt sincerity and for the favor of granting me special permission, so that I may be free from the turmoil and dust of the mundane world and roll up the traces of my shadow from human society in order to keep company with herds of elk and deer and to follow groups of wild ducks and cranes, while I dwell on a piece of stone and take shelter in the shade of a tree. [I would] keep watch on the ape-like mind and contemplate the reality of all things, so that the thieves of the four Māras and the nine bonds should have nowhere to break through or to climb over the wall to cause disturbances. The mind of the Five Endurances and the Ten Deeds should originate from this to form a path gradually leading to Bodhi and be a good cause for crossing over to yonder shore. Thus I shall not be an external encumbrance to imperial edification but shall internally increase my own good deeds. If I may do so until the end of my life, it will be a favor from the Emperor. If I am granted my request, I shall follow the example of the good behavior of Huiyuan of Lu Mountain and continue the pure moral integrity of Daolin of Yan Hill. But I still hope to engage myself from time to time in translating scriptures in leisure hours left after practising meditation, which I would be very glad to do. With respect I come to the palace to submit this letter to your Presence, and by doing so I may have

> imprudently caused offence to imperial prestige. I deeply regret this with increasing trembling.

After reading the letter, the Emperor did not give his consent.

On the twenty-first day of that month the Emperor personally wrote a reply with his Divine Pen, saying:

> By reading your letter we have come to know that you wish to live a retired life in the mountains amid springs after the example of Daolin and Huiyuan of past ages and to engage in practising meditation in tranquillity along the tracks of Buddhacinga and Kumārajīva to set up a standard for the present time. We admire your pure moral integrity with veneration; it is truly what we appreciate and hold in esteem. We are devoid of knowledge and have acquired little learning, having never studied what is lofty and profound. But with our shallow judgement and superficial experience, we do not see the advisability of your proposal. Serving as a ferry or a bridge in the Three Worlds to conduct and guide all beings of the Four Modes of Birth, with bright intelligence issuing from the lamp of your mind, with your mentality crystalized like tranquil water by the practice of contemplation, Your Reverence cannot be obstructed by the dusts of sentiment, so how can the waves of mental agitation startle you? As you
> 274b abide in morality, there is no need for you to go to live in the overlapping ranges of Taihua Mountain. Since you can make a lodging out of voidness and tranquility, Shaoshi Mountain with its layers of peaks is not the only retreat in which you can stay. Pray put away what you have said and do not make the request again. Then the public marketplace will be a great hermitage, to be valued not only by ancient sages alone. Moreover, you may greatly increase your knowledge to win the esteem of the present age.

Since the imperial decree ordered him to cut short his request, the Master did not venture to say anything more.

After receiving the decree, he wrote a letter of thanks, saying:

I, Śramaṇa Xuanzang, beg to say that the messenger Li Junxin has arrived with the decree written personally by Your Majesty for me. The vigorous strokes of your handwriting are beautiful in the characters written in vermilion, and the wise phrases are as splendid as the mystic diagram that emerged from the Yellow River. The words appear like rocks piled together in the shapes of mountains and hills, and they seem to be suffused with the vitality of wind and clouds. I never expected that in the autumnal days of my life I might read literary writing as beautiful as flowers in springtime or that while staying between the Yi and Luo Rivers I would all of a sudden see a piece of precious jade from the Kunlun and Jin Mountains. I held it in both hands and danced with delight. Formerly, when (Wu Zhi, alias) Jizhong received a letter from the Lord of Wei, it only expressed friendly feeling at their being parted from each other, while the letter sent by the Emperor of the Jin dynasty to Huiyuan merely ordered that the monk be provided with rice. In their letters no such idea as making a lodging out of voidness and tranquillity is seen; neither is there the friendly emotion of the instruction that the public marketplace can be a great hermitage. From this I certainly know that the bosom of Your Majesty cherishes everything in both the mundane and the supermundane categories to the utmost degree. [The letter] contains the theories of both existence and nonexistence, greatly surpassing [the ancient Emperors] Fuxi and Xuanyuan and overtopping the Wei and Jin dynasties still more. But I am of the disposition of white silk and particularly fear the colors red and blue; my body is of the nature of kudzu and climbing plants that really need pine and willow trees to depend upon. I think of and wish to compare myself with the mist and clouds in the twilight at Shaoshi Mountain. I wish to keep company with the streams and rocks in the recesses of Mount Song, where my wish to avoid being drowned [in the sea of rebirth] might be realized and my ambition to prevent the fire [of desire] be fulfilled.

> Therefore I ventured with utmost ignorance to submit a report at the risk of my life, in the hope that the compassion of a sage monarch ruling over his country would not forsake even a wild duck or a quail, and that the moistening effect of clouds and rain would not desert a spider or a root-eating insect. But the illustrious decree arrived without granting me permission; however, it still favored me with praise and preserved my glory in a roundabout way. As my five sentiments are trembling, I do not know by which one I should abide. Since I have put aside my request, I dare not repeat it. I am respectfully writing this letter to express my thanks, shuddering more and more in fear.

In the winter, on the fifth day of the eleventh month, the first birthday anniversary of Prince Buddha Light, the Master again presented a religious robe to him, with a letter saying:

> I, Śramaṇa Xuanzang, beg to say that I have heard that one who passes by orchids blooming in the Purple Garden will surely feel happy, and that when one comes across a cassia tree flourishing beside a stream of bluish water, one will be delighted by its fragrance. If even a plant or a tree possesses such [a gladdening effect], it is needless to speak of a human being, and an imperial offspring at that. I humbly believe that the Emperor and the Empress, having imbibed divine and wise endowments, possess the virtues of Heaven and earth, placating and pacifying the various regions of the empire and fostering all their subjects as their children. At the same time, they have constructed a large number of monasteries and have widely performed meritorious deeds in order to make the Throne constant and unchangeable and to strengthen the destiny of the empire and make it as
> 274c strong as a diamond. It is their wonderfully good way of spiritual cultivation that makes the Crown Prince more and more intelligent and energetic day by day. As for the Prince of Luzhou, his extraordinary talent is becoming ever more brilliant. Prince Buddha Light's youthful wisdom has

augmented his luster, which may be said to have overtopped the Zhou and excelled the Shang dynasties to match the Yellow Emperor in sublimity. This is a matter for celebration by descendants for ten thousand years into the future.

Though a humble person of lowly position, I have been allowed the privilege of having interviews from time to time with the Prince and others, to my delight, real joy, and happiness at the bottom of my heart. As today is the first birthday of Prince Buddha Light, gifts must be offered in accordance with social etiquette, and so out of my benighted sincerity, I solemnly present a religious robe to him. I respectfully wish the Prince to be protected by ten thousand deities, sustained by a hundred blessings, and in peace and felicity whether awake or asleep. May he have a balanced appetite for his feedings of milk. May he perpetuate and make prosperous the Triple Gem, subjugate the four Māras, practise the Way of a Bodhisattva, and succeed to the causes of a Tathāgata. I am extremely happy to see a jade calyx on the celestial branch with beautiful and exuberant flowers. I beg to submit this letter, together with the religious robe, to your Presence. I may have imprudently offended the dignity of Your Majesty, for which I shiver with deep fear.

The Master was then engaged in translation at Jicui Palace. As he labored without even momentary stops, he fell ill from constant overwork. When this was reported to the Emperor, he was unhappy to hear about it, and dispatched, by imperial order, the palace physician Lü Hongzhe to comfort the Master. With incessant feelings of pain and joy intermingled, the Master wrote a letter of thanks to the Emperor, saying:

I, Śramaṇa Xuanzang, beg to say that the envoy Lü Hongzhe and others have arrived with an imperial order to console me while I am suffering from illness and to permit me to go out of the palace for recuperation. When the gracious edict suddenly arrived, my feeble body instantly stood up as if I were in the presence of the Crown, with awe as if I were placed on the thin ice over a deep pond. As my way of conserving good health is contrary to regular methods, disease and illness have befallen me. Since I left your Presence, I have felt doubly troubled by a pain in the heart, a depressed sensation in the back, bone-sore and painful muscles, abrupt loss of appetite, insomnia, and weaker and weaker breath. Fearing that something unthought-of might happen to defile the buildings of the palace, I thought of moving out and discarding myself in gullies, but I feared that it might cause alarm to Your Majesty; thus I dared not report the matter to the Throne. With the aid of my gate registration, I went out of the palace to the monastery, where, due to exhaustion and fatigue, my disease became critical, and my mind was also separated from the present time of good governance. Then the court physician Zhang Dezhi of the Palace Medical Department treated me with acupuncture, by which I was gradually cured of my ailment; it also enabled me to preserve my head. Recollecting the guilt of having taken arbitrary action, I am awaiting condign punishment.

I humbly believe that the sun and the moon, with their brightness, always forgive me for my stupidity and awkwardness, and that the moistening effect of the rivers and the sea has been specially lenient toward my faults; but how can imperial grace be extended to a humble person, distorting the law in favor of a common institution? I hope that justice will be upheld, so as to maintain the solemnity of the judiciary. A miscarriage of justice can be lightly done, but the use of the axe is a great matter. My remnant soul
275a and decaying body are still under the illumination of imperial favor, and I pat my chest to remember your sayings, which are engraved on my flesh and bones. I consider that I am not lying in my sickbed because of a common ailment. Even though I have no worry about death, my hope to live is exhausted. But my regret is that I could not repay [your] great kindness before the collapse of my humble life.

> I respectfully think that Your Majesty is assiduous, sparing no pains to take part personally in hunting expeditions and to inspect military forces in order to train the troops. You have shown kindness both in releasing a unicorn and in recording the merit of one who offered a phoenix, for which people assembled from far and near to celebrate. Both the high and low were simultaneously joyous, while the god of wind swept away dust and the mountain deities protected the wilderness. I respectfully think that whether active or inactive you will always be extremely happy and fortunate. When you went to pronounce the explicit Precepts for a hundred days, you [completed the mission and] returned in twelve days. You disdained travelling around on fine horses (like the eight reputed steeds of King Mu of the Zhou dynasty) and would turn back from a nearby place. The Imperial Carriage may be halted, but your constant remembrance is a comfort to me. In managing affairs I hesitate, for fear that I might commit dereliction of duty at the end of my life. With utmost gratitude and dread, I am respectfully submitting this letter for your hearing while awaiting punishment. In perplexity and trepidation, not knowing what to do, I am crouching to listen to your edict.

The Emperor was quite pleased to read the letter. Three days later he dispatched an envoy to welcome the Master to the palace, where he was entertained with the four requisites of a monk for many days in succession. Then the Master was sent back by imperial order to Jicui Palace to continue his task of translation.

In the winter, in the twelfth month, the palace at Luoyang was made the Eastern Capital. Because the area delimited for the capital was too small, portions of the counties of Sishui in Zhengzhou and Heyang in Huaizhou in the east were incorporated into the environs of the capital, while in the west Guzhou was abrogated and Yiyang, Yongning, Xinan, Mianchi, and such counties were taken and put under the jurisdiction of the metropolis. As the position of the Master's hometown was thereby elevated, he wrote a letter of thanks to the Emperor, saying:

> I, Śramaṇa Xuanzang, beg to say that I have heard that the Quail's Head demarcated the boundary of the State of Qin as a testimony of God presaging that (the Qin Emperor's reign would be as strong as) a golden city, and that the scripts presented by a tortoise to the Emperor of the Xia dynasty opened a hole through which to peep at the Jade Spring in the imperial city. From this we may know that the purpose of divine gifts is apparently the Emperor's edification. Good praise forecasts the distant future, and a light is placed high to shine to the utmost limit. One should sincerely act according to that edification. I humbly believe that the Emperor and the Empress manage everything, adjudicate all matters, and pacify the secular world with impartiality. You have repaired to an important habitable place in the middle of the land and settled there in the course of a pleasure trip. Following the example of the preeminent and glorious old system, an outer city wall has been built after the fashion of the capital [of the Zhou dynasty] at Hao. But a plain and simple palace was still cherished in your mind, and hard labor was substituted for the service system of old days. As you were absorbed in riding your galloping horse, you detested living in comfort and rose early in the morning. This is certainly not a compromise between the Flowery Empire and the foreign tribes to uniformize different systems of supplying corvee. How can one indulge in the Emperor's kind consideration shown in his announcement of his irrevocable decree? Thus when the order was first issued, the luxuriant mountains and rivers changed their appearance. At the beginning of the development of the system, the flying mist and clouds altered their colors. The lofty ridges of the palace halls are brilliant in the sunshine, and the imperial highway is peaceful with a gentle breeze. The deities responded to prayers, and moral

relations among the people were agreeable and harmonious. If Your Majesty wishes to compose a poem on the bream of Wuchang and take pleasure in shifting the imperial residence, I will vie with the crane standing in a pavilion on the heights to attend the imperial auxiliary carriages. I will imme-
275b diately slight the dependence of the State of Zheng upon the State of Jin and depreciate the tactics of Liu Ba toward Zhang Fei. Some former kings [of the Zhou dynasty] who were narrow-minded established Fen and Luoyi as their capitals at different times; but our lord, who is in control of everything, constructed both the Yi Valley and Xianyang as his seats of government simultaneously. The brilliant imperial clan will be prosperous, and the destiny of the empire will last to the distant future. It will certainly pacify Pingluo in the east and reach the Jianzhang Palace in the west. The standing musician played the *sheng* to wish for a long life; and peace and happiness are recorded in elegant language that is spread far and wide through intonation. Great is your perfect justice, and lofty are your deeds that are seldom narrated! Being a man of no use, I am unable to render any service. My fear about this is becoming deeper and deeper. But my native village is included in the suburbs of the capital in the region of the Three Rivers. This honor, which will last a thousand years, makes it a prosperous new town. My poor cottage has vanished, but my humble life is still in existence. I am glad that my native place is incorporated into the capital area, though I was not embarrassed to live outside the pass. Moreover, jubilation of nationwide stability is a matter for common rejoicing far and near, and the good health of Your Majesty is what the humble people specially bear in mind. Being overwhelmed by extreme gladness, I respectfully submit this letter to express my gratitude for your hearing.

In the first month, in the spring of the third year (658), the Emperor returned to the Western Capital, and the Master also followed him back.

Fascicle X

Beginning with His Return to the Western Capital with the Emperor from Luoyang in the First Month of the Third Year of Xianqing and Ending with His Demise at Yuhua Palace in the Second Month of the First Year of Linde

In the first month of the third year of Xianqing (658), the Emperor returned from the Eastern Metropolis to the Western Capital; and the Master also returned with him.

In the seventh month, during the autumn, an edict was again issued, asking the Master to move his residence to Ximing Monastery. This monastery was constructed on the nineteenth day of the eighth month, in the autumn of the first year of Xianqing (656). A decree had previously been announced that one Taoist temple and one Buddhist monastery should be built in the name of the Crown Prince at the site of the old house of the Prince of Pu on Yankang Street. The Master was asked to make a preliminary inspection of the place; and he reported after his inspection that the site was too narrow to contain two establishments. Thus the whole site was used for the construction of the Buddhist monastery, while the Taoist temple was separately built on Puning Street. The Buddhist monastery was built first; and the construction was completed in the sixth month, during the summer of the same [third] year.

The monastery was 350 *bu* on each side, with a circumference of several *li*. On both the left and the right sides there were thoroughfares, while in the front and at the back there were markets and hamlets. Green locust trees were planted in rows

outside the buildings, and a brook of limpid water flowed through the compound. With many imposing and spacious buildings con-
275c structed exquisitely, this was the most magnificent Buddhist monastery in the capital. The corridors, halls, storeyed houses, and terraces were so tall that they would frighten flying birds and touch the Galaxy. The gilded door knockers and the beams painted in colors were as dazzling as the glow of sunlight. There were ten courtyards with more than four thousand rooms. The whole establishment was so splendidly decorated that neither Tongtai Monastery of the Liang dynasty nor Yongning Monastery of the Wei dynasty could surpass it.

The Emperor had previously instructed the authorities to select fifty learned monks, each with an attendant. Later he also ordered that one hundred fifty youths who were practising moral deeds be chosen by examination to be ordained as monks. On the thirteenth day of that month a ceremony of ordination was performed in the monastery, and the Master was invited to supervise the ordination. On the fourteenth day of the seventh month, in the autumn, the monks were welcomed into the monastery, with a procession of people holding banners and umbrellas and playing music, just as when the Master and the imperial inscription were welcomed into Ci'en Monastery. The Emperor ordered Ximing Monastery to furnish one of its best rooms for the use of the Master, with ten of the newly ordained *śramaṇera*s (novices), Haihui and the others, to be his disciples. As the Master had been respected by the preceding ruler, the reigning Emperor, after succeeding to the Throne, venerated him all the more. Palace messengers and courtiers were sent to inquire after him without cessation. A total of more than ten thousand rolls of floss silk, damask, and brocade, together with several hundred monks' garments, patchwork vestments, and cassocks, were offered to him as alms at different times. After receiving these gifts, the Master spent them all for the construction of pagodas, for copying scriptures or making images of the Buddha for the benefit of the country, or for alms to the poor as well as to foreign Brahamanic guests. Whatever he received he gave to others immediately, without hoarding anything. He made a vow to make ten *koṭis*—one *koti* being one million—of images of the Buddha, which all were made.

In the Eastern Country the *Mahāprajñāpāramitā Sūtra* was highly esteemed. Although it had been translated into Chinese during a previous dynasty, the translation was incomplete, so the people requested that the Master kindly translate it anew. But as this sutra was a voluminous work, the Master feared that if he stayed in the capital where there were many distractions, [then,] human life being ephemeral, he might not be able to fulfil the task. Thus he asked for permission to live at Yuhua Palace to translate the sutra, and the Emperor consented.

In the tenth month, during the winter of the fourth year (659), the Master left the capital for Yuhua Palace, together with other learned monk-translators and disciples. All their supplies were provided for them as in the capital. Upon his arrival there he was lodged at the Sucheng Court.

On the first day of the first month, in the spring of the fifth year (660), he started to translate the *Mahāprajñāpāramitā Sūtra,* the original Sanskrit text of which consisted of two hundred thousand verses. Since it was a work of such vast magnitude, his disciples often requested that he produce an abridged version of it. In
276a compliance with their wishes, the Master planned to translate the text in the way that Kumārajīva did his translations, by deleting the superfluities and cutting out the repetitions. Having thought so, he had a dream one night in which he saw some extremely fearful things as warnings to him, such as [himself] sailing in a dangerous boat or walking on a precipitous peak, or a fierce animal pouncing upon him. He managed to escape these predicaments with trembling and perspiration. After awakening he was frightened and told his disciples, while making up his mind to translate the text in full. In the night he saw various Buddhas and Bodhisattvas emitting light from the middle of their eyebrows, shining over his body, and making him feel happy and pleasant. The Master also saw that he [himself] held flowers and lamps to offer to the Buddhas, or that he ascended a high pulpit to preach the Dharma to an assembly of many people who surrounded and

praised him with veneration. Or he dreamed that some people offered him famous fruits. When he awoke he felt pleased and happy, and dared not make any alteration or abridgement but translated the work exactly as the Sanskrit text was.

The Buddha preached this sutra at four different places, namely: (1) Vulture Peak near the city of Rājagṛha, (2) the garden of Anāthapiṇḍika, (3) the Heavenly Palace of the Paranirmita-vaśavartins, and (4) the Veṇuvana Vihāra in the city of Rājagṛha. It consists of a total of sixteen parts combined into one book. The Master had obtained three different versions of this text in the Western Region, and at the time of translating it he compared the three versions to fix the correct wording whenever he came across dubious or mistaken points in the text. He made attentive researches before he put it into Chinese; his scrupulosity and carefulness had no parallel since ancient times. Whenever he hesitated at some peculiar phrase or obscure meaning, he would always feel an unusual mental state, as if someone were solving his doubts. His mind would suddenly become clear, as if he were seeing the sun when the clouds opened up. He said, "Such powers of understanding are not due to my shallow knowledge; they are due to the spiritual assistance of the Buddhas and Bodhisattvas."

In the first part of the sutra, there is the Chapter on the Adornment and Purification of Buddha Lands, in which it is related that various Bodhisattvas and *Mahāsattva*s, for the sake of the *prajñāpāramitā* (the acme of wisdom) and by their supernatural powers, carried the best gems and jewels, all kinds of wonderful incense and flowers, food and drink of a hundred tastes, garments, music, and all excellent things produced at will that are pleasant to the five senses, as well as various other offerings of the great chiliocosm, to adorn the places where the Dharma was preached. During that night Huide, abbot of Yuhua Monastery, and Jiashang, a monk-translator, had a similar dream in which they saw that Yuhua Monastery was broadly and extensively decorated and purified, with beautiful adornments of pennants and curtains, precious carts, flowery banners, and musicians performing music everywhere in the monastery. They also saw that innumerable

monks, holding flowery canopies and offerings like those described above, came together to offer them to the *Mahāprajñāpāramitā Sūtra*. All the alleyways and walls in the monastery were decorated with gorgeous brocade; and famous flowers, on which the monks stepped and walked, were scattered over the ground. As for the Court for Translating Scriptures, it was doubly fine and exquisite, just like the land with precious adornments depicted in the scripture. They also heard that sermons were being given in three halls of the court, with the Master preaching in the middle one. Upon seeing this sight, they felt delighted and awoke. They both sent to see the Master and told him about their dream. The Master
276b said, "As we are just now translating this chapter, the Bodhisattvas must have offerings for it. Since Your Reverences have seen it, do you not believe it?"

Beside the hall there were two apple trees that suddenly blossomed several times out of season in a very lovely manner, with six-petalled flowers of brilliant red and white colors. The monks discussed the matter in detail, saying that it was a sign of the revival of the theory of *prajñā,* and that the six petals signified the Six *Pāramitā*s of reaching the other shore. But at the time of translating this scripture, the Master was constantly worried about the impermanence of human life. He said to the monks, "I am sixty-five this year, and I am sure I shall end my life here in this monastery. As this sutra is a voluminous work, I have often feared that I might not be able to complete the translation. So every one of us should work hard with more effort and spare no pains."

On the twenty-third day of the tenth month, in the winter of the third year of Longshuo (663), the translation was completed in six hundred fascicles altogether, with the title *Da-bo-re-jing* (*The Scripture of Great Wisdom*) in Chinese. Closing his palms together with exhilaration, the Master told his disciples, "This sutra has a special relationship with the land of the Han people. It is on account of this sutra that I have come to this Yuhua Monastery. If I had stayed as before in the capital, where there were many miscellaneous affairs to distract my mind, how could I have finished the work in time? It is with the spiritual assistance of the Buddhas and under the protection of the dragons and deities that I have completed the task. As this is a text that will guard the nation and a great treasure of men and heavenly beings, you all should rejoice and be glad at its completion." After the celebration ceremony was over, Jizhao, the duty distributor of Yuhua Monastery, prepared a feast as an offering [to the monks].

On that day the sutra was taken from Sucheng Hall to Jiazhou Hall, where the feast was arranged, for exposition and recitation. When the sutra was being taken, this work on *prajñā* emitted a light and flowers rained from Heaven, while music was heard in the air accompanied by an unusual fragrance. Having witnessed these spiritual auspices, the Master was greatly pleased and said to his disciples, "It is recorded in the sutra itself that in this country there will be people taking delight in Mahayana teachings. All kings, ministers, and followers of the four groups who copy, receive, and keep it, as well as recite and circulate it will be reborn in the heavens and obtain ultimate emancipation. Since there is such a passage, we must not keep silent about it."

On the twentieth day of the eleventh month, he asked his disciple Kuiji to write a report to the Emperor entreating him to compose a preface for the sutra. On the seventh day of the twelfth month, Feng Mao, a court secretary, announced an imperial decree consenting to the request.

After translating the *Prajñā Sūtra,* the Master felt physically exhausted. Knowing that death was approaching, he said to his disciples, "I came to Yuhua Monastery on account of the *Prajñā Sūtra.* Since I have now completed the affair concerning the sutra, my career has also come to an end. After my death you should manage my funeral in a simple and frugal way. You may just wrap my body in a coarse bamboo mat and dispose of it in some quiet corner of the mountains. Do not put it near the palace or any monastery. The impure body should be discarded far away." Upon hearing these words, his disciples wept piteously. While wiping their tears, they said, "Your health is still tolerably good and your
276c countenance is as usual. Why do you suddenly say such things?" The Master said, "I know it myself. How can you understand it?"

On the first day of the first month, in the spring of the first year of Linde (664), the monk-translators and other monks of Yuhua Monastery earnestly requested that the Master translate the *Mahā-ratnakūṭa Sūtra* into Chinese. Upon seeing the sincerity of the monks, he exerted himself to translate the sutra; but after doing just a few lines he closed the Sanskrit text and stopped the task. He told the monks, "This sutra is as voluminous as the *Mahā-prajñāpāramitā Sūtra*. Estimating my own strength, I shall not be able to complete this work. I am approaching my time, and it is not far-off. Now I wish to go to the Lanzhi Valley and other places to pay my last homage to a *koti* of Buddha's images." Then he went out with his disciples, and the monks looked at one another with tearful eyes. After worshipping the images, he returned to the monastery and engaged exclusively in practising the Way, doing no more translation.

On the eighth day his disciple Xuanjue, a monk from Gao-chang, dreamed that a tall and magnificent pagoda suddenly collapsed. He was surprised at the sight and got up to tell the Master, who said, "It has nothing to do with you. It is a sign of my dissolution." In the evening of the ninth day, when the Master was crossing a ditch behind his room, he tumbled and slightly injured his shin. Then he was confined to bed by an illness, and his breath gradually weakened.

On the sixteenth day he said in a dreaming condition, "There is a white lotus flower as large as a dish, pure and lovely, before my eyes." On the seventeenth day, he again dreamed that he saw hundreds and thousands of men, gigantic in stature and all clad in silk, bringing with them gorgeous embroideries, beautiful flowers, and valuable jewels to decorate the Master's bedroom up to the whole Court for Translating Scriptures inside and out. Even the hills and woods behind the court were decked with banners and pennants in a colorful way, and music was played. He also saw outside the gate numberless precious carriages, carrying hundreds and thousands of different varieties of fragrant food and delicious fruits, not products of the human world, to be offered to the Master. The Master declined the offerings and said, "Such delicious food can be enjoyed only by those who have attained supernatural powers. Not having attained to such a stage, how dare I accept it?" In spite of his declining, the food was offered to him without stop.

When his attendant coughed, he awakened and opened his eyes. Thus he related the foregoing dream to Huide, the abbot of the monastery. The Master also said, "According to this phenomenon it seems that what blessedness and wisdom I have cultivated in my life have not been acquired in vain. I believe that the law of causality as taught by the Buddha is not false."

277a Then he asked the Venerable Jiashang to make a list of the scriptures and commentaries he had translated into Chinese, which amounted to a total of 74 works in 1,338 fascicles. It was also recorded that he had painted pictures of Bhṛkuṭī and Maitreya, each 1,000 times, as well as ten *koṭi*s of clay statues. He had also transcribed the *Vajracchedikāprajñāpāramitā Sūtra,* the *Bhaiṣajyaguru Sūtra,* the *Ṣaḍmukhadhāraṇī Sūtra,* and other scriptures, each 1,000 times. He had given alms to more than 10,000 poor people, made offerings to more than 10,000 monks, lighted hundreds and thousands of lamps, and redeemed the lives of tens of thousands of living creatures. When the list had been made, he asked Jiashang to read it out. Having heard it, he closed his hands palm to palm with happiness and jubilation. He also told his disciples, "The time of my passing away is approaching, and I wish to make a confession of the offences I have committed against the disciplinary rules in the presence of the community of monks. Let all the monks who are able to come be assembled here." Then he gave up his robes and other property to make more images and invited the monks to perform a ceremony.

On the twenty-third day a feast was prepared for the monks and alms were offered to them. On the same day [the Master] also asked the sculptor Song Fazhi to erect an image of the Buddha in the posture of attaining enlightenment in the Jiazhou Hall. When the skeleton had been finished, he happily bade farewell to the monks of the monastery and the monk-translators as well as his disciples, saying, "This pestilent body of mine is deeply abominable. Since my work has been done, it is unnecessary for me to live any longer. I wish to share the merits of the blessedness and wisdom I have cultivated with all living beings, so that we all may be reborn in the Tuṣita Heaven to serve Maitreya Bodhisattva together with his inner retinue. [Then] when the [future] Buddha descends to the human world we may also come down with him to perform Buddhist affairs extensively until we attain Supreme Enlightenment."

After having said farewell, he concentrated his right thought in silence, while he murmured, "The aggregate of matter is void; and the aggregates of perception, conception, volition, and consciousness are also void. The realm of sight is void; and [all sense realms] up to the realm of mind are also void. The realm of sight-perception is void; and [all sense-perception realms] up to the realm of the mental faculty are also void. Ignorance is void; and [all *nidānas*] up to old age and death are also void. Even enlightenment is void; and voidness itself is also void." He also uttered a stanza and taught the people to repeat, "Homage to Maitreya Tathāgata, the Fully Enlightened One! May I and all living beings be speedily present before your compassionate countenance! Homage to the inner residents in the Abode of Maitreya Tathāgata! May I be reborn among them after I have forsaken my present life!"

At that time the abbot Huide again dreamed that he saw a thousand golden figures coming from the east and alighting at the Court for Translating Scriptures, while the air was filled with fragrant flowers.

At midnight on the fourth day of the second month, Mingzang, a master of meditation who tended the Master during his illness, saw two men, both about ten feet in height, holding together a white lotus flower the size of a small wheel with three layers of petals and a leaf more than one foot long, very clean and lovely, which was brought into the presence of the Master. Those who held the flower said, "All the evil deeds you have done to harm others from time without beginning have been annulled on account of
277b your indisposition. You should rejoice at it." The Master looked at them and put his hands palm to palm for a long while. Then he supported his head with his right hand, stretched his left hand

over his left thigh, and lay down on his right side with his feet relaxed one on the other. He remained in this posture until his death; and he did not move nor drink or eat anything.

At midnight of the fifth day, his disciples Puguang and others inquired of him, "Are you sure, Reverend Sir, that you will be reborn in the inner court of Maitreya's abode?" The Master replied, "I am sure to be reborn there." After he had said so, he panted and his breath gradually diminished. In another moment, his spirit passed away without being perceived by his attendants. When a piece of new floss was placed at his nostrils, they found [that he had already expired]. His body gradually became cool from the feet up to the top, which was the last spot that remained warm. His countenance was of a pinkish white color with an unusually relaxed and pleasant expression. [The body] did not change for seven weeks, nor did it have any offensive smell. If he had not adorned himself with meditation and wisdom and guarded himself with the fragrance of the disciplinary rules, how could he have attained to such a condition?

In Ci'en Monastery there was a monk Minghui, who practised good deeds diligently and ascetically and recited scriptures or walked in meditation during the first, the middle, and the last parts of the night without being idle or negligent. On the night of the Master's demise, he was walking around the Buddha hall to practice the Way after midnight when he saw four white rainbows stretching from the north toward the south, brightly and distinctly through Gemini, right over the pagoda in Ci'en Monastery. He wondered what they meant and remembered that when the Tathāgata entered nirvana, twelve white rainbows stretched from the west right through the constellation Tai-wei, whereupon the Great Saint passed away. "Now might this phenomenon be a symbol signifying the death of the Master at Yuhua Monastery?" At dawn he told the monks what he had seen, and they all thought it strange. On the morning of the ninth day, tidings of the Master's death, which had coincided with the occurrence of the phenomenon, actually reached the capital. Those who heard about it were amazed at the unusual spiritual event.

The Master was over seven feet in stature, and his body was of a pinkish white color with broad eyebrows and bright eyes. He was as dignified and solemn as a sculpture and as handsome as a figure in a painting. His voice was clear and far-reaching; and he spoke elegantly and sonorously, so that his listeners were never bored. Whether he was with his disciples or entertaining guests, he would sit for half a day without movement. He liked to wear Gandhāra costume cut out of fine felt only, neither too tight nor too loose. When he walked he carried himself gracefully, looking straight ahead, never glancing sideways. His magnificent manners were like the Great River flowing over the earth, and his brilliant wisdom resembled a lotus flower growing in the water. Moreover, he always observed the disciplinary rules in the same strict manner from the beginning [of his monkhood] to the end [of his life]. He took better care of the disciplinary rules than he would take of a floating bag when crossing a river, and he held to the rules more tightly than he would bind a bundle of cogon grass. He loved contentment and natural simplicity and did not like social life. Once he entered a place for practising the Way, he would not come out unless there was a summons from the court.

After the death of the Master, during the period of Qianfeng (666–68), the Vinaya Master Daoxuan, the abbot of Ximing Monastery, who had the power of communicating with divine beings, once saw a deity appearing before him. The deity avowed himself to be a disciple, saying, "I am a son of General Weito among the heavenly beings, and I am in charge of ghosts and divine beings.
277c When the Tathāgata was about to enter nirvana, he instructed this disciple of yours to guard and maintain his bequeathed Dharma in Jambudvīpa. I have recently seen that you are pure and strict in observing the disciplinary rules, that you pay attention to the texts of the Vinaya *Piṭaka,* and that people of the four quarters who have doubts come to consult you for a solution. But there are to be found from time to time abnormal and erroneous points in the commentaries you have written on the major and minor Precepts. As you are getting advanced in age, you have been incorrect in your writings, which might mislead people of later generations. Thus

I have come to let you know the Buddha's intention." Then he pointed out the errors and mistakes in the commentaries and exegeses Daoxuan had written on the major and minor Precepts, and asked him to correct them. Upon hearing this, Daoxuan trembled with both grief and joy. Then he asked about various dubious and ambiguous points found in the scriptures, disciplinary rules, and commentaries to which he could not find a solution. The deity solved them all for him. Again, he asked about the morality of the monks who had transmitted the Dharma since ancient times; and he also inquired about the Master. The deity said in reply, "Since ancient times teachers have been either strong in understanding the Dharma but weak in practising it, or weak in understanding but strong in practice, without a unitary standard. The Venerable Xuanzang alone cultivated the deeds of both blessedness and wisdom in nine lives. In every incarnation he was always learned and erudite, intelligent and eloquent, always the first and foremost in the land of Cīna in Jambudvīpa. Such were his blessed virtues also. His translations are good both in literary style and in quality, and are not inconsistent with the Sanskrit texts. Owing to the power of his good deeds, he has now been reborn in the inner court of Maitreya in the Tuṣita Heaven, where he will hear the Dharma with comprehension and understanding, and he will never again be born in the human world. After inquiring about the Dharma from Maitreya, he will gain comprehension and understanding and attain to sainthood." Having received these words of the deity, Daoxuan took his leave and returned; and he recorded this event in several fascicles that are now stored at Ximing Monastery. Based on this account we may say that if it were not for the deity, who would know the Master's high talents and excellent virtue? How could the mind of an ordinary man conjecture them?

When the Master was ill, Xu Xuanbei, an official sent to inspect the translation of scriptures, submitted a memorial to the Emperor on the third day of the second month in that year, saying that the Master had been ill because of an injury to his foot. On the seventh day of that month, a decree was issued to the effect that the Palace Service Department should send physicians to attend him with

medicine. The authorities immediately dispatched the imperial physicians Chang Dezhi and Cheng Tao to go posthaste with medicine to see the Master. But when they arrived, the Master has already passed away, and it was too late to give him any medical treatment. Then Du Shilun, Prefectural Magistrate of Fangzhou,
278a reported the demise of the Master to the Emperor, who was so much grieved at the sad news that he suspended court affairs and said, "We have lost a national treasure." At that time all the civil and military officials wept piteously, and the Emperor, after uttering the remark, also could not refrain from sobbing mournfully. On the next day the Emperor said again to his ministers, "What a pity that our country has lost the Venerable Xuanzang. Although he was only one man, it may be said that a pillar of the community of monks has collapsed and that all living beings of the Four Modes of Birth have lost their guide. It is like a host that has suddenly sunk in the vast sea of suffering, or a lamp that has gone out in a dark room." After saying so, the Emperor sobbed without cease.

On the twenty-sixth day of that month, an imperial edict was issued, saying:

> It is reported by Du Shilun that the Venerable Monk Xuanzang of Yuhua Monastery has passed away. All requirements for the funeral service should be provided at public expense.

On the sixth day of the third month another decree was issued, saying:

> Since the Venerable Xuanzang of Yuhua Monastery has died, his translation work should be suspended. The scriptures he had already translated into Chinese should be copied by the government as usual, while the other untranslated texts should be handed over to Ci'en Monastery for safekeeping and must not be lost. Those of the Master's disciples and co-translators who were not formerly resident monks at Yuhua Monastery should be allowed to return to their original monasteries.

On the fifteenth day of the third month there was another decree, saying:

> On the day of the funeral of the late Venerable Monk Xuanzang of Yuhua Monastery, the monks and nuns in the capital should be permitted to make banners and canopies to escort his remains to the cemetery.

Being a person learned in the Way and highly virtuous, the Master was deeply adored by the reigning monarch, who therefore issued decrees repeatedly in favor of him after his death. None of the ancients could be compared with him in this respect.

Then his disciples, in compliance with his last instructions, made a hearse out of bamboo mats and carried the coffin back to the capital, where it was placed in the Hall for Translating Scriptures in Ci'en Monastery. Several hundred of his disciples cried so piteously that they shook the earth; and the monks and laymen in the capital who hurried to the place, weeping and sobbing, amounted to hundreds and thousands every day.

On the fourteenth day of the fourth month, when the burial was to take place east of the Chan River, the monks, nuns, and laypeople in the metropolis arranged a funeral procession, holding more than five hundred articles, such as unadorned canopies and white banners, curtained carriages used on the occasion of nirvana, a golden coffin kept inside a silver one, the śāla trees, and so forth, arrayed in the streets one after another like clouds touching the Galaxy, while funeral music sounded mournfully in the air up to the sky. Over a million people in the capital city and from various states within a radius of five hundred *li* attended the funeral procession. Although the funeral affairs were arranged gorgeously, the Master's coffin was carried in a bamboo-mat hearse. The silk traders of the Eastern Market used three thousand rolls of silk fabrics to make a nirvana bier decorated with resplendent jade ornaments in an extremely fine manner, and asked that the Mas-
278b ter's coffin be placed on it. Fearing that it might be contrary to their teacher's wishes, the disciples did not consent. Thus they placed the Master's three regular robes, as well as a patch-robe worth a

hundred pieces of gold and offered by the state, on the bier to proceed in front, while the bamboo-mat hearse followed behind it. All the onlookers shed tears and were choked with sobs. On that day over thirty thousand people, both monks and laymen, spent the night in the cemetery.

On the morning of the fifteenth day, when the coffin pit had been filled up, a feast was prepared at the cemetery for the people before they dispersed. At that time the sky darkened and the earth changed color, and the birds and beasts cried in lamentation. If even the animals felt so sorrowful, it is needless to say how sad the hearts of human beings felt. They all remarked that the boat of compassion had suddenly sunk in the deep river of passion and that the light of the Lamp of Wisdom had gone out when the long night was still dark. They were as pained at the departure of the Master as if they had lost their own eyes. It was not merely comparable to the collapse of a mountain or the ruin of an arbor. How piteous it was!

On the eighth day of the fourth month in the second year of Zongzhang (669), an edict was issued that the tomb of the Master be shifted to the plain north of the Fan River, where a pagoda and a temple were constructed. This was because the original tomb was too near the capital and was visible from the imperial palace, so that the Emperor was often grieved at the sight of it. Thus another site was chosen for the tomb. The ceremony for the reburial was duly performed. The disciples were moved by sadness; and wayfarers felt deep sorrow and were just as mournful as before. Alas!

> *Comment by Shi Huili:* We observe that stars at dusk and the moon at night continue the brightness of the sun that has sunk in the west, and that the three rivers and nine streams help expand the sea in the east. Such is the way that things assist each other. There is no difference between them and men in the transmitting of tradition. Since the brilliance of the King of the Dharma faded away and Ānanda presided over the Assembly of Elders, a thousand years have elapsed and ten generations have passed away. During

this time saints and sages appeared now and then, and men of outstanding talent emerged one after another. Each of them cherished his own great ambition, and all of them were profuse in superior wisdom. They carried on their shoulders the teachings bequeathed by the Buddha and guided heavenly beings and men, while their Way could becalm a whirlwind and their spirit could overturn the seas and mountains. Some of them could stretch a finger to produce moistening rain, or issue a marvellous light to illumine another one's rooms. Others subjugated the heavenly Māra with a pair of corpses, or answered the questions of the reigning lord with a single reply. Others wished to spread the Dharma at a frontier monastery, risking winds and waves on the dangerous journey, and still others were open-minded in dealing with others and sought provisions to travel to deadly places. They finally enriched the Stream of the Way and benefited an unlimited number of people. This was good for the transmission of the Lamp of the Dharma, and it coincided with the instruction of the Buddha. According to former books, is this not true? As the source of purity is inexhaustible, we now have the Master who has succeeded to the tradition.

The Master was endowed with the spirit of the stars and imbued with the ascending vitality of the great mountains; his talents surpassed the bamboo arrows of the east [a synonym for men of genius], and his reputation was as good as that of the bronze vessels of the south. His refined character was unusually prominent, and his strong virtue was unparalleled. He assumed the salvation of all beings of the Four Modes of Birth as his own responsibility and regarded the establishment of the Right Dharma as his personal duty. So lofty was he! like the Song and Hua Mountains supporting the vault of Heaven! And so immaculate was he! resembling carnelian shining under the clear water of the sea! His intelligence and great talents origi-
278c nated spontaneously, while his appreciation of the Way and

his disdain of worldly glory arose out of his natural tendencies. As regards the profundity of his versatility and wide learning, he capped and was even higher than Daoheng and Sengzhao, and his ability to scrutinize abstrusity and perceive what was subtle outstripped and went even farther than that of Daosheng and Daorong. How great and magnificent he was! He was truly an extraordinary person to perpetuate and make prosperous the teachings of the Buddha. He will make the edification of the Image Period shine again during the Period of Decadence. That was why a man of such brilliance and virtue was born in this world.

The Master believed that although the virtuous teachers of ancient times and in his day all based their expositions of the scriptures and commentaries on the holy teachings, they had cited different texts and caused theoretical disputations in a confused manner for a long time. More than a hundred topics were in dispute, such as whether the *ālaya-vijñāna* (receptacle consciousness) suffers retribution or not, whether a transformed person has mind or not, whether or not the sin of those who repeatedly threaten the harmony of the Sangha might be absolved by hearing or through the influence of the Dharma, and so forth. All these are complicated subjects in the Tripiṭaka and the *Four Āgama*s and were key problems for both the Greater and the Lesser Schools, which were not solved by former sages and commonly caused doubt among present savants. The Master, too, was hesitant about these points, and this made him unhappy. He sighed with emotion and remarked, "The scriptures and commentaries we have in this land are but branches of the Gate of the Dharma; they are not the roots. The various teachers, moreover, hold different views; they cannot dispel the doubts in their minds. The full texts must be obtained, and we shall probably be able to get the decisions only at Jetavana Grove."

Thus he cherished a lofty aspiration and made up his mind to travel to a foreign land. In the eighth month, in the

autumn of the third year of Zhenguan (629), he made a vow and packed up to go his way at once. He reached Nālandā Monastery in Central India, where he met a great teacher named Śīlabhadra, meaning Eminent in Virtue, who practised both of the two schools of Buddhism and whose unusual discernment was profound and far-reaching, since he was well versed in the Tripiṭaka and adept at the Four Vedas. He was most proficient in and familiar with the *Saptadaśabhūmi Śāstra*. As this treatise was the crown of all scriptures, it was specially favored and frequently taught and preached. It was originally composed by Maitreya Bodhisattva, and being the root system of all Mahayana Teachings, it was what the Master had made up his mind to seek. All of the sixteen great states turned toward it with adoration, and the students who studied its theories always numbered over ten thousand people. When the Master went to visit the teacher to study with him, they were pleased to meet each other at first sight and regretted that they did not meet sooner. Thus the Master listened to the teacher's lectures and accepted his instructions with full conviction. He also consulted with the teacher to solve his doubts. Whatever he had heard once, he could repeat without omission, just as Mengsi takes in the water of all rivers, or as Mengzhu lake absorbs all the water of the swamps of Yun-meng. The
279a teacher sighed with surprise and remarked that he had never seen such a prodigy before. He said, "We rarely hear even the name of such a person, not to say discuss the mysterious teachings with him at this time!"

Since then the Master's fame spread to west of the Pamir Ranges, and his name was known in the eight countries. Having heard about his renown, the elder teachers and eminent scholars of those countries, all being experienced writers of profound learning, came to debate with him. Their carriages, proceeding one after another like a line of flying geese or a school of fish swimming in file, congested the road and made pedestrians touch shoulders. Although challenges of controversy fell upon the Master like rain pouring down from a cumulonimbus, he defended himself and explained his views in a leisurely manner. He turned his opponents' arguments against them, as if he were thrusting their own spears against their shields. All of them found their way of reasoning defeated and laughed merrily in submission, remarking that this revered gentleman was endowed with genius by Heaven and that it was difficult to rebut his propositions. Upon seeing him, King Śīlāditya and others applauded with delight, prostrated themselves before him with their elbows on the ground to kiss his feet, and offered him all the valuables they had in their possession.

When the congregation was over, the Master continued to study Sanskrit texts and various scriptures and treatises, including all of the Vaipulya teachings spoken by the Tathāgata during his lifetime on Gṛdhrakūṭa Mountain; the incomplete (Hinayana) texts taught at the Deer Park; the works written by the later saints Aśvaghoṣa, Nāgārjuna, Asaṅga, and Vasubandhu; and even the heterogeneous views of the eighteen schools of the Gokulikas, etc., and the ultimate gists of the five groups of Mahayana texts of the superior Way, which he collected and did research into to understand their essence and grasp their literary meanings. He also visited those places where the Buddha had left his traces during his lifetime, such as the wood of evergreen śāla trees where he entered nirvana, the Bodhi tree under which he subjugated Māra the Evil One, the lofty stupa (tope) built by Ajātaśatru, and the hill where the Buddha left his shadow. The Master paid homage in person to all those spots and saw all of the spiritual wonders without omission.

Having fulfilled his expectations and completed his studies, the Master was about to return to his homeland; he had copied over six hundred Mahayana and Hinayana texts and obtained seven statues of the Buddha and more than a hundred grains of *śarīra* relics. On the twenty-fifth day of the first month, in the spring of the nineteenth year of the present reign (of Zhenguan, 645) of the Tang dynasty, he returned to Chang'an. The monks and laity rushed out to welcome him, and all the markets in the capital closed for the day. At that time the mist disappeared and the fog rolled away, unveiling beautiful scenery with a light breeze wafting gently. Precious curtains filled the streets, and ornamental banners covered up the sun. Auspicious clouds emitted colorful rays in the sky in a rich and luxuriant manner, and the common people and scholars sang praises on the thoroughfares in booming and sonorous voices. Evil winds were then suppressed, and the Sun of Wisdom was conspicuously brilliant once again. Although it was not as joyful as when the World-honored One descended from the Trāyastriṃśa Heaven to Jambudvīpa, it may well be called a happy occasion that happens once in a thousand years.

On this journey the Master travelled tens of thousands of *li* through various kinds of hardships and perils. As for the frozen and icy cold mountains; the rivers with surging billows and turbulent waves; the extremely toxic vapors of black winds; the herds of lions, wolves, and hyenas; the country where Faxian lost his travelling companions; and the place where Zhiyan parted company with his friends, these were places not visited by Ban Chao nor toured by Zhang Hai. But the Master travelled alone by himself without fear of obstacles, spreading the virtues of Tang beyond the eight rivers and propagating the national culture among
279b the five regions of India. Thus he made the lords and kings of distant lands turn their minds toward the Emperor of China and the chieftains of faraway quarters admire the celestial capital. Although rare merit as was achieved by the Master is not to be seen in every generation, it is also due to the influence of the power and prosperity of the imperial dynasty.

The Emperor, holding the mystic diagrams in his hand, ascended the Throne in accordance with the preordained order of succession and coincided with the red prediction that he would rule over the people as supreme lord. He slaughtered vicious persons to save the populace and swept away the clouds and rainbows to let the sun and moon shine brightly. He put right the broken pillars at the four quarters and quelled the overflow of the great sea to set up the universe anew and cast it again in another mold. The nine functions of his government included all those of the Yu and Xia dynasties (2155–1767 B.C.), and his seven martial virtues crowned those of the Han and Wei dynasties (208 B.C.–A.D. 265). The country was in such a peaceful condition that the great sea was calm and the Yellow River became clear, while the weather was propitious and produced rich harvests. No faraway people were disloyal to him, and all those who were near him lived in safety. Everything was achieved spontaneously without effort, peace reigned in his domain, and both men and divine beings rejoiced happily. Moreover, as the sun and moon are attached to the sky, the significance of the three good [roots] may become prominent, and as his ministers are loyal and assiduous, it is fitting to sing their praises. The weight of his exploits is so heavy that it has reached the limit of the carrying capacity of the earth, and his virtue has moved Heaven above. The purple ganoderma bloomed at the jade steps, and the fruit trees blossomed beside the crimson pavilion. [His virtue] is also like the auspicious rock found at West Prefecture or the supernatural omen shown on a piece of jade in Song County, which recorded the one thousand years' reign of the sagacious monarch and manifested the deeds to be succeeded to by the Crown Prince. Sentences are being written by talented scholars that are as rarely seen as the feathers of a phoenix; and compositions concerning the Superior Fruit of the Sun of the Buddha, which have not been heard of for numerous generations in the past, are now appearing during the reign of the present Emperor. Is not this a sign of the divinities assisting the Virtuous One and of Heaven blessing the members of the imperial family?

On the other hand, the Master fixed his attention on the ultimate truth and protected the Five Vehicles like a city wall and its moat. He remembered the features of Gṛdhrakūṭa Mountain and recalled the sermon delivered by the Ajitavatī River. Thus the Buddha's image with purple hair arrived brilliantly, as auspiciously as when a phoenix appeared at the imperial court, and eminent monks learned in the superior texts arrived, adding radiance to each other. Clouds of compassion spread over the whole world, and the drum of the Dharma sounded throughout the three thousand great chiliocosms, with heavenly flowers flying in propitious winds, and emerald mist sharing the fragrance of the smoke of incense. So those who are submerged in the stream of mundanity may hope to get ashore in time, and those who are pursuing spirituality and practising mysticism can see the three voidnesses not far away. It is said that by means of the compass that points the road, those who have lost their way may find directions, and that when the autumnal wind blows through a forest, all hollows sound by themselves. The Master's great virtue was like that, and he was living at a time such as this! He was not like Faya or Buddhatuṅga, who cherished the Way but met with the two cruel and ferocious rulers Shi Le and Shi Hu [of the later Zhao period, 319–51]; nor was he like Dao'an or Kumārajīva, who transmitted the scriptures though theirs was the time of the two usurpers Fu Jian [founder of the former Qin dynasty, 351–94] and Yao Chang [founder of the later Qin dynasty, 384–417]. To compare the depth of their learning, they were but ditches beside a road, while the Master resembled a river or a lake. To contrast their brilliance, one was the morning sun while the others were glowworms.

Formerly, when a penannular jade ring from Zhong Mountain arrived, Emperor Wen of the Wei dynasty (220–64) offered to write a rhapsodic poem in praise of it. When a phoenix presented itself, Jia Kui composed a verse to describe its marvellous appearance. If even such humble

things as a bird and an inanimate object were exalted in poems in days of yore, how can we keep silent at the present time, when an enlightened ruler is on the Throne, without saying anything to eulogize the Master's immortal deeds and his great function as a pillar of the state? I am ashamed to compare my learning with that of the past sages, and as far as virtue is concerned, I am not like the prominent
279c persons of former times. It is simply because we shared the same teachings of the Buddha of the Image Period, and because I had the good fortune to join the Sangha as a junior member, that my mind of admiration for him is a hundred times more than that of ordinary persons. Therefore I made the effort, despite my mediocrity and stupidity, to write this biography. As regards the beauty of his pure character and good repute, and the traces of his unprecedented and unrepeatable journey, they will be recorded separately by other great men of the pen and cannot be fully described here. I hope gentlemen of clear discernment will refrain from sneering at me.

The eulogy says:

Perishable are the senses of living beings;
The Great Saint has shifted his spirit.
Nobody but a sage
Can continue his heritage.
Aśvaghoṣa propagated it at first,
And Āryadeva expounded it afterward;
Just as when the sun has sunk,
The bright moon will appear.
Serene and majestic was the Master's deportment;
Surely he was a man of integrity
More elegant than celestial beings
And unhampered by worldly defilements.
Having thoroughly mastered the profound teachings,
And being also learned in Confucian principles,
He was as pure as brilliant pearl,

With virtues as fragrant as orchids and angelica.
He regretted that the scriptures were deficient
And feared that there might be wrong meanings.
He risked his life to seek more texts,
Climbing over peaks and walking across valleys.
Magnanimous was his personality,
Gallant, sincere, and scrupulous.
His name resounded in the Western Region,
And to the guesthouse he returned with merits.
His time was one when good government prevailed
in the empire,
Which was ruled by none other than our Emperor.
The Jade Mirror of wise judgement hung high again;
The Pearl Bags were awarded once more to
ministers of rank.
Having explained the Three Vehicles,
He also elucidated the Ten Stages of
Bodhisattvahood,
So that the Sun of Wisdom
Might become brighter [and emerge] out of obscurity.
A common and insignificant man am I,
But lucky [enough] to follow in the dust he raised.
I was brought up in a humble hut,
Neither painted in colors nor spacious.
I respect him for his virtue high as a mountain.
I eagerly admire his noble character pure as a
stream.
I wish to climb and depend upon him,
As a creeping vine on a tree.

A Note by Shi Yancong: I have observed that since the introduction of Buddhism to the Eastern Land, tens of thousands of talented and intelligent people have renounced their homes to enter the Way, but few of them have been versatile in an all-round way, though some of them may have had one or two good points. The Tripiṭaka Master possessed such good qualities as regular features, perfect faculties of sight, hearing, and speech, erudition, and a retentive memory. He disregarded his life for the sake of the Way and travelled far to extremely distant regions. His moral integrity was as upright as pine trees and bamboo. He cherished lofty ambitions stronger than metal and stone. At a time when groups of independent warlords attempted to create trouble in the country, he turned his mind toward the Emperor as sunflowers always face the sun.

I have also heard that the Tripiṭaka Master never perspired at the height of summer, nor would he shiver in times of severe cold. He never curled up or stretched himself and never yawned or sneezed. This was because he could not adapt to circumstances; it should not be taken as a measure to judge saints or sages. Moreover, when he was ill at the Northern Palace, all amusements and elaborate formalities were suspended. On the day when he was about to pass away, his color and features looked amiable and pleasant.

There was also something difficult to interpret. About month after his demise, a man came with some sandalwood powder and asked permission to rub it over the Tripiṭaka Master's body in the manner of the western countries. But all the monks would not allow him to do so. That man changed countenance and said, "This disciple has come by special order. If you teachers do not permit me to do this, you may write a report to the Emperor!"

Then the monks gave consent. When they opened the coffin and unbuttoned the shroud, they smelled a strange fragrance like the odor of lotus flowers. They asked one another about it in amazement, and all of them said that
280a they had also sensed it. The man who had just come took off the shroud, leaving only the underclothes on the body. All the monks saw that the features of the Tripiṭaka Master remained as if he were alive, and they cried most piteously while they looked at the corpse. When the man had rubbed the body with sandalwood powder, redressed it in

the cerement, and closed the coffin again, he instantly disappeared to nowhere. The monks suspected that he was a heavenly being.

Considering the Tripiṭaka Master's long-cherished mind, and in view of his recent activities, if he was not a *Mahāsattva,* what else could he have been? I hope my fellow monks will hold him in deep respect. Let us try our best to do so!

Glossary

Abhidharma [*Piṭaka*]: the section of the Buddhist canon containing philosophical commentaries.

ācārya: a preceptor.

āmra: a mango.

amṛta: Sweet Dew, ambrosia.

arhat: a perfect saint who has freed himself from the bonds of samsara by eliminating all passions and desires.

asaṃkhyeya kalpa: an immeasurable length of time.

Asura: a kind of demon, an evil spirit.

Avaraśaila: Western Hill.

Avīci: the hell of uninterrupted suffering.

Bhadrakalpa: the Good Aeon, in which a thousand Buddhas are to appear.

bhikṣu: a Buddhist monk.

bhikṣuṇī: a Buddhist nun.

birth-and-death (samsara): the cycle of repeated births and deaths in which deluded sentient beings exist.

Bodhi: enlightenment.

Bodhisattva: the seeker in Mahayana (q.v.) who perfects the virtues of wisdom and compassion for the sake of liberating all sentient beings from suffering.

bu: six feet.

Buddha nature: the seed of Buddhahood or enlightenment.

caitya: a shrine.

Cakravartin (Wheel-turning King): a universal monarch; the emperor of the earth.

deva: a god.

Deva Bodhisattva: Āryadeva, a disciple of Nāgārjuna.

dhāraṇī: an incantation.

Dharma-body. *See* Dharmakāya.

Dharmakāya (Dharma-body): the body of Truth, one of the three bodies of a Buddha. The other two bodies are Nirmāṇakāya (Transformation-body) and Saṃbhogakāya (Enjoyment-body).

Dharma nature: the quintessence, or true nature, of all things.

Dharma *Piṭaka:* a collection of Buddhist texts.

Dharmarāja: a Buddhist king.

dhyāna: meditation, trance.

dou: approximately eighteen liters.

Eight Emancipations: emancipation from attachment to forms and desires through eight types of meditation.

Eight Erroneous Practices: the practices that are against the Eightfold Noble Path (q.v.).

Eightfold Noble Path: (1) right view, (2) right thought, (3) right speech, (4) right action, (5) right livelihood, (6) right effort, (7) right mindfulness, and (8) right concentration.

Ekayāna (One Vehicle): also called the Buddhayāna (Buddha Vehicle); the Mahayana (q.v.) doctrine which contains the final and complete Dharma of the Buddha and not merely a part, or a preliminary stage, as in the Hinayana. It is often identified with the teaching of the *Lotus Sutra.*

fen: one tenth of an inch.

Field of Blessedness: a figurative term for those such as Buddhas and monks who deserve offerings. Just as a field can yield crops, so donors can obtain good karmic results through their offerings to them.

Five Endurances: the five stages through which a Bodhisattva deepens his insight into the Dharma: (1) before the Ten Stages of Bodhisattvahood (q.v.), (2) the first, second, and third stages of the Ten Stages, (3) the fourth, fifth, and sixth stages of the Ten Stages, (4) the seventh, eighth, and ninth stages of the Ten Stages, and (5) the tenth stage and the stage of Buddhahood.

Five Precepts: (1) not to kill, (2) not to steal, (3) not to commit adultery, (4) not to speak falsely, and (5) not to drink intoxicants.

Five Sciences: grammar, mathematics, medicine, logic, and philosophy.

Five Vehicles: the vehicles of (1) humans, (2) gods, (3) *Śrāvaka*s, (4) *Pratyekabuddha*s, and (5) Bodhisattvas.

Five Virtuous Elements: almsgiving, keeping the precepts, patience under insult, zeal or progress, and meditation.

Four *Dhyāna*s: the four stages of meditation that correspond with the four *dhyāna* heavens, which are still in the realms of samsara.

Four Endurances: the understanding of the following four: (1) all things do not arise, (2) all things do not perish, (3) all things do not have self-nature, for they exist because of causes and conditions, and (4) all things are such that one should not let his mind dwell on them.

Four Inverted Views: the four wrong views entertained by deluded beings: (1) to regard the impermanent as permanent, (2) to regard suffering as happiness, (3) to regard impurity as purity, and (4) to regard non-self as self.

Four Kalpas: the four periods of time, each consisting of twenty small *kalpas* (q.v.), during which the worlds go through formation, destruction, and annihilation: (1) the Kalpa of Existence (*vivarta-siddha kalpa*), during which the sun and moon rise, sexes are differentiated, heroes arise, the four castes are formed, and social life evolves; (2) the Kalpa of Destruction (*saṃvarta kalpa*), during which fire, water, and wind destroy everything except the Fourth *Dhyāna* Heaven; (3) the Kalpa of Annihilation (*saṃvarta-siddha kalpa*), during which nothing exists; and (4) the Kalpa of Formation (*vivarta kalpa*), during which worlds and the beings on them are formed.

Four Modes of Birth: (1) viviparous, as with mammals; (2) oviparous, as with birds; (3) moisture- or water-born, as with worms and fishes; and (4) metamorphic, as with moths from the chrysalis, or with spirits into heavens or hells.

Four Noble Truths: (1) life is suffering; (2) defilements are the cause of suffering; (3) all suffering can be ended; and (4) the way to end suffering is the Eightfold Noble Path (q.v.).

Four Unlimited Mental States: (1) boundless kindness, (2) boundless pity, (3) boundless joy, and (4) limitless indifference to distinctions of friend and enemy, love and hate, etc.

gāthā: a stanza.

Great Vehicle. *See* Mahayana.

Hetuvidyā: logic, one of the Five Sciences (q.v.).

Hinayana ("Lesser Vehicle"): a derogatory term applied by Mahayanists to various schools of Buddhism that teach the attainment of an arhat (q.v.).

hu: approximately 180 liters.

Jambudvīpa: the world.

Jeta Wood: Jetavana.

kalpa: an immense period of time, an aeon.

Kalpa of Destruction. *See* Four Kalpas.

Kalpa of Existence. *See* Four Kalpas.

Kalpa of Formation. *See* Four Kalpas.

karma: a person's actions and the consequences of those actions.

kāṣāya: a Buddhist monastic robe.

Kāśyapa-Mātaṅga: a monk who introduced Buddhism to China.

koṭi: an extremely large number, usually ten million, sometimes one million.

kṣatriya: the governmental caste, the warrior caste; one of this caste.

Kuṇāla: Aśoka's son.

Land of Endurance: Sahā world; the world of suffering.

Lesser Vehicle. *See* Hinayana.

li: approximately 1/3 mile.

Mahācīna: China.

Mahāsattva ("great being"): a Bodhisattva (q.v.) with great wisdom and compassion.

mahat: intellect.

Mahayana ("Great Vehicle"): the teaching on the attainment of enlightenment or Buddhahood; the seeker of enlightenment is the Bodhisattva (q.v.).

Maitreya Bodhisattva: the future Buddha, presently in the Tuṣita heaven (q.v.).

maṇi: pearl.

Māra: demon; the Devil.

Middle Way: the truth of nonduality that Śākyamuni taught; the truth of neither existence nor nonexistence.

mou: approximately a hundred square meters.

nāga: a dragon.

One Vehicle. *See* Ekayāna.

pāramitā: spiritual perfection.

pippala: a long pepper.

Piṭaka: a collection of Buddhist texts.

prajñā: wisdom; one of the Six *Pāramitā*s (q.v.).

prajñāpāramitā: the acme of wisdom.

Pratyekabuddha: a self-enlightened Buddha.

Pure Land: the name of the Buddha Amitābha's land.

Pūrvaśaila: Eastern Hill.

rākṣasī: an ogress.

Śabdavidyā: grammar and composition; one of the Five Sciences (q.v.).

Sadāpralāpa: Sadāprarudita, a Bodhisattva mentioned in the *Prajñāpāramitā Sūtra*s.

Śākya Bodhisattva: (later) Śākyamuni Buddha.

samādhi: contemplation, deep trance.

saṃghāṭi: outer robe of a monk.

Saṃmitīya ("correct measures") school: one of the early schools of Buddhism, which was formed approximately three hundred years after the passing of Śākyamuni.

Sangha: the Buddhist Order.

śarīra: a relic.

Śāstrin: a teacher, a learned person.

Seven Links of Enlightenment: (1) mindfulness, (2) discrimination between the true and the false, (3) vigor, (4) joy, (5) ease of body and mind, (6) concentration, and (7) equanimity.

sheng: one pint (approximately).

sheng: a musical instrument.

Six Arts (of Confucianism): rites, music, shooting, horse-riding, writing, and mathematics.

Six Defilements: six qualities that are the cause of all impurity, i.e., sight, sound, smell, taste, touch, and idea.

Six *Pāramitās*: six spiritual perfections: giving, precept-keeping, patience, effort, meditation, and wisdom.

six supernatural powers: (1) supernatural vision, (2) supernatural hearing, (3) the power to know others' thoughts, (4) the power to know the past lives of oneself and others, (5) the power to perform miracles, such as appearing anywhere at will, and (6) the power totally to eradicate defilements.

śramaṇa: a Buddhist monk.

Śrāvaka: a disciple.

stupa: a tope, a reliquary.

Suchness. See *tathatā.*

Sumeru: the highest mountain in the world.

śūnyatā. See voidness.

Sutra ("thread"): a discourse of the Buddha.

Tathāgata ("Thus-come or Thus-gone"): a title of the Buddha.

tathatā (Suchness): absolute truth, or ultimate reality; the content of wisdom-insight into things, just as they are, i.e., empty and dependently co-arisen.

Ten Capabilities: ten masteries possessed by a Buddha or Bodhisattva concerning (1) lengthening or shortening life span, (2) *samādhi,* (3) material things, (4) actions, (5) births, (6) aspiration (or vow), (7) understanding, (8) supernatural abilities, (9) wisdom, and (10) teachings.

Ten Good Deeds: (1) not to kill, (2) not to steal, (3) not to engage in illicit sexual practices, (4) not to lie, (5) not to utter harsh words, (6) not to utter words that cause enmity among people, (7) not to engage in idle talk, (8) not to be greedy, (9) not to be angry, and (10) not to have wrong views.

Ten Powers: the ten powers of the Buddha, giving complete knowledge of (1) what is right or wrong; (2) the past, present, and future karmas of all sentient beings; (3) all forms of meditation; (4) the powers and faculties of all sentient beings; (5) the desires, or moral direction, of every being; (6) the different levels of existence; (7) the results of various methods of practice; (8) the transmigratory states of all sentient beings and the courses of karma they follow; (9) the past lives of all sentient beings and nirvana; and (10) the destruction of all evil passions.

Ten Stages of Bodhisattvahood: the stages of Bodhisattva practice: (1) the stage of joy, in which one experiences the joy of entering on the path to Buddhahood; (2) the stage of stainlessness, in which one is liberated from all possible defilement; (3) the stage of bright radiance, the stage of further enlightenment; (4) the stage of blazing fire; (5) the stage that is difficult-to-conquer, in which one masters final difficulties; (6) the stage of presence, the open way of wisdom above definitions of impurity and purity; (7) the stage of reaching afar, in which one gets above ideas of self in order to save others; (8) the stage of imperturbability; (9) the stage of subtle wisdom, in which one possesses the finest discriminatory wisdom, knowing where and how to save beings, and the ten powers; and (10) the stage of the Dharma-cloud, in which one attains to the fertilizing power of the Dharma-cloud.

Three Clear Insights: (1) insight into the previous births of self and others; (2) insight into future births; and (3) insight into present sufferings so as to overcome all passions and realize nirvana.

three kinds of pure meat: meat from an animal not seen to be killed for oneself, not heard to have been so killed, of which one has no suspicion of such killing.

Three Refuges: the Buddha, the Dharma, and the Sangha.

Three Studies: discipline, meditation, and wisdom.

Three Vehicles: the three paths to enlightenment: (1) the *Śrāvaka*-vehicle, (2) the *Pratyekabuddha*-vehicle, and (3) the Bodhisattva-vehicle.

Three Worlds: (1) the desire world, which is the sphere of sensuous desire, of sex and food; (2) the form world, which is above the desire world and comprises part of heaven; and (3) the formless world, which is the sphere of pure spirit.

Trayastriṃśa: the thirty-three gods who live on the top of Mt. Sumeru in the second heaven of the desire world.

Tripiṭaka (three baskets): the Buddhist canon.

Triple Gem: the Buddha, the Dharma, and the Sangha.

Tuṣita heaven: the fourth of the six heavens in the desire world.

Two Adornments: (1) adornment of wisdom and (2) adornment of good deeds such as alms-giving and keeping the precepts.

upadeśa: a form of Buddhist literature for instruction.
upādhyāya: a teacher.
upāsaka: a Buddhist layman.
Vaipulya ("broad"): Mahayana (q.v.).
Vārāṇasī (city): Benares.
Vedas: Hindu scriptures.
vihāra: a hall, a monastery.
Vinaya: Buddhist monastic rules.
voidness (*śūnyatā*): the absence of permanent essence in things.
Wheel-turning King. See *Cakravartin.*
yakṣa: a kind of spirit or demon.
yāna: a vehicle.
yin and *yang:* two primal forces, negativity and positivity.
yojana: one day's journey in an ox cart.
Yonghui period: A.D. 650–55.

Selected Bibliography

Grousset, René. *In the Footsteps of the Buddha.* Translated by Mariette Leon. London: Routledge & Sons, 1932.

Hiuen Tsiang. *Si-Yu-Ki.: Buddhist Records of the Western World.* Translated by Samuel Beal. London: Trubner, 1884; reprint, Delhi: Motilal Banarsidass, 1981.

Hsüan-tsang. *Mémoires sur les contrées occidentales, traduits du sanscrit en chinois, en l'an 648, par Hiouen-thsang.* Translated into French by Stanislas Julien. Paris: Imprimerie imperiale, 1857–58.

Hui-li. *Histoire de la vie de Hiouen-Thsang et de ses voyages dans l'Inde, depuis l'an 629 jusqu'en 645, par Hoei-li et Yen-thsong: Suivie de documents et d'eclaircissements geographiques tirés de la relation originale de Hiouen-Thsang.* Translated into French by Stanislas Julien. Paris: Imprimerie imperiale, 1853.

Hui-li. *The Life of Hsuan-tsang, the Tripitaka-Master of the Great Tzu En Monastery.* Translated by Li Yung-hsi. Peking: Chinese Buddhist Association, 1959.

Waley, Arthur. *The Real Tripitaka.* London: Allen and Unwin, 1952.

Watters, Thomas. *On Yuan Chwang's Travels in India, 629–645 A.D.* London: Royal Asiatic Society, 1904–5; reprint, San Francisco, 1975.

Index

Abhayadaṃṣṭra (monk), 115
Abhayasiddhi Śāstra, 127
Abhidharma
monks, 68
Piṭaka. See under *Piṭaka*(s)
works, 48, 250
Abhidharmajñānaprasthāna Śāstra, 15, 48, 67, 308
Abhidharmakośa Śāstra, 17, 39, 40, 48, 62, 70, 76, 101, 155, 159, 232
Abhidharmamahāvibhāṣā Śāstra, 1
Abhidharmanyāyānusāra Śāstra, 232
Abhidharmaprakaraṇaśāsana Śāstra, 67
Abhidharmasamuccaya Śāstra, 15, 16
Abhidharmasamuccayavyākhyā Śāstra, 155
Abhidharmasamudāya Prakaraṇa Śāstra, 76, 101, 169
Abhidharmasamudāyavyākhyā Śāstra, 67
Abhidharmavibhāṣa Śāstra, 64
Ācāra (arhat), 113
Ācārya, 230, 266
Accumulated Stones, Mountain of, 161
Action(s), 77, 133, 176, 184, 204, 225, 241, 267, 282, 285, 293, 309, 321. *See also* Karma
Adbhuta (stupa), 59
Āgamas, Four, 48, 244, 314, 341
Aghadarśanabheda Śāstra, 135, 144
Ahaṃkāra. See Self-consciousness
Ahicchattra (country), 71
Ajātaśatru (king), 95, 97, 99, 343
Ajitavatī River, 6, 84
Ālaya-vijñāna, 341
Alms bowl, 50, 56, 57, 85, 124, 251, 302
Āmra (elder), 93
Āmrapālī (courtesan), 86
Āmravana Garden, 7, 195, 210
Amṛta, 13. *See also* Sweet Dew
Analytical Exposition of Grammar, 102
Ānanda (Śākyamuni's disciple), 5, 63, 68, 84, 88, 97, 98, 339
Ānandapura (country), 123
Anāthapiṇḍika (wealthy elder), garden of, 81, 328
Anavatapta Lake, 161, 204, 234
Ancheng, Marquis of, 263
Andarāb (country), 158
Andhra (country), 113
Anfu Gate, 218, 219, 283
Aṅgulimāla (transgressor), 81
Annals of the Jin Kingdom, 177
Anujñānaprasthāna Śāstra, 71
Apalāla Dragon Spring, 58
Araurak (city), 170
Arhat(s), 60, 63, 69, 80, 98, 113, 114, 121, 125, 161–67
999 great, 97
Arhatship, 68, 97, 113
Arini (country), 159
Āryadāsa (monk), 50
Āryasena (monk), 50
Āryavarman (monk), 52
Asaṃgamanirvāṇa Śāstra, 127
Asaṃkhyeya kalpa, 53
Asaṅga (*śāstra* master), 2, 57, 75, 80, 343
Āścarya ("Extraordinary") Monastery, 39
Asita (*ṛṣi*), 82
Aśoka
Hell of, 87, 123
King, 53, 58–61, 72, 73, 75, 79–85, 87, 88, 97–99, 109–12, 114, 116, 119, 121–25, 158, 164, 225
tree, 76
Aṣṭadhātu Śāstra, 102
Asura, 114
Asvabhāva (*śāstra* master), 216
Aśvaghoṣa (poet), 161, 200, 343, 347
Aśvajit (monk), 96
Aṭali (country), 123
Ātmane (voice), 103
Audumbatira (country), 124
Aurṇika cape, 154
Avakan (country), 157
Avalokiteśvara (bodhisattva), 23, 26, 27, 59, 89, 92, 101, 105, 109
Avaṇḍa (country), 124

Avaraśaila ("Western Hill") Monastery, 113
Avataṃsaka Sūtra, 250
Avīci. *See* Hell
Ayamukha (country), 78
Ayodhyā (country), 75, 76

Badakshan (country), 159
Bālāditya (king), 92, 94, 99
Balapati (country), 126
Balkh (country), 47–49
Bālukā (country), 41
Balūra (country), 161
Bamboo Grove (monastery), 97, 285
Bāmīyān (country), 49, 50
Ban Chao (marquis), 185, 344
Ban Gu (historian), 177
Baochang (monastery), 180
Baocheng (nun), 265, 266
Bhadrakalpa, 67, 82, 85, 88, 89, 114
Bhadraruci (*śāstra* master), 125, 126
Bhadra Vihāra, 73
Bhāgya (city), 164
Bhaiṣajyaguru Sūtra, 332
Bhallika (city), 48
Bharukacchapa (country), 122
Bhāvaviveka (*śāstra* master), 114
Bhikṣu(s), 81, 83, 96, 125, 149, 150, 162, 230, 233, 235, 251
Bhikṣuṇī(s), 68, 80, 265, 266
Bhūtas (heretics), 132
Bianji (monk), 180
Bianzhou (region), 180
Bimbisāra (king), 32, 87, 99, 100
Bing (state), 8, 194
Birth
  –and-death, 200, 203, 225, 243
  Four Modes of, 312, 317, 337, 340
Bodhi. *See* Enlightenment
  Temple, 128, 130
  tree, 36, 54, 76, 88, 89, 99, 129, 141, 168, 250, 253, 343
Bodhimaṇḍa (seat of enlightenment), 89
Bodhimegheśvara (monk), 115
Bodhiruci (Tripiṭaka master), 179, 216, 263, 311, 315
Bodhisattva
  deeds of, 86, 139
  images/statue of, 89, 105
  practices, 223, 227
  Precepts, 223, 224, 266
  stage of, 194. *See also under* Stage(s)
  Way/path, 58, 60, 93, 151, 119, 320
Bodhisattvahood, Tenth Stage of. *See under* Stage(s)
Bodhisattvapiṭaka Sūtra, 86, 181, 209, 211
Bone(s). *See* Buddha(s), bone/tooth of; Relic(s)
Book of Changes, 187, 200, 201, 210, 238, 258, 284, 285, 300
Book of Filial Piety, 12
Book of Songs, 300
Bowang (region), Marquis of, 177, 185
Brahmā, 72, 102, 146
Brahman(s), 54, 57, 65, 66, 81, 93, 99, 101, 102, 113, 122, 132, 134, 135, 145, 146, 151, 152
Brahmapura (country), 71
Buddha(s)
  alms bowl of, 57, 85, 124
  bone/tooth of, 47, 50, 54, 111. *See also* Relic(s)
  Dharma, 9, 89, 119, 140, 141, 143, 149, 154, 164, 177, 245, 249, 251
  Dharma-body of, 249
  footprint(s) of, 59, 87
  four past, 57, 58, 65, 75, 85, 99, 106, 109, 111, 121, 177
  image(s)/statue of, 21, 32, 38, 39, 50, 54, 72, 76, 79, 81, 85, 89, 99, 100, 110, 115, 119, 125, 146, 147, 152, 156, 160, 164–67, 169, 173, 174, 218–20, 222, 227, 326, 327, 331, 332, 346
  lands, 285
  Light (prince), 298, 300, 303, 304, 306, 319, 320
  nature, 105, 224
  one thousand, 67, 89, 229, 306
  One, Vehicle, 5. *See also under* Vehicle(s)
  robe of, 54, 56
  seven, 122
  staff of, 54
  of the Superior Dragon Race, 251. *See also* Mañjuśrī

Three Bodies of, 139
Tooth Temple, 119
Buddhabhadra (monk), 91, 92, 311
Buddhabhūmi Sūtra, 181, 182
Buddhaciṅga (monk), 317
Buddhadāsa (*śāstra* master), 73
Buddhagupta (king), 93
Buddhahood, 60, 89, 114
Buddhasiṃha (translator), 253, 269
Buddhatuṅga (translator), 182, 247
Bukhārā (country), 45

Caitya, 48, 276
Cakravartin King, 209, 233, 314
Calmadana (country), 170
Camel(s), 24, 29, 124, 125, 158, 170
Campā (country), 107
Campaka flowers, 79
Candrabhāgā (river), 64
Candrachattra (monk), 302
Candraprabha (king), 60, 156
Candrasiṃha (monk), 130
Candravarman (monk), 67
Canglang (river), 184
Caotang Monastery, 228
Caritra (city), 111
Categories of cognition (*padārthas*), 133
Chakuka (country), 163
Chandaka (groom), 84
Chang'an (city), 14, 17, 20, 22, 30, 44, 168, 173, 180, 218, 283, 344
Chan River, 338
Chanting, 57, 146, 157, 204, 219, 269
Chenliu (region), 11
Chu (region), 15, 182, 259
Chui (craftsman), 208
Chu Suiliang (chief privy councillor), 193, 194, 219, 226
Ci'en Monastery, 3, 216–18, 222, 244, 262, 263, 275, 280, 283, 284, 326, 334, 337, 338
Cīnabhukti (country), 67
Cīna-deva-gotra (Divine Stock of Han), 161
Ciñcā (Brahmin woman), 81
Colya (country), 114
Concise Analytical Exposition of Grammar, 102
Confucius (sage), 178, 189, 246, 313
Correlation (*samavāya*), 133
Crane Grove, 184, 240, 250
Crown Prince, 99, 203, 206, 207, 209, 216, 218–21, 262–64, 299, 301, 319, 325, 345
Cui Guang (premier), 263
Cuiwei Palace, 221
Cunda (blacksmith), 84, 223
Cuzhou (region), 223

Dai (region), 30, 262, 311
Dai's, two, 260
Dāna, 225
Dantaloka Mountain, 250
Dao'an (monk), 177, 192, 247, 346
Daobiao (monk), 192
Daogong (monk), 212, 213
Daoheng (monk), 192, 341
Daoshen (monk), 17, 180
Daoxuan (monk), 180, 335, 336
Daoyin (monk), 180
Daozhuo (monk), 180
Darada (valley), 60
Deeds, Ten Good, 43, 48
Deer Park, 7, 85, 166, 174, 198, 204, 267, 285, 343
Defilement(s), 15, 205, 214, 246, 347
Six, 198, 205
Deity (-ies), 28, 51, 52, 61, 70, 76, 78, 113, 115, 138, 149, 164, 175, 176, 293, 297, 298, 301, 304, 305, 310, 320, 322, 323, 330, 335, 336. See also *Deva*(s)
Deva(s), 122, 125. *See also* Deity (-ies)
temple, 81, 110–12, 120, 121
Deva (*śāstra* master), 69, 79, 112, 114
Devadatta (monk), 81, 95, 109
Devaśarman (arhat), 80
Devasena (arhat), 69, 144
Deye Nunnery, 266
Dhānakaṭaka (country), 113
Dhanapāla (elephant), 95
Dhāraṇī Piṭaka. See under *Piṭaka*(s)
Dharma
–body, 249, 259
Buddha, 9, 89, 119, 140, 141, 143, 149, 154, 164, 177, 245, 249, 251
nature, 204, 205, 210
Piṭaka(s). See under *Piṭaka*(s)

rain, 34, 205, 267
Stream of, 196, 204, 210, 217, 304
Wheel of, 5, 85, 166, 174, 220, 248
Dharma (monk), 21
Dharma-dhātu(s), 200
Dharmadīrgha (monk), 229, 230, 233
Dharmagupta (school), 58, 174
Dharmākara (Hinayana Tripiṭaka master), 49
Dharmalakṣaṇa (school). *See* Faxiang/Dharmalakṣaṇa
Dharmanandi (translator), 263
Dharmapāla (*śāstra* master), 2, 80, 93, 114
Dharmapriya (Hinayana Tripiṭaka master), 49
Dharmarakṣa (translator), 34
Dharmāraṇya (monk), 6, 253
Dharmasaṃgha (monk), 46
Dharma Store. *See* Śīlabhadra/Right Dharma Store
Dharmatrāta (*śāstra* master), 57
Dhruvabhaṭa (king), 123, 152, 155
Dhyāna(s), 205, 311
Four, 210
Diagrams, Eight, 238, 260, 276
Diamond
Ranges, 211
Samādhi, 89
Seat, 88, 89, 229
Wheel(s), 57, 88
Dignāga (*śāstra* master), 113
Dingyuan (region), 185
Dingzhou (region), 180
Dīpaṃkara (Buddha), 53, 55
Dragon(s), 59, 60, 63, 83, 85, 93, 94, 170, 174–76, 273, 279, 299, 330
Cave, 174
–elephant, 251
king, 55, 63
Palace, 211, 267, 271, 276, 285, 294
Six, 270, 272
Draviḍa (country), 114, 120
Dravya. *See* Substance
Dubhe, 281
Dunhuang (region), 21, 25, 169
Duobao Monastery, 180
Durgā (goddess), 76
Du Shenglun (governor), 223
Dvādaśāṅgapratītyasamutpāda Śāstra, 127
Dvārapatī (country), 110

Ego, 34, 80, 244
Non-, 80
Ekayāna (One Vehicle). *See under* Vehicle(s)
Emperor
Fuxi, 209, 276, 318
Guangwu, 179
Ming, 210, 271, 278, 285
Shun, 188, 189, 205, 220
Taizong, 176
Wu of Han, 191
Wu of Liang, 212
Wu of Wei, 287
Wu of Zhou, 179, 205
Xiaowen, 179, 311
Xuanyuan, 183, 209, 281, 318
Yang, 14
Yao, 183, 188, 205
Yellow, 320
Yu, 188
Zhou of Shang, 179, 189
Emptiness, 6, 273, 281. *See also* Voidness(es)
Endurances
Eight, 312
Five, 316
Four, 197
Enlightenment, 7, 48, 54, 82, 89, 90, 93, 114, 115, 147, 163, 182, 208, 211, 223, 225, 235, 246, 247, 250, 282, 302, 312, 313, 316, 332, 333
Seven Links of, 248
Supreme [Perfect], 89, 162, 250, 333
Evil One. *See* Māra(s); Pāpīyān
Exposition of the Mahāyānasaṃgraha Śāstra, 216
Exposition of the Pañcaskandha Śāstra, 67
Exposition of the Vidyāmātrasiddhitri-daśakārikā Śāstra, 67

Fahai Monastery, 180
Fairy Lady Yunyin, 273
Fajiang Monastery, 180
Fang Xuanling (imperial regent), 170, 173, 180, 263

Faxian (monk), 18, 182, 247, 344
Faxiang/Dharmalakṣaṇa (school), 2, 50, 180
Faya (monk), 346
Feng (area), 190
Fengde Monastery, 180
Field of Blessedness, 153, 212, 213, 225, 292, 295
Fiery Island, 190
Final Period, 227, 245, 250, 291
Fire worshippers, 42
Footprint(s). *See under* Buddha(s)
Four Āgamas. See *Āgamas, Four*
Fu, House of, 247, 262
Fu-fa-zang-[yin-yuan]-zhuan, 5
Fufeng (place), 167
Fu Jian (ruler), 177, 192, 263, 346
Fuju Monastery, 180
Fu Sheng (scholar), 167
Fuxi (emperor). *See under* Emperor

Gandhāra (country), 57, 63, 75, 102, 335
Ganges (river), 7, 69, 71–73, 75, 76, 78, 85–87, 106, 107, 109, 142, 145, 151, 152, 200, 205, 211, 215, 224, 240, 250
Gao Jifu (court officer), 207
Gāthā, 59
Gaz (country), 49
Ge (city), 191
Gem, Triple, 5, 79, 122, 123, 195, 211, 221, 239, 248, 249, 251, 295, 297, 320. *See also* Refuge(s), Three
Generality (*sāmānya*), 133
Ghoṣila (wealthy elder), 79, 155
Ghūr (country), 46, 159
Gokulika(s) (school), 343
Golden Wheel King, 50
Gopa (arhat), 80
Gopāla (dragon king), 55
Gṛdhrakūṭa Mountain/Vulture Peak, 7, 34, 76, 96, 166, 168, 174, 184, 187, 198, 200, 204, 209, 224, 227, 240, 250, 271, 284, 294, 328, 343, 346
Great Mystery Classic, 241
Great Source of Intellect, 133, 134
Great Tang Dynasty Preface to the Holy Teachings of the Tripiṭaka, 195
Great Tang Dynasty Record of the Western Regions, 185
Great Wall, 190
Grosapam (city), 157
Gross elements, 133
Guangwu (emperor). *See under* Emperor
Guilin (region), 184
Guṇa. See Quality
Guṇabhadra (monk), 52
Guṇaprabha (*śāstra* master), 69–71, 125
Guoxi Monastery, 8
Guozhou (region), 180
Gūrjara (country), 123
Gūzgānān (country), 49

Haṃsa (stupa), 100
Han
  court/royal house, 43, 49, 197
  descent, 28
  dynasty, 11, 184, 188, 191, 210, 227, 247, 253, 256, 262, 271, 277, 278, 285, 287, 300, 345
  Eastern, dynasty, 179
  land of, 155
  language, 44
  people, 329
Han (river), 294
Hao (region), 190, 259, 323
Harṣavardhana (king), 72
Hayamukha (country), 76
Heavenly Ladder, 36, 155
Helin Nunnery, 265, 266
Hell, 40, 81, 87, 123
  Aśoka's, 87, 123
  Avīci, 78
Henan (region), 226
Hengzhou (region), 223
Hepu (region), 184
Heretic(s), 7, 66, 69, 79–81, 95, 110–12, 114, 120–22, 130, 132, 133, 145–47, 152, 231, 234, 248, 253, 254, 302
Hetuvidyā (logic), 113, 126, 174, 245, 249, 251, 255, 256
Hetuvidyā Śāstra, 62, 101, 113, 115, 127, 237, 240, 242
Hiḍḍa Mountain, 59
Himatala (country), 149, 159

Hinayana (Lesser Vehicle), 47. *See also under* Vehicle(s)
adherents/followers, 79, 85, 130, 140, 145, 147, 149
doctrines/teachings, 17, 52, 69, 72, 75, 106, 107, 109, 121, 122, 124, 131, 145
masters/teachers, 48, 49, 51, 80, 130, 131
monastery, 51, 165
schools/sects, 7, 34, 50, 70, 80, 100, 109, 120, 123, 126, 131, 229
text(s), 47, 48, 75, 180, 205, 343
theories, 148, 229, 234
views, 131
Hiraṇyavatī River, 184, 250, 254
History of Xia, 183
Hongfa-yuan (palace building), 216
Hongfu Monastery, 173, 175, 179, 180, 182, 205, 207, 215, 219, 237
Horiṣmīka (country), 45
Hotan (country), 163
Hot Sea, 42, 168
Houmochen Shi (general), 173
Hrom (country), 124
Hu
man/people, 22, 23, 44, 45, 164
merchants, 38
tribe(s), 21, 22, 28, 163
Huichang Monastery, 180
Huigui (monk), 180
Huili (author of this biography), 2, 3, 8, 181, 244, 246, 339
Huixuan (monk), 212, 213
Huns (nomads), 163, 191
Huo Qubing (general), 191
Huśkara (temple), 61
Hvamna (country), 163

Ice Mountains, 41, 42, 49
Image Period, 90, 228, 233, 277, 279, 285, 292, 301, 341, 347
Indra (god), 72, 93, 102, 146
Indraśailaguhā Mountain, 100
Indriya(s). *See* Organs
Indus (river), 57, 60, 167, 233, 235
Inflection, 102, 103
Insights, Three Clear, 34, 276
Institute for the Expansion of Culture, 196
Īraṇaparvata (country), 75, 104, 106, 107
Iron Gate, 45, 46, 168
Īśānapura (country), 110
Īśvaradeva (god), 152

Jāguḍa (country), 157
Jajhoti (country), 124
Jālandhara (country), 155
Jambudvīpa (continent), 71, 88, 107, 116, 139, 158, 160, 335, 336, 344
Jayagupta (monk), 69
Jayapura (city), 64
Jayasena (*śāstra* master), 126–28
Jayendra Monastery, 62
Jetavana
Garden/Park, 34, 184, 208, 233, 266, 272, 273, 277
Grove/Wood, 81, 270, 341
Vihāra, 200
Ji (empress), 276
Jia Dunze (governor), 223, 225
Jiangxia (prefecture), 218
Jianzhou (region), 180
Jicui Palace, 306, 307, 320, 322
Jie (ruler), 13
Jin, 210, 256
dynasty, 207, 296, 318
Mountains, 318
region, 30, 182
State of, 185, 324
Jinabandhu (monk), 63
Jinan (region), 167
Jinaputra (*śāstra* master), 125
Jinatrāta (monk), 63
Jincheng (region), 184
Jing (monk), 15
Jing (state), 15, 194
Jingfa Monastery, 180
Jingmai (monk), 180, 240
Jingming (monk), 180
Jīvaka (physician), 96
Jñānacandra (monk), 40
Jñānaprabha (monk), 131, 229, 230
Jumna (river), 69, 78, 151, 152
Jumo
land of, 170
River, 169
Jūṭaka(s) (heretics), 132, 133
Jyotiṣka (wealthy elder), 99

Kabandha (country), 161
Kajuṅghira (country), 109, 142
Kali (king), 58
Kaliṅga (country), 111
Kalpa
of Destruction, 53
of Existence, 102
of Formation, 102
Kāmalāṅkā (country), 110
Kāmarūpa (country), 107, 135
Kāñcīpura (capital), 114, 115
Kaniṣka (king), 57, 58, 63
Kanyākubja (country), 37, 72, 123, 145, 152, 229, 234, 277
Kāpālika(s) (heretics), 130, 132
Kapilavastu (country), 31, 82, 175, 176, 205, 239, 240, 250, 271, 282
Kapiśā (country), 44, 51, 55, 156, 157, 168
Kapitha (country), 71, 174
Kapotaka Monastery, 104
Karaṇḍa Bamboo Grove, 96
Karma, 133, 289, 299. *See also* Action(s)
Karṇasuvarṇa (country), 72, 109
Karpūra tree, 116
Kārttika (name of month), 84
Kashgar (country), 46, 161, 163, 167
Kaśmīra (country), 61, 66, 70, 101, 131, 149, 150, 156, 157, 164, 165, 184
Kāśyapa (Buddha), 48, 82, 85, 162
Kāśyapa/Mahākāśyapa (Śākyamuni's disciple), 6, 84, 97, 98, 232
Kāśyapa-Mātaṅga (monk), 6, 34, 181, 247, 253
Kāśyapīya (school), 58, 157, 174
Kātyāyana (*śāstra* master), 15, 48, 67
Kauṇḍinya (Śākyamuni's disciple), 86
Kauśāmbī (country), 79, 155, 169, 174
Khamdādh (city), 160
Kharghan (country), 45
Kheḍa (country), 123
Khost (country), 159
Khotan (country), 46
Kokālika (monk), 81
Koṅgoda (country), 111, 130
Koṅkaṇapura (country), 120
Konyodha (country), 141
Korea, 191
Kośakarakā Śāstra, 70
Kou (heavenly teacher), 259
Krīta caste, 149
Kṛṣma (country), 159
Kṣānti Ṛṣi, 58
Kṣāntisiṃha (Sarvāstivāda teacher), 106
Kṣatriya (caste), 51, 112, 121, 123, 126
Kuafu (traveler), 185
Kucha (country), 33, 38, 39, 167
Kuiji (Xuanzang's disciple), 2, 330
Kukkuṭārāma (monastery), 88, 187, 209
Kulūta (country), 67
Kumāra (king), 135, 137, 138, 140–42, 144, 146, 147, 152–55
Kumārajīva (Sautrāntika school's founder), 161
Kumārajīva (translator), 34, 182, 216, 247, 253, 261, 263, 269, 317, 327, 346
Kumāralāta (Sautrāntika teacher), 60
Kuṇḍikā (bathing pot), 106
Kunlun Range, 190, 245, 318
Kurān (country), 159
Kuśāgrapura (city), 95, 99
Kusānika (country), 45
Kuśinagara (country), 84, 86, 211
Kustana (country), 163, 164, 165, 167–70
Kusumapura (city), 87

Lampāka (country), 53, 64, 157
Land of Endurance, 5
Laṅgala (country), 124
Laṅkā Mountain, 120
Laṅkāvatāra Sūtra, 120
Laozi (sage), 15, 285, 290
Lāṭa (country), 122
Li Chang (prefect), 21
Li Daoyu (governor), 223
[Li] Daozong (prince), 218
[Li] Hong (prince), 262
Li Shushen (prefect), 173
Li Qianyou (magistrate), 173, 219
[Li] Zhi (crown prince), 206
[Li] Zhong (crown prince), 262
Liang
district, 34, 262

dynasty, 212, 263, 326
state, 194
Liangguo (region), 170, 173, 180
Liao (city), 191
Liao (river), 170, 178
Liaodong (country), 214
Lingrun (monk), 180
Lokāyatika (school), 132
Lokottaravāda (school), 50
Longguo Nunnery, 266
Lop Nor (lake), 161
Lu Ban (craftsman), 208
Lü Cai (chief of the Imperial Medical Bureau), 237, 245, 248, 255
Lulan (country), 170
Luo (region/state), 34, 182, 194
Luo (river), 13, 190, 280, 306, 318
Luofu (region), 247
Luohan Monastery, 180
Luoyang
capital, 12, 25, 176, 178, 180, 183, 188, 309, 311, 322, 325
Palace, 212, 306
Luozhou (region), 181
Lu Shang (statesman), 192

Mādhyamika Śāstra, 66, 101, 129
Madhyāntavibhāga Śāstra, 75
Madhyāntika (arhat), 60, 63
Magadha (country), 87, 93, 95, 122, 126, 174, 230, 239
Mahābhūta(s). *See* Gross elements
Mahābodhi (great enlightenment), 211. *See also* Enlightenment
Mahābodhi Monastery, 229, 233
Mahābodhisattvapiṭaka Sūtra, 182
Mahābrahmā (god), 72
Mahācampā (country), 110
Mahācīna (China), 61, 229
Mahākāśyapa (Śākyamuni's disciple). *See* Kāśyapa/Mahākāśyapa
Mahāmāyā/Māyā (Śākyamuni's mother), 71, 82
Mahāparinirvāṇa Sūtra, 13, 15, 19
Mahāprajñāpāramitā Sūtra, 1, 19, 96, 327, 329, 331
Mahārāṣṭra (country), 121
Mahāratnakūṭa Sūtra, 331
Mahāsāṃghika (school), 50, 58, 63, 98, 114, 158, 174
Mahāsattva(s), 100, 328, 350
Mahāsattva (prince), 60
Mahat. See Great Source of Intellect
Mahātāra(s) (attendant officials), 155
Mahayana (Great Vehicle), 46, 52, 53, 149, 174. *See also under* Vehicle(s)
believers/followers/students, 68, 130, 148
doctrine(s)/theories, 34, 76, 131, 145, 206
master/monk/teacher, 52, 63, 131
monastery, 51, 52, 157
school(s), 7, 34, 119, 120, 126, 229, 254
teaching(s), 17, 39, 52, 69, 71, 72, 75, 87, 94, 100, 109, 111, 121, 123, 125, 130, 131, 134, 135, 138, 144, 145, 147, 148, 164, 234, 256, 330, 342
text(s), 40, 75, 114, 163, 174, 180, 205, 229, 343
Mahāyānabheda Śāstra, 130
Mahāyānābhidharmasaṃyukta-samudāya Śāstra, 181, 182
Mahāyānadeva (Xuanzang's honorary title), 149, 250
Mahāyānaprabha (monk), 289, 293
Mahāyānasaṃparigraha Śāstra, 13, 15–17, 19, 76, 129, 155, 169
Mahāyānasūtrālaṃkāra Śāstra, 75
Mahendra (monk, Aśoka's younger brother), 119
Maheśvarapura (country), 124
Mahīśāsaka (school), 52, 58, 75, 174
Maitreya (future Buddha), 21, 40, 60, 69, 70, 75, 77, 85, 89, 92, 105, 114, 121, 175, 176, 332–36
Maitreya (*śāstra* master), 193, 342
Maitrībala (king), 59
Malakūṭa (country), 116
Mālava (country), 122
Malaya Mountain, 116
Manasabhidheyatā Śāstra, 127
Maṅgala (city), 58, 59
Maṇi (pearl), 166, 234
Mañjuśrī (bodhisattva), 68, 92, 127, 223, 251
Manojñaghoṣa (Tripiṭaka master), 52
Manoratha (*śāstra* master), 57
Manqian (sage), 256
Manṭhaka (text), 102
Maoxian (sage), 256

Māra(s), 89, 248, 340, 343. *See also* Pāpīyān
Ma Rong (scholar), 167
Mathurā (country), 68
Matipura (country), 69
Maudgalyāyana (Śākyamuni's disciple), 79, 90
Ma Xuanzhi (layman), 168
Māyā. *See* Mahāmāyā/Māyā
Mianzhou (region), 180
Middle Way, 255
Ming (emperor). *See under* Emperor
Mingjue (monk), 240
Mingyan (monk), 180
Miscellaneous *Piṭaka*. See under *Piṭaka*(s)
Mitrasena (monk), 71
Mleccha (frontier lands), 53
Mohoyan Desert, 20, 26
Mokṣācārya (Xuanzang's honorary title), 229, 230
Mokṣa-deva (Xuanzang's honorary title), 149
Mokṣagupta (monk), 38–41
Mongolian Desert, 191
Mu (empress), 179
Mūlābhidharma Śāstra, 114, 126
Mūlasthānapura (country), 125
Munjān (country), 159
Music, 7, 39, 43, 138, 141, 143, 144, 152, 163, 165, 187, 206, 208, 220, 241, 278, 281, 284, 285, 297, 301, 326, 328, 330, 331, 338
Musician, 324
Muye (battle), 179

Nāga Palace, 200
Nagaradhana Monastery, 67
Nagarahāra (country), 53, 174
Nāgārjuna (*śāstra* master), 67, 112, 113, 161, 200, 231, 343
Nairañjanā (river), 88, 210
Nālandā Monastery, 90, 93, 95, 99, 101, 126, 127, 129–31, 141, 145, 147, 150, 342
Nanguo (scholar), 249
Nārasiṃha (city), 65
Nārāyaṇadeva (*śāstra* master), 57
Nārikeladvīpa (island country), 120
Narmadā (river), 122
Navāpa (country), 170
Navasaṃghārāma (monastery), 47, 48
Nikāyasaṃgraha Śāstra, 130
Nina (city), 170
Ningyin Palace, 295
Nirgrantha(s) (heretics), 137, 138
Nirvana, 25, 48, 50, 63, 67, 75, 83, 84, 86, 87, 88, 89, 93, 97, 98, 113, 119, 133, 162, 163, 170, 177, 181, 194, 225, 248, 334, 335, 338, 343. See also *Parinirvāṇa*
Nüwa (empress), 183
Nyāyadvāratāraka Śāstra, 67
Nyāyamukha Śāstra, 237
Nyāyānusāra Śāstra, 62, 70, 101, 106

Odun (country), 163
Organs (*indriyas*), 133
Ormus (city), 124
Oxus (river), 45–47, 159, 160

Padārtha(s). *See* Categories of cognition
Palāśa (tree), 65
Pamir
  Range, 31, 35, 41, 44, 46, 160, 162, 168, 181, 185, 239, 342
  Valley, 160, 168
Pāṇini (*ṛṣi*), 102
Panmu (mount), 183
Pāpīyān, 285, 303. *See also* Māra(s)
Paramārthasatya Śāstra, 64
Pāramitā(s), 43
  Six, 204, 211, 238, 270, 285, 329
Paranirmita-vaśavartins (gods), 328
Parasmai (voice), 103
Pārghar (country), 159
Parinirvāṇa, 86. *See also* Nirvana
Pāriyātra (country), 68
Parṇotsa (country), 64
Pārsa (country), 124
Pārśva (monk), 57, 63
Particularity (*viśeṣa*), 133
Parvata (country), 69, 125
Pāṭaliputra (country), 87, 99
Pāṭāsila (country), 124
Path,
  Bodhisattva. *See under* Bodhisattva
  Eightfold Noble, 5, 181, 214, 224, 238, 246, 253, 270, 286, 313
Pei Fangyan (magistrate), 218
Period of Decadence, 341

Pima (city), 169, 170
Pippala tree, 57, 89
Pirates, 76–78
Piṭaka(s)
  Abhidharma, 64, 98
  Dhāraṇī, 98
  Dharma, 5, 97, 98, 262, 276
  Miscellaneous, 98
  Sūtra, 64, 98
  Vinaya, 64, 98, 250, 335
Pi Zhao (sage), 259
Postscript, 209, 228
  to Preface by emperor, 226
Potalaka Mountain, 101
Power(s), supernatural, 60, 77, 97, 112, 114, 116, 119, 163, 230, 253, 254, 328, 332
Prabhākaravardhana (king), 72
Prabhāpāla (bodhisattva), 85
Prabhāraṇa (translator), 263
Prāgbodhi Mountain, 174
Prajāpatī (Śākyamuni's stepmother), 80
Prajñā, 225, 250, 282, 315, 329, 330
Prajñābhadra (monk), 126
Prajñādeva (monk), 229, 230, 233
Prajñāgupta (Brahmin teacher), 130
Prajñākara (Tripiṭaka master), 48, 49, 51–53
Prajñāpāramitā, 328
Prajñāpāramitāhṛdaya Sūtra, 26
Prajñāpāramitā Sūtra, 305
Prajñāpāramitā Sūtra of the Benevolent King, 32
Prajñā Sūtra, 330
Prakaraṇāryavācā Śāstra, 76, 80, 101, 181, 182
Prakṛti. See Self-nature
Prasenajit (king), 32, 80, 81
Pratītyasamutpāda Sūtra, 216
Pratyekabuddha(s)
  stage of, 193
  tooth of, 50
Prayāga (country), 78, 151, 155, 168
Precept(s), 22, 37, 45, 57, 141, 192, 322, 335, 336
  Bodhisattva, 223, 224, 266
  Five, 22, 37, 48, 78
Preceptor, 126, 266
Preface to the Holy Teachings of the Tripiṭaka, 226
Puguang Monastery, 180, 290
Pujiu Monastery, 180
Puṇḍravardhana (country), 109
Pure Land, 198, 238
Pūrṇavarman (king), 100, 126
Purple Palace, 267
Puruṣa (grammatical example), 104
Puruṣa (spirit), 133, 134
Puruṣapura (capital), 57
Pūrvaśaila Monastery, 113
Puṣkalāvatī (city), 58
Puxian (monk), 180

Qi dynasty, 263
Qin dynasty, 181, 184, 284, 296, 323, 346
Qin Jing (envoy), 6
Qixuan (monk), 180
Qiyan Monastery, 180
Quality (*guṇa*), 133
Qu Lake, 208

Rāhula (Śākyamuni's son), 68, 99
Rājagṛha (city), 87, 88, 95, 99, 100, 168, 185, 250, 266, 328
  Small, 47
Rājapura (country), 64
Rajas (foulness), 133
Rājyavardhana (Harṣavardhana's brother), 72
Rākṣasī(s), 119
Raktamṛttikā Monastery, 110
Rāmagrāma (country), 82
Ratnākāra, 86
Rebirth, 127, 244, 273, 312, 318
Record of the Nine States, 185
Record of the Western Regions, 119, 123, 183, 186
Red Book, 209
Refuge(s), Three, 37, 301, 303. *See also* Gem, Triple
Relic(s), 60, 68, 226. *See also under* Buddha(s)
  of the Buddha, 48, 54, 57, 61, 83, 84, 87, 97, 111, 128, 129, 149, 150, 156, 173, 219, 343
  of Kāśyapa Buddha, 82
Religions, three, 194
Right Dharma Store. *See* Śīlabhadra/Right Dharma Store
Rocky Pass, 60, 61

Rohitaka Stupa, 59
Rohu (country), 159
Ṛṣi (hermit), 82, 102, 112, 124
Ruo River, 184

Śabda Śāstra, 257
Śabdavidyā (grammar), 126, 174
Śabdavidyāsaṃyukta Śāstra, 115
Śabdavidyā Śāstra, 62
Sadāpralāpa (bodhisattva), 31, 227
Saddharmapuṇḍarīka Sūtra, 96, 174
Saddharmasaṃparigraha Śāstra, 126
Ṣaḍdvāradhāraṇī Sūtra, 181, 182
Ṣaḍmukhadhāraṇī Sūtra, 332
Sāgaramati (monk), 131
Śākala (city), 64
Śakrāditya (king), 93
Śākya Bodhisattva, 53, 82
Śākyamuni (Buddha), 5, 50, 58, 67, 85, 124, 162, 170, 226, 239, 247, 292, 302
Śāla Grove, 84
Śālāka (monastery), 51, 53
Śāla trees, 6, 34, 198, 200, 247, 250, 253, 270, 271, 338, 343
Śalātura (city), 102
Samādhi of the Cessation of Mentality, 161–63
Sāmānya. See Generality
Samarkand (country), 44
Samataṭa (country), 110
Samavāya. See Correlation
Śāmbhī (country), 160
Saṃdhinirmocana Sūtra, 2
Saṃghabhadra (*śāstra* master), 70, 71
Saṃghakīrti (monk), 62, 63
Saṃghāṭi robe, 50, 54
Sāṃkhya(s) (heretics), 132, 133
Sāṃkhya Śāstra, 257
Saṃmitīya (school), 80, 85, 109, 122, 123, 126, 130
Samuccayapramāṇa Śāstra, 101, 113
Saṃyuktābhidharmahṛdaya Śāstra, 39
Śāṇakavāsa (teacher), 50, 232
Sangha, 58, 88, 90, 186, 299, 341, 347
Saṅghavarman (translator), 34
Saptadaśabhūmi Śāstra, 18, 342. See also *Yogācārabhūmi Śāstra*
Śāriputra (Śākyamuni's disciple), 68, 81, 96
Śarīra(s), 124, 343
Sarvasiddhārtha (prince), 120, 166
Sarvāstivāda (school), 52, 58, 63, 67, 69–71, 75, 85, 106, 126, 165, 174
Sarvāstivāda Vinaya, 241
Śaśāṅka (king), 72, 141
Śatadharmavidyānikāya Śāstra, 216
Śatadru (country), 68
Śata Śāstra, 66, 101, 129
Ṣaṭpādābhidharma Śāstra, 48
Sattva (virtue), 133
Satyaśāsana Śāstra, 126
Satyasiddhi Śāstra, 17
Sautrāntika (school), 60, 161
Sautrāntikavibhāṣā Śāstra, 69
Sciences, Five, 63
Script
  Chinese style(s), 286–87
  imperial edict in red, 278
  on palm leaves, 6
  Sanskrit, 181
  in shapes of birds, 209
  on tortoise shells, 209
Scriptures
  of Nine Divisions, 233
  of Twelve Divisions, 223
Self-consciousness (*ahaṃkāra*), 133
Self-nature (*prakṛti*), 133, 134
Senghui (monk), 182
Sengjing (monk), 13, 14
Shangguan Yi (scholar), 195
Shang-yang bird, 261
Shanshan (region), 169
Shaolin Monastery, 179, 311, 312
Shaoshi Mountain/Peak, 179, 311, 315, 317, 318
Shazhou (region), 170
Shenfang (monk), 180
Sheng (river), 249, 260
Shentai (monk), 180, 240, 241
Shiji Monastery, 180
Shun (emperor). *See under* Emperor
Śikni (country), 160
Śīlabhadra/Right Dharma Store (Xuanzang's teacher in India), 90–92, 95, 101, 116, 126, 128–32, 135, 139–41, 229, 231, 342
Śīlāditya (king), 73, 79, 100, 101, 121–23, 126, 127, 130, 132, 137, 138, 140–44, 146–48, 150, 152, 153, 155, 343

Silver Mountain, 38
Sima Qian (historian), 177
Siṃhacandra (monk), 155
Siṃhala (country), 111, 112, 115, 116, 119, 120
Siṃhaprabha (monk), 129–31, 155
Siṃhapura (country), 60, 155
Sindhu (country), 125, 211
Sindhu (river), 156
Sītā River, 161, 163
Six Classics, 241, 276
Slave, 134, 135, 149
Small Isolated Hill, 106
Snow Mountains, 49, 51, 157, 165, 168, 177, 184, 205, 243, 269, 272
Song Mountain, 179, 241
Song Xingzhi (magistrate), 218
South Kosala, 112
Spirit (*puruṣa*), 133
Śramaṇa(s), 76, 77, 82, 110, 119, 145, 147, 151, 229
Śrāmaṇera(s), 33, 35, 45, 54, 65, 83
Śrāvaka(s), 193
Śrāvastī (country), 80, 210, 233
Śrīgupta (would-be assassin), 96
Śrīkrītāti (country), 163
Śrīkṣetra (country), 110
Śrīmālādevīsiṃhanāda Sūtra, 56
Śrotakoṭīviṃśa (arhat), 121
Śrughna (country), 68
Stage(s)
of complete/incomplete nirvana, 194
four, of *Dhyāna,* 270
of [no more] learning, 97, 98
of non-retrogression, 211
of *Pratyekabuddhas*, 193
of sainthood, 163
seventeen, of Bodhisattvahood, 193
of *Śrāvakas*, 193
Ten, of Bodhisattvahood, 197, 205, 299, 348
Ten, of the Perfect Sect, 5
Tenth, of Bodhisattvahood, 139, 221, 239, 244
of wisdom, 204
States, nine, 190, 194, 195, 200, 276
Sthāneśvara (country), 68
Sthavira (school), 82, 110–12, 115, 119, 174
Sthiramati (*śāstra* master), 126
Stickwood Hill, 126, 127
Story of the Scripture of Requiting Favors, 305
Studies, Three, 17
Subanta (verb paradigm), 102, 103
Śubhavastu River, 58
Subhūti (monk), 114
Subhūti (Śākyamuni's disciple), 189
Substance (*dravya*), 133, 134
Subtle Elements (*tanmātras*), Five, 133
Suchness, 269, 278
Sudāna (prince), 73
Sudatta (Aśoka's brother), 81
Śuddhodana (Śākyamuni's father), 82, 166
Sudhana (seeker), 31
Sugatamitra (Sarvāstivāda monk), 63
Sui dynasty, 8, 11, 13, 14, 30, 191, 214, 215, 263, 265, 306, 309
Sumeru (mountain), 18, 54, 77, 210, 225, 239
Śūnyapuṣpa (heretic), 130
Surāṣṭra (country), 124, 126
Suraṭṭha (country), 123
Sūrya (monk), 114
Sūryadeva (monk), 63
Sūryalabdha (layman), 230
Sūryavarman (Buddhist sage), 73
Sūtrālaṃkāra Śāstra, 127
Sūtra *Piṭaka.* See under *Piṭaka*(s)
Sūtraśata Śāstra, 67
Sutṛṣṇa (country), 44
Sūyāb (city), 42
Suzhou (region), 212
Śvetapura (city), 86
Swat River, 58
Sweet Dew, 13, 31, 166, 211

Taibo (prince), 262
Tai-wei, constellation of, 334
Tai Xuan Jing. See *Great Mystery Classic*
Taizong (emperor). *See under* Emperor
Tajiks (tribe), 160, 184
Ṭakka (country), 64, 66
Takṣaśilā (city), 60, 156, 161, 164
Tāla trees, 121
Tamas (ignorance), 133
Tamasāvana Monastery, 67
Tamasthiti (country), 159, 160
Tāmralipti (country), 110

Tang (dynasty), 14, 191, 230, 232, 233, 238, 344
Tanmātra(s). *See* Subtle Elements
Taoism, 194, 291
Taras (city), 44
Tardu Shad (Yehu Khan's son), 46
Tathāgata, 5, 13, 33, 48, 49, 53–57, 59–61, 63, 67, 68, 72, 79–81, 83–85, 87–89, 93, 94, 96–100, 112, 119, 120, 123–25, 162, 166, 173–76, 207, 223, 225, 227, 244, 253, 301, 320, 333–35, 343
Tathāgatagupta (Sarvāstivāda teacher), 106
Tathatā, 203, 244
Tattva(s). *See* True Entities
Tattvasandeśa Śāstra, 71
Tattvasatya Śāstra, 69, 71
Telāḍhaka Monastery, 88
Thousand Springs (region), 44
Three Rivers, 143, 182, 324
Tiangong Monastery, 181
Tiladhāka Monastery, 126
Tiṅanta (verb paradigm), 102, 103
Toṣasana Monastery, 67
Trapuṣa (city), 48
Trāyastriṃśa Heaven, 208, 344
Treatise on the Essential Realities of the Holy Teaching, 80
Triṃśikā, 2
Tripiṭaka, 1, 3, 7, 8, 48, 49, 52, 63, 67, 69, 71, 73, 88, 97, 98, 111, 114, 126, 131, 157, 167, 179, 199, 200, 204, 228, 230, 233, 239, 240, 242, 244, 251, 254, 252, 314, 315, 341, 342, 348–50
  Master, 239, 250
True Entities (*tattvas*), 133, 134
Truth(s)
  Four Noble, 247
  ultimate, 5, 197, 223, 224, 239, 247, 255, 270, 282, 346
Tukhāra (country), 46, 49, 53, 149, 158, 159, 170
Turbidities, five, 292
Turks, 43, 46, 159
Tuṣita (heaven/palace), 60, 69, 75, 77, 105, 114, 175, 176, 250, 333, 336

Uḍakhāṇḍa (city), 58, 60, 156
Udayana (king), 79, 81, 169, 174
Udita (king), 154, 155
Uḍra (country), 111, 126, 130, 131, 134
Udyāna (country), 58, 60, 157
Ujjayanī (country), 123
Uṇādi (text on grammar), 102
Upadeśa, 6
Upadeśa Śāstra, 64
Upādhyāya, 91, 92
Upagupta (arhat), 68, 125, 232
Upāli (Śākyamuni's disciple), 68, 98
Upāsaka, 126, 230, 251
Urasā (country), 61
Usar (country), 162
Uttara (arhat), 114
Uttarāṣāḍhā (name of month), 82

Vadi (country), 45
Vaipulya, 5, 31, 229, 254, 343
Vaipulyaśata Śāstra, 79
Vairocana (arhat), 165
Vaiśākha (name of month), 84
Vaiśālī (country), 86, 88, 99, 144, 174, 246, 250
Vaiśeṣika (school), 132, 133, 258
Vaiśravaṇa (god), 164
Vaiṣya (caste), 72
Vajra (king), 94
Vajra (Nirgrantha), 137
Vajracchedikāprajñāpāramitā Sūtra, 215, 216, 332
Vakula (*yakṣa* king), 106
Valabhi (country), 123
Vāṇi (minister), 72
Varaṇa (country), 157
Vārāṇasī (country), 57, 85, 174, 211, 277
Vāśibhā Monastery, 109
Vasubandhu (*śāstra* master), 2, 57, 63, 64, 70, 71, 75, 80, 216, 343
Vasumitra (Sarvāstivāda monk), 63
Veda(s), 66, 94, 126, 229, 239, 342
Vehicle(s)
  Five, 195, 214, 254, 261, 346
  Great, 197, 231, 314. *See also under* Mahayana
  Lesser, 197, 231, 314. *See also under* Hinayana
  One/Unique [Buddha] (Ekayāna), 5, 181, 198, 200, 205, 241, 247, 285, 298

Three, 5, 231, 240, 312, 348
of truth, 210
Veṇuvana Vihāra, 328
Vermilion Bird Street, 173, 175
Vibhāṣāprakaraṇapāda Śāstra, 67
Vibhāṣā Śāstra, 39, 40, 47–49, 70, 73, 101, 106
Vidyābhadra (monk), 147
Vihāra, 59, 72, 79, 80, 81, 96, 200
Vijñānakāyapāda Śāstra, 80
Vijñānamātraparikalpana Śāstra, 127, 129
Vijñānamātratā Śāstra, 80
Vijñānavāda. *See* Faxiang/Dharmalakṣaṇa
Vijñaptimātratāsiddhi Śāstra, 2, 76, 115, 155
Vilaśāṇa (country), 71, 155
Vimalakīrti (layman), 86, 139, 189, 223, 245, 248, 251
Vimalakīrtinirdeśa Sūtra, 86
Vimalamitra (*śāstra* master), 70
Vimalanetra (monk), 302
Vinaya *Piṭaka.* See under *Piṭaka*(s)
Vinayavibhāṣā Śāstra, 64
Vinītaprabha (monk), 67
Vīryasena (Tripiṭaka master), 73
Viṣaka (country), 80
Viśeṣa. See Particularity
Viśuddhasiṃha (monk), 63
Voidness(es), 196, 203, 238, 240, 247, 248, 255, 291, 317, 333
three, 197, 253, 298, 346. *See also* Emptiness
and tranquillity, 318
true, 254
twofold, 7, 224
Vṛjisthāna (country), 157
Vulture Peak. *See* Gṛdhrakūṭa Mountain/Vulture Peak
Vyākaraṇa (text), 102

Wang Mang (usurper), 14, 179
Wangmu, 183
Wang Xiang (captain), 24–26
Wang Xizhi (calligrapher), 207
Wang Xuance (envoy), 128
Wang Zun (envoy), 6, 49
Wannian (city), 218
Washing stone of the Tathāgata, 59
Weeping Kylin and the Lamenting Phoenix, 284
Weibei (region), 180
Wei Hong (sage), 259
Wei Qing (general), 191
Weishi (school). *See* Faxiang/Dharmalakṣaṇa
Weito (general), 335
Wende (empress), 207, 208, 267
West [Great] Women's Country, 119, 124
White Horse Monastery, 210, 228, 278
White Water (city), 44
Worlds
Three, 97, 127, 277, 278, 291, 317
Three Thousand, 34, 253, 285
three thousand Dharma, 210, 239
Worship
of the Bodhi tree, 76, 89, 129, 168
of the Buddha's shadow, 55, 56
of crown, 120
of deities/*devas*/divine beings, 78, 91, 122, 125
of fire, 42, 44
of goddess Durgā, 76
of holy sites, 53, 58, 61, 64, 88, 90, 95, 101, 109, 114, 138, 139, 144, 155, 157, 184
of [image of] Bodhisattva(s), 92, 105
of [image of the] Buddha(s), 32, 37, 39, 45, 55, 77, 153, 160, 165, 220, 222, 290, 295, 314, 331
of Maitreya, 70, 92
of Master [Xuanzang], 19, 21, 29, 32, 42, 78, 143, 157, 171
of relics, 47, 48, 128, 129, 150
of stupa, 83
Wu (emperor). *See under* Emperor
Wu (state), 15, 17, 25, 34, 182
Marquis of, 219

Xia dynasty, 191, 281, 323, 345
Xiang (state), 194
Xian-yun (tribe), 190
Xiao-lian (honorary post), 11
Xiao Rui (governor), 223
Xiaowen (emperor). *See under* Emperor
Ximing Monastery, 325, 326, 335, 336

Xingshan Monastery, 181
Xingyou (monk), 180
Xixuan (monk translator), 237, 241
Xuanmu (monk), 181
Xuanying (monk), 181
Xuanyuan (emperor). *See under* Emperor
Xuanzang, 1–3, 11, 21, 25, 33, 140, 167, 181, 183, 184, 186, 192, 197, 200, 205, 206, 211, 213, 217, 227, 230, 233, 235, 239, 250, 263, 269, 275, 277, 280, 284, 286, 288, 289, 292, 293, 295, 296, 298, 300, 303, 304, 306, 309, 310, 312, 318–20, 323, 336–38
Xuanze (monk), 181
Xuanzhong (monk), 180
Xue (nun), 265

Yakṣa(s), 59, 64, 106, 111, 133, 243
Yamanadvīpa (country), 110
Yamgān (country), 159
Yan (Xuanzang's teacher), 13
Yāna (s), 5. *See also* Vehicle(s)
Yang (emperor). *See under* Emperor
Yang (state), 194
Yangzi (river), 294
Yanjue Monastery, 180
Yanran Mountain, 191
Yao (emperor). *See under* Emperor
Yao, House of, 247, 263
Yao Xing (ruler), 192, 263
Yaxartes (river), 44
Yehu Khan (khan), 42, 46, 159
Yellow Emperor. *See under* Emperor
Yellow River, 13, 190, 240, 273, 300, 318, 345
Yi
- region/state, 16, 194
- tribe, 183

Yiluan Hall, 176
Yin and *yang*, 168, 196, 238, 241, 258
Yi Yin (statesman), 192
Yizhou (region), 180
Yogācārabhūmi Śāstra, 2, 18, 40, 75, 77, 91, 92, 101, 111, 115, 116, 125–27, 129, 139, 143, 169, 181, 188, 193, 194, 232. See also *Saptadaśabhūmi Śāstra*
Yogaparikalpana Śāstra, 155
Yong (state), 194
Yonghui period, 128, 203, 222, 237, 282, 290
Yongzhou (region), 173
Youzhou (region), 181
Yu (emperor). *See under* Emperor
Yuddhapati (country), 86
Yu dynasty, 191, 345
Yuhua Monastery, 328–31, 334, 337, 338
Yuhua Palace, 188, 325, 327
Yumen Pass, 20, 23, 211, 254
Yunhe (mount), 187

Zhang (Queen Mother), 32
Zhang family, 309
Zhang Qian (marquis), 177, 185
Zhangsun Wuji (duke), 177, 178, 194, 266
Zhangye (region), 184
Zhang Yun (traveller), 185
Zhao (state), 219, 247, 263
Zhaoren Monastery, 181
Zhenguan period, 3, 8, 18, 168, 173, 181, 203, 205, 211, 263, 282, 290, 342, 344
Zheng Xuan (scholar), 167
Zhenxiang Monastery, 180
Zhiyan (monk), 18, 182, 344
Zhongchi Monastery, 181
Zhongnan Mountain, 180, 268
Zhou dynasty, 179, 181, 188, 191, 253, 263, 271, 278, 297, 300, 301, 320, 322–24
Zhou of Shang (emperor). *See under* Emperor
Zhuan script, 209
Zi (river), 249, 260
Ziwei Hall, 216
Zumathān (country), 49

A List of the Volumes of the BDK English Tripiṭaka (First Series)

Abbreviations

Ch.: Chinese
Skt.: Sanskrit
Jp.: Japanese
T.: Taishō Tripiṭaka

Vol. No.		Title	*T.* No.
1, 2	*Ch.* *Skt.*	Ch'ang-a-han-ching (長阿含經) Dīrghāgama	1
3–8	*Ch.* *Skt.*	Chung-a-han-ching (中阿含經) Madhyamāgama	26
9-I	*Ch.*	Ta-ch'eng-pên-shêng-hsin-ti-kuan-ching (大乘本生心地觀經)	159
9-II	*Ch.* *Skt.*	Fo-so-hsing-tsan (佛所行讃) Buddhacarita	192
10-I	*Ch.*	Tsa-pao-ts'ang-ching (雜寶藏經)	203
10-II	*Ch.*	Fa-chü-p'i-yü-ching (法句譬喩經)	211
11-I	*Ch.* *Skt.*	Hsiao-p'in-pan-jo-po-lo-mi-ching (小品般若波羅蜜經) Aṣṭasāhasrikā-prajñāpāramitā-sūtra	227
11-II	*Ch.* *Skt.*	Chin-kang-pan-jo-po-lo-mi-ching (金剛般若波羅蜜經) Vajracchedikā-prajñāpāramitā-sūtra	235

Vol. No.		Title	*T.* No.
11-III	*Ch.*	Jên-wang-pan-jo-po-lo-mi-ching (仁王般若波羅蜜經)	245
	Skt.	Kāruṇikārājā-prajñāpāramitā-sūtra (?)	
11-IV	*Ch.*	Pan-jo-po-lo-mi-to-hsing-ching (般若波羅蜜多心經)	251
	Skt.	Prajñāpāramitāhṛdaya-sūtra	
12-I	*Ch.*	Ta-lo-chin-kang-pu-k'ung-chên-shih-san-mo-yeh-ching (大樂金剛不空眞實三麼耶經)	243
	Skt.	Adhyardhaśatikā-prajñāpāramitā-sūtra	
12-II	*Ch.*	Wu-liang-shou-ching (無量壽經)	360
	Skt.	Sukhāvatīvyūha	
12-III	*Ch.*	Kuan-wu-liang-shou-fo-ching (觀無量壽佛經)	365
	Skt.	Amitāyurdhyāna-sūtra	
12-IV	*Ch.*	A-mi-t'o-ching (阿彌陀經)	366
	Skt.	Sukhāvatīvyūha	
12-V	*Ch.*	Ti-ts'ang-p'u-sa-pên-yüan-ching (地藏菩薩本願經)	412
	Skt.	Kṣitigarbhapraṇidhāna-sūtra (?)	
12-VI	*Ch.*	Yao-shih-liu-li-kuang-ju-lai-pên-yüan-kung-tê-ching (藥師琉璃光如來本願功德經)	450
	Skt.	Bhaiṣajyaguruvaiḍūryaprabhāsapūrvapraṇidhānaviśeṣavistara	
12-VII	*Ch.*	Mi-lê-hsia-shêng-ch'êng-fo-ching (彌勒下生成佛經)	454
	Skt.	Maitreyavyākaraṇa (?)	
12-VIII	*Ch.*	Wên-shu-shih-li-wên-ching (文殊師利問經)	468
	Skt.	Mañjuśrīparipṛcchā (?)	
13-I	*Ch.*	Miao-fa-lien-hua-ching (妙法蓮華經)	262
	Skt.	Saddharmapuṇḍarīka-sūtra	
13-II	*Ch.*	Wu-liang-i-ching (無量義經)	276
13-III	*Ch.*	Kuan-p'u-hsien-p'u-sa-hsing-fa-ching (觀普賢菩薩行法經)	277
14–19	*Ch.*	Ta-fang-kuang-fo-hua-yen-ching (大方廣佛華嚴經)	278
	Skt.	Avataṃsaka-sūtra	

Vol. No.		Title	*T.* No.
20-I	*Ch.*	Shêng-man-shih-tzŭ-hou-i-ch'eng-ta-fang-pien-fang-kuang-ching (勝鬘師子吼一乘大方便方廣經)	353
	Skt.	Śrīmālādevīsiṃhanāda-sūtra	
20-II	*Ch.*	Chin-kuang-ming-tsui-shêng-wang-ching (金光明最勝王經)	665
	Skt.	Suvarṇaprabhāsa-sūtra	
21–24	*Ch.*	Ta-pan-nieh-p'an-ching (大般涅槃經)	374
	Skt.	Mahāparinirvāṇa-sūtra	
25-I	*Ch.*	Fo-ch'ui-pan-nieh-p'an-liao-shuo-chiao-chieh-ching (佛垂般涅槃略説教誡經)	389
25-II	*Ch.*	Pan-chou-san-mei-ching (般舟三昧經)	418
	Skt.	Pratyutpannabuddhasammukhāvasthitasamādhi-sūtra	
25-III	*Ch.*	Shou-lêng-yen-san-mei-ching (首楞嚴三昧經)	642
	Skt.	Śūraṅgamasamādhi-sūtra	
25-IV	*Ch.*	Chieh-shên-mi-ching (解深密經)	676
	Skt.	Saṃdhinirmocana-sūtra	
25-V	*Ch.*	Yü-lan-p'ên-ching (盂蘭盆經)	685
	Skt.	Ullambana-sūtra (?)	
25-VI	*Ch.*	Ssŭ-shih-êrh-chang-ching (四十二章經)	784
26-I	*Ch.*	Wei-mo-chieh-so-shuo-ching (維摩詰所説經)	475
	Skt.	Vimalakīrtinirdeśa-sūtra	
26-II	*Ch.*	Yüeh-shang-nü-ching (月上女經)	480
	Skt.	Candrottarādārikāparipṛcchā	
26-III	*Ch.*	Tso-ch'an-san-mei-ching (坐禪三昧經)	614
26-IV	*Ch.*	Ta-mo-to-lo-ch'an-ching (達摩多羅禪經)	618
	Skt.	Yogācārabhūmi-sūtra (?)	
27	*Ch.*	Yüeh-têng-san-mei-ching (月燈三昧經)	639
	Skt.	Samādhirājacandrapradīpa-sūtra	
28	*Ch.*	Ju-lêng-ch'ieh-ching (入楞伽經)	671
	Skt.	Laṅkāvatāra-sūtra	

Vol. No.		Title	T. No.
29-I	*Ch.*	Ta-fang-kuang-yüan-chio-hsiu-to-lo-liao-i-ching (大方廣圓覺修多羅了義經)	842
29-II	*Ch.*	Su-hsi-ti-chieh-lo-ching (蘇悉地羯羅經)	893
	Skt.	Susiddhikaramahātantrasādhanopāyika-paṭala	
29-III	*Ch.*	Mo-têng-ch'ieh-ching (摩登伽經)	1300
	Skt.	Mātaṅgī-sūtra (?)	
30-I	*Ch.*	Ta-p'i-lu-chê-na-ch'êng-fo-shên-pien-chia-ch'ih-ching (大毘盧遮那成佛神變加持經)	848
	Skt.	Mahāvairocanābhisambodhivikurvitādhiṣṭhāna-vaipulyasūtrendrarāja-nāma-dharmaparyāya	
30-II	*Ch.*	Chin-kang-ting-i-ch'ieh-ju-lai-chên-shih-shê-ta-ch'eng-hsien-chêng-ta-chiao-wang-ching (金剛頂一切如來眞實攝大乘現證大教王經)	865
	Skt.	Sarvatathāgatatattvasaṃgrahamahāyānābhi-samayamahākalparāja	
31–35	*Ch.*	Mo-ho-sêng-ch'i-lü (摩訶僧祇律)	1425
	Skt.	Mahāsāṃghika-vinaya (?)	
36–42	*Ch.*	Ssŭ-fên-lü (四分律)	1428
	Skt.	Dharmaguptaka-vinaya (?)	
43, 44	*Ch.*	Shan-chien-lü-p'i-p'o-sha (善見律毘婆沙)	1462
	Pāli	Samantapāsādikā	
45-I	*Ch.*	Fan-wang-ching (梵網經)	1484
	Skt.	Brahmajāla-sūtra (?)	
45-II	*Ch.*	Yu-p'o-sai-chieh-ching (優婆塞戒經)	1488
	Skt.	Upāsakaśīla-sūtra (?)	
46-I	*Ch.*	Miao-fa-lien-hua-ching-yu-po-t'i-shê (妙法蓮華經憂波提舍)	1519
	Skt.	Saddharmapuṇḍarīkopadeśa	
46-II	*Ch.*	Fo-ti-ching-lun (佛地經論)	1530
	Skt.	Buddhabhūmisūtra-śāstra (?)	
46-III	*Ch.*	Shê-ta-ch'eng-lun (攝大乘論)	1593
	Skt.	Mahāyānasaṃgraha	
47	*Ch.*	Shih-chu-p'i-p'o-sha-lun (十住毘婆沙論)	1521
	Skt.	Daśabhūmika-vibhāṣā (?)	

Vol. No.		Title	T. No.
48, 49	*Ch.* *Skt.*	A-p'i-ta-mo-chü-shê-lun (阿毘達磨俱舍論) Abhidharmakośa-bhāṣya	1558
50–59	*Ch.* *Skt.*	Yü-ch'ieh-shih-ti-lun (瑜伽師地論) Yogācārabhūmi	1579
60-I	*Ch.* *Skt.*	Ch'êng-wei-shih-lun (成唯識論) Vijñaptimātratāsiddhi-śāstra (?)	1585
60-II	*Ch.* *Skt.*	Wei-shih-san-shih-lun-sung (唯識三十論頌) Triṃśikā	1586
60-III	*Ch.* *Skt.*	Wei-shih-êrh-shih-lun (唯識二十論) Viṃśatikā	1590
61-I	*Ch.* *Skt.*	Chung-lun (中論) Madhyamaka-śāstra	1564
61-II	*Ch.* *Skt.*	Pien-chung-pien-lun (辯中邊論) Madhyāntavibhāga	1600
61-III	*Ch.* *Skt.*	Ta-ch'eng-ch'êng-yeh-lun (大乘成業論) Karmasiddhiprakaraṇa	1609
61-IV	*Ch.* *Skt.*	Yin-ming-ju-chêng-li-lun (因明入正理論) Nyāyapraveśa	1630
61-V	*Ch.* *Skt.*	Chin-kang-chên-lun (金剛針論) Vajrasūcī	1642
61-VI	*Ch.*	Chang-so-chih-lun (彰所知論)	1645
62	*Ch.* *Skt.*	Ta-ch'eng-chuang-yen-ching-lun (大乘莊嚴經論) Mahāyānasūtrālaṃkāra	1604
63-I	*Ch.* *Skt.*	Chiu-ching-i-ch'eng-pao-hsing-lun (究竟一乘寶性論) Ratnagotravibhāgamahāyānottaratantra-śāstra	1611
63-II	*Ch.* *Skt.*	P'u-t'i-hsing-ching (菩提行經) Bodhicaryāvatāra	1662
63-III	*Ch.*	Chin-kang-ting-yü-ch'ieh-chung-fa-a-nou-to-lo-san-miao-san-p'u-t'i-hsin-lun (金剛頂瑜伽中發阿耨多羅三藐三菩提心論)	1665
63-IV	*Ch.* *Skt.*	Ta-ch'eng-ch'i-hsin-lun (大乘起信論) Mahāyānaśraddhotpāda-śāstra (?)	1666

Vol. No.		Title	T. No.
63-V	*Ch.* *Pāli*	Na-hsien-pi-ch'iu-ching (那先比丘經) Milindapañhā	1670
64	*Ch.* *Skt.*	Ta-ch'eng-chi-p'u-sa-hsüeh-lun (大乘集菩薩學論) Śikṣāsamuccaya	1636
65	*Ch.*	Shih-mo-ho-yen-lun (釋摩訶衍論)	1668
66-I	*Ch.*	Pan-jo-po-lo-mi-to-hsin-ching-yu-tsan (般若波羅蜜多心經幽賛)	1710
66-II	*Ch.*	Kuan-wu-liang-shou-fo-ching-shu (觀無量壽佛經疏)	1753
66-III	*Ch.*	San-lun-hsüan-i (三論玄義)	1852
66-IV	*Ch.*	Chao-lun (肇論)	1858
67, 68	*Ch.*	Miao-fa-lien-hua-ching-hsüan-i (妙法蓮華經玄義)	1716
69	*Ch.*	Ta-ch'eng-hsüan-lun (大乘玄論)	1853
70-I	*Ch.*	Hua-yen-i-ch'eng-chiao-i-fên-ch'i-chang (華嚴一乘教義分齊章)	1866
70-II	*Ch.*	Yüan-jên-lun (原人論)	1886
70-III	*Ch.*	Hsiu-hsi-chih-kuan-tso-ch'an-fa-yao (修習止觀坐禪法要)	1915
70-IV	*Ch.*	T'ien-t'ai-ssŭ-chiao-i (天台四教儀)	1931
71, 72	*Ch.*	Mo-ho-chih-kuan (摩訶止觀)	1911
73-I	*Ch.*	Kuo-ch'ing-pai-lu (國清百録)	1934
73-II	*Ch.*	Liu-tsu-ta-shih-fa-pao-t'an-ching (六祖大師法寶壇經)	2008
73-III	*Ch.*	Huang-po-shan-tuan-chi-ch'an-shih-ch'uan-hsin-fa-yao (黄檗山斷際禪師傳心法要)	2012 A
73-IV	*Ch.*	Yung-chia-chêng-tao-ko (永嘉證道歌)	2014
74-I	*Ch.*	Chên-chou-lin-chi-hui-chao-ch'an-shih-wu-lu (鎭州臨濟慧照禪師語録)	1985
74-II	*Ch.*	Wu-mên-kuan (無門關)	2005

Vol. No.		Title	*T.* No.
74-III	*Ch.*	Hsin-hsin-ming (信心銘)	2010
74-IV	*Ch.*	Ch'ih-hsiu-pai-chang-ch'ing-kuei (勅修百丈清規)	2025
75	*Ch.*	Fo-kuo-yüan-wu-ch'an-shih-pi-yen-lu (佛果圜悟禪師碧巖録)	2003
76-I	*Ch.* *Skt.*	I-pu-tsung-lun-lun (異部宗輪論) Samayabhedoparacanacakra	2031
76-II	*Ch.* *Skt.*	A-yü-wang-ching (阿育王經) Aśokarāja-sūtra (?)	2043
76-III	*Ch.*	Ma-ming-p'u-sa-ch'uan (馬鳴菩薩傳)	2046
76-IV	*Ch.*	Lung-shu-p'u-sa-ch'uan (龍樹菩薩傳)	2047
76-V	*Ch.*	P'o-sou-p'an-tou-fa-shih-ch'uan (婆藪槃豆法師傳)	2049
76-VI	*Ch.*	Pi-ch'iu-ni-ch'uan (比丘尼傳)	2063
76-VII	*Ch.*	Kao-sêng-fa-hsien-ch'uan (高僧法顯傳)	2085
76-VIII	*Ch.*	T'ang-ta-ho-shang-tung-chêng-ch'uan (遊方記抄:唐大和上東征傳)	2089-(7)
77	*Ch.*	Ta-t'ang-ta-tz'ŭ-ên-ssŭ-san-ts'ang-fa-shih-ch'uan (大唐大慈恩寺三藏法師傳)	2053
78	*Ch.*	Kao-sêng-ch'uan (高僧傳)	2059
79	*Ch.*	Ta-t'ang-hsi-yü-chi (大唐西域記)	2087
80	*Ch.*	Hung-ming-chi (弘明集)	2102
81–92	*Ch.*	Fa-yüan-chu-lin (法苑珠林)	2122
93-I	*Ch.*	Nan-hai-chi-kuei-nei-fa-ch'uan (南海寄歸内法傳)	2125
93-II	*Ch.*	Fan-yü-tsa-ming (梵語雑名)	2135
94-I	*Jp.*	Shō-man-gyō-gi-sho (勝鬘經義疏)	2185
94-II	*Jp.*	Yui-ma-kyō-gi-sho (維摩經義疏)	2186
95	*Jp.*	Hok-ke-gi-sho (法華義疏)	2187

Vol. No.		Title	*T.* No.
96-I	*Jp.*	Han-nya-shin-gyō-hi-ken (般若心經秘鍵)	2203
96-II	*Jp.*	Dai-jō-hos-sō-ken-jin-shō (大乘法相研神章)	2309
96-III	*Jp.*	Kan-jin-kaku-mu-shō (觀心覺夢鈔)	2312
97-I	*Jp.*	Ris-shū-kō-yō (律宗綱要)	2348
97-II	*Jp.*	Ten-dai-hok-ke-shū-gi-shū (天台法華宗義集)	2366
97-III	*Jp.*	Ken-kai-ron (顯戒論)	2376
97-IV	*Jp.*	San-ge-gaku-shō-shiki (山家學生式)	2377
98-I	*Jp.*	Hi-zō-hō-yaku (秘藏寶鑰)	2426
98-II	*Jp.*	Ben-ken-mitsu-ni-kyō-ron (辨顯密二教論)	2427
98-III	*Jp.*	Soku-shin-jō-butsu-gi (即身成佛義)	2428
98-IV	*Jp.*	Shō-ji-jis-sō-gi (聲字實相義)	2429
98-V	*Jp.*	Un-ji-gi (吽字義)	2430
98-VI	*Jp.*	Go-rin-ku-ji-myō-hi-mitsu-shaku (五輪九字明秘密釋)	2514
98-VII	*Jp.*	Mitsu-gon-in-hotsu-ro-san-ge-mon (密嚴院發露懺悔文)	2527
98-VIII	*Jp.*	Kō-zen-go-koku-ron (興禪護國論)	2543
98-IX	*Jp.*	Fu-kan-za-zen-gi (普勧坐禪儀)	2580
99–103	*Jp.*	Shō-bō-gen-zō (正法眼藏)	2582
104-I	*Jp.*	Za-zen-yō-jin-ki (坐禪用心記)	2586
104-II	*Jp.*	Sen-chaku-hon-gan-nen-butsu-shū (選擇本願念佛集)	2608
104-III	*Jp.*	Ris-shō-an-koku-ron (立正安國論)	2688
104-IV	*Jp.*	Kai-moku-shō (開目抄)	2689
104-V	*Jp.*	Kan-jin-hon-zon-shō (觀心本尊抄)	2692
104-VI	*Ch.*	Fu-mu-ên-chung-ching (父母恩重經)	2887

Vol. No.		Title	T. No.
105-I	*Jp.*	Ken-jō-do-shin-jitsu-kyō-gyō-shō-mon-rui (顯淨土眞實教行証文類)	2646
105-II	*Jp.*	Tan-ni-shō (歎異抄)	2661
106-I	*Jp.*	Ren-nyo-shō-nin-o-fumi (蓮如上人御文)	2668
106-II	*Jp.*	Ō-jō-yō-shū (往生要集)	2682
107-I	*Jp.*	Has-shū-kō-yō (八宗綱要)	蔵外
107-II	*Jp.*	San-gō-shī-ki (三教指帰)	蔵外
107-III	*Jp.*	Map-pō-tō-myō-ki (末法燈明記)	蔵外
107-IV	*Jp.*	Jū-shichi-jō-ken-pō (十七條憲法)	蔵外